Francis Horace Teall

English Compound Words and Phrases

A Reference List with Statement of Principles and Rules

Francis Horace Teall

English Compound Words and Phrases
A Reference List with Statement of Principles and Rules

ISBN/EAN: 9783744716949

Printed in Europe, USA, Canada, Australia, Japan

Cover: Foto ©Thomas Meinert / pixelio.de

More available books at **www.hansebooks.com**

ENGLISH
COMPOUND WORDS
AND PHRASES

A REFERENCE LIST, WITH STATEMENT OF
PRINCIPLES AND RULES

BY

F. HORACE TEALL

AUTHOR OF "THE COMPOUNDING OF ENGLISH WORDS," AND DEPARTMENT EDITOR OF
FUNK & WAGNALLS' STANDARD DICTIONARY

PRINTED IN THE UNITED STATES

New York
FUNK & WAGNALLS COMPANY
LONDON AND TORONTO

1892

PREFACE.

THE original list of which this is a revision was made for guidance in the preparation of the Standard Dictionary, and adopted after many competent critics had expressed their approval of it.

In the preface of the author's earlier book, "The Compounding of English Words," the making of a list of all common compounds was said to be impracticable. The reason for that assertion holds good, and the present is not such a list. Compounds that are practically common have been used in English literature, and others equally good are continually made, in such numbers that the dictionaries can never record all that are in current use.

All terms of the kind in question found in our fullest dictionaries are here gathered, besides many others, with the hope that the list may be advantageous to all who desire to attain reasonable consistency in the matter of compounding. Careful selection of the forms most in accordance with the best literary usage has been the aim of the author, and he has endeavored to show fully the analogies upon which the selection is based.

Many good writers object to frequent use of the hyphen, but even they may find the list useful—if for no other reason, because of its record of common solid words each made of two words. Our language has many such words, unquestionably correct in the close form, that are frequently separated into two words in print. Such separation, in many cases, should not be possible as anything but the merest accident.   Continual reference to a full list seems to promise a practical reform.

There is nothing in the history of **our language** to indicate a probability that English writers will ever universally omit the hyphen in compounding. On the contrary, our grammarians and philologists all give evidence in favor of hyphened compounds, the only difficulty in the case being that they are not systematic or thorough in this matter. W. D. Whitney, for instance, in his book on "The Life and Growth of Language," speaks of "a process which the general history of language shows to be more important than any other," and then says : "It is the composition of words, the putting two independent elements together to form a single designation." He shows that he means hyphened as well as continuous compounds by citing *rest-day, learning-knights, head-dress;* and his book abounds in hyphened compounds—many of them improperly so written. Max Müller's books are very much like Professor Whitney's in this respect, and so are the works of all our best writers.

Is it not well, then, to find and settle upon the principles that should guide us in the use of the hyphen? These principles the author has tried to set forth clearly in "The Compounding of English Words." For the fullest reasoning about that subject of which he is capable, inquirers must be referred to that book; but a practical work for constant reference seemed to be required, and this one is made for such use.

ENGLISH COMPOUND WORDS AND PHRASES.

CUSTOM VERSUS PRINCIPLE.

In the English language it is very common to name a thing, or express an attribute, or assert an action or a manner of action, by omitting minor or connecting parts of a full expression, and using only the principal elements in more or less arbitrary association and frequently in inverted order. Thus, instead of "a box for hats," "the cover of a book," "one who picks pockets," "having red hair," "to break (a colt) to the halter," "in the manner of one having a broad mind," we select the most prominent words from each full expression, and use only *hat* and *box, book* and *cover, pick* and *pocket, red* and *haired* (substituting *-ed* for "having"), *halter* and *break*, and *broad* and *mindedly* (substituting *-ed* for "having" and *-ly* for "in the manner").

How do we determine whether words used together as *hat* and *box* are to name a box, or as any of the others instanced, are to be written as two words, as a hyphened compound, or as one continuous word—*hat box, hat-box*, or *hatbox*, etc. ?

The impression is not uncommon that "usage" or "custom" determines the form; and probably those who would answer the question in this way would, on occasion, consult a dictionary to ascertain the results of inquiry regarding usage or custom as there shown.

Unfortunately, custom in this matter is simply confusion. That this is true is amply shown in the author's earlier book, " The Compounding of English Words," in which also many details of principle and usage are discussed much more fully than is possible here.

Mr. Benjamin Drew, who has had much experience both in proof-reading and in teaching, says, in his book entitled " Pens and Types " :

"To search for authority, then, in the matter of compounding words, will avail next to nothing. . . . Thus it appears that, in regard to compounding (by which we mean inserting the hyphen between the parts of a compound word), the proof-reader is left to his own discretion, and can do very much as he pleases. He should, however, adopt some method by which he can approximate to uniformity in his own work ; for as to agreeing with anybody else, that is out of the question."

Mr. Drew tells the bare truth in affirming that our common dictionaries (for they are the sources of authority he had chiefly in view) afford no reasonable guidance. But proof-readers are not always left to their own discretion, for it was probably an order to "follow copy" which occasioned the appearance in a recent book of *wood pile*, *wood-pile*, and *woodpile* in close succession, and which produces the same result in many other instances.

Probably no familiar phrase could be selected which can not be found somewhere written as a compound word. A very forcible illustration of this is *above-all*, given in Worcester's dictionary as a compound adverb, although it is really the two words *above all*, preposition regularly governing its noun—with one adverbial meaning, yet never properly written as anything but two words. Per contra, our most familiar compounds are often printed with the elements separated.

Some of the most eminent writers join a certain pair of words into one by means of a hyphen, others equally eminent keep these words separate although the meaning intended to be conveyed by them is the same, and still others'join them as one continuous word. All the current dictionaries except the "Webster's International" have *thunder-storm*, Appleton's "American Cyclopædia" has *thunder storm*, and the "Encyclopædia Britannica" has *thunderstorm*, and at least one of the other forms, *thunder-storm*. Now, one of these three forms *must* be more reasonable than either of the others; and if the dictionary does not determine which is best, how is the person who there seeks information on this point benefited by his quest?

Every writer chooses, for a term of the kind here discussed, that one of the three forms which he thinks to be prescribed by custom; and custom certainly should be a proper criterion in such matters. In order, however, to be the basis of decision, custom should be founded on principle. The difficulty in this case arises from the fact that, beginning apparently with the very earliest period of the language, word-forms have been selected according to individual conceptions of custom concerning the one term in hand, without sufficient recognition of its analogy with other like terms. Formulation of principles has been neglected or slighted, so that no adequate teaching on the subject has been available, and the fact that one combined term is commonly written in a certain form has not been, and is not now, universally taken as an indication that another exactly similar term should have the same form.

Of the makers of the works mentioned above, those who

wrote *thunder-storm* would doubtless claim that that is the customary form, while each of the other forms would be upheld by its users on the same plea. Can all three forms be supported by custom? Certainly all three are in use, as are also three forms of many other terms; therefore the following paragraph from a large popular dictionary may be nearly (though not quite) a true record :

"*Paper* is often used adjectively or in combination, having commonly an obvious signification; as *paper* cutter or *paper-*cutter; *paper* knife, *paper-*knife, or *paper*knife; *paper* maker, *paper-*maker, or *paper*maker; *paper* mill or *paper-*mill; *paper* weight, *paper-*weight, or *paper*weight, etc."

From the fact that in each instance the two-word form is the first given, we may conclude that the writer of the paragraph prefers that form; but we can not tell why. What was his reason for noting *papermaker* as a solid word, and not *papercutter* or *papermill?* The form is as good for any one as for either of the others. Where did he find *paperknife* in print? Why oes not the same dictionary tell us that *honey suckle* has been printed as two words? Why does it not mention *golden rod*—the name of a plant, and not a rod at all—as two words (so found in some newspapers)?

Of course, however, the dictionary can *not* tell in individual entries why the forms given are preferred, and the only possible basis for a reasonably consistent practical record is principle.

The accompanying list of word-forms is based upon a close inductive study of principles. Many terms of all possible constructions were selected from a wide range of standard literature, and classified analogically, with the result here shown. It is believed that every form given is analogically indicated by usage, and that most of the forms actually predominate in usage.

Necessarily the list embodies some seeming inconsistencies. Many words taking one form may seem at first thought to be just the same in nature as some others that have here a different form, and yet still another and a larger selection of terms shows a much closer analogy to those in question. The *closest* analogy has been sought in all cases as the basis for similarity of form. Absolute logical consistency, however, is impossible.

A FEW IMPORTANT HISTORICAL FACTS.

IN the very beginning of our written language some words were used together, just as they are now, in locutions so different from their rulable association that pairs were frequently united in form, and treated as one word made by joining two—one compound word. It has been asserted that in making these joinings our forefathers never used the hyphen, and that this mark is a modern innovation. Research does not confirm this opinion.

Our etymological dictionaries and our books on grammar contain many Anglo-Saxon compounds as written with hyphens, though whether as actually copied from the manuscripts or not is somewhat uncertain.

Tyrwhitt's edition of Chaucer—presumably the best edition as to preservation of Chaucer's own word-forms— contains many hyphened compound words. Some of these forms noted at the time of writing are *not-hed* (nut-head), *wood-craft*, *out-rider*, *love-knotte*, *fote-mantel* (foot-mantle), *gat-tothed* (gat-toothed), *nose-thirles* (nostrils), *even-song*, *box-tree*, *arm-gret* (arm-great), *out-renne* (out-run), *barme-clothe*, *cole-black*, *Pater-noster*, *Vaine-glorie;*

and there are many others. It is noticeable, however, that Chaucer's language is so constructed that compounding is comparatively little needed. Chaucer also wrote many continuous compounds, as *baggepipe, plowman, quick-silver, brimston, fourtenight;* and a term now thoroughly familiar in the continuous form appears as two words in his *twelve month*.

Our etymological dictionaries record most of the compound words of the Middle English period in the continuous form; but it is reasonable to conclude that the hyphen was frequently used in compounding.

A photographed facsimile of the Shakespeare folio of 1623 has hyphened compounds on almost every page, among which are *eye-ball, Noone-tide, Rye-straw, Sea-marge, heart strings, fore-head, after-love, over-taketh, Mill-wheeles, Bore-spritt* (bowsprit), *sea-sorrow, mid-night, grand-mother, top-Maste, bote-swaine, hony-combe, sea change, non-pareill, Vice-royes, pouncet-box, Brine-pits, on-set, Male-content, Water-spaniell, Waiting-Gen-tlewoman.*

Chaucer's writing and Shakespeare's were very much alike in this respect. Both poets wrote many hyphened compounds, and it is unreasonable to suppose that they were simply whimsical in so doing, because their words are quite systematic.

No writing of the highest rank as to style or idiom has been found by the author, in any period of our literature, in which expressions of the kind under discussion are systematically printed in the separated form. On the other hand, none has appeared in which such terms are systematically shown in the continuous form, though there are and have been writers who insist that when words are joined at all they should have that form. Dr.

Latham gave in his dictionary many such forms that never had any currency, and the following paragraph from the author's earlier book, "The Compounding of English Words," exhibits some curious work of this kind by another lexicographer.

"No dictionary of English has yet exhibited the language precisely in the forms, throughout its range, which even the maker himself would use in writing, unless it might have been so in the case of a work published by a Mr. Jodrell in 1820, entitled 'Philology *on* the English Language.' Mr. Jodrell evidently thought that a term made of two words, if joined at all, should be solidified into one continuous word. His work was made as supplementary to the other dictionaries of his time—to explain terms not given in them—and he gave such one-word forms as *battlepainting, camelswallower, courtparasite, deepprojecting, fellowcandidate, foundlinghospital, islandempress, latelypurchased, marriagesettlement, promontoryshoulder, procurationmoney, pulpitsophistry, restlessrolling, stagegesture, tapestryhanging,* and almost countless others just as odd; and he even gave this solid form to all such words in quotations from authors who undoubtedly had written the terms as hyphened compounds in some instances and as two words in others."

It seems needless to say that Mr. Jodrell never found any support in literature for his oddities. His work apparently died a very natural early death.

All the weight of the best usage favors the insertion of a hyphen between certain words under certain circumstances. Also, usage favors the retention of the hyphen in certain joinings, with no reasonable possibility of change to the continuous form.

WHAT IS THE REASONABLE BASIS FOR COMPOUNDING?

ACCENTUATION in pronouncing the pairs of words most commonly joined in form differs so much, and so naturally, from that of pairs commonly left separated, that many writers have mistakenly accepted pronunciation as a guide in deciding the proper form. Under ordinary circumstances, for instance, a noun following an adjective is pronounced with a stress easily noted as stronger than that of the adjective ; if the stronger accentuation is given to the adjective, it is generally so by way of emphasis. Thus, we speak of a *good boy'* and of a *prom''inent man,* when not contrasting two of different character or standing ; but in emphasizing the boy's character, as by way of contrast, we say *good' boy,* and in emphasizing the man's prominence we say *prom'inent man''.*

Emphasis and accent should be carefully distinguished. Emphasis is occasional ; accent is permanent.

Taking the names made by omitting particles from phrases, as instanced above, we find the accent always falls naturally on the first element in the pair—*hat' box, book' cover, pick' pock''et, red' haired, broad' mind''edly ;* and this recession of accent, which is a permanent feature of the spoken words, has been taken as making each pair become *one* word in speech. Presence or absence of the hyphen in writing the words makes no difference. The word *hyphen* means literally "into one," and in its current nominal use "that which marks the fact that two or more elements are joined or compounded so as to be *one word.*"

Writers who have made rules based on accentuation have usually to some extent presupposed that their readers know when a compound form is to be written, and their rules distinguish between hyphened and continuous compounds only. No note, or almost none, seems to have been made of the fact that there are two kinds of forms in which the hyphen is not used.

Soule and Wheeler's "Manual of English Pronunciation and Spelling" gives such rules as follows :

"When each of the parts of a compound word is pronounced with a distinct accent, they should be joined with a hyphen."

"When one of the words of which a compound is formed is pronounced without a distinct accent, no hyphen should be inserted between them."

Very plausible these rules seem before testing them ; but their authors did not apply them in their own work, as witness words from their vocabulary in the same book —*blameworthy, thankworthy, flapdragon, bookbinder, loveletter, note-worthy, sea-worthy, snap-dragon, sea-farer, water-wort, glasshouse, lifeblood, milkpail, scarf-skin, bull-dog, fire-fly, hill-side, key-board.*

In Drew's "Pens and Types" the same direction is given thus :

"Perhaps as good a rule as can be laid down on this subject is to close up the word when compounding changes the accentuation ; otherwise, insert the hyphen. Thus, 'quartermaster' has a different accentuation from the two words 'quarter master'; therefore make one word of it, without the hyphen. 'Head-assistant' is accented like the two words 'head assistant,'—therefore insert the hyphen. By this rule 'schoolhouse' and 'blackboard' should be severally closed up; 'salt-mine' takes the hyphen,—'saltsea' (adjective) does not."

Nothing could bring out more plainly than this citation

the fact that its author does not afford reasonable guidance. The two words *quarter master* are never used as two words, and therefore have no accentuation as such. There is no reason whatever for writing *head-assistant*, although it is sometimes so written. Mr. Drew's rule properly applied would give *saltmine* and *salt-sea*—the reverse of his own forms.

Many philologists insist that some of our most familiar and fully established compound words have no disparity of accent, and this amounts simply to an assertion that in speech each of the terms in question constitutes two words. This fact and the other facts noted of misapplication of rules seem to indicate clearly that accent can not be taken as the only guide to the formation of compound words.

The alternative, here accepted and applied, is purely grammatical.

PRINCIPLES AND RULES.

COMPARISON of forms as found in the best literature discloses, as regards differences of sense conveyed in the three forms (two words, hyphened compound, and continuous compound), distinctions like the following : *iron fence*, a fence made of iron ; *iron-saw*, a saw used to cut iron; *ironwood*, a tree with wood like iron. The first of these terms is an adjective and a noun—the fence itself is noted as differing in composition from other fences ; the second is two nouns in literal sense—the saw is not described in the name (it might be any kind of saw, except arbitrarily, so far as the name indicates), and *iron* is merely the name of what is cut ; the third is an adjective and a noun combined in a very arbitrary use, naming neither iron nor wood, but a tree.

These distinctions are not artificial inventions, but are shown predominatingly in the language as it is actually written. Anything bordered with lace has a *lace border*, the bordering pattern on figured lace is a *lace-border*, and a certain moth is called a *laceborder* because its wings have lace-like borders. The head of a sheep is a *sheep's head*, a certain porgy with some resemblance to a sheep's head is called *sheep's-head porgy*, and another fish with such resemblance is called the *sheepshead*. A house for children to play with is a *toy house*, and a business house dealing in toys is a *toy-house*. Other distinctions, varying with the grammatical variation, are generally analogous to these, and analogy indicates the following

GENERAL PRINCIPLES.

1st. That all words should be separate when used in regular grammatical relation and construction, unless they are jointly applied in some arbitrary way.

2d. That abnormal association of words generally indicates unification in sense, and hence compounding in form.

3d. That no expression in the language should ever be changed from two or more words into one (either hyphened or solid) without change of sense.

RULES FOR COMPOUND NOUNS.

Rule 1.—Two nouns used together as one name, in such a way that the first does not convey a descriptive or attributive sense, or so that the two are not in apposition, form a compound noun.

Seeming Exceptions.

Nearly all uses in which nouns might seem to be exceptions to this rule if left separate are provided for in the clause "in such a way that the first does not convey a descriptive or attributive sense." When the first of a pair of nouns *does* represent such a sense the two should not be connected in form, either by a hyphen or continuously.

Many English nouns are placed before other nouns to give ideas that would be expressed by the use of adjectives if we had the adjectives; and whenever this effect is real in the use of a pair of nouns, even to the extent of straining a point to make it so, the first of the pair is reasonably held to be an adjective. In such a name as *book-cover* this is not the case, there being no possibility of any adjective construing of *book;* the name is simply an elliptical inversion of *cover of a book*, and *book* and *cover* are, in this joint use, two nouns compounded into one. Such is the true standing of all pairs used in the same way, as *hat-box, grape-sugar, rifle-ball, pistol-shot, sewing-machine, office-seeker*, etc. These are real compounds, from a grammatical point of view, no matter how they are written. *Business man, insane asylum, insane pavilion, cold wave*, and *hot wave* are a few terms coming closest to being real exceptions to the rule; but, though each of them is commonly spoken like one word, with the stress on the first of the pair, it would be pedantic to insist upon the compounding of any of them.

Some uses in which the first of two nouns really stands as an adjective are as follows :

1. With the sense "made of," as in *silk dress, brick house, feather bed, pumpkin pie, stone wall*, etc.

2. With the sense "having the shape or the character or quality of," as in *barrel vault, alligator forceps, companion picture, he bear, man milliner, man servant, boy bishop, bull calf, brother officer, fellow citizen, mesh structure*, etc.

3. With the sense "pertaining to, suitable for, or repre-
senting," as in *parlor clock, city officer, district attorney,
government employee, railroad company, insurance
office, church furniture*, etc.

4. With the sense "characterized by," as in *diamond
ring, cylinder press, cupola furnace*, etc.

5. With the sense "situated in, having a character
naturally implied from situation or connection," as in
*mountain streams, country gentleman, ocean steamer,
school etiquette, society manners*, etc.

[In specific names of this kind, however, compounding
is indicated by the fact of specification, which is merely
naming; and for some common compounds other than
such purely specifying names no reason is apparent, unless
accent be here taken as a reason, or unless we conclude
that the indefinable border-line that exists in all human
affairs is here encountered. Thus (1) we have *sea-anem-
one, sea-gull, field-mouse, house-fly, mountain-fringe*
(a plant), etc., and, (2) while we say and write as two
words *o"cean steam'er*, we say as one word *wa'ter-
an"imal*, and it should be so written.]

6. With the sense "acting in support of, advocating,"
as in *Jackson voters, silver advocates, silver man, pro-
hibition speaker*, etc.

7. With the sense "residing, existing, or originating in,
or coming from (a place)," as in *Brooklyn politics, Bath
brick, New York schools, Florida oranges*, etc.

8. With the sense "originated or made by, or named
after," as in *Armstrong gun, Williams College*, etc.

Apposition.—Placing two nouns in apposition is very
nearly the same in effect as using the first as an adjective,
the difference being that in a case of real apposition either

word may be used alone for the thing named, as in *monarch oak, knight templar, knight companion,* etc.

No term strictly analogical with any of the above enumeration should be compounded.

Sub-rule 1. *When the sense is clearly literal, the two nouns are commonly joined by a hyphen.*

Notes.—(1) The only possible rule for two nouns used jointly, each with its primary naming sense, is simply that they form a compound word, and should not be written as two words; but the number of such terms commonly written without the hyphen is *comparatively* small, though some others may become solid through establishment in familiar use, and occasionally one may be properly a solid word from the start, because some name closely analogous is a solid word. Thus *hat-box, paint-brush, salt-mine, slaughter-house, thunder-shower,* etc., are hyphened compounds, each being simply two nouns selected from a phrase like " box for a hat (or for hats)," and should always remain so; *eyelid, sunbeam,* and many others at least apparently similar to those above, are established as solid words; and *guncotton* was a perfectly justifiable form the first time the name was used, because *gunpowder* was already an established form.

(2) Some words are so frequently used after and in intimate union with others, in a way that somewhat generalizes them in sense, that they are instinctively treated as if they were mere suffixes, and the unified term is written in solid form. Among these are *boy* as in *footboy, cowboy,* etc.; *man* as in *coachman, footman, hackman,* etc.; *stick* as in *candlestick* and *drumstick; stand* as in *inkstand; tree* as in *axletree, crosstree,* etc.; *weed* as in *milkweed, seaweed,* etc.; *work* as in *brickwork, clockwork,* etc.; *ware*

as in *earthenware, chinaware,* etc.; *way* as in *railway, speedway, stairway,* etc.

(3) Some other words are so commonly used as the latter element in many special names, that the names are always compounded, mostly with the hyphen. Some of these names are *blackbird, canary=bird,* etc.; *blackfish, gold-fish* (all specific names with *fish* and another monosyllable are made continuous in our list), *balloon=fish,* etc.; *apple=shell, needle=shell,* etc.; *apple=tree, pear=tree,* etc.

Sub=rule 2. When the application is purely arbitrary, as in arrowhead, *a plant with leaves like arrow=heads, as in* cotton-wood, *a tree, etc., the joining should be close—with no hyphen.*

Rule II.—Every name apparently composed of a plain noun and a noun of agent or a verbal noun, but really conveying the sense of a phrase with the suffix -er, -or, or -ing added, should be written as a compound.

Note.—Some such names are written continuously (as *housekeeper, shoemaker*), and almost any short one may become established in that form ; but the only rule that can be formulated is that such a name should *not* be written as *two words*, no matter how new it is nor how long.

Rule III.—Many possessive phrases are used as specific names, mostly of plants, and in such use the phrase becomes a compound word.

Notes.—(1) Such names have not appeared in print systematically as compounds, even books in which some of them are joined containing others in the two=word form. In most dictionaries they are all compounded, mainly with a hyphen ; but here, as in other cases, most dictionaries are inconsistent. The "Webster's International Dictionary" gives fifty=four hyphened compounds like *bear's=ear, bear's foot, wolf's=foot, crane's=bill, parrot's=bill, hare's=tail,* and *cat's-tail*, all names of plants.   Other plant-names in the same work are *elephant's ear, goat's foot, lion's foot, heron's bill, stork's bill, lion's tail;* there are at least seventy in this form.   Probably the inconsistency is based upon the fact that literature is inconsistent ; but there is evidence of editorial recognition of analogy in the fact that all such names with the same possessive word are treated similarly.   Thus, *bear's-breech, bear's-ear, bear's foot,* and *bear's paw,* all names with *cat's,* and all with *dog's* are hyphened, while all with *goat's, lady's, lion's,* etc., are given in the separated form. Analogy in the latter part of such terms, and in the term as a whole, is ignored.

The evil of this is that it affords no guide to a decision but the remembering of arbitrary differences, which is no guide at all.   Such names should all have the same form, except as noted in the next paragraph.

(2) Some, though comparatively few, of these names have already become established as continuous words. Prominent instances of solidifying are *ratsbane, sheepshead.*   A form not so thoroughly established is *catspaw,* instead of which *cat's-paw* is often used.   *Catspaw* has, however, sufficient currency to support it as a preferred form.

Rule IV.—Any phrase used as a specific name, in any arbitrary application not simply figurative, is properly in that use a compound noun.

Notes.—(1) The commonest names covered by this rule consist of an adjective and a noun in arbitrary specific application; as, *blackberry*, a certain black berry; *bluecoat*, a person wearing a blue coat.   All short names like these (with possibly a few exceptions) should have the solid form.

(2) In speaking of a woman as *queen of the prairie,*

the idea of an actual queen is presented in a merely figurative application; in using the same phrase as a specific name for a plant, the same kind of figurative application is made, but so arbitrarily that compounding is indicated—*queen-of-the-prairie.* A familiar name of this kind is *forget me-not,* always written with the hyphens. The reason for the use of hyphens in this name is equally applicable to any other name like it.

Rule V.—A pair of words used as one name, of which the second is a noun, but the first is not really an adjective, should be compounded.

Notes.—(1) The reason of this rule is the same as that of the first rule. If the first word of a pair really qualifies, it should remain a separate word—it is an adjective; if it does not inherently note quality, position, characteristic, or limitation, it is *not* an adjective. Thus we have such compounds as *foster-brother, know-nothing* (*foster* and *know* are verbs), *down-town, up-town, after-consideration, after-ages* (*down, up,* and *after* are prepositions), etc.; but in *down train, through passenger,* and all really similar terms, the first word is a qualifier and properly separate—the sense is "downward (down-going) train," "through-going passenger," etc.

(2) Many familiar continuous compounds consist of a verb and an objective noun; as, *pickpocket, breakwater, catchpenny,* etc. No such term should have any other form, except that occasionally a hyphen may well enough be used because of unfamiliarity or awkward appearance as a solid word. Thus, one who interferes with the pleasure of others has been called a *spoil-sport,* and might be called a *mar-pleasure, mar-sport,* or *spoil-pleasure;* for a scribbler the name *spoil-paper* has been used, and

for a malicious person *spit=poison.* All established solid words of this kind are given in the list.

Rule VI.—Any two words other than nouns should be compounded when arbitrarily associated as a name.

Note.—The continuous form is most usual in such joinings, as *lockup, breakdown, outlook, lookout,* etc.; but the hyphen is sometimes inserted, generally for an obvious reason, as in *make-up, tie=up, shake=up,* etc.

Rule VII.—A noun or an adjective made by adding a suffix to a proper name composed of two words should be compounded; as, an East-Indian, a New-Yorker.

Note.—The names without inflection should *never* be compounded. Thus, a *New York* man, *East India* Company, etc.

COMPOUNDS OTHER THAN NOUNS.

Rule.—Any pair or series of words arbitrarily associated, in a joint sense not properly inherent in them as separate words, should be compounded.

Note.—This rule really covers *all* compounding, including that of nominal words; and the analogies shown under the rules for nouns apply equally well all through, with slight change according to the part of speech under consideration. The following are a few special points:

1. When *like* placed after a noun simply indicates resemblance to the thing named, a hyphen is used in the compound; but all compounds in which *like* has a force similar to that of the suffix *-ly* are continuous—as *warlike, businesslike,* etc., meaning "like that which pertains to business," etc. Similar distinction is equally reasonable in any similar case.

2. Compound adjectives containing an adjective or a

noun as first element, and a participle or a participial form as the second, are usually written with a hyphen; as, *feeble-minded, hard-hearted, close mouthed, hammer-headed*, etc. Some very familiar words of this kind are always written continuously, and some others may well enough be so written, especially when used not far from a similar word familiar in the solid form. All that appear to have been used by the best writers as solid words are so given in the list.

3. An adjective and a participle used jointly are just as properly a compound in the predicate as in the attributive position. Thus, we should write "the man was *good-looking*" (as every one *does* write "a *good-looking* man"), "her hair is *jet-black*," "it went up *sky-high*," etc. In the first of these uses, the error of separation—as, "the man was *good looking*"—is not very uncommon; but there is no reason for a difference.

HOW THE LIST IS MADE.

IN selecting forms for the list, the fact that English writers and English readers object to very frequent hyphening has been duly recognized; but another fact has also claimed and received recognition—that all writers use some compound words, and the only means of knowing when to compound is analogy. Thus, because *hat-box* is a compound is a sufficient reason for so writing *coal-box*, *paper-box*, *pill-box*, and all other such names of boxes; and because the *boxes* are so treated is a sufficient reason for similarly treating names of other things.

Naturally, this reasoning applied all through the language gives many compound words; but a good means of avoiding their frequent use in ordinary writing, and to some extent even in technical matter, is available in the use of the full phrases instead of compounds. Thus, it is better to write "speed of a lathe" than to write "lathe-speed," "a body of bishops" is much better than "bishop-body," and "arm of a chair" is at least sometimes better than "chair-arm." Full phrases may be used advantageously even instead of very familiar compounds of this kind.

Following are explanations of the peculiarities in the list:

1. Some terms properly written as separated words are included, in some cases merely for exemplification, in others because of frequent mistaken compounding in literature. The list is by no means full as regards such terms.

2. Words marked with an asterisk (as *Aaron's-beard**) are compounds in their purely arbitrary application only.

Thus, *Aaron's-beard* is the name of a plant; for "the beard of Aaron," *Aaron's beard* should be written.

3. Where an obelisk(†) is used, with a word ending in *-er* or *-ing*, the word having the other suffix takes the same form as the one with which the mark is given.   Thus, *body-snatcher†* indicates *body-snatching* to be the proper form.

4. The double obelisk is used after the word *after-ages* as a reminder that in the normal use of the preposition and noun the words should be separate; as, "*after ages* had gone by," etc.   This mark is used but once in the list, but the fact noted by it applies in all similar cases.

5. Since every word made of an adjective or noun and another element ending in *-ed*, or with any participle as the second element, is written as a compound, the list gives one such word in each instance, with "etc." to indicate that all others should have the same form.   "Etc." is added sometimes simply to provide for possible words that may be made at any time.

6. The explanatory parentheses given with some names, as "a plant" or "a fish," are intended to indicate in each instance "the name of a particular species" or "of a kind with peculiar characteristics."

7. Such a parenthesis with "etc." indicates that the name is used for other things also; thus, *grayback* is used for a man, a snipe, a body-louse, a whale, and two kinds of duck.

8. When a word ending with *flower* has "(plant)" after it, the meaning is that the name is given to the plant and

not merely to the flower.   Thus, *Mayflower* is the name
of a plant as well as of its flower.

9. Terms without explanation should always have the
form given in the list.

10. Words like *childish-mindedness* are omitted. They
should have the same form as the word without the suffix
-ness.

11. No one should decide that compounding is not indicated because a term is not found in this list.   It is simply
impossible to make such a list absolutely exhaustive ; and
this one includes merely the terms of its kind that are re-
corded in dictionaries, with a few others that are common.

A

Aaron's-beard*
Aaron's-rod*
abat-jour
abat-vent
abat-voix
abbey-counter
abbey-laird
abbey-land
abbey-lubber
abbot-general
abb-wool
abel-tree
able-bodied
about-sledge
aboveboard
abovedeck
Abraham-man
abscess-root
absent-minded
absorption bands
absorption lines
absorption spectrum
abutment crane
acceleration-diagram
accommodation bill
accommodation cramp
accommodation ladder
accommodation lands
accommodation road
accommodation train
accommodation works
accordion-player†
accountant-general
account-book
account-day
acheweed
ach-root
acid green
acid magenta
acid-pump

acid yellow
ackman
ack-pirate
a-cockbill
acorn-cup
acorn-duck
acorn-moth
acorn-oil
acorn-shell
acorn-weevil
acorn-worm
acquittance-roll
acre-dale
action sermon
action-taking
acuyari-wood
Adam's-flannel*
addendum circle
adder-bead
adder-bolt
adder-fish
adder-fly
adder-gem
adder-grass
adder-pike
adder's-fern*
adder's-flower*
adder's-meat*
adder's-mouth*
adder-spit
adder's-spear*
adder-stone
adder's-tongue*
adder's-violet*
adder's-wort*
adding-machine
addlebrain (a person)
addle-headed
addlepate (a person)
addle-pated

addleplot (a person)
addle-pool
addressing-machine
adhesion-car
adit-level
adjusting-cone
adjusting-screw
adjusting-tool
adjutant-bird
adjutant-crane
adjutant-general
adjutant-stork
admiral-shell
advance-note
advantage-ground
adverb phrase
advice-boat
adz-plane
affeeringman
aforegoing
aforehand
aforementioned
aforenamed
aforesaid
aforethought
aforetime
after-ages (ages that
    come after a cer-
    tain time)‡
afterbirth
after-body
afterbrain
afterclap
aftercome
aftercrop
after-damp
after-egg
after-eye
afterfeed
aftergame

after=gland
afterglow
aftergrass
aftergrowth
afterguard
afterhind
after=hold
after=hood
after=image
aftermath
afternoon
afternoon=ladies (plant)
after=note
after=pains
afterpiece
after=rake
aftershaft
afterthought
after=time
after=wale
afterwash
afterwash=cistern
after=wise
after=wit
after=witted
after=years
aft=gate
agal=agal
agar=agar
agaric=gnat
agate=glass
agate=shell
agate=snail
agate=ware
age=prayer
aggry=beads
ague=bark
ague=cake
ague=drop
ague=fit
ague=grass
ague=proof
ague=root
ague=spel
ague=tree
agueweed
aide=de=camp
aid=prayer
aigue=marine

aiming=drill
aiming=stand
air=bag
air=balloon
air=bath
air=bed
air=bladder
air=blast
air=bone
air=box
air=brake
air=braving†
air=breather†
air=brick
air=bridge
air=brush
air=bucket
air=buffer
air=bug
air=built
air=camel
air=cane
air=carbureter†
air=casing
air=castle
air=cavity
air=cell
air=chamber
air=chambered
air=cock
air=compressor†
air=cone
air=cooler†
air=course
air=crossing
air=cushion
air=cylinder
air=dew
air=drain
air=drawn
air=dried
air=drill
air=drum
air=duct
air=endway
air=engine
air=equalizer†
air=escape
air=exhauster†

air=faucet
air=filter
air=flue
air=fountain
air=funnel
air=furnace
air=gas
air=gate
air=gauge
air=gossamer
air=governor
air=grating
air=gun
air=heading
air=heater†
air=hoist
air=holder†
air=hole
airing=stage
air=injector†
air=jacket
air=level
air=line
air=lock
air=locomotive
air=logged
air=machine
air=manometer
air=meter
air=oven
air=passage
air=pipe
air=pit
air=plant
air=poise
air=port
air=pressure
air=proof
air=pump
air=pyrometer
air=receptacle
air=regulator†
air=reservoir
air=sac
air=scuttle
air=setting
air=shaft
air=slaked
air=solar

air=space
air=spring
air=stack
air=stove
air=strake
air=thermometer
air=thread
air=tight
air=trap
air=trunk
air=tube
air=tumbler
air=turbine
air=valve
air=vesicle
air=vessel
air=washings
airway
air=wood
aitchbone
aitchpiece
à=la=grecque, n.
à la mode
à la morte
alarm=bell
alarm=bird
alarm=clock
alarm=compass
alarm=funnel
alarm=gauge
alarm=gun
alarm=lock
alarm=post
alarm=watch
albion=metal
albumin beer
albumin paper
alcohol=engine
alder=buckthorn
alderman=lizard
ale=bench
aleberry
ale=brewer
ale=conner
ale=cost
ale=draper
ale=drinking†
ale=fed
. ale=garland

ale=gill
ale=house
ale=pot
alerce=tree
ale=silver
ale=taster†
ale=vat
ale=washed
alewife
ale=yard
alfa=grass
alienation=office
alkali=stiff
alk=gum
all=amort
allbone, n.
aller=float
aller=trout
alley=taw
alleyway
All=father
all=fired
all=fours (a game)
allgood (a plant)
all=hail
All=hallow
Allhallowe'en
Allhallowmass
All=hallown
All=hallows
Allhallow=tide
allheal (a plant)
allice=shad
alligator=apple
alligator=fish
alligator forceps
alligator=pear
alligator=terrapin
alligator=tortoise
alligator=tree
alligator=turtle
alligator=wood
alligator wrench
allmouth (a fish)
all=over (a button plat-
    ed all over)
all=overishness
alloy balance
allseed (a plant)

all=sorts (a beverage)
allspice
allwhere
allwhither
Almain=rivet
almond=cake
almond=eyed
almond=furnace
almond=oil
almond paste
almond=tree
alms=bag
alms=box
alms=chest
alms=deed
alms=dish
alms=drink
alms=fee
alms=folk
alms=gate
almsgiver†
almshouse
almsman
alms=pot
almucantar=staff
aloes=wood
aloe=tree
alongshore
alongshoreman
alongside
altar=board
altar=bread
altar=card
altar=carpet
altar=cavity
altar=chime
altar=cloth
altar=cross
altar=curtain
altar=cushion
altar=desk
altar=dues
altar=fire
altar=frontal
altar=herse
altar=lantern
altar=ledge
altar=light
altarpiece

altar-protector†
altar-rail
altar-screen
altar-side
altar-slab
altar-stairs
altar-stole
altar-stone
altar-table
altar-thane
altar-tomb
alt-horn
alto-relievo
aludel furnace
alum-battery
alum-earth
alum-rock
alum-root
alum-stone
amaranth-feathers
amargoso-bark
amber-fish
amber-seed
amber-tree
amendment-monger
amidships
ammer-goose
ammunition-chest
ammunition bread
ammunition shoes
ammunition stockings
amœba-movement
ampere-meter
ampulling-cloth
amputating-knife
amputating-saw
amy-root
anchor-ball
anchor-bolt
anchor-chock
anchor-drag
anchor-gate
anchor-hold
anchor-hoy
anchor-ice
anchor-lift
anchor-lining
anchor-oven
anchor-plate

anchor-ring
anchor-rocket
anchor-shackle
anchor-shot
anchor-stock
anchor-tripper†
anchor-watch
anchor-well
anchovy-pear
andira-guaca
andiroba-oil
an-end
angel-fish
angel-light
angel's-eyes*
angel-shot
angel's-trumpets*
angel-water
angica-wood
angili-wood
angle-bar
angle-bead
angle-beam
angle-bevel
angle-block
angle-brace
angle-bracket
angle-brick
angle-capital
angle-chuck
angle-cock
angle-float
angle-iron
angle-meter
angle-modillion
angle-plane
angle-pod
angle-rafter
angler-fish
angle-shades
angle-splice
angle-staff
angle-tie
angle-valve
angleworm
animal-clutch
animal-trap
anise-camphor
aniseed

anise-tree
ankle-bone
ankle-boot
ankle-clonus
ankle-deep
ankle-jack
ankle-jerk
ankle-joint
ankle-reflex
ankle-tie
annealing-arch
annealing-box
annealing-color
annealing-furnace
annealing-lamp
annealing-oven
annealing-pot
anon-right
ant-bird
ant-catcher†
ant-cow
ant-eater†
ant-egg
anthemion frieze
anthemion molding
ant-hill
ant-hillock
antic-mask
antimony-blende
antimony-bloom
antimony-furnace
antimony-glance
ant-king
ant-lion
ant-skrike
ant's-wood*
ant-thrush
ant-tree
ant-worm
ant-wren
anvil-block
anvil-cupper
anvil-dross
anvil-vise
anybody
anyhow
any one
anything
anyway, *adv.*

anywhere
anywhither
ape=man
apes=on=horseback (a
   plant)
apex=beat
aphis=lion
aphis=sugar
appleberry
apple=blossom
apple brandy
apple=bud
apple butter
apple=core
apple=corer†
apple=curculio
apple=green
apple=headed
applejack
apple=John
apple=juice
apple=mint
apple=mose
apple=moth
apple=parer†
apple=peel
apple pie (a pie)
apple=pie (a plant)
apple=pie order
apple=pulp
apple=quarterer†
apple=scoop
apple=seed
apple=shell
apple=snail
apple=tree
application=lace
apron=lining
apron=man
apron=piece
apron=roll
apron=string
apse=aisle
apse=chapel
arachis=oil
arbor=chuck
arbor=day
arbor=vine
arbor=vitæ

arc=cosecant
arc=cosine
arch=band
arch=bar
arch=board
arch=brick
arch=buttress
archer=fish
arch=moulding
arch=stone
arc=light
are=piece
arc=secant
arc=sine
arc=tangent
arctic=bird
argan=oil
argan=tree
argle=bargle
Argus=eyed
argus=pheasant
argus=shell
ark=shell
arle=penny
arm=band
arm=board
arm=bone
armchair
arm=chest
arm=gaunt
arm=great
arm=guards
armhole
arming=buckle
arming=doublet
arming=point
arming=press
arming=spear
arming=sword
armor=clad, a.
armorclad, n.
armor=grating
armor=plate
armor=plated
armor=plating
armor=shelf
armpit
arm=rack
arm=rest

arm=saw
arm=scye
arm's end
arm's length
arm=sling
arm=span
arm's reach
arm=sweep
army=cloth
army=corps
army=list
army=worm
arris=fillet
arris=gutter
arris=piece
arris=rail
arrow=grass
arrow=head (head of an
   arrow)
arrowhead (a plant)
arrow=headed
arrowleaf (a plant)
arrow=poison
arrowroot
arrow=shaped
arrow=stone
arrow=tie
arrow=wood (wood of
   which arrows are
   made)
arrowwood (a plant)
arrow=worm
arsenic=black
arsenic=furnace
arsenic=glass
arse=smart
arsy=versy
artery=forceps
artillery=carriage
artillery=level
artillery=plant
artist=like
art=union
art=worm
asbestos=stove
as=ducat
ash=barberry
ash=barrel
ash=bead

ash=bin
ash=cake
ash=candles
ash=color
ash=colored
ash=fire
ash=fly
ash=furnace
ash=hole
ash=key
ash=leach
ash=pit
ash=plate
ash=shoot
asparagus=bean
asparagus=beetle
asparagus=stone
asparagus=tongs
asper=artery
asphaltum=furnace
assagai=wood
assai=palm
assay=furnace
assay=master
ass=ear
assembly=room
ass=head
assize sermon
ass's=ear*
ass's=foot*
astragal=plane
astragal=tool
atlas=folio
atocha=grass
atone=maker†

attachment=screw
attorney=general
attorney=generalship
auction pitch
auction pool
audience=chamber
audience=court
audit=house
audit=office
auger=bit
auger=faucet
auger=gauge
auger=hole
auger=making†
auger=shell
auger=stem
auger=twister†
aulin=scouty
aurora=shell
autumn=bells
avant=courier
average=adjuster†
average=stater†
average=taker†
away=going
awestruck
awl=bird
awl=clip
awl=shaped
awl=tree
axe=blank
axe=grinder†
axe=handle
axe=head
axe=helve

axe=maker†
axemaster
axe=shaped
axe=stone
axis=cylinder
axis=deer
axle=adjuster†
axle=arm
axle=bar
axle=block
axle=box
axle=clip
axle=collar
axle=gauge
axle=guard
axle=hook
axle=making†
axle=nut
axle=packing
axle=pin
axle=saddle
axle=seat
axle=setting†
axle=skein
axle=sleeve
axle=tooth
axletree
axletree=clamp
axle=yoke
ay=green
ayni=wood
ay=word
azo=blue
azo=erythrin
azure=stone

B

babbitting-jig
Babington's-curse (a plant)*
baby-carriage
baby-clothes
baby-farm
baby-farming†
baby-house
baby-jumper†
baby-pin
baby-walker†
bacaba-palm
bachelor's-buttons*
backache
backache-brake
backache-root
back-action
back-balance
back-band
back-bar
back-block
back-bond
back-bone (bone of the back)
backbone (figurative uses)
back-casing
back-cast
back-center
back-chain
back-cloth
back-comb
back door
back-end
back-fillet
back-flap
back-frame
back-friend
back-game
backgammon

backgammon-board
backgammon-playing†
back-gear
background
backhand
backhanded
backhead
backhouse
backing-boards
backing-deals
backing-hammer
backing-iron
backing-metal
backing-pan
back-joint
backlash
back-lining
back-link
backlog
back look
back-lye
back-mill
back-mold
back-overman
back-painting
backpiece
backplate
back pressure
back-racket
back-raking
back-rent
back-rest
back-return
back room
backrope
back-saw
back-scraper†
back-scratcher†
backset
back-settler

back-shift
backside
back-sight
back-skin
back slang
backslide
back-speed
back-splinting†
back-spring
back-staff
back-stair, a.
back stairs
back-stairs, a.
back-stall
backstay
back-step
backstitch
backstone
back-stop
back-strap
back-strapped
back-stream
back-string
back-stroke
back-swimmer†
back-sword
back-tack
back-tool
back-trick
back-washed
backwater, n.
backwood (part of carpenters' plane)
backwoods (unsettled wooded country)
backwoodsman
backworm
backwort
back-wounding†
bacon-beetle

bacon=weed
badak=tapa
badger-baiting†
badger=dog
badger=hound
badger=legged
badger=plane
badger's=bane*
baff=ends
baffle=plate
baff=week
bagasse=furnace
bagatelle=board
bagatelle=playing†
bagatelle=table
bag=clasp
bag=fastener†
bag=filler†
bag=filter
bag=fox
bag=frame
baggage=car
baggage=check
baggageman
baggage=master
baggage=truck
bag=holder†
bag=lock
bag=machine
bag net
bagnut
bagpipe
bag press
bag=pudding
bag pump
bag=reef
bag=room
bag=tie
bag trousers
bag=weigher†
bag wig
bag=worm
bail=bond
bail=dock
bail=piece
bail=scoop
bairntime
bairnwort
bait=box

bait=fish
bait=fishing†
bait=mill
bait=poke
bait=rod
baked=apple (a certain
    dried fruit)
bakehouse
baker=foot
baker=kneed
baker-legged
bakestone
baking=powder
balaam=basket
balaam=box
balance=bar
balance=barometer
balance=beam
balance=bob
balance=book
balance=bridge
balance=crane
balance=frames
balance=dynamometer
balance=electrometer
balance=engine
balance=fish
balance=frame
balance=gate
balance=knife
balance=level
balance=pit
balance=plow
balance=reef
balance=rudder
balance=rynd
balance=section
balance=sheet
balance=step
balance=thermometer
balance=valve
balance=vise
balance=wheel
balata=gum
balata=tree
bald=faced
baldhead (a person)
bald=headed
baleen=knife

bale=fire
bale=hook
bale=tie
baling=machine
baling=press
balk=line
balk=staff
ballad=maker†
balladmonger
ballad=opera
ballad=singer†
ballan=wrasse
ballast=car
ballast=engine
ballast=getter†
ballast=hammer
ballast=heaver†
ballast=hole
ballast=lighter
ballast=port
ballast=shovel
ballast=trim
ball=bearing
ball=block
ball blue
ball=calibre
ball=cartridge
ball=caster
ball cock
ball=cover
ball=field
ball=flower
ball=game
ball grinder
ball gudgeon
balling=furnace
balling=gun
balling=iron
balling=machine
balling=tool
ball ironstone
ball joint
ball=lever
ball=mine
ball mounting
balloon boiler
balloon=fish
balloon=jib
balloon=net

balloon=sail
balloon=vine
ballot=box
ball=player†
ball=proo
ball=rack
ballroom
ball=screw
ball=seater
ball=stock
ball=train
ball=trimmer†
ball=trolly
ball=turning†
ball valve
ball=vein
balm=cricket
balm=oil
balsam=apple
balsam=bog
balsam=herb
balsam=poplar
balsamroot (a plant)
balsam=tree
balsamweed
baluster=shaft
baluster=stem
bamboo=brier
bamboo palm
bamboo=partridge
banana=bird
banana=cater†
banana=peel
banana=plant
banana=quit
banana=skin
band=axis
band-bird
bandbox
band=brake
band=coupling
band=cutting†
band=driver
bandfish
banding=machine
banding=plane
banding=ring
band=lacing
band=linen

band=master
band=mounting
band=nippers
bandoleer=fruit
band=pulley
band=robin
band=saw
band=setter†
bandsman
band spectrum
band=string
band=wheel
band=work
bandy-ball
bandy=jig
bandy=legged
bandyman
baneberry
banewort
bang=beggar
banghy=post
banghy=wallah
bangle=ear
bangle=eared
bang=pitcher
bang=straw
bang=up
banister=cross
banjo=frame
banjo=player†
banjo=string
bank=account
bank=bait
bank=bill
bank=book
bank=credit
bank fence
bank=game
bank=head
bank=holiday
bank=hook
banking=file
banking=pin
banking=wax
bank=level
bank=martin
bank=note
banko ware
bank=plate

bank=post
bank=protector †
bank=shot
bank=stock
bank=swallow
bank=work
banner=plant
banner=roll
banner=stone
banner=vane
bannock=fluke
banquet=hall
banquet=house
banqueting=hall
banqueting=house
banqueting=room
Bantam=work
banyan=tree
barathea=cloth
Barbados=pride
barb=bolt
barber=boat
barber=chirurgeon
barber=fish
barberry
barberry=fungus
barber=surgeon
barber=surgery
barb=feathers
barb=pigeon
bar=cutter †
bareback
barebacked
barebone
bareboned
barefaced
barefoot
barefooted
bare=gnawn
barehanded
bareheaded
bare=legged
bare=necked
bare=picked
bare=pump
bare=ribbed
bare=worn
bar=fee
bar=fish

bar=frame
bargain=chop
bargainman
bargain=work
barge=board
barge=couple
barge=course
bargeman
bargemaster
barge=rafter
bar=goose
bar=gown
bar iron
bark bed
bark=bound
bark=cutting†
barkceper†
bark=feeder†
bark=galled
barking=ax
barking=bill
barking=bird
barking=iron
barking=mallet
barking=tools
bark=louse
bark=mill
bark=paper
bark path
bark=pit
bark=planing†
bark=rossing†
barkstone
bark=stove
bark=tanned
bark walk
bar=lathe
barley=bigg
barley=bird
barley=brake
barley=bree
barley=broo
barleycorn
barley fever
barley=fork
barley=island
barley=meal
barley=mill
, barley=sick

barley=sugar
barley=water
barley=wine
bar lift
bar=loom
bar magnet
barmaid
barman
barmaster
barmbrack
barm=cloth
bar=mining
barmy=brained
Barnaby=bright
barnacle=goose
barn door
bar=net
barney=pit
barn=gallon
barn=grass
barnman
barn=owl
barns=breaking
barnstormer†
barn=swallow
barn=yard
barometer=flowers
barometer=gauge
baron=court
bar=post
bar=pump
bara=boat
barrackmaster
barrel=bayonet
barrel=bellied
barrel=bolt
barrel=bulk
barrel curb
barrel drain
barrel=prier†
barrel=filler†
barrel=fish
barrel=gauge
barrel=head
barrel=hooks
barrel=hoop
barrel=hooping†
barrel=lifter†
barrel loom

barrel=making†
barrel organ
barrel pen
barrel pier
barrel=plate
barrel=roller†
barrel=saw
barrel=screw
barrel=setter†
barrel=shaped
barrel vault
barrel=vise
barrel=washer†
barrel=work
barren=spirited
barret=cap
barrfish
barrier=gate
barring out
bar=roll
barroom
barrow=coat
barrowman
barrow=pig
barrow=pump
barrow=tram
barrow=truck
barrowway
bars gemel
bar=shear
bar=shoe
bar=shooting†
bar=shot
bar=sight
bar=tailed
Bartholomew=tide
bar=weir
basal=nerved
bascule bridge
base=bag
baseball
base=board
base=born
base=bred
base broom
base=burner†
base=court
base=dance
base=hearted, etc.

base-hit
base-line
basement story
base-moulding
base-plate
base-ring
base-rocket
base-running†
bashi-bazouk
basil-oil
basil-thyme
basil-weed
basin-cock
basin-grate
basining-cloth
basin-plug
basin-stopper
basin-trap
basin-waste
basin-wrench
basket-beagle
basket button
basket carriage
basket couching
basket-fern
basket-fish
basket grate
basket-handle
basket-hare
basket hilt
basket-hilted
basket-hood
basket-lizard
basket-oak
basket-making†
basket-of-gold (a plant)
basket-palm
basket-urchin
basket-withe
basketwood (a plant)
basketwork
basket-worm
basking shark
bas-relief
bass-bar
basset-horn
bass-goose
bass mat
bass-rope

basswood
basting-machine
bast-palm
bast-tree
bat-bolt
bate-breeding
batement-light
batfish
bat-fowler†
bath-cock
bath-furnace
bath-heater†
bath-house
bathing-box
bathing-dress
bathing-house
bathing-machine
bathing-suit
bathing-tub
bath-kol
bathroom
bath-sponge
bath-spring
bathtub
bathwort
batman
bat-money
baton-cross
bat-printing†
bat-shell
batsman
battalion drill
batten door
batter-head
battering-charge
battering-gun
battering-piece
battering-ram
battering-rule
battering-train
batter-level
batter-rule
battery-box
battery-brush
battery-gun
battery-head
battery-shooting
battery-wagon
bat-tick

batting-block
batting-machine
batting-staff
battle-axe
battle-bolt
battle-brand
battle-club
battle-cry
battle-field
battle-flag
battle-ground
battle-lantern
battle-mace
battle-piece
battle-scarred
battle-shout
battle-song
battle-writhen
battoule-board
bauchee-seed
bawdy-house
baw-money
bay-antler
bayberry
bayberry-tallow
bay-birds
bay-bolt
bay-breasted
bay-cod
bay-gall
bay-goose
bay-leaf
bay-mahogany
bayman
bay-oil
bayonet-clasp
bayonet clutch
bayonet joint
bayonet-scabbard
bay-porpoise
bay rum
bay-salt
bay-stall
bay-tree
bay window
bay-winged
bay-wood
bay-yarn
bazaar maund

beach-birds	beam-light	bearing-binnacle
beach-clam	beam-line	bearing-cloth
beach-comber	beam-platform	bearing-feeler
beach-flea	beam-roll	bearing-neck
beach-grass	beam-room	bearing-note
beachman	beam-trawl	bearing-rein
beachmaster	beam-tree	bearing-robe
beach-pea	beam-truss	bear-leader
beach-plum	bean-brush	bear-moss
beach-wagon	bean-cake	bear-mouse
beacon-blaze	bean-caper	bear-oak
beacon-fire	bean-cod	bear-pig
beacon-tower	bean-crake	bear-pit
bead-furnace	bean-curd	bear's-bed*
bead-house	bean-dolphin	bear's-bilberry
bead-loom	bean-feast	bear's-breech*
beadman	bean-fed	bear's-ear*
bead-mould	bean-fly	bear's-foot *
bead-moulding	bean-goose	bear's-garlic
bead-plane	bean-harvester†	bear's-grape *
bead-proof	bean-king	bearskin
bead-roll	bean-meal	bear's-weed
bead-sight	bean-mill	bear-whelp
beadsman	bean-pole •	bearwood
bead-snake	bean-sheller†	bearwort
bead-stuff	bean-shooter†	beast-hide
beadswoman	bean-shot	beast's-bane*
bead-tool	bean-stalk	beat-ax
bead-tree	bean-tree	beater-press
beadwork	bean-trefoil	beating-bracket
beadwork-lathe	bean-weevil	beating-engine
beaker-cells	bear-animalcule	beating-hammer
beakhead	bear-baiting	beating-machine
beaking-joint	bearbane	beau-ideal
beak-iron	bearberry	beaumont-root
beak-rush	bearbine	beau-peruke
beak-sheath	bear-caterpillar	beau-pot
beam-bird	bear-cloth	beau-semblant
beam-board	beard-grass	beauty-of-the-night (a
beam-caliper	bearding-line	plant)
beam-center	beard-moss	beauty-sleep
beam-compass	bear-dog	beauty-spot
beam-engine	beardtongue (a plant)	beauty-wash
beam-feather	bearer-bar	beaver-poison
beam-filing	bearer-pin •	beaver-rat
beam-gudgeon	bear-garden	beaverroot (a plant)
beam-hook	bear-grass	beavertongue (a plant)
beaming-machine	bearherd	beaver-tree
beam-knife	bear-hound	bêche-de-mer

beck=harman	bedstock	bee=garden
beck=iron	bedstone	bee=glue
becuiba=nut	bedstraw	bee=gum
bed=ale	bed-thrall	bee=hawk
bed=board	bedtick	bee=herd
bed=bolt	bedticking	beehive
bed=bottom	bedtime	beehouse
bedbug	bed=tool	beekeeper†
bed=chair	bed-vein	bee=killer†
bedchamber	bedway	bee=king
bed=clip	bedwork	bee=line
bedclothes	bed=wrench	bee=louse
bedcover	bee=bird	bee=martin
bedda=nut	bee=block	beemaster
bedding=moulding	bee=bread	bee=moth
bedding=plant	beech=coal	bee=nettle
bedding=stone	beech=cherry	bee=orchis
bedfast	beechdrops	bee=parasite
bedfellow	beech=fern	beer=barrel
bed=frame	beech=finch	beer=brewery
bedgown	beech=fungus	beer=brewing†
bed=hangings	beech=gall	beer=drinking†
bed=key	beech=hopper	beer=engine
bed=lathe	beech=marten	beer=faucet
bed=linen	beech=mast	beer=float
bed=lounge	beechnut	beer=fountain
bedmaker†	beech=oil	beer=garden
bedmate	beech=owl	beer=glass
bed=moulding	beech=wheat	beer=hopper
bed=pan	bee=culture	beer=house
bedplate	bee=eater†	beer=machine
bedpiece	beef=brained	beer=measure
bedpost	beef=cattle	beer=money
bed=presser†	beef=eater†	beer=preserver†
bedquilt	bee=feed	beer=pull
bedridden	bee=feeder†	beer=pump
bed=right	bee=fumigator†	beer=saloon
bed=rite	beef=herd	beer=selling†
bed=rock	beef=kid	beer=shop
bedroom	bee=flower	beerstone
bed=sacking	bee=fly	beer=swilling†
bed=screw	beef=measle	beer=vat
bedside	beefsteak	bee=scap
bed=sore	beefsteak=fungus	bee=skep
bedspread	beefsteak=plant	beeswax
bed=spring	beefsuet=tree	beeswing
bedstead	beef tea	beet=chards
bedstead=fastener†	beef=witted	beet=fly
bed=steps	beefwood	beetle=brow

beetle-browed
beetlehead (a person, a
    bird)
beetle-headed
beetle-mite
beetle-stock
beetlestone
beetling-machine
beetmaster
beetmister
beet-press
bee-radish
beet-rave
bee-tree
beet-root
bee-wolf
bee-worm
beforehand
beggar-my-master
beggar's-basket*
beggar's-lice*
beggar's-needle*
beggar's-ticks*
beggarweed
being-place
bel-accoil
belaying-bitt
belaying-pin
belfry-owl
belfry-turret
bell-animal
bell-animalcule
bellasombra-tree
bell-bind
bell-bird
bell-bloom
bell-bottle
bell-boy
bell-buoy
bell-cage
bell-call
bell-canopy
bell-chamber
bell-chuck
bell-cord
bell-cote
bell-crank
belles-lettres
bellflower

bell-founder†
bell-foundry
bell-gable
bell-gamba
bell-gastrula
bell glass
bell-hanger†
bell harp
bell jar
bell-magnet
bell-magpie
bellman
bell-mare
bell-metal
bell-metronome
bell mouth (a mouth or
    mouthpiece of bell
    shape)
bell-mouth (mouth of
    a bell)
bellmouth, v.
bell-mouthed
bell-nosed
bellows-camera
bellows-fish
bellows-pump
bellows-sound
bell-pepper
bell-polyp
bell-pull
bell pump
bell-punch
bell-ringer†
bell roof
bell-rope
bell-rose
bell screw
bell-shaped
bell-sound
bell telegraph
bell-tower
bell trap
bell-turret
bell-wether
bell-work
bellwort
bellyache
belly-band
belly-boards

belly-bound
belly-brace
belly-button
belly-cheat
belly-cheer
belly-cheering, etc
belly-churl
belly-doublet
belly-god
belly-guy
belly-piece
belly-pipe
belly-rail
belly-roll
belly-slave
belly-stay
belly-timber
belly-vengeance
belly-wash
belly-worm
belt-clamp
belt-clasp
belt-coupling
belt-cutter†
belt-lacing
belt-mouldir
belt-pipe
belt-punch
belt-punching†
belt-rail
belt-saw
belt-screw
belt-shifter†
belt-shipper†
belt-speeder†
belt-splicing†
belt-stretcher†
belt-tightener†
belt-tool
belt-weaving†
bench-clamp
bench-drill
bench-forge
bench-hammer
bench-hook
bench-lathe
bench-level
bench-mark
benchmaster

bench=plane
bench=reel
bench=screw
bench=shears
bench show
bench=stop
bench=strip
bench=table
bench=vise
bench=warrant
bending=machine
bending=strake
bend=leather
bendy=tree
Ben=Israel
benjamin=bush
benjamin=tree
ben=kit
ben=nut
ben=oil
benne=oil
ben=teak
bent=grass
benting=time
bequia=sweet
bergamot=oil
berth=brace
berth=deck
berthing=rail
berth=room
berth=latch
betel=box
betelnut
betel=pepper
bettering=house
between=decks
bevel=gear
bevel=hub
bevelling=board
bevelling=edge
bevelling=frame
bevelling=machine
bevel=jack
bevel=joint
bevel=plater†
bevel=protractor†
bevel=rest
bevel=square
bevel=tool

bevel=ways
bevel=wheel
bevel=wise
bez=antler
bezoar=goat
bias=drawing
bib=cock
Bible=clerk
Bible=oath
bible=press
bidding=prayer
bidet=pan
bid=hook
bidri=ware
bidri=work
bid=stand
bier=balk
bier=right
bigeye (a fish)
bigfoot (a bird)
bighead (a fish, a person
bighorn (a sheep)
bigwig (a person, as one
    who wears a big
    wig)
bilberry
bile=cyst
bile=duct
bile=pigment
bilestone
bilge=board
bilge=coad
bilge=free
bilge=keel
bilge=keelson
bilge=piece
bilge=plank
bilge=pump
bilge=water
bilgeways
bill=board
bill=book
bill=broker
bill=chamber
billet=cable
billet=doux
billet=head
billetting=roll

billet=master
billet=moulding
billfish
bill=hawk
bill=head
bill=hook
billiard=ball
billiard=cloth
billiard=cue
billiard=marker†
billiard=player†
billiard=room
billiard=table
bill=poster†
bill=scale
bill=sticker
billy=gate
billy=goat
billy=piercer†
billy=roller†
billy=web
binder=frame
binding=cloth
binding=guide
binding=joist
binding=piece
binding=post
binding=rafter
binding=screw
binding=strakes
binding=wire
bind=rail
bindweb
bindweed
bindwith
bindwood (a plant)
bingstead
birch broom
birch=camphor
birch=oil
birch=water
birch wine
bird=baiting†
bird=bolt
bird=cage
bird=call
bird=catcher†
bird=dog
bird=duffer

bird=eye
bird=eyed
bird=fancier
bird=fauna
bird=foot
bird=house
birding=piece
birdlike
birdlime
bird=louse
birdman
bird=net
bird=organ
bird=pepper
bird=plant
bird's=bread*
bird=seed
bird's=eye*
bird's=foot*
bird=shot
bird's=mouth*
bird's nest
bird's=nest (soup)
bird's=nesting
bird=spider
bird's=tares*
bird's=tongue*
bird=tick
bird=trap
bird=witted
birtfish
birth=child
birthday
birth=hour
birthland
birthmark
birthnight
birthplace
birth=rate
birthright
birthroot (a plant)
birth=sin
birth=song
birth=strangled
birthwort
biscuit=oven
biscuit=root
bishop=bird
bishop's=cap*

bishop's=elder*
bishop's=hat*
bishop's=leaves*
bishop=sleeve
bishop's length
bishop's=mitre*
bishop's=weed*
bishopweed
bismuth=blende
bismuth=furnace
bismuth=glance
bit=brace
bitch=wood
bit=key
bit=pincers
bit=stock
bit=strap
bitterblain
bitterbloom (a plant)
bitterbush (a certain
    plant)
bitter earth
bitter end
bitter=end (cable=end
    abaft the bitts)
bitter=grass
bitterhead (a fish)
bitter=herb
bitter=king
bitternut (a tree)
bitterroot (a plant)
bitter salt
bitter=spar
bitterstem (a plant)
bitterstick (a plant)
bitter=sweet (in literal
    senses)
bittersweet (a plant)
bitter vetch
bitterweed
bitterwood (a tree or its
    wood)
bitterwort
bitt=head
bitting=harness
bitting=rigging
bitt=pin
bitt=stopper†
blackback (bird, fish)

blackball, n. (in any
    sense other than
    "a black ball")
blackball, v.
blackband (a kind of
    iron ore)
black bass
black=beetle
blackbelly (a fish)
blackberry
blackbird
blackboard
blackbonnet (a bird)
blackboy (a tree)
blackbreast (a bird)
black=browed, etc.
black=brush, a.
blackbur (a plant)
blackcap (a person, a
    bird, a plant, a
    black=roasted ap-
    ple)
black=cat (a marten)
black cattle
blackcoat (one who
    wears a black coat)
blackcock
black damp
black=draught
black=drop
black=dye
black=extract
blackfin (a fish with
    black fins)
blackfish
blackfisher†
black=flea (a turnip=flea)
black=fly (a gnat, a
    plant=louse)
blackfoot (a person)
black=fox (a marten)
black friar
black=grass
blackguard
blackhead (a duck, a
    fish)
blackheart (a cherry, a
    certain kind of
    wood)

black-hearted (wood)
black helmet
black hole
black-horse (a fish)
blacking-box
blacking-brush
blacking-case
black-jack
black-knot (a fungus)
black lead
blacklead, v.
blackleading-machine
blackleg (a person)
black letter
black-liquor (a crude
acetate of iron)
black list
blacklist, v.
black-mack
blackmail
black-match
blackmouth (a person)
black-mouthed
black mullet
blacknob (a person)
black-pigment
black plate
black-pot (a kind of
crockery)
black pudding
black-quarter
black-rod (a person)
blackroot (a plant)
black-salter
black salts
black-sampson
blackseed (a plant)
black-shell (a mollusk)
blacksize, v.
blacksmith
blacksnake (name of
certain black
snakes)
black-spaul
black-spot (a rose-bush
disease)
black-strap (a bever-
age)
black-stripe (beverage)

blacktail (a fish, a deer)
blackthorn (a plant, or
its wood)
black-tongue (a dis-
ease of cattle in
which they have a
black tongue)
black turpeth
black-varnish tree
black-wad
black-ward
black-wash
black-water
black whale
blackwood (one of cer-
tain trees, or the
wood of one)
blackwork
blackwort
blackytop (a bird)
bladder-blight
bladder-brand
bladder-campion
bladder-fern
bladder-gastrula
bladder-green
bladder-herb
bladder-kelp
bladder-ketmia
bladdernose (a hooded
seal)
bladder-nosed
bladdernut (a plant)
bladderpod (a plant)
bladder-senna
bladdersnout (a plant)
bladder-worm
bladderwort
bladder-wrack
blade-bone
bladefish
blade-metal
blade-mill
blade-ore
blade-spring
blae-linen
blameworthy
blanch-farm
blanch-holding†

blanching-liquor
blanc-mange
blank book (a book
that is blank)
blank-book (a book of
blanks—printed
forms to be filled)
blanket-bar
blanket-clause
blanket-deposit
blanketleaf (a plant)
blanket mortgage
blanket-piece
blanket sheet
blanket-sluice
blanket-washer†
blanking-press
blast-box
blast-engine
blast-furnace
blast-gate
blast-hearth
blast-hole
blasting-cartridge
blasting-fuse
blasting-gelatin
blasting-mixture
blasting-needle
blasting-oil
blasting-powder
blasting-tools
blasting-tube
blast-lamp
blast-machine
blast-meter
blast-nozzle
blast-orifice
blast-pipe
blast-recorder†
blay-linen
blazing-star (a plant)
bleach-field
bleaching-liquid
bleaching-powder
bleareye (a disease)
blear-eyed
blear-witted
bleedhearts (a plant)
bleeding-heart (a plant)

bleeding-tooth (a mollusk)
blendcorn
blendwater (a disease of cattle)
blessed-herb (avens, a plant)
blight-bird
blindage-frame
blind-ball
blind-born
blind-fast
blindfish
blindfold
blind-Harry
blind-lift
blindman (a reader of blind writing)
blind man's ball
blind man's bellows
blind man's buff
blind man's holiday
blind - operator (that which operates a blind)
blind-slat
blindsnake
blind-stile
blindstitch, v.
blind-story
blind-tooling
blind-wiring†
blindworm
blink-beer
blink-eyed
blinking chickweed
blister-beetle
blister-fly
blister-plaster
blister-steel
blobber-lip
blobber-lipped
blob-lipped
blockade-runner†
block-bond
block-book
block coal
block-colors
block-furnace

blockhead
blockhouse
blocking-course
blocking-hammer
blocking-kettle ·
blocking-machine
blocking-press
blocklike
block-machine
block-making†
block-plane
block-printing†
block-ship
block tin
block-trail
block-truck
blond-lace
blond-metal
blood-baptism
blood-bespotted, blood-consuming, etc.
blood-cell
blood-corpuscle
blood-cups
blood-curdling
blood-disk
blood-drier†
blood-finch
blood-fine
bloodflower (a plant)
blood-guiltiness
blood-guiltless
blood-guilty
blood-heat
blood-horse
blood-hot
bloodhound
blood-leech
bloodlet, v.
blood-mare
blood-money
blood-orange
blood-pheasant
blood-plaque
blood-plate
blood-poisoning
blood pudding
blood-red
blood-relation

blood-relationship
bloodroot (a plant)
blood-sacrifice
bloodshed
bloodshedder
bloodshedding
bloodshot
blood-sound
blood-spavin
blood-spiller†
blood-stain
blood-stanch
blood-stick
blood-stone
blood-strange
blood-stroke
blood-sucker (one who sucks blood)
bloodsucker (a lizard)
blood-sucking
blood-swelling
bloodthirstiness
bloodthirsty
blood-tree
blood-vascular
blood-vessel
blood-warm
blood-wite
bloodwood (a tree, or its wood)
bloodworm
bloodwort
bloody-bones (a bugbear)
bloody-man's-finger (a plant)
bloody-red
bloody-warrior (plant)
bloomer-pit
bloom-hook
blooming-mill
blooming-sally (plant)
bloom-tongs
blossompecker (a bird)
blossomrifler (a bird)
blotting-book
blotting-pad
blotting-paper
blow-ball

blow=cock
blow=fly
blow=gun
blow-hole
blowing=charge
blowing=cylinder
blowing=engine
blowing=fan
blowing=furnace
blowing-house
blowing=iron
blowing=machine
blowing=pipe
blowing=pot
blowing=snake
blowing=tube
blow=milk
blow=off
blowout
blow=over, n.
blowpipe
blow=point
blow=through
blow=tube
blow=up
blow=valve
blow=well
blubber=lip
blubber=lipped
blubber=spade
blueback (a fish)
bluebell (a plant)
blueberry (a plant, or
    its fruit)
bluebill (a duck)
blue=billy
bluebird
blue=black
blue=blazer (a drink)
blue=blind   [bird)
bluebonnet (a person, a
bluebottle (a plant, an
    insect, a person)
bluebreast (a bird)
bluebuck (an antelope)
bluebush (a shrub)
bluebuttons (a person)
bluecap (a fish, a plant,
    a person)

bluecoat (one who
    wears a blue coat)
blue cod
blue creeper
blue=curls (a plant)
blue devils
blue=disease
blue=eyed, blue=laid,
    etc.
bluefin (a fish)
bluefish
blue glede
bluegown (a person)
blue=grass
blue=gum (a gum=
    disease, a tree)
blue=hafit
blue hawk
bluehearts (an herb)
blue=hot
bluejack (an oak=tree)
bluejacket (a sailor)
blue=john
bluejoint=grass
blue kite
blue=laws
blueleg (a person)
blue mantle (a person)
blue mass
blue=mould (a fungus)
bluenose (a person)
blue ointment
blue=paidle
blue=paper (blue=pro=
    cess paper)
blue perch
blue peter
blue pie
blue=pigeon (a sound-
    ing-lead)
blue pike
blue pill
blue=pipe (a lilac)
bluepod (a weed)
bluepoker (a fish)
blue=pot (a crucible)
blue pox
blue=print
blue=printing†

blue racer
blue rock
blue ruin
bluesides (a harp=seal)
blue snapper
blue=spar
bluestart (a bird)
bluestem (a grass)
bluestocking (a person)
bluestockingism
bluestone
bluetail (a lizard)
bluetangle (a plant)
bluethroat (a bird)
blueweed
bluewing (a duck)
bluewood (a tree)
bluff=bowed, etc.
blunderhead
blunthead (a serpent)
blunt=witted, etc.
blush=rose
blushwort
boa=constrictor
board=clip
board=cutter†
boarding=clerk
boarding=gauge
boarding=house
boarding=joist
boarding=machine
boarding=netting
boarding=officer
boarding=pike
boarding=school
board=rack
board=rule
board school
board=wages
boarfish
boar=hunting†
boar=spear
boar=stag
boar's=tusk*
boasting=chisel
boatbill (a bird)
boat=builder†
boat=car
boat=davit

boat·fly
boat·hook
boat·house
boat·insect
boat·keeper†
boat·lowering
boatman
boat·race
boat·racing†
boat·rope
boat's gripes
boat·shaped etc
boat·shell
boat·skid
boat·song
boattail (a bird)
boat·tailed
boatwright
bobbin·lace
bobbin·net
bobbin·stand
bobbin·winder†
bobbin·work
bob·cherry·
bob·fishing†
bob·lincoln
bob·sled
bob·sleigh
bobstay
bobstay·piece
bobtail
bobtail wig
bob·white
bob·wing
bock beer
bock·pot
boco·wood
bode·wash
bodhi·tree
bodkin·work
bod·worm
body·bag
body·bolster
body·cavity
body·cloth
body·clothes
body·coat
body·color
body·guard

body·hoop
body·horse
body·loop
body·louse
body·oil
body·plan
body·post
body·servant
body·snatcher†
body·varnish
body·wall
body·whorl
bog·asphodel
bog·bilberry
bog·bean
bog·blitter
bog·bluiter
bog·bull
bogbumper (a bittern)
bog·butter
bog·cutting†
bog·earth
boggle·de·botch
bog·glede
bogjumper (a bittern)
bog·land
bog·manganese
bog·moss
bog·myrtle
bog·oak
bog·onion
bog·orchis
bog·ore
bog·rush
bog·spavin
bogsucker (a wood-
    cock)
bog·trotter†
bog·violet
bog·wood
bogwort
boiler·alarm
boiler·clamp
boiler·feeder†
boiler·float
boiler·furnace
boiler·house
boiler·iron
boiler·keelson

boiler·making†
boiler·meter
boiler·plate
boiler·protector†
boiler·prover†
boiler·shell
boiler·shop
boiler·tube
boiling·furnace
boiling·point
bold·face type
boldface (a person)
bold·faced, etc.
bollard·timber
boll·rot
boll·worm
bolster·plate
bolster·spring
bolsterwork
bolt·auger
bolt·boat
bolt·chisel
bolt·clipper†
bolt·cutter†
bolter·cloth
bolt·extractor†
bolt·feeder†
bolt·head
bolt·header†
bolt·hole
bolt·hook
bolting·chest
bolting·cloth
bolting·cord
bolting·house
bolting·hutch
bolting·mill
bolting·millstone
bolting·tub
bolt·knife
bolt·making†
bolt·rope
bolt·sawing†
bolt·screwing†
bolt·strake ·
bolt·threader†
bomahnut
bombardier·beetle
bombard·man

bombard-phrase
bomb-chest
bomb-fuse
bomb-ketch
bomb-lance
bomb-proof
bombshell
bomb-vessel
bonace-tree
bond-cooper
bond-creditor
bond-debt
bondfolk
bondholder†
bondland
bondmaid
bondman
bond-paper
bond-servant
bond-service
bond-slave
bondsman
bond-stone
bondswoman
bond-tenant
bond-timber
bonduc-seeds
bondwoman
bone-ace
bone-ache
bore-ash
bone-bed
bone-binder
bone-black
bone-breaker†
bone-breccia
bone-brown
bone-cartilage
bone-cave
bone-dog
bone-dust
bone-earth
bone-eater†
bone-elevator†
bonefish
bone-glass
bone-glue
bone-lace
bone-manure

bone-mill
bone-naphtha
bone-nippers
bone-oil
bone-phosphate
bone-pot
boneset
bone-setter†
bone-shark
bone-spavin
bone-spirit
bone-turquoise
bone-waste
bone-yard
boning-rod
bonnet-block
bonnet-fluke
bonnet-grass
bonnet-laird
bonnet-limpet
bonnet-macaque
bonnet-making†
bonnet-monkey
bonnet-pepper
bonnet-piece
bonnet-rouge
bonnet-shark
bonnet-shell
bonnet-string
bonnet-worm
bonnyclabber
bonny-dame (a plant)
bonte-quagga
bon-ton
bony-fish (a menhaden)
booby-hatch
booby-hut
booby-hutch
book-account
book-back
bookbinder†
bookbindery
book-buyer†
bookcase
book-clamp
book-debt
book-edge
book-fair
book-folding†

book-formed
book-holder†
book-hunter†
booking-clerk
booking-machine
booking-office
book-ink
bookkeeper†
book-knowledge
bookland
book-learned
book-learning
book-lore
book-louse
book-lover†
book-madness
book-maker†
bookman
book-mark
bookmonger
book-muslin
book-name
book-notice
book-oath
book-plate
book-post
book-rack
book-scorpion
bookseller†
book-sewing†
book-shop
book-slide
book-stall
book-stand
book-stone
book-store
book-trade
book-tray
book-trimmer†
book-work
bookworm
bookwright
boom-boat
boom-iron
boom-jigger
boom-mainsail
boomslang
boom-tackle
boon-day

boon=loaf
boon=work
bootblack
boot=calk
boot=catcher†
boot=channelling†
boot=clamp
boot=closer†
boot=crimp
boot=crimping†
boot=cuff
boot=edge
boot=grooving†
boot=heel
boot=holder†
boot=hook
boot=hose
booting=corn
bootjack
boot=lace
boot=last
boot=leg
bootmaker†
boot=pattern
boot=powder
boot=rack
boot=seam
boot=shank
boot=stocking
boot=stretcher†
boot=top
boot=topping†
boot=tree
boot=ventilator†
bo=peep
bordering=wax
border=knife
border=land
border=lights
border=plane
border ruffian
border=stone
border tower
border warrant
bord=halfpenny
bord=land
bord=lode
bord=service
bore=tree

bore=worm
boring=anchor
boring=bar
boring=bench
boring=bit
boring=block
boring=collar
boring=dust
boring=gauge
boring=head
boring=lathe
boring=machine
boring=mill
boring=rod
boring=sponge
boring=table
borough court
borough English
borough=head
borough=holder†
boroughmaster
boroughmonger
boroughmongering
borough=reeve
borough sessions
borough town
borrow=head
borrowing=days
bosom=board
bosom=folder†
bosom=spring
bosom=staff
bot=fly
both=sided
botthammer
bottle=bellied, etc.
bottle=bird
bottle=boot
bottle=brush
bottle=brushing†
bottle=bump
bottle=carrier†
bottle=case
bottle=charger†
bottle=chart
bottle=clip
bottle=coaster†
bottle=cod
bottle=companion

bottle=conjurer
bottle=dropsy
bottle=faucet
bottle=filler†
bottle=fish
bottleflower (a plant)
bottle=friend
bottle=glass
bottle=gourd
bottle=grass
bottle=green
bottle=holder†
bottle=imp
bottle=jack
bottle=mould
bottle=moulding†
bottlenose (a whale)
bottlenose=oil
bottle=ore
bottle=pump
bottle=rack
bottle=screw
bottle=stand
bottle=stoop
bottle=stopper
bottle=tit
bottle=track
bottle=tree
bottle=washer†
bottle=wax
bottling=machine
bottling=room
bottom=captain
bottom=fish
bottom=fishing†
bottom=glade
bottom=grass
bottom=ice
bottoming=hole
bottoming=tap
bottom=land
bottom lift
bottom=plate
bottom=tool
bough=house
bough=pot
boulder=clay
boulder=head
bouldering=stone

boulder-paving
boulder-stone
bouncing-bet
bound bailiff
bounty-jumper†
bouquet-holder¡
bour-tree
bouse-team
bow-arm
bow-backed, etc.
bow-bearer†
bow-bent
bow-boy
bow-brace
bow-case
bow-chaser†
bow-clavier
bow-compass
bow-drill
Bow dye
bowed-embowed
bower-anchor
bower-bird
bower-eaves
bower-maid
bower-thane
bower-woman
bow-fast
bow file
bow-grace
bow-hand
bow-harpsichord
bowhead (e whale)
bowie-knife
bow-instrument
bow-iron
bow-kail
bow-knot
bowl-alley
bowline
bowline-bridle
bowline-cringle
bowline-knot
bowling-alley
bowling-crease
bowling-green
bowling-ground
bowl-machine
bowman's-root

bow net
bow-oar
bow-pen
bow-pencil
bow-piece
bow-pin
bow-saw
bow-shot
bowsprit-cap
bowstaff
bowstring
bowstring bridge
bowstring girder
bow-timbers
bow window
bow-wise
bow-wood
bow-wow
box barrow
box beam
box bed
box car
box-coat
box coil
box-crab
box-day
box drain
box-elder
boxfish
box frame
box girder
boxhaul
box-hook
boxing-day
boxing-glove
boxing-machine
boxing-match
boxing-night
boxing-off
box-iron
box-keeper†
box-key
box-lobby
box-lock
box-making†
box-metal
box-money
box-office
box-opener†

box-packing†
box plait
box-plaiting†
box-scraper†
box-seat
box-set
box-setter†
box-slater†
box slip
box snuffers
box stall
box-strap
box-thorn
box-tortoise
box trap
box-turning†
box-turtle
box valve
boxwood
boy bishop
boy-blind
boy-queller†
boy's-love*
boy's play
brace-drill
brace-head
brace-key
brace-mould
brace-pendant
brace-stake
bracing-chain
bracket-crab
bracket-trail
brad-awl
brad-driver†
brad-setter†
braid-comb
braiding-machine
braid-polishing†
braid-sizing†
brain-bladder
brain-box
brain-case
brain-cavity
brain coral
brain-fag
brain fever
brain-maggot
brainpan

brain=racking†
brainsand
brain=sick
brainstone
brainstone coral
brain throb
brain=tumor
brain=wave
brain=work
brain=worm
brake=band
brake=bar
brake=beam
brake=block
brake=hanger
brake=head
brake=hopper
brakeman
brake=shaft
brake=shoe
brake=sieve
brakesman
brake=spool
brake=strap
brake=van
brake=wheel
braking=machine
brambleberry
bramble=bond
bramble=bush
bramble=finch
bramble=net
bramble=rose
bramble=worm
bran bread
branch chuck
branch=leaf
branch=pilot
branch=point
brand=goose
branding=iron
brand=iron
brand=mark
brand=new
brand=spore
bran=duster†
brandy=bottle
brandy=fruit
brandy=pawnee

brandy=snap
brantail (a bird)
brant=fox
brant=goose
brass blacking
brass band
brass bass
brass=color
brass=finisher†
brass=foil
brass=founder†
brass=furnace
brass=leaf
brass=paved, etc.
brass=powder
brass=smith
brass=wind
brattice=cloth
brawn=fallen
brazen=browed, etc.
brazenface (a person)
brazil=cock
Brazil=nut
Brazil=root
brazil=wood
brazing=tongs
breaching=battery
bread=barge
bread=basket
breadberry
bread=corn
bread=crumb
breadfruit
breadfruit=tree
bread=knife
bread=making†
breadmeal (berghmehl)
bread=rasp
breadroot (a plant)
bread=slicer†
breadstuff
breadth=line
bread=tray
bread=tree
bread=weight
breadwinner†
breakax
breakbones
breakcircuit

breakdown, n.
breakfast
breakfast=cap
breakfast=dishes
breakfast=set
breakfast=table
breakfast=time
break=in
breaking=diameter
breaking=engine
breaking=frame
breaking=weight
break=iron
break=lathe
breakneck, a. and n.
break=off
breakpromise (a person)
breakshare
break=signal
breakstaff
breakstone (a plant)
break=up
break=van
breakwater
breamflat (a fish)
breast=backstay
breast=band
breast=beam
breast=board
breast=bone
breast=chains
breast=collar
breast=deep
breast=drill
breast=fast
breast=gasket
breast=harness
breast=height
breast=high
breast=hook
breasting=knife
breast=knee
breast=knot
breast=line
breast=moulding
breast=pain
breast=pang
breastpin
breastplate

breast-plow
breast-pump
breast-rail
breast-strap
breast-summer
breast-wall
breastweed
breast-wheel
breast-wood
breastwork
breathing-hole
breathing-mark
breathing-place
breathing-pore
breathing-sound
breathing-space
breathing-spell
breathing-time
breathing-tube
breathing-while
breath-sound
breech-band
breach-barrow
breech-block
breech-clout
breeches-buoy
breeching-bolt
breeching-hook
breeching-loop
breech-loader†
breech-mechanism
breech-piece
breech-pin
breech-screw
breech-sight
breech-wrench
breeding-cage
breeding-pen
breeding-place
breeding-season
breeze-fly
breeze-oven
brent-fox
brent-goose
brent-new
brequet-chain
brew-house
brew-kettle
bribe-pander

bribery oath
bribe-taker†
bric-à-brac
brick-axe
brick-barrow
brickbat
brick-built
brick-clamp
brick-clay
brick-drier†
brick-dust
brick-earth
brick-elevator†
brick-field
brickfielder
brick-furnace
brick-klin
bricklayer†
brick-machine
brickmaker†
brick-mason
bricknog
bricknogging
brick-oil
brick-press
brick ten
brick-tile
brick-trimmer†
brick-truck
brickwork
brick-yard
bridal-wreath (a plant)
bride-cake
bride-chamber
bride-day
bridegroom
bridemaid
brideman
bridesmaid
bridesman
bridewort
bridge-bar
bridge-board
bridge-deck
bridge-head
bridge-islet
bridge-pile
bridge-pit
bridge-rail

bridge-stone
bridge-tower
bridge-tree
bridge-truss
bridge-ward
bridging-floor
bridging-joist
bridging-piece
bridle-bit
bridle-chains
bridle-hand
bridle-path
bridle-port
bridle-rein
bridle-road
bridle-rod
bridle stricture
bridleway
bridle-wise, a.
brier-bird
brier-root
brier-rose
brier-wood
brigade major
brigadier-general
bright-cut
bright-eyed, etc.
brightwork
brim-sand
brimstone
brimstonewort
brindle-moth
brine-evaporator†
brine-pan
brine-pit
brine-pump
brine-shrimp
brine-spring
brine-valve
brine-worm
bristle-fern
bristle-grass
bristle-herring
bristle-moss
bristle-pointed
bristletail (an insect)
bristlewort
Bristol-board
Britain crown

britterworts
brittle=star (a starfish)
broaching=press
broach=post
broach=turner
broad arrow
broadaxe
broad=based, broad=
    billed, etc.
broadbill (a bird)
broadbrim (a Quaker)
broadcast
broadcloth
broad=gauge (having a
    broad gauge)
broadhorn (a flatboat)
broadleaf (a tree)
broadleaf=tree
broadmouth (a bird)
broad=piece
broad seal
broad=seal, v.
broadside
broad=spoken, etc.
broad=spread
broadstone (ashler)
broadsword
broadtail (a parrot)
broadthroat (a bird)
broad tool
brock=faced
broken=backed, etc.
brome=grass
bronze=backer (a bass)
bronze=gold
bronze=liquid
bronze=liquor
bronze=paint
bronze=powder
bronzewing (a pigeon)
bronzing=machine
bronzing=salt
brood=bud
brood=capsule
brood=cavity
brood=cell
brood=mare
brood=pouch
brood=space

brook=fish (any fish in
    brooks)
brookfish (a killifish)
brooklime (a plant)
brook=mint
brook=moss
brook=pickerel
brook=runner
brookside
brook=trout
brookweed
broom=brush
broom=bush
broom=corn
broom=crowberry
broom=grass
broom=handle
broom=head
broom=palm
broom=pine
broom=rape
broom=root
broom=sedge
broom=sewing†
broomstaff
broomstick
broom=tree
broom=vise
broomweed
brother german
brother=in=law
brother officer
brotherwort
brow=ague
brow=antler
brow=band
browbeat
brow=bound
brownback (a bird)
brown=backed, etc.
brown=bess
brownbill (a halbert)
brown blaze
brown coal
brownstone
brown stout
brownwort
brow=post
browse=wood

brow=snag
browspot
brow=transom
bruisewort
bruising=machine
bruising=mill
brush=bird
brush=burn
brush=cherry
brush=hat
brushing=machine
brush=jack
brushman
brush=monkey
brush=ore
brush=plow
brush=puller†
brush=tailed
brush=tongued
brush=turkey
brush=wheel
brushwood
buaze=fiber
bubble=shell
bubble=trier
bubbling=fish
buck=ague
buck=and=ball
buck=basket
buck=bean
buckboard
bucket engine
bucket=hook
bucket=lift
bucket=making†
bucket=pitch
bucket=rod
bucket=shop
bucket=valve
bucket=wheel
buckeye
buck=eyed
buck=fever
buckfinch
buckhorn
buckhorn=sight
buck=hound
bucking=iron
bucking=kier

bucking-plate
bucking-stool
buck-jumper
buckle-beggar
buckle-chape
buckle-horns
buckler-fern
buckler-fish
buckler-headed
buckler-mustard
buckling-comb
buck-log
buck-mackerel
buck-moth
buckpot
buck-saw
buck's-beard*
buck's-horn*
buckshot
buckskin
buck-stall
Bucktail
buckthorn (a plant, a
   tooth)
buck-tooth
buck-wagon
buckwash, v.
buckwashing
buckwheat
buckwheat-field
buckwheat-huller†
buckwheat-tree
bud-cell
budding-knife
bud-finch
budge-barrel
buffalo-berry
buffalo-bird
buffalo-bug
buffalo-chips
buffalo-clover
buffalo-cod
buffalo-fish
buffalo-gnat
buffalo-grass
buffalo-jack
buffalo-nut
buffalo-perch
buffalo robe

buff-coat
buffer-bar
buffer-beam
buffer-block
buffer-head
buffer-spring
buffet-stool
buffing-block
buffing-lathe
buffing-machine
buffing-spring
buffing-wheel
buff jerkin
buff-laced
buff leather
buffle-duck
bufflehead (a duck)
buffle-headed
buffle-horn
buffle-wood
buff-stick
bugbear
bug-bite
bugeye
bugfish
buggerow-boat
buggy-boat
buggy cultivator
buggy plow
bugle-call
bugle-cap
bugle-horn
bugle-rod
bugleweed
buglewort
bugseed (a plant)
bug-shad
bugwort
buhl-saw
buhl-work
buhr-dresser†
buhr-driver†
buhrstone
building-block
building-iron
building lease
building-mover
building-slip
building-stance

building-wax
bukkum-wood
bulgeways
bulkhead
bull-baiting
bullbat
bull-beef
bullbeggar
bull-boat
bullbrier
bull calf (a male calf)
bull-calf (a person)
bullcomber
bull-dance
bulldog
bulldoze
bullen-bullen
bullen-nail
bullet-bag
bullet-extractor†
bullet-headed
bullet-hook
bulletin-board
bullet-ladle
bullet-machine
bullet-making†
bullet-mould
bullet-moulding†
bullet-probe
bullet-proof
bullet-screw
bullet-shell
bullet-tree
bullet-wood
bull-faced, bull-head-
   ed, etc.
bull-feast
bull-fight
bull-fighter†
bullfinch
bullfish
bullfist
bullfly (a gadfly)
bullfrog
bull-fronts
bull-head, a.
bullhead (a fish, an in-
   sect, a plover)
bullhead-plover

bullhoof (a plant)
bulling=shovel
bullion=bar
bullion=fringe
bullion=point
bull=neck
bull=net
bullnose (a clam)
bullnut (a hickory=
  tree)
bullock's=eye*
bullock's=heart*
bullock=shell
bull=pine
bull=pout (a fish)
bull=pump
bull=ring
bull=roarer
bull=rope
bulls=and=cows (plant)
bull=segg
bull's=eye*
bull's=foot*
bull's=mouth*
bull=snake
bull's=nose*
bull=spink
bull=stag
bull=stang
bull=terrier
bull=trout
bullweed
bull=whack
bull=whacker†
bull=wheel
bull=whip
bullwort
bully=cod
bully=head
bully=tree
bumblebee
bumbleberry
bumble=foot (a club=
  foot)
bumblefoot (a disease
  of fowls)
bumble=footed
bumbler=box
bumble=staff

bumboat
bum=clock
bumper=timber
bumping=post
bum=wood
bunchberry (a plant)
bunch=fish
bunchflower (a plant)
bunch=grass
bunch=whale
bundle=pillar
bundle=sheath
bundling=machine
bundling=press
bung=borer†
bung=cutter†
bung=drawer†
bung=hole
bungo=tree
bung=starter†
bung=stave
bung=vent
bunker=plate
bunko=game
bunko=joint
bunko=man
bunko=steerer†
bunt=ear (a smut of
  wheat)
bunter=sandstein
bunt=gasket
bunting=crow
bunting=finch
bunting=iron
bunting=lark
bunt=jigger
buntline=cloth
bunt=whip
bunya=bunya
buoy=rope
buoy=safe
bur=bark
burbot=eel
bur=brick
bur=chisel
bur=cutter†
burden=bearer†
burdock=grass
bur=dresser†

bur=drill
bur=driver†
burfish
bur=gauge
burgage=tenant
burgage=tenement
burghermaster
burghmaster
burglar=alarm
burglar=proof
bur=grass
burial=case
burial=ground
burial=mound
burial=place
buri=nut
burling=iron
burling=machine
bur=marigold
bur=millstone
burnet=moth
burnet=rose
burning=bush (a plant)
burning=fluid
burning=glass
burning=house (a kiln)
burning=lens
burning=mirror
bur=nipper†
burnishing=machine
burnt=ear (a smut of
  wheat)
burnt offering
burnt sacrifice
burnt=stone
burnwood (a plant)
bur=oak
bur=parsley
bur=pump
burras=pipe
burrawang=nut
bur=reed
burrel=fly
burrel=shot
burring=machine
burring=saw
burring=wheel
burrow=duck
bursting=charge

burstone
burstwort
bur=thistle
burton=tackle
bur=tree
burying=beetle
burying=ground
burying=place
bush=babbler
bush=bean
bush=block
bushbuck (an antelope)
bushcat (a serval)
bushchat (a bird)
bush=chirper
bush=creeper
bush=dog
bushel=barrel (a half=
  barrel)
bushelman
bushelwoman
bush=extractor†
bush=fighting†
bush=goat
bush=hammer
bush=harrow
bush=hook
bush=lark
bush=lawyer
bushman
bushmaster
bush=metal
bush=oven
bush=quail
bushranger†
bush=scythe
bush=shrike
bush=tailed
bush=tit
bushwhacker†
businesslike
busybody
butcher=crow
butcher=knife
butcher=meat
butcher's=broom*
butcher's=prickwood
but=gap
butment=cheek

butt=bolt
butt=chain
butt end
butter=ale
butter=and=eggs (a
  plant)
butterball (a duck)
butter=bean
butter=bird
butter=boat
butter=box
butterbump (a bittern)
butterbur (coltsfoot)
butter=color
buttercup
butter=daisy
butter=dock
butter=duck
butter=fingered
butter=fingers
butter=firkin
butter=fish
butterflip (a bird)
butterflower (a plant)
butterfly
butterfly cock
butterfly=fish
butterfly=gurnard
butterfly=nose
butterfly=orchis
butterfly=pea
butterfly=plant
butterfly=ray
butterfly=shaped
butterfly=shell
butterfly valve
butterfly=weed
butter=knife
butter=making†
butterman
buttermilk
butter=mould
buttermunk (a heron)
butternut
butter=pat
butter=plate
butter=pot
butter=print
butter=scotch

butter=shag
butter=stamp
butter=store
butter=tongs
butter=tooth
butter=tree
butter=trier†
butter=tub
butterweed
butterwife
butterwoman
butter=worker†
butterwort
buttery=bar
buttery=book
buttery=hatch
butt=hinge
butt=howel
butting=joint
butting=machine
butting=ring
butting=saw
butt=joint
butt leather
buttock=line
buttonball (a tree)
button=blank
button=brace
button=bush
button=ear
button=fastener†
buttonflower (a plant)
buttonhole
buttonhole=machine
button=hook
button=lathe
button=mould
button=nosed
button=piece
button=quail
button=riveting†
button=solder
button=soldering†
button=tool
button=tree
buttonweed
buttonwood (a tree)
buttress=tower
butt=strap, v.

butt=weld
buttwoman
butty=collier
butty=gang
buzzard=clock
buzzard=hawk
buzzard=moth
buzz=saw
by=aim
by=altar
by=ball
by=bidder
by=blow
by=book
by=business
by=cause
by=comment
by=concernment
by=corner
by=dependency
by=design
by=drinking
by=dweller

by=election
by=end
by=fellow
by=fellowship
bygone
by=hour
by=interest
by=intimation
by=lane
by=law
by=lead
by=legislation
by=matter
by=motive
by=name
by=ordinary
by=pass
by=passage
by=passer
by=past
by=path
by=place
byplay

by=plot
by=product
by=purpose
by=report
byrlaw=court
byrlaw=man
by=road
by=room
by=speech
bystander
by=street
by=stroke
by=talk
by=term
by=time
by=turning
by=view
by=walk
by=walker
by=wash
bywater
byway
byword

C

caaing=whale
cabbage=bug
cabbage=butterfly
cabbage=flea
cabbage=fly
cabbage=maggot
cabbage=moth
cabbage=oil
cabbage=palm
cabbage=palmetto
cabbage=rose
cabbage=tree
cabbage=wood
cabbage=worm
cabin=boy
cabinet=maker†
cabin=mate
cable=bend
cable=buoy
cable=carrier†
cable=current
cable=drilling†
cable=gripper†
cable=hook
cable=laid
cable=locker†
cable=moulding
cable=nipper†
cable=railroad
cable=road
cable=screw
cable=shackle
cable's length
cable=stopper†
cable=tier
cable=tools
cableway
cab=driver†
cabman
cab=stand

cacao=butter
cacao=nut ·
cache=pot
caddis=fly
caddis=shrimp
caddis=worm
cade=oil
cade=worm
cadmium yellow
cage=bird
cage=guides .
cage=seat   ⁻
cage=shuts
cahinca=root
Cain=and=Abel (a plant)
cain=colored
cairn=tangle
caisson=disease
cake=alum
cake=baker†
cake=basket
cake=bread
cake=copper
cake=cutter†
cake=lake
cake=mixer†
cake=steamer†
cake=urchin
cake=walk
calabar=skin
calabash=tree
calabur=tree
calamander=wood
calcination=pot
calcining=furnace
calcium=light
calc=sinter
calc=spar
calc=tuff
calculating=machine

calendar=clock
calendering=machine
calendering=rubber
calf=bone
calfkill (a plant)
calf=lick
calf=like
calf=love
calf's=foot*
calf's=head*   .
calfskin   ·
calf=snout
calf=ward
caliatour=wood
caliber gauge
caliber rule
caliber square
calicoback (a bird)
calico bass
calico=bush
calico=printer†
calico=wood
calking=anvil
calking=chisel
calking=iron
calking=mallet
calking=tongs
calk=sharpener†
calk=swage
call=bell
call=bird
call=box
call=boy
call=button
call=changes
calley=stone
calling crab
calling hare
call=loan
call=me=to=you (a plant)

call=note
callous=beaked
calm=belt
calm=latitudes
calves'=snout*
calves'=tongue*
camara=wood
camass=rat
camber=beam
cambering=machine
camber=keeled
camber=slip
camber=window
cambric=grass
cambric=muslin
cam=cutter†
camel=backed, etc.
camel=bird
camel=cricket
camel=driver†
camel=grass
camel=insect
camel=locust
camel's=thorn (a shrub)
cameo=conch
cameo=glass
cameo=press
cameo=shell
cameotype
cameo=ware
camera=lens
camera=stand
camp=ceiling
camp=chair
camp=drill
camp=fight
camp=fire
camp=follower†
camphor=oil
camphor=tree
camphor=wood
camphor=wood oil
camp=kettle
camp=kit
camp=meeting
camp=mill
camp=stool
camp=stove
camp=table

camp=vinegar
cam=shaft
cam=wheel
canal=boat
canal=coal
canal=lift
canal=lock
cananga=oil
canary=bird
canary=creeper
canary=finch
canary=grass
canary=moss
canary=seed
canary=stone
canary=weed
canary=wood
can=bottle
can=buoy
can=cart
cancelling=press
cancelling=stamp
cancer=bandage
cancer=cell
cancer=juice
cancer=mushroom
cancerroot (a plant)
cancerweed
cancerwort
candle=balance
candle=beam
candle=bearer†
candleberry
candleberry=myrtle
candleberry=tree
candle=bomb
candle=case
candle=coal
candle=dipping†
candle=end
candle=fir
candle=fish
candle=flame
candle=fly
candle=holder†
candle=light
Candlemas=bell (a plant)
candle=mine

candle=mould
candlenut
candle=power
candle=rush
candlestick
candle=tree
candle=waster†
candle=wick
candlewood (a tree)
candy=sugar
candytuft
cane=borer†
cane=brake
cane=colored
cane gun
cane=harvester†
cane=hole
cane=juice
cane=killer†
cane=knife
canella=wood
cane=mill
cane=rush
cane=polishing†
cane=press
cane=scraper†
cane=splitter†
cane=stripper†
cane=sugar
cane=trash
cane=working†
can=frame
can=hook
canister=shot
canjica=wood
canker=bit
canker=bloom
canker=blossom
canker=dort
canker=fly
canker=nail
canker=rash
cankerroot (a plant)
canker=worm
cannel=coal
cannon=ball
cannon=bit
cannon=bone
cannon=casting†

cannon=lock
cannon=metal
cannon=pinion
cannon=proof
cannon=range
cannon=shot
cannon=stove
can not
canoe=birch
canoe=cedar
canoeman
canoewood (a tree)
canon=bit
cañon=wren
can-opener†
can=roving†
can=soldering†
cant=block
cant=board
cant=body
cant=chisel
cant=dog
canterbury=bell (a
   plant)
cant=fall
cant=file
cant=frames
cant=hook
cantick=quoin
canting=coin
canting=wheel
cant=moulding
cant=piece
cant=purchase
cant=rail
cant=robin
cant=spar
cant=timber
canvasback (a duck)
canvas=backed
canvas=cutter†
canvas=stretcher†
canvas=work
cap=a=pie
caper=berry
caper=bush
caper=cutting†
caper=plant
caper sauce

caper=spurge
caper=tea
caper=tree
capeweed
capitan=pacha
capon's=feather*
capon's=tail*
cap paper (a size of
   paper)
cap=paper (for making
   caps)
cap=piece
capping=brick
capping=plane
cap=pot
cap=pudding
cap=rock
cap=screw
cap=scuttle
cap=sheaf
cap=shore
cap=sill
cap=square
capstan=bar
capstan=barrel
capstone
captaincy=general
captain=general
captain=generalcy
captain=pasha
carana=palm
caravan boiler
car=axle
car=basket
carbine=thimble
carbon=black
carbon=bronze
carbon=button
carbonization=bed
carbonizing=furnace
carbon=paper
carbon=point
carbon=print
carbon=printing†
car=brake
car=buffer
car=bumper
carcass=flooring
carcass=roofing

carcass-saw
carcel=lamp
car=coupling†
cardamom=oil
card=basket
cardboard
cardboard=press
card=case
card catalogue
card=clothing
card=cutter†
carder=bee
card=grinder†
cardinal=bird
cardinal=flower (a
   plant
cardinal=red, a.
carding=bee
carding=engine
carding=machine
card=maker†
card=match
card=party
card=player†
card=rack
card=press
card=printing†
car=driver†
card=setting†
card=sharper
card=table
card=tray
care=crazed, etc.
caretaker
care=worn
cargo=block
car=heater†
car=horse
caricature=plant
car=indicator
car=jack
carl=cat
carl=crab
car=lamp
car=lantern
carl=hemp
carling=knee
car=load
car=lounge

car=tangle
carnal=minded
carnation=grass
carn=tangle
carob=bean
carp=bream
carpenter=moth
carpenter's=herb
carpetbag
carpetbagger
carpet=beater†
carpet=bedding
carpet=beetle
carpet=broom
carpet=brush
carpet=cleaner†
carpet=dance
carpet=fastener†
carpet=friend
carpet=knight
carpet=lining
carpet=loom
carpetmonger
carpet=moth
carpet=rod
carpet=sewer†
carpet=snake
carpet=strainer†
carpet=stretcher†
carpet=sweeper†
carpet=tack
carpet=thread
carpetweed
carpet=worsted
carp=louse
carp=mullet
carp=sucker
car=replacer†
carriage=bolt
carriage=brake
carriage=bridge
carriage=coupling
carriage=free
carriage=guard
carriage=jack
carriage=lock
carriage=piece
carriage=shackle
carriage=spring

carriage=top
carriageway
carriage=wheel
carrick=bend
carrick=bitt
carrier=bird
carrier=pigeon
carrier=ring
carrier=shell
carrion=beetle
carrion=buzzard
carrion=crow
carrion=feeder†
carrion=flower
carrion=hawk
carrion=vulture
carron=oil
carrot=tree
carryall (a wagon)
carrying=on
car=seal
car=seat
car=spring
car=standard
car=stake
car=starter†
car=stove
car=swallow
cart=aver
cart=body
carte=de=visite
cart=horse
cartilage=bone
cart=jade
cart=ladder
cart=load
carton=pâte
carton=pierre
car=track
cartridge=bag
cartridge=belt
cartridge=block
cartridge=box
cartridge=capper†
cartridge=case
cartridge=filler†
cartridge=gauge
cartridge=loader†
cartridge=paper

cartridge=pouch
cartridge=primer†
cartridge=retractor†
cartridge=wire
car=truck
car=truss
cart=saddle
cart=tail
cartway
cartwright
carvel=built
carvel=joint
carvel=work
carving=chisel
carving=fork
carving=knife
carving=lathe
carving=machine
carving=table
car=wheel
car=window
case=bay
case=bearer†
case=binding
case=bottle
case=char
case=ending
case=harden
case=hardened
case=hardening
case=knife
case=lock
case=maker†
caseman
casemate=carriage
casemate=gun
casemate=truck
case=paper
case=rack
case=shot
caseweed
case=work
case=worm
cash account
cash=book
cash=box
cash=boy
cash=carrier†
cash=credit

cash=day
casher=box
cashew=bird
cashew=nut
cashew=tree
cash=girl
cash=keeper†
cash=note
cassavawood (a tree)
casse=paper
casserole=fish
cassia=buds
cassia=lignea
cassia=oil
cassia=pulp
caster=wheel
cast=gate
casting=bottle
casting=box
casting=glass
casting=ladle
casting=net
casting=pit
casting=pot
casting=press
casting=slab
casting=table
casting vote
casting=weight
cast iron
cast=iron, *a.*
cast knitting
castle=builder†
castle=guard
castle=stead
castle=town,
castle=ward
cast=net
cast=off, *a.*
castor=bean
castor-oil
castrating=clamp
cast shadow
cast steel
cast=steel, *a.*
cataract=knife
cataract=forceps
cataract=needle
cataract=spoon

cat=back (a rope)
catbird
cat=blash
cat=block
cat=boat
catbrier (smilax)
catcall
cat=castle
catchall, *n.*
catch=bar
catch=basin
catch=bolt
catch=club
catch=drain
catch=feeder
catch=fly
catch=hook
catching bargain
catch=land
catch=lever
catch=line
catch=match
catch=meadow
catchment=basin
cat=chop
catchpenny
catchpoll
catchwater, *n.*
catchweed
catch=weight
catchword
catchwork
cater=cornered
cater=cousin
caterpillar=catcher†
caterpillar=eater†
caterpillar=fungus
caterpillar=hunter†
cat=eyed, cat=footed,
    etc.
cat=fall
catfish
cat=foot
cat=gold
catgut
catgut=scraper†
cat=hammed
catharine=wheel
cat=harpin

cat=haws
cat=head, *n.*
cathead, *v.*
catheter=gauge
cat=hole
cat=hook
cat=ice   •
cat=in=clover (a plant)
cat=lap
catlike
catmint
cat=nap
catnip
catnut
cat=o'=mountain
cat=o'=nine=tails
cat=owl   ,
cat=pipe
cat=rake
cat=rig
cat=rigged
cat=rope
cat=rush
cat=salt
cat's=brains*
cat's=claw*
cat's=cradle*
cat's=ear*
cat's=eye*
cat's=foot*
cat=shark
cat's=head*
cat=silver
cat's=milk*
catspaw
cat's=purr*
cat=squirrel
cat's=tail*
cat=stane
cat=stick
cat=stopper
cat=tackle
cattail (a plant)
cat=thrasher
cattle=farm
cattle=feeder†
cattle=guard
cattle=heron
cattle=leader†

cattle=louse
cattle=marking†
cattle=pen
cattle-plague
cattle=pump
cattle=range
cattle=run
cattle=show
cattle=stall
cattle=tie
caudle=cup
cautery=electrode
cauting=iron
caution=money
cave=bear
cave=cricket
cave=dweller†
cave=fish
cave=hyena
cave=keeper†
cave=lion
caveman
cave=pica
cave=swallow
cave=tiger
caving=rake
cavinna=wood
cavo=rilievo
cedar=apple
cedar=bird
cedar=gum
cedar=lark
cedar=oil
cedar=pine
cedar=tree
cedar=wood
ceiling=boards
ceiling=joist
ceiling=plate
celery=pine
cell=animal
cellar=book
cellar=flap
cellarman
cellar=rat
cellar=snail
cell=capsule
cell=development
cell=enamel

cell=membrane
cell=mouth
cell=parasite
cell=parasitism
cell=protoplasm
cell=sap
cell=space
cell=substance
cementation=box
cementation=furnace
cement=copper
cement=duct
cement=gland
cementing=furnace
cementing=oven
cement=mill
cement=stone
census=paper
centre=bar
centre=bit
centre=block
centreboard
centre=chisel
centre=chuck
centre=drill
centre=fire
centre=gauge
centre=guide
centre=lathe
centre=mould
centrepiece
centre=pin
centre=plate
centre=punch
centre=rail
centre=saw
centre=second
centre=table
centre=tools
centre=valve
centre=velic
centre=wheel
centring=gauge
centring=machine
centring=tool
century=plant
certosina=work
cesspool
cetin=claic

cetain=elaine
cevadilla=oil
chack=bird
chackstone (a jack-
 stone)
chafewax
chafeweed
chaff=cutter†
chaff=engine
chaff=flower
chaff=halter
chaffseed
chaffwax
chaffweed
chafing=board
chafing=check
chafing=dish
chafing=gear
chafing=plate
chain=ball
chain=bearer†
chain bit
chain=boat
chain=bolt
chain bond
chain bridge
chain cable
chain=chest
chain coral
chain=coupling†
chain=fastening†
chain=fern
chain=gang
chain=gear
chain=grate
chain=guard
chain=hook
chain=inclinometer
chain=knot
chain=lifter†
chain lightning
chain=lock
chain=locker†
chain=loom
chain mail
chain=moulding
chain=pier
chain=pin
chain=pipe

chain-plate
chain-pulley
chain-pump
chain-rule
chain-saw
chain-shot
chainsmith
chain-snake
chain-stitch
chain-stopper†
chain syllogism
chain-timber
chain-towing
chain-wale
chain-well
chain-wheel
chainwork
chair-arm
chair-back
chair-bearer†
chair-bed
chair-bolt
chair-days
chair-leg
chair-maker†
chairman
chair-organ
chair-rail
chair-seat
chair-spring
chair-web
chalice-case
chalice-cells
chalice-pall
chalice-spoon
chalice-veil
chalk-box
chalk-cutter†
chalk-drawing†
chalk-engraving†
chalk-line
chalk-mark
chalk-pit
chalkstone
chamber-council
chamber-counsel
chamber-counsellor
chamber-fellow
chamber-gauge

chamber-hangings
chamber-kiln
chambermaid
chamber-master
chamber-music
chamber-organ
chamber-piece
chamber-practice
chamber-story
chancel-aisle
chancel-arch
chancel-rail
chancel-screen
chancel-table
chance-medley
chandelier-tree
change-house
change-pump
change-ratio
change-ringing†
changerwife
change-wheel
changing-house
chank-shell
channel-bar
channel-bass
channelbill (a cuckoo)
channel-board
channel-bone
channel-cat
channel-duck
channel-goose
channelling-machine
channel-iron
channel-leaved
channel-plate
channel-stone
channel-wale
chaparral-cock
chap-book
chapel-cart
chapel-clerk
chapel-de-fer
chapelmaster
chapel text
chapfallen
chapter-head
chapter-heading
chapter-house

chapter-lands
char-à-bancs
character-monger
charcoal
charcoal-black
charcoal-burner†
charcoal-cooler†
charcoal-drawing†
charcoal-filter
charcoal-furnace
charcoal-iron
charcoal-paper
charcoal-pencil
charcoal-pit
charcoal-plates
charcoal-tree
charger-pit
charge-sheet
chariot-man
chariot-race
charity boy
charity child
charity girl
charity school
charly-mufty
charnel-house
char-oven
charring-chisel
Charter boy
Charter brother
charter-land
charter-master
charter-party
chart-room
charwoman
charwork
chase-gun
chase-mortise
chase-port
chase-ring
chasing-chisel
chasing-hammer
chasing-lathe
chasse-marée
chaste-eyed, etc.
chaste-tree
chat-roller
chatterbasket (a chat-
terer)

chatterbox (a chatterer)
chatter-water
chat-thrush
chat-wood
chaud-medley
chaud-mille
chauk-daw
chaw-bacon
chaw-stick
Chebacco-boat
check-book
check-bridge
check-chain
check-clerk
check-cord
check-end
checkerberry
checker-board
checkering-file
checker-roll
checker-tree
checkerwork
check-hook
check-key
check-line
check-list
check-lock
checkmate
check-nut
check-rail
check-rein
check-roll
check-rope
check-rower†
check-stop
check-strap
check-string
check-taker†
check-valve
cheek-band
cheek-blade
cheek-block
cheek-bone
cheek-piece
cheek-pouch
cheek-strap
cheek-tooth
cheese-cake
cheese-cement

cheese-cloth
cheese-cutter†
cheese-fly
cheese-hoop
cheesehopper (a maggot)
cheese-knife
cheese-maggot
cheese-maker†
cheesemaker (a plant)
cheese-mite
cheese-mould
cheesemonger
cheese-pale
cheese-paring†
cheese-press
cheese-rennet
cheese-room
cheese-running†
cheese-scoop
cheese-shelf
cheese-taster†
cheese-toaster†
cheese-turner†
cheese-vat
chef-d'œuvre
chenille-machine
chenille-needle
cherry-bird
cherry-blight
cherry-blossom
cherry bounce
cherry brandy
cherry-chopper†
cherry-coal
cherry-cob
cherry-coffee
cherry-colored
cherry cordial
cherry-finch
cherry-gum
cherry-laurel
cherry-net
cherry-oil
cherry-pepper
cherry pie
cherry-pit
cherry-plum
cherry rum

cherry-snipe
cherry-stick
cherry-stone
cherry-stoner†
cherry-tree
cherry wine
chess-apple
chess-board
chessman
chess-player†
chess-rook
chess-tree
chess-type
chest-bellows
chest-founder
chest-lock
chest-measure
chest-measurer†
chestnut-brown
chestnut-bur
chestnut coal
chestnut-meal
chestnut-oak
chestnut-tree
chest-register
chest-rope
chest-saw
chest-tone
chest-voice
cheval-de-frise
cheval-glass
cheval-screen
chevaux-de-frise
chevron-bone
chevron-moulding
chevron-work
chewing-ball
chewing-gum
chew-stick
chichling-vetch
chicken-bird
chicken-breasted, etc
chicken-cholera
chicken-feeder†
chicken-halibut
chicken-hawk
chicken-heart
chicken-pox
chicken's-meat*

chicken=snake
chicken=tortoise
chickenweed
chick=house
chick=pea
chickstone (a bird)
chickweed
chicle=gum
chief justice
chief=justiceship
chief=rent
chiffchaff (a bird)
chiffon=work
child=bearing
childbed
childbirth
child bishop
child=crowing
childish=minded
child=killing
child=learnt
childlike
child wife
chill=hardening
chilli=coyote
chilli=pepper
chime=barrel
chime=bell
chime=ringing
chiming=machine
chimneyboard
chimney=breast
chimney=can
chimney=cap
chimney=collar
chimney=corner
chimney=head
chimney=hook
chimney=jack
chimney=jamb
chimney=money
chimneypiece
chimney=pot
chimney=shaft
chimney=stack
chimney=stalk
chimney=swallow
chimney=sweep
chimney=sweeper†

chimney=swift
chimney=top
chimney=valve
chimney=work
china=ale
china=clay
china=grass
Chinaman
Chinaman's=hat*
china=root
chinar=tree
china=shell
china=shop
china=stone
china=token
china=tree
chinaware
china=withe
chin=band
chinch=bug
chin=cloth
chin=cough
chine=hoop
chining=machine
chin=jerk
chinkapin=oak
chinkapin=perch
chin=piece
chin=scab
chinsing=iron
chin=strap
chin=welk
chip=axe
chip=bird
chip=breaker†
chip=chop, a.
chipchop, n.
chipping=bird
chipping=chisel
chipping=knife
chipping=machine
chipping=piece
chipping sparrow
chipping squirrel
chipping up
chisel=draft
chisel=edge
chisel=point
chisel=shaped

chisel=tooth
chit=book
chit=chat
chittagong=wood
chittamwood (a tree)
chive=garlic
chock=a=block
chock=and=block
chock=block
chock=full
chocolate cake
chocolate=house
chocolate=mill
chocolate=root
chocolate=tree
choice=note
choir=boy
choir=office
choir=organ
choir=pitch
choir=ruler
choir=screen
choir=service
choir=tippet
chokeberry
choke=bore
choke=cherry
choke=damp
choke=full
choke=pear
choke=pondweed
choke=strap
chokeweed
chokewort
chola=plant
choosing=stick
chop=boat
chop=cherry
chop=dollar
chop=hammer
chop=house
chop=logic
chop=nut
chopper=cot
chopping=block
chopping=board
chopping=knife
chopping=mill
chopping note

chopping-tray
chop-sticks
choral-book
chorda-animal
chorus-master
chow-chow
chowder-beer
choy-root
chrism-child
Christ-child
christ-cross
christcross-row
Christmas-tide
chrome-alum
chrome black
chrome-color
chrome green
chrome-iron
chrome-ironstone
chrome-mica
chrome-ochre
chrome orange
chrome-oxide
chrome red
chrome yellow
chrysalis-shell
chub-cheeked, etc.
chub-mackerel
chub-sucker
chuck-a-by
chuck-farthing
chuck-full
chuckie-stone
chucking-machine
chuck-lathe
chuckle-head (a head)
chucklehead (a person)
chuckle-headed
chuck-will's-widow
chum-drill
chump-end
chunkhead (a snake)
chunk-yard
church-ale
church-bred
church-bug
church dues
church-gang
church-garth

churchgoer†
church-haw
church-hay
church-house
church-land
churchlike
church-litten
church-loaf
churchman
churchmanlike
church-member
church-mouse
church-outed
church-owl
church-quack
church-rate
church-scot
church-town
church trustee
church-wake
church-warden
churchway
churchwoman
church-work
church-writ
churchyard
churl's-head*
churl's-treacle*
churn-dasher
churn-drill
churn-jumper
churn-milk
churn-owl
churn-power
churn-staff
churr-worm
chyle-bladder
chyle-corpuscle
chyle-intestine
chyle-space
chyle-stomach
chyme-mass
cider brandy
cider-mill
cider-press
cider-tree
cider vinegar
cigar-bundler†
cigar-case

cigarette-filler†
cigarette-machine
cigarette-paper
cigar-fish
cigar-holder
cigar-lighter†
cigar-machine
cigar-maker†
cigar-plant
cigar-press
cigar-steamer†
cigar-store
cigar-tree
cigar-tube
cinchona-tree
cinder-bed
cinder-cone
cinder-fall
cinder-frame
cinder-notch
cinder path
cinder pig
cinder-sifter†
cinder-tub
cinder-wench
cinder-woman
cinder-wool
cinnabar-green
cinnamon-brown
cinnamon-fern
cinnamon-oil
cinnamon-stone
cinnamon-suet
cinnamon-water
cinq-trou
cinque-cento
cinque-pace
cinque-port
cinque-spotted
ciper-tunnel
ciphering-book
ciphering-slate
cipher-key
cipher-tunnel
circle-cutter†
circle-iron
circle-reading†
circle-squarer†
circuit-breaker†

circuit-closer†
circuit-rider†
circulation-coil
circulation-stove
circus-ring
cirl-bunting
cirrus-sac
cirrus-sheath
citril-finch
citron-oil
citron-tree
citron-water
citron-wood
citron-yellow
citrus-tree
civet-cat
civil-suited
clack-box
clack-dish
clack-door
clack-goose
clack-mill
clack-piece
clack-seat
clack-valve
claim-notice
claire-cole
clair-obscure
clambake
clamber-skull
clam-cod
clam-cracker†
clamming-machine
clamp-cell
clamp-connection
clamp-coupling
clamp-dog
clamp-iron
clamp-kiln
clamp-nail
clamp-screw
clam-scraper†
clam-shell
clam-tongs
clam-worm
clang-color
clang-tint
clansman
clapboard

clapboard-gauge
clap-bread
clap-dish
clapmatch (an old seal)
clap-net
clapperbill (a stork)
clapperclaw
clapper-stay
clapper-valve
clap-sill
clap-stick
claptrap
claret-cup
claret-red
claribel-flute
clarinet-stop
claro-obscuro
clary-water
clasp-hook
clasp-knife
clasp-lock
clasp-nail
class-day
class-fellow
class-leader
classman
classmate
classroom
class-shooting
clatter-goose
clause-rolls
clawback (a back-
    scratcher)
claw-balk
claw-bar
claw-foot
claw-hammer (a ham-
    mer)
clawhammer (a coat)
claw-hand
claw-joint
claw-sick
claw-wrench
clay-band
clay-bead
clay-brained, clay-
    built, etc.
clay-clot
clay-cold

clay-course
claying-bar
clay-kiln
clay-mill
clay-pit
clay-pulverizer†
clay-screening†
clay-stone
clay-yellow
cleaching-net
clean-cut, clean-hand-
    ed, etc.
cleaning-hydrant
cleaning-machine
cleaning-valve
cleansing-days
cleansing-round
cleansing-square
cleansing-vat
cleansing-week
clean-up
clear-cut, clear-eyed,
    etc.
clearer-bar
clearing-battery
clearing-beck
clearing-house
clearing-nut
clearing-pan
clearing-plow
clearing-ring
clearing-sale
clearing-screw
clearing-stone
clear-melting
clear-seer†
clearstarch
clearstarcher
clearstory
clearweed
clearwing (a sphinx-
    moth)
cleavage-cavity
cleavage-cell
cleavage-globule
cleavage-mass
cleaving-knife
cleaving-saw
clecking-time

cleft-graft
cleft-grafting
clench-bolt
clench-nail
clench-ring
clergyman
clergywoman
click-beetle
click-pulley
click-wheel
cliff-brake
cliff-limestone
cliff-swallow
climbing boy
climbing fern
climbing-fish
climbing-irons
climbing-perch
clinch-built
clincher-built
clincher-plating
clincher-work
clingstone (a peach)
clink-shell
clinkstone (a phonolite)
clinkum-clankum
clinometer-level
'clip-candlestick
clip-chair
clip-finch
clip-hook
clipper-built
clipper-ship
clippfish
clipping-machine
clipping-shears
clipping-time
clip-plate
clip-pulley
clip-swage
clip-yoke
clish-clash
cloak-anemone
cloak-bag
cloak-room
clock-alarm
clock-beetle
clock-case
clock-face

clock-maker†
clock-movement
clock-oil
clock-pillar
clock-setter†
clock-spring
clock-star
clock-stocking
clock-tower
clock-turret
clock-watch
clockwork (mechanism)
clod-breaker†
clod-crusher†
clod-fishing†
clodhopper†
clodpate
clodpated
clodpoll
clog-almanac
clog-burnisher†
clog-dance
clog-dancer†
cloghead
clog-hornpipe
clog-pack
clogweed
cloister-garth
close-banded, close-bodied, etc.
close-fights (bulkheads)
close-hug (scapular arch of a fowl)
close-plane
close-point
close quarters
close-quarters (bulkheads)
close-reef
close-season
close-stool
close-time
close-work
closh-hook
closing-hammer
closing-machine
cloth-creaser†

cloth-dressing†
cloth-drying†
clothes-basket
clothes-brush
clothes-drier†
clothes-horse
clothes-line
clothes-moth
clothes-pin
clothes-press
clothes-sprinkler†
clothes-wringer†
cloth-finishing†
cloth-folding†
cloth-hall
cloth-lapper†
cloth-measure
cloth-measuring†
cloth-paper
cloth-plate
cloth-press
cloth-prover†
cloth-shearer†
cloth-shop
cloth-sponger†
cloth-stitch
cloth-stretcher†
cloth-teazler†
cloth-tester†
cloth-varnishing†
cloth-wheel
cloth-worker†
cloth-yard
cloud-bank
cloud-born, cloud-capped, etc.
cloudburst
cloud-compeller†
cloud-drift
cloud-kissing
cloudland
cloud-rack
cloud-ring
clough-arch
clout-nail
clove-bark
clove-cinnamon
clove-gillyflower
clove-hitch

clove=hook
clovenberry
cloven=footed
cloven=hoofed
clove=nutmeg
clove=orange
clove=pink
clover=grass
clover=huller†
clover=leaf
clover=seed
clover=sick
clover=thresher†
clover=weevil
clovewort
clownheal
clown's=treacle*
club=ball
club=compasses
club=fisted
club=foot (the foot itself)
clubfoot (distortion of foot)
club=footed, club=headed, etc.
club=grass
clubhaul
club=house
club=law
clubman (who uses a club)
club=man (member of club)
club=master
club=moss
club=palm
clubroom
clubroot
club=rush
club=shaped
club=skate
club=topsail
clucking=hen (a crying= bird)
clue=garnet
clue=iron
clue=jigger
clue=line

clue=net
clump=block
clump=boot
clumsy=boots (a person)
clumsy=cleat
cluster=cups (fungi)
cluster=pine
cluster=spring
clutch=drill
clutch=lamp
clutchtail (a monkey)
coachbell (an earwig)
coach=bit
coach=box
coach=colors
coach=currier
coach=dog
coachfellow
coach=founder†
coach=horse
coach=leaves
coachmaker†
coachman
coachmaster
coach=office
coach=screw
coach=stand
coach=trimmer†
coach=wheel
coach=whip (a whip)
coachwhip (a snake, a pennant)
coachwhip=snake
coachwood (a tree)
coal=backer
coal=barge
coal=basin
coal=bed
coal=bin
coal=black
coal=boring†
coal=box
coal=brand
coal=brass
coal=breaker†
coal=bunker
coal=car
coal=carrier†
coal=cart

coal=chute
coal=cutting†
coal=drop
coal=dumping†
coal=dust
coal=field
coalfish
coal=fitter
coal=gas
coal=goose
coal=heaver†
coal=hod
coal=hole
coal=hood
coal=hoodie
coal=hulk
coalman
coalmaster
coal=measures
coal=meter
coal=mine
coal=miner†
coal=mouse
coal=note
coal=oil
coal=passer†
coal=pipe
coal=pit
coal=plant
coal=sack
coal=screen
coal=scuttle
coal=ship
coal=slack
coal=sledge
coal=smut
coal=staith
coal=stone
coal=stove
coal=tar
coal=tit
coal=tongs
coal=trimmer†
coal=viewer†
coal=whipper†
coal=workings
coal=works
coaly=hood
coarse=grained, etc.

coast-guard
coast-ice
coast-line
coast-pilot
coast-rat
coast-waiter
coat-armor
coat-button
coat-collar
coat-link
coat-money
coat-pocket
coat-sleeve
coat-tail
cobalt-bloom
cobalt blue
cobalt-bronze
cobalt-crust
cobalt-glance
cobalt green
cobalt-ochre
cobalt-vitriol
cobalt yellow
cobbler-fish
cobblestone
cob-horse
cob house
cob-iron
cob-joe
cob-loaf
cobnut
cob-poke
cobra-de-capello
cobra-monil
cob-stacker
cobstone
cob wall
cobweb
cobworm
cock-a-hoop
cock-ale
cock-and-bull, a.
cock-bead
cockbill
cockboat
cock-brass
cock-bread
cock-broth
cockchafer

cockcrow
cockcrowing
cocked-hat (bowling)
cockeye
cock-feather
cock-fight
cock-fighter†
cock-garden
cockgrass
cockhead
cock-hedge
cockhorse
cockie-leekie
cocking-main
cock-laird
cockle-boat
cockle-brained, etc.
cockle-brillion
cockle-bur
cockle-garden
cockle-hat
cockle-oast
cockle-sauce
cockle-shell
cockle-stair
cockle-stove
cockle-wife
cock lobster
cockloft
cock-master
cock-match
cockmate
cock-metal
cock-nest
cock-penny
cockpit
cockroach
cockscomb
cockscomb-grass
cockscomb-oyster
cocksfoot-grass
cockshead (a plant)
cockspur
cockspur-grass
cockstone
cock-sure
cocktail
cock-up, a.
cockup (a fish)

cock-water
cockweb
cockweed
cockyoly-bird
cocoanut
cocoanut-crab
cocoanut-oil
cocoanut-tree
cocoa-oil
cocoa-plum
cocoa-powder
cocoa-tree
coco-de-mer
coco-wood
cocum-butter
cocum-oil
cocus-wood
coddy-moddy
codfish
codfish ball
codfish cake
cod-fisher†
cod-fishery
cod-glove
cod-line
codling-moth
codlins-and-cream
cod-liver
cod-murderer†
cod-piece
cod-pole
cod-sound
cœlom-epithelium
coffee-bean
coffee-berry
coffee-biggin
coffee-blight
coffee-borer†
coffee-bug
coffee-cleaner†
coffee-corn
coffee-cup
coffee-grinding†
coffee-house
coffee-huller†
coffee-making†
coffee-man
coffee-mill
coffee-nib

coffee=nut
coffee=polisher†
coffee=pot
coffee=pulper†
coffee=roaster†
coffee=room
coffee=sage
coffee=shop
coffee=stand
coffee=tree
coffer=dam
coffer=fish
cofferwork
coffin=boat
coffin=bone
coffin=carrier†
coffin=fish
coffre=fort
cog=bells
cog=rail
cogware
cog=wheel
cogwood (a tree)
cohune=oil
coil=plate
coin=assorter†
coin=balance
coin=counter†
coining=press
coin=weighing†
coke=barrow
coke=furnace
coke=making†
coke=omnibus
coke=oven
coke=tower
coking=kiln
coking=oven
colander=shovel
cola=nut
cola=seed
cold=blooded, cold=
  drawn, etc.
cold=chisel
cold=cream
cold=hammer, v.
cold=kind
cold=moving
cold=pale

cold=short
cold=shot
cold=shut
cold=sore
cold=stoking
cold=sweating
cold=tankard
cold=tinning
cole=rape
cole=seed
cole=slaw
cole=tit
colicroot (a plant)
collar=awl
collarbags (smut of
  wheat)
collar=beam
collar=bird
collar=block
collar=bolt
collar=bone
collar=box
collar=button
collar=cell
collar=check
collar=harness
collar=launder
collar=nail
collar=plate
collar=swage
collar=tool
collar=work
collecting=bottle
collecting=cane
collecting=net
collector magistrate
college pudding
collery=stick
colly=brand
color=bearer†
color=blind
color=blindness
color=box
color=chart
color=circle
color=combination
color=comparator
color=cone
color=contrast

color=cylinder
color=diagram
color=doctor
color=equation
color=guard
coloring=matter
coloring=tool
color=lake
color=line
colorman
color=party
color=printing†
color=reaction
color=sensation
color=sense
color=sergeant
color=striker†
color=triangle
color=variation
color=variety
colt=ale
colter=neb
colt=evil
colt=like
colt=pixy
coltsfoot (a plant)
colt's=tail*
column=lathe
column=rule
column=skulls
comb=bearer†
comb=broach
comb=brush
comb=cap
comb=cutter†
comb=frame
comb=honey
combination lock
combing=machine
comb=jelly
comb=paper
comb=pot
comb=rat
comb=saw
come=at=ability
come=at=able
come=down
come=off
come=outer

comet=finder†
comet=seeker†
coming=floor
commandancy=general
commander=in=chief
comma=tipped
commissary=court
commissary=general
commissary=sergeant
commission agent
commission merchant
committeeman
committee=room
commonplace=book
common=sense, *a.*
commonsensible
commonweal
commonwealth
communication=plate
communication=valve
communion=cloth
communion=cup
communion=rail
communion=table
commutation ticket
companion=ladder
companionway
compass=bar
compass=board
compass=bowl
compass=box
compass=brick
compass=card
compass=dial
compass=headed
compass=joint
compass=needle
compass=plane
compass=plant
compass roof
compass=saw
compass=signal
compass=timber
compass=window
compensation balance
compensation bars
compensation pendu-
   lum
composing=frame

composing=machine
composing=room
composing=rule
composing=stand
composing=stick
compression casting
compression=cock
compression=machine
compromise wheel
comptroller=general
concert grand
concert=master
concert music
concert piece
concert pitch
concho=grass
conch=shell
concrete=press
condenser=gauge
condensing=coil
conditioning=house
conduct=money
conductor=head
cone=billed
cone bit
cone clutch
coneflower (a plant)
cone=gamba
cone=gear
cone=granule
cone=in=cone
cone=joint
cone=nose
cone=plate
cone pulley
cone=seat
cone=shell
cone=valve
cone wheel
confection=pan
confession=chair
configuration=diagram
congee=house .
congee=water
conger=doust
conger=eel
congo=eel
Congressman
conic=acute, *a.*

conic=ovate, *a.*
conjugating=tube
conjuring=cup
connate=perfoliate
connecting=cell
connecting=link
connecting=rod
conning=tower
conscience=smitten
consecration=cross
console=table
construction=way
consulate=general
consul=general
contact=breaker†
contact=level
contact=lever
cont=line
contour=feather
contour=hair
contour=line
contraction=rule
contrary=minded
contrast=diagram
contre=ermine
contre=lettre
contre=vair
control=experiment
controller=general
controlling=nozzle
cont=splice
convention coin
convention dollar
conversation=tube
converting=furnace
cony=burrow
cony=fish
cony=wool
coo=in=new
cook=book
cook=conner
cook=house
cooking=range
cooking=stove
cook=maid
cook=room
cook=wrasse
cool=cup
cool=headed, etc.

cooling=cup
cooling=floor
cool=tankard
coolweed
coolwort ·
coon=bear
coonda=oil
coon=heel
coon=oyster
coonskin
cootfoot (a bird)
coot=footed
coot=grebe
copaiba=oil
cope=chisel
copepod stage
copperbell (a snake)
copperbelly (a snake)
copper=bit
copper=bottomed, etc.
copper captain
copper=furnace
copper=glance
copperhead (a snake)
copper=nickel
coppernose (a sunfish)
copperplate
copper=powder
copper=rose (a poppy)
coppersmith
copper=wall
copperwing (butterfly)
copperwork
copper=works
copper=worm
copping=plate
copping=rail
copping=crown
copple=dust
copsewood
cop=tube
copy=book
copyhold
copyholder (one who
  has a copyhold)
copy=holder (one who
  holds copy)
copying=ink
copying=lathe

copying=machine
copying=paper
copying=pencil
copying=press
copying=ribbon
copy=money
copyright
coquilla=nut
coquito=oil .
coralberry
coral=fish
coral=insect
coral=mud
coral=plant
coral=polyp
coral=rag
coralroot (a plant)
coral=snake
coral=stitch
coral=tongs
coral=tree
coral=wood
coralwort
coral=zone
corbel=piece
corbel=steps
corbel=table
corbie=crow
cordate=lanceolate
cordate=oblong
cordate=sagittate
cord=covering†
cord=drier†
cor-de-chasse
cord=grass
cord=leaf
cord=machine
cord=sling
cord=stitch
cord=wood
core=barrel
core=box
core=lifter†
core=piece
core=print
core=valve
core=wheel
corf=house
coriander=seed

cork=bark
cork=black
cork=board
corkbrain (a person)
cork=brained, etc.
cork=clasp
cork=cutter†
cork=fastener†
cork=faucet
cork=fossil
corking=machine
corking=pin
cork=leather
cork=machine
cork=oak
cork=press
cork=presser†
cork=pull
cork=puller†
corkscrew
cork=tree
corkwood (a tree)
corn=badger
corn ball
corn=beetle
cornbells (a fungus)
cornbind (a plant)
cornbottle (a plant)
cornbrash
corn bread
corn cake
corn=chandler
corn=cleaner†
corn=cob
corn=cockle
corn=coverer†
corn=cracker†
corn=crake
corn=crib
corn=cultivator†
corn=cutter†
corn dodger
corn=drill
cornea=lens
cornea=reflex
corn=eater†
cornel=tree
corner=chisel
corner=cutter†

corner-drill
cornering-machine
corner-piece
corner-plate
corner-punch
corner-saw
corner-stone
corner-tooth
corner-valve
cornet-à-pistons
cornet-stop
corn exchange
corn-factor
corn-field
corn-flag
corn-floor
corn-flower
corn-fly
corn fritter
corn-goose
corn-grater†
corn-growing†
corn-harp
corn-harvester†
corn-hook
corn-huller†
corn-husk
corn-husker†
cornice-hook
cornice-plane
cornice-ring
corning-house
Cornishman
corn-juice
corn-knife
corn-land
corn-law
corn-lift
corn-loft
corn-marigold
corn-meter
corn-mill
corn-mint
corn-moth
corn-muller
corn-oyster
corn-parsley
corn-pipe
corn-planter†

corn-plaster
corn-plow
corn pone
corn-popper†
corn-poppy
corn-rent
corn-rig
corn-rose
corn-row
corn-salad
corn-sawfly
corn-sheller†
corn-shuck
corn-shucking†
corn-snake
corn-stalk
corn-starch
cornstone
corn-stripping
corn-thrips
corn-van
corn-violet
corn-weevil
corn-worm
coronation-oath
coronation-roll
corporal-case
corporal-cloth
corporal-cup
corporation stop
corpse-candle
corpse-cooler†
corpse-gate
corpse-light
corpse-plant
corpse-preserver†
corpse-sheet
correcting-plate
corset-maker†
corundum-point
corundum-tool
costal-nerved
cost-book
costean-pit
coster-boy
costermonger
cost-free
cost-sheet
costus-root

cot-bed
cotbetty
Côte-rôtie
cot-roller
cottar-town
cotter-drill
cotter-file
cotter-plate
cotton-bale
cotton-blue
cotton-broker
cotton-brush
cotton-cake
cotton-chopper†
cotton-cleaner†
cotton-elevator
cotton-fibre
cotton-floater†
cotton-gin
cotton-grass
cotton-hook
cotton-lord
cotton-machine
cotton-manufactory
cotton-manufacture
cotton-mill
cottonmouth (a snake)
cotton-opener†
cotton-picker†
cotton-plant
cotton-planter†
cotton-plantation
cotton-powder
cotton-press
cotton-rat
cotton-rush
cotton-scraper†
cotton-sedge
cottonseed
cottonseed-cleaner†
cottonseed-mill
cottonseed-oil
cotton-shrub
cotton-stainer†
cotton-sweep
cottontail (a rabbit)
cotton-thistle
cotton-topper†
cotton-tree

cottonweed
cottonwood (a tree)
cotton=wool
cotton=worm
cot-town
couch=fellow
couch=grass
couching=needle
coughwort
coulomb=meter
coumu=oil
council=board
council=book
council=chamber
council=house
councilman
council=table
counsel=keeper†
counting=house
counting room
count=out
country=base
country=bred
country=dance
countryman
country=rock
country=seat
countryside
countrywoman
count=wheel
county=seat
coupe=gorge
couple=close
coupling=box
coupling=link
coupling=pin
coupling=pole
coupling=strap
coupling=valve
coupon=killer†
coursing=hat
coursing=joint
coursing-trial
court=baron
court=bred
court=card
court chaplain
courtcraft
court=day

court dress
court=dresser
court favor
court fool
court guide
court=hand
court=house
court=lands
court=leet
court=like
court-marshal
court martial
court=martial, v.
court mourning
court=plaster
court=rolls
court=shift
court sword
court=tennis
courtyard
cous=cous
couvre=nuque
cove=bracketing
covenant=breaker†
coventry=bell
Coventry blue
coventry=rape
cove=plane
cover=cloth
cover=glass
covering=board
covering=seed
covering=strap
cover=point
cover=side
cover=slip
covert=baron
covert=feather
cowbane
cow=beck
cow=bell
cowberry (a plant)
cowbird
cow=blackbird
cow=blakes
cowboy
cow=bunting
cow calf
cowcatcher

cow=chervil
cow=cress
cowdie=gum
cow=doctor
cow=feeder†
cowfish
cow=gate
cow=grass
cow=heel
cow=herb
cowherd
cowhide
cow=hitch
cow=hocked
cow=horn
cow=house
cow=keeper†
cow=killer†
cow=leech
cow=leeching
cowlick
cowlike
cowl=muscle
cowlstaff
cow=man
cow=milker†
cow=oak
cow=paps
cow=parsley
cow=parsnip
cow=path
cow=pea
cowpen=bird
cow=pilot
cow=plant
cowpock
cow=poison
cow=pony
cowpox
cowquakes (grass)
cowrie=pine
cow=shark
cowslip
cow=stone
cow=tree
cow=troopial
cowweed
cow=wheat
crab=apple

crab-catcher† (one who catches crabs)
crabcatcher (a bird)
crab-eater† (one who eats crabs)
crabeater (a bittern, a fish)
crab-farming†
crab-grass
crab-lobster
crab-louse
crab-oil
crab-pot
crab-roller
crab's-claw*
crabs'-eyes*
crabsidle
crab-spider
crabstick
crabstock
crabstone
crab-tree
crab-winch
crab-wood
crab-yaws
crack-brained
cracker-baker†
crackle china
crackle glass
crackle porcelain
crackle ware
crackskull (a person)
cracksman
cracktryst (a person)
cradle-bar
cradle-cap
cradle-clothes
cradle-hole
cradle-rocker†
cradle-scythe
cradle vault
craftsman
craftsmaster
cragsman
craig-fluke
crail-capon
crakeberry (a plant)
crake-herring
crake-needles (a plant)

crambo-clink
crambo-jingle
cramp-bark
cramp-bone
cramp-drill
crampfish
cramp-iron
cramp-joint
cramp-ray
cramp-ring
cramp-stone
cranberry
cranberry-gatherer†
cranberry-tree
crane-fly
crane-ladle
crane-line
crane-necked
crane-post
cranesbill (a plant)
crane-shaft
crane-stalk
crank-axle
crankbird
crank-brace
crank-hatches
crank-hook
crank-pin
crank-plane
crank-puller†
crank-shaft
crank-sided
crank-wheel
crape-cloth
crape-fish
crape-hair
crape-myrtle
craping-machine
crappit-head
cratch-cradle
cravat-goose
crawfish
crawl-a-bottom (a fish)
crawleyroot (a plant)
crayon-board
crayon-drawing†
crazy-bone
crazy-quilt
crazyweed

crazy-work
cream-cake
cream cheese
cream-colored
creamcups (a plant)
cream-faced
cream-freezer†
creamfruit
creaming-pan
cream-jug
cream-laid
cream-nut
cream-pan
cream-pitcher
cream-pot
cream-slice
cream ware
cream-white
cream-wove
creasing-hammer
creasing-tool
credence-table
credit-union
creedsman
creek-duck
creekfish
creel-frame
creep-hole
creeping-disk
creeping-jack
creeping-jenny
creeping-sailor (plant)
creeping-sheet
creeping-sickness
creep-mouse
creosote-bush
creosote-water
crêpe-lisse
cresset-light
cresset-stone
cress-rocket
crestfallen
crest-tile
crevasse-stopper
crewel-stitch
crewel-work
cribbage-board
cribbage-player†
crib-biter†

cribble=bread
crib=dam
crib=muzzle
cribrate=punctate
crib=strap
cribwork
cricket=ball
cricket=bat
cricket=bird
cricket=club
cricket=field
cricket=frog
cricket=game
cricket=ground
cricket=iron
cricket=player†
cricket=shoes
crimping=board
crimping=house
crimping=iron
crimping=machine
crimp=press
crimson=warm
crinkum=crankum
crisping=iron
crisping=pin
crisscross=row
crochet=hook
crochet=lace
crochet=needle
crochet=type
crochet=work
crock=saw
crocodile=bird
crookback (a person)
crooked=backed, etc.
crook=neck (squash)
crook=rafter
crop=ear
crop=eared
cropfish
crop=hide
crop=ore
cropple=crown
cropweed
croquet=ball
croquet=ground
croquet=mallet
croquet=player†

cross=action
cross=aisle
cross=armed, etc.
cross=axle
cross=banister
cross=bar
cross=bar shot
crossbeak (a bird)
cross=beam
cross=bearer†
cross=bearings
cross=bedding
cross=belt
cross=bill (a bill, in law,
    crossing another)
crossbill (a bird)
cross=birth
cross=bit
cross=bond
cross=bone
crossbow
crossbowman
cross=breed
cross=breeding
cross=bun
cross=buttock
cross=chock
cross=cloth
cross=clout
cross=country
cross=course
cross=curve
cross=cut, n. and a.
crosscut, v.
cross=days
cross=examination
cross=examine
cross=examiner†
cross=eye
cross=eyed, etc.
cross=fertilizable
cross=fertilization
cross=fertilize
cross=file
cross=fire
crossfish
crossflower (a plant)
cross=flucan
cross=fox

cross=frog
cross=furrow
cross=garnet
cross=guard
cross=hair
cross=hatching
cross=head
cross=hilt
cross=interrogatory
cross=jack
cross=lode
cross=loop
cross=loophole
cross=marriages
cross=mouth
cross=multiplication
cross=nervure
cross=pawl
crosspiece
cross=pile
cross=piled
cross=pollination
cross=purpose
cross=quarters
cross=question
cross=reference
cross=road (a road that
    crosses another)
crossroads (place where
    roads cross)
cross=row
cross=ruff
cross=rule
cross=section
cross=set
cross=shed
cross=sill
cross=spider
cross=springer
cross=staff
cross=stitch
cross=stone
cross=summer
cross=tail
cross=tie
cross=timber
cross=tining
crosstree
cross=valve

cross-vaulting
cross-vein
cross-vine
cross-way
cross-weaving
cross-webbing
cross-week
cross-wire
crosswort
croton-bug
croton-oil
crouchback (a person
crouch-clay
crouch-ware
crow-bait
crowbar
crowbells (a plant)
crowberry
crow-blackbird
crow-corn
crowdie-time
crow-flight
crowflower (a plant)
crowfoot
crowfoot-halyard
crown-antler
crown-arch
crown-badge
crown-bar
crownbeard (a plant)
crown-crane
crow-needles (a plant)
crow-nest
crow-net
crown-face
crown-gate
crown glass
crown-grafting
crown-head
crown-imperial (a
   plant)
crown land (land
   owned by the
   crown)
crownland (a province)
crown-net
crown-palm
crown-paper
crown piece (coin)

crownpiece
crown-pigeon
crown-post
crown prince
crown-saw
crown-scab
crown-sheet
crown-shell
crown-sparrow
crown-summit
crown-thistle
crown-tile
crown-valve
crown-wheel
crownwork
crow-quill
crow-roost
crow's-bill*
crow's-foot*
crow-shrike
crow-silk
crow's-nest*
crow-steps
crowstone
crowtoe (a plant)
crozing-machine
crucian carp
cruciate-complicate
cruciate-incumbent
crucible-mould
crucible-oven
crucible-tongs
crue-herring
cruet-stand
crumb-brush
crumb-cloth
crumb-knife
crumb-of-bread (a
   sponge)
crumb-remover
crupper-chain
crusher-gauge
crush-hat
crushing-machine
crush-room
crust-hunt
crust-hunter†
crust-lizard
crutch-handle

crutch-handled
crutch-palsy
crying-bird
cubbridge-head
cubby-hole
cubby-house
cubby-yew
cub-drawn
cubeb-pepper
cube ore
cube powder
cube-spar
cubit-bone
cubit-fashion
cucking-stool
cuckold-maker†
cuckold's knot
cuckold's-neck*
cuckoo-ale
cuckoo-bee
cuckoo-dove
cuckoo-fish
cuckooflower (a plant)
cuckoo-fly
cuckoo-grass
cuckoo-gurnard
cuckoo-pint
cuckoo's-bread*
cuckoo-shell
cuckoo-shrike
cuckoo's-maid*
cuckoo's-mate*
cuckoo's-meat*
cuckoo-spit
cuckoo-spittle
cucumber-beetle
cucumber-oil
cucumber-root
cucumber-tree
cudgel-play
cudgel-proof
cudweed
cue-ball
cue-button
cue-rack
cue-tip
cuff-button
cuff-frame
cuir-bouilli

cul=de=four
cul=de=lampe
cul=de=sac
culm=bar
culture=bulb
culture=cell
culture=fluid
culture=medium
culture=oven
culture=tube
cultus=cod
culver=dung
culverfoot (a plant)
Culver's=physic*
Culver's=root*
culvertail
culverwort
cumberground
cumin=seed
cunning man
cunning woman
cup=and=cone
cup=and=saucer, a.
cup=anvil
cup=bearer†
cupboard
cup coral
cupel=dust
cup=gall
cup guard
cup=hilted, etc.
Cupid's=wing*
cup=laud
cup=leather
cup=lichen
cupman
cup=moss
cup=mushroom
cupola furnace
cupping=glass
cupping=machine
cupping=tool
cup=plant
cup purse
cuprea=bark
cuprose (a poppy)
cupseed (a plant)
cup=shrimp
cup=sponge

cup valve
curaçao=bird
curb=bit
curb=chain
curb=key
curb=pin
curb=plate
curb roof
curb=sender
curbstone
curculio=trap
curcuma=paper
curd=breaker†
curd=cutter†
curd=mill
cur dog
cure=all
curfew=bell
curiosity=shop
curl=cloud
curlewberry
curlew=jack
curlew=knot
curling=iron
curling=stone
curling=tongs
curl=pate
curly=headed, etc.
curly=pate
currant=borer†
currant=clearwing
currant=gall
currant=moth
currant=tree
currant=worm
current=breaker†
current=fender†
current=gauge
current=meter
current=mill
current=regulator†
current=sailing
current=wheel
curry=card
currycomb
currying=glove
curry=leaf
curry=powder
curtail=step

curtain=angle
curtain=lecture
curtain of mail
curtain=paper
curtain=wall
cuscus=oil
cushew=bird
cushie=doo
cushion=capital
cushion=carom
cushion=dance
cushion=pink
cushion=rafter
cushion=scale
cushion=star
cushion=stitch
cuss=word
custard=apple
custard=cups (a plant)
custom=house
customs duty
customs union
cutaway
cut=chundoo
cut drop
cut=grass
cutheal (valerian)
cutlas=fish
cutlips (a fish)
cut=lugged
cut=mark
cut=off
cut=out
cut=pile
cutpurse
cut=splay
cutter=bar
cutter=grinder†
cutter=head
cutter=stock
cutthroat
cutting=board
cutting=box
cutting=compass
cutting=engine
cutting=file
cutting=gauge
cutting=line
cutting=lipper (a fish)

cutting=nippers
cutting=out, a.
cutting=plane
cutting=pliers
cutting=press
cutting=punch
cutting=shoe
cutting=spade
cutting=thrust
cutting=tool
cuttlebone
cuttlefish
cuttlefish=bone
cuttoo=plate
cutty=gun
cutty=quean
cutty=stool
cutty=wren

cutwater
cutweed
cut=work
cutworm
cyan blue
cyclone=pit
cylinder=axis
cylinder=bit
cylinder=bore
cylinder car
cylinder=cock
cylinder=cover
cylinder desk
cylinder engine
cylinder escapement
cylinder=face
cylinder gauge
cylinder glass

cylinder=grinder
cylinder=mill
cylinder=milling
cylinder=port
cylinder=power
cylinder press
cylinder=snail
cylinder=snake
cylinder=staff
cylinder=tape
cylinder=wrench
cymbal=doctor
cypress=knee
cypress=moss
cypress=root
cypress=tree
cypress=vine
cyprus=bird

D

dabbing-machine
dabchick
dab-wash
daddy-long-legs
daddy-sculpin
dado-plane
dagger-fibre
dagger-knee
dagger-knife
dagger-moth
dagger-plant
dagger-thrust
dag-lock
dairy-farm
dairymaid
dairyman
dairywoman
daisy-bush
daisy-cutter†
dale-land
dale-lander
dalesman
damask-loom
dame-school
dame's-violet*
dam-head
dammar-gum
dammar-pitch
dammar-resin
damper-pedal
damper-regulator
damping-machine
dam-plate
damsel-fly
dam-stone
dance-music
dancing-disease
dancing girl
dancing-girls (a plant)
dancing-master

dancing-room
dancing-school
dandy-brush
dandy-cock
dandy-fever
dandy-hen
dandy-horse
dandy-note
dandy-rig
dandy-roller
daneflower (a plant)
danesblood (a plant)
daneweed
danewort
danger-signal
dangleberry
dapple-bay
dapple-gray
daredevil
daredeviltry
dark-arches (a moth)
darkling-beetle
dark-slide
darning-ball
darning-last
darning-needle
darning-stitch
daroo-tree
darter-fish
dart-moth
dart-sac
dart-snake
dashboard
dasher-block
dash-guard
dash-lamp
dash-pot
dash-rule
dash-wheel
date-line

date-mark
date-palm
date-plum
date-shell
date-sugar
date-tree
date wine
datum-line
datum-plane
daughter-cell
daughter-in-law
David's-root*
davit-fall
daw-dressing
dawfish
dawpate (a simpleton)
dayberry (a plant)
day-blindness
day-book
daybreak
day-coal
day-dream
day-dreamer†
day-dreamy
day-feeder†
day-flier†
dayflower (a plant)
day-fly
day-hole
day-house
day-labor
day-laborer
day-level
daylight
day-lily
dayman
daymare
day-nurse
day-nursery
day-owl

day-peep
day-room
day-rule
day-scholar
day-school
dayshine
daysight
daysman
dayspring
day-star
day-tale
daytaleman
daytaler
daytime
daywoman
day-work
day-writ
dead-angle
dead-beat, a.
dead-born
dead-centre
dead-clothes
dead-coloring
dead-dipping
dead-door
deadeye
deadfall
dead-file
dead-flat
dead-ground
dead-hand
dead-head (mechanical)
deadhead (a person)
deadhead, v.
dead-house
dead-latch
deadlight
dead-line
dead-lock (a door-lock)
deadlock (stoppage of progress)
· deadly-handed
deadly-lively.
dead-man's-hand (a plant)
dead-march
dead-men's-bells (a plant)

dead-men's-fingers (a plant)
dead-men's-lines (a plant)
dead-neap
dead-nettle
dead-oil
dead-plate
dead-pledge
dead-point
dead-reckoning
dead-rise
dead-rising
dead rope
dead set
dead-sheave
dead-shore
dead-small
dead's part
dead-spindle
dead-stroke
dead-thraw
dead-tongue
dead-water
dead-weight
dead-well
dead-wind
dead-wood
dead-wool
dead-work
dead-works
deaf-adder
deaf-dumbness
deaf-mute
deaf-muteness
deaf-mutism
dealfish
deal-frame
deal-tree
dear-bought
death-adder
death-agony
death-bed
death-bell
death-bird
death-blow
death-cord
death-damp
death-dance

death-day
death-fire
death-grapple
death-hunter
deathlike
death-mask
death-point
death-rate
death-rattle
death-ruckle
death's-head
death's-herb*
deathsman
death-sough
death-stroke
death-struck
death-throe
death-tick
death-token
death-trance
death-trap
death-warrant
death-watch (literal)
deathwatch (a beetle)
death-wound
decarbonizing-furnace
deck-beam
deck-bridge
deck-cargo
deck-carline
deck-cleat
deck-collar
deck-curb
deck-feather
deck-feed
deck-flat
deck-hand
deckhead
deck-hook
deck-house
deckle-edged
deckle-strap
deck-light
deck-load
deck-moulding
deck-nail
deck-passage
deck-passenger
deck-pipe

deck=planking
deck=plate
deck=pump
deck=sheet
deck=stopper
deck=tackle
deck=transom
decomposing=furnace
decoy bird
decoy duck
decrescent-pinnate
deed=box
deed=doer†
deep=laid
deep=mouthed, etc.
deep=sea, a.
deerberry (a plant)
deer=fold
deer=grass
deer=hair
deerherd
deerhound
deer=lick
deer=mouse
deer=neck
deer's=hair*
deerskin
deer=stalker†
deer's=tongue*
deer=tiger
delivery=roller
delivery=valve
Della=Cruscan
delta=metal
dentate=ciliate
dentate=serrate
dentate=sinuate
den=tree
depositing=dock
deposit=receipt
depthening=tool
depth=gauge
derm=skeleton
derrick=car
derrick=crane
descant=viol
desert=chough
desert=falcon
desert=hare

desert=mouse
desert=palm
desert=pea
desert=snake
desk=cloth
desk=knife
desk=maker†
desk=room
desk=work
despatch=boat
despatch=box
despatch=tube
dessert=spoon
desulphurizing=fur-
    nace
detaching=hook
detector=lock
detent=joint
detonating=tube
deux=temps
devil=bean
devil=bird
devil=bolt
devil=carriage
devil=dodger
devil=fish
devil=in=a=bush (plant)
devil=may=care, a.
devil's=apple*
devil's=apron*
devil's=bird*
devil's=bit*
devil's=claw*
devil's=club*
devil's=cotton*
devil's=cow*
devil=screecher
devil's=dung*
devil's=dust*
devil's=ear*
devil's=fig*
devil's=finger*
devil's=guts*
devil's=horse*
devil's=milk*
devil's=shoestring*
devil=tree
devilwood
devil=worship

devil=worshipper
dew=beater†
dewberry (a plant)
dew=besprent, etc.
dew=claw
dew=cup
dew=drink
dew=drop
dewfall
dew=grass
dewlap
dew=plant
dew=point
dew=ret
dew=rot
dew=shoe
dewstone (a limestone)
dewworm
diabase=porphyrite
diadem=lemur
diadem=spider
diagonal=built
dial=bird
dial=lock
dial=plate
dial=resistance
dial=telegraph
dial=wheel
dial=work
diamondback (a turtle)
diamond=backed, etc.
diamond=beetle
diamond=bird
diamond=breaker†
diamond=cutter†
diamond=draft
diamond=drill
diamond=dust
diamond=finch
diamond=flounder
diamond=gauge
diamond=knot
diamond=mortar
diamond=plaice
diamond=plate
diamond=point
diamond=powder
diamond=setter†
diamond=snake

diamond=spar
diamond=truck
diamond=weevil
diamond=wheel
diamond=work
diaper=work
diaphragm=faucet
diaphragm=plate
diaphragm=pump
diaphragm=valve
diatom=prism
dibbling=machine
dib=hole
dibstone
dice=box
dice=coal
dice=player†
dicing=house
dick=cissel
dick=dunnock
dicky=bird
die=away
die=back
die=holder†
die=sinker†
die=stock
diet=bread
diet=drink
diet=kitchen
die=work
difference=engine
difference=equation
difference=gauge
diffraction grating
diffraction spectrum
diffusion=osmose
diffusion=tube
diffusion=volume
digger=pine
digger=wasp
digging=machine
dika=bread
dike=grave
dike=reeve
dillweed
dilly-dally
diluting=roller
diminishing=rule
diminishing=scale

dimishing=stuff
dindle=dandle
dingle=dangle
dining=room
dinner=hour
dinner=table
dinner=time
dinner=wagon
Diogenes=crab
Diogenes=cup
dip=bucket
dip=circle
dip=head
dip=net
dipper=clam
dipping=compass
dipping=frame
dipping=house
dipping=liquor
dipping=needle
dipping=pan
dipping=tube
dipping=vat
dipping=wheel
dip=pipe
dip=regulator†
dip=rod
dip=roller
dip=sector
dipsey=line
dip=splint
dip=tray
dip=tube
direct=action, a.
direct=draught, a.
directing=circle
dirk=knife
dirt=bed
dirt=board
dirt=cheap
dirt=eating†
dirt=scraper†
dirty=allen
discharge=valve
discharging=arch
discharging=gear
discharging=rod
discharging=tongs
discount broker

discovery=claim
disengaging=gear
dish=catch
dish=cloth
dish=clout
dish=faced
dish=heater†
dish=holder†
dish=rack
dish=rag
dish=towel
dish=washer†
dishwasher (a bird)
dish=water
disk armature
disk clutch
disk dynamo
disk=gastrula
disk harrow
disk=owl
disk=shell
disk telegraph
disk valve
disk=wheel
dispart=sight
displacement=diagram
display=letter
display=line
display=stand
display=type
dissecting=forceps
dissecting=knife
dissecting=microscope
distance=block
distance=judge
distance=piece
distance=post
distance=signal
distemper=brush
distemper=ground
distributing=machine
distributing=table
dita=bark
ditch=bur
ditch=dog
ditch=fern
ditch=grass
ditching=machine
ditching=plow

ditching=tools
ditch=water
dithering=grass
ditto=suit
ditty=bag
ditty=box
diversion=cut
dividing=engine
dividing=iron
dividing=machine
divi=divi
diving beetle
diving=bell
diving bird
diving buck
diving=dress
diving=net
diving spider
diving=stone
divining=rod
divining=staff
division=board
division=catheter
division=mark
division=plate
divot=spade
do=all
dobby=machine
dock=block
dock=charges
dock=cress
dock=dues
dockmaster
dock=rent
dock=warrant
dockyard
doctor=box
doctor=fish
doctor=gum
dodder=grass
dodder=seed
doeskin
doffing=cylinder
doffing=knife
dog and chain
dog ape
dogbane (a plant)
dog bee
dog=belt

dogberry (a berry, a
    tree)
dogberry=tree
dog=biscuit
dogblow (a plant)
dogbrier (the dogrose)
dog=cart
dog=catcher†
dog=cheap
dog=cherry
dog=collar
dog=daisy
dog=days
dog=draw
dog=eared, dog=faced,
    etc.
dog=fancier†
dog=fennel
dogfish
dog=fly
dog fox (a male fox)
dog=fox (animal like
    both dog and fox,
    as *Vulpes corsac*)
dog=gone
dog=goned
dog=grass
dog=grate
dog=head
dog=hole
dog=hook
dog=house
dog=kennel
dog=Latin
dog=leech
dog=letter
dog=lichen
doglike
dog=louse
dog=lover†
dog=mad
dog=man
dog=muzzle
dog=nail
dog=nose
dog=pan
dog=parsley
dog=pig
dog=poison

dog=powder
dog=power
dog=ray
dogrose (a plant)
dog=salmon
dog's=bane*
dog's=body*
dog's=chop*
dog's=ear*
dog's=fennel*
dog's=grass*
dog's=guts*
dog=shark
dogshore
dog=show
dog=sick
dogskin
dog=sleep
dog's meat
dog's=mercury*
dog's=nose*
dog's-tail grass
dog=star
dog=stone
dogstones (a plant)
dog's=tongue*
dog's-tooth grass
dog=stopper
dog=tent
dog=tick
dog=tired *
dog=tooth (a tooth)
dogtooth (a shell or a
    punch)
dog=tooth spar
dog=tooth moulding
dog=tooth violet
dog=town
dog=tree
dog=trick
dog=trot
dog=vane
dog=watch
dog=weary
dog=wheat
dog=whelk
dog=whipper†
dogwood
dogwood=bark

dogwood=oil
dogwood=tree
dog=worship
dole=fish
dole=meadow
dollar=bird
dollar=fish
dollar=mark
dollee=wood
dolly=bar
dolly=shop
dolly=tub
dolphin=flower (a
   plant)
dolphin=fly
dolphin=striker†
domba=oil
dome=cover
dome=head
donation party
donkey=engine
donkey=pump
donkey=rest
do=nothing
dood=wallah
dool=tree
doom=palm
doomsday
door=alarm
door=bell
door=case
door=cheek
door=fastener†
door=frame
door=guard
door=hanger†
door=hawk
door=jamb
doorkeeper†
door=knob
door=knocker
door=latch
door=lock
door=mat
door=nail
door=piece
door=pin
door=plate
door=post

door=pull
door=roller
door=shaft
door=sill
door=spring
door=step
door=stone
door=stop
door=strap
door=strip
doorway
doorway=plane
doorweed
dooryard
dop=chicken
dopper=bird
dor=beetle
dor=bug
dor=fly
dor=hawk
dormer=window
doss=house
dotting=pen
dot=wheel
double=acting
double=bank, v.
double=banked, etc.
double=banker
double=bass
double=biting, a.
double=bitt, v.
double=breather†
double=charge, v.
double=concave, a.
double=cone, a.
double=convex
double=crown
double=darken
double=dealer†
double=decker
double=dye, v.
double=dyeing
double=eagle
double=ender
double=face
double=first
double=gear
double=gild
double=header

double=hung
double=lock, v.
double=man
double=meaning, a.
double=quick
double=ripper
double=ruff
double=runner
double=shade, v.
double=shining
double=shot
double=snipe
double=stop
double=stopping
double=struck
double=time
double=tongue, v.
double=topsail, a.
double=touch
doubletree
double=trouble
doubling=frame
doubling=nail
dough=baked, etc.
dough=balls
dough=bird
dough=brake
doughface (a person)
doughing=machine
dough=kneader†
dough=maker†
dough=mixer†
doughnut
dough=raiser†
dough=trough
doughty=handed
dousing=chock
dousing=rod
dove=color
dove=cote
dove=dock
dove=eyed, etc.
dove=house
dove=like
dove=plant
dove's=foot*
dovetail
dovetail=box
dovetail=cutter†

dovetail joint
dovetail=marker†
dovetail moulding
dovetail=plane
dovetail plates
dovetail=saw
dove=wood
dowel=bit
dowelling=machine
dowel=joint
dowel=pin
dowel=pointer
dower=house
downbear
down=beard
down bed
down=by
downcast
downcome
down=draught
downdraw
down=east, a.
down=easter
downfall
downhaul
downhearted
downhill
downland
downlooked
downlying
downpour
downright
downrush
downset
down=share
downsitting
down=stairs
down=stream
downtake
downthrow
down=town
down=tree
downtrodden
downweed
downweigh
draft=animal, etc.
   See *draught=ani-*
    mal, etc.
drag=anchor

drag=bar
drag=bench
drag=bolt
drag=chain
drag=driver
drag=hook
drag=hound
drag=hunt
drag=link
dragman
drag=net
dragon=arum
dragon=beam
dragon=fish
dragon=fly
dragon=leech
dragon=piece
dragonroot (a plant)
dragon's=blood*
dragon's=eye*
dragon's=head*
dragon=shell
dragon's=tail*
dragon=standard
dragon=tree
✓ dragon=water
dragonwort
dragoon=bird
drag=rake
drag=rope
drag=sail
drag=saw
drag=seine
drag=sheet
dragsman
drag=spring
drag=staff
drag=twist
drag=washer
drainage=basin
drainage=tube
drain=cap
drain=cock
drain=curb
drain=gauge
drain=gate
draining=auger
draining=engine
draining=machine

draining=plow
draining=pot
draining=pump
draining=tile
draining=vat
drain=pipe
drain=tile
drain=trap
drain=well
drake=fly
drakestone
draught=animal
draught=bar
draught=board
draught=box
draught=cattle
draught=compasses
draught=engine
draught=equalizer†
draught=eye
draught=furnace
draught=hole
draught=hook
draught=horse
draught=net
draught=ox
draught=regulator†
draught=rod
draughtsman
draught=spring
draught=tree
draught=tug
drawback
draw=bar
draw=bays
draw=bench
draw=bolt
draw=bore, *n.*
drawbore, *v.*
draw=boy
drawbridge
draw=cut
drawfile, *v.*
draw=gate
draw=gear
draw=glove (a glove)
drawglove (a game)
draw=head
draw=horse

drawing=awl	dreamland	drill=extractor†
drawing=bench	dream=while	drill=gauge
drawing=block	dream=world	drill=harrow
drawing=board	dredge=boat	drill=holder
drawing=book	dredge=box	drill=husbandry
drawing=compass	dredgeman	drilling=jig
drawing=engine	dredge=net	drilling=lathe
drawing=frame	dredging=box	drilling=machine
drawing=glove	dredging=machine	drill=jar
drawing=hook	drenching=horn	drill=master
drawing in	dress=circle	drill=pin
drawing=knife	dress coat	drill=plate
drawing=lift	dress=goods	drill=plow
drawing=machine	dress=guard	drill=press
drawing=master	dressing=bench	drill=rod
drawing=materials	dressing=case	drill=sergeant
drawing=paper	dressing=floor	drill=spindle
drawing=pen	dressing=frame	drill=stock
drawing=pencil	dressing=gown	drill=tongs
drawing=pin	dressing=jacket	drink=a=penny
drawing=point	dressing=knife	drinker=moth
drawing=press	dressing=machine	drinking=bout
drawing=rolls	dressing=room	drinking=fountain
drawing=room	dressing=sack	drinking=horn
drawing=table	dressing=table	drink=money
draw=kiln	dressmaker†	drink=offering
draw=knife	dress parade	drip=joint
draw=lid	dress=spur	dripping=pan
draw=link	dress uniform	drip=pipe
draw=loom	drift=anchor	drip=pump
draw=net	drift=bolt	drip=stick
drawn=work	drift=current	dripstone
draw=plate	drift=ice	drip=tray
draw=point	drift=land	drive=boat
draw=poker	drift=lead	drive=bolt
draw=rod	drift=mining	driver=ant
drawshave	drift=net	driver=boom
draw=spring	drift=netter†	driveway
draw=stop	drift=piece	drive=wheel
draw=taper	drift=pin	driving=axle
draw=timber	drift=sail	driving=band
draw=tongs	driftway	driving=bolt
draw=tube	driftweed	driving=box
draw=well	driftwood	driving=cap
dray=cart	drill=barrow	driving=chisel
dray=horse	drill=bit	driving=gear
drayman	drill=bow	driving=gloves
dreadnaught	drill=chuck	driving=rein
dream=hole	drill=clamp	driving=shaft

driving=spring
driving=wheel
drone=bass
drone bee
drone=beetle
drone=cell
drone=fly
drone=pipe
drongo=cuckoo
drongo=shrike
drop=bar
drop=black
drop=bottom
drop=box
drop=curls
drop=curtain
drop=drill
drop=elbow
drop=fingers
drop=flue
drop=fly
drop=forging
drop=glass
drop=hammer
drop=handle
drop=keel
drop=letter
drop=light
drop=meter
drop=net
dropping=bottle
dropping=tube
drop=press
drop=ripe
drop=roller
drop=scene
dropseed=grass
drop=shutter
dropstone
drop=table
drop=tee
drop=the=handkerchief
drop=tin
drop=worm
dropwort
drowsy=headed
drug=mill
drug=sifter†
drug=store

druid=stone
drum armature
drum=beat
drumble=drone
drum=call
drum=corps
drum=curb
drum=cylinder
drumfish
drum=guard
drumhead
drum=major
drumming=log
drum=saw
drum=sieve
drum=skin
drumstick
drumstick=tree
drum=wheel
drumwood (a tree)
dryasdust
drybone
dry=boned
dry=casting
dry=castor
dry=cup
dry=cupping
dry=cure
dry dock
dry=eyed, dry=shod,
    etc.
dryfoot, *adv.*
dry=gilding
dry=goods
dry=grinding
dry=house
drying=box
drying=case
drying=chamber
drying=floor
drying=house
drying=machine
drying off
drying=oven
drying=plate
drying=room
drying=stove
drying=tube
dry=multure

dry=nurse
dry=pipe (for dry
    steam)
dry=point
dry=pointing
dry=press, *v.*
dry=rent
dry=rot
dry=rub
dry=salt, *v.*
drysalter
dry=sand, *v.*
dry=stone
dry=stove
D string
dub=a=dub
dubbing=tool
duchy=court
duck=ant
duck=barnacle
duckbill (an animal)
duck=billed, duck=
    legged, etc.
duck=hawk
ducking=gun
ducking=sink
ducking=stool
duckmeat
duck=mole
duck=oak
duck's=bill*
duck's=egg*
duck's=foot*
duck=shot
duck's=meat*
duck=snipe
duckweed
duck=weight
ductor=roller
dudgeon=tree
due=bill
dugout, *n.*
dug=way
duke's=meat*
dule=tree
dull=brained, dull=
    eyed, etc.
dullhead (a blockhead)
dumb=bell

dumb=bidding
dumb=cake
dumb=cane
dumb=cbalder
dumb=craft
dumb=plate
dumb show
dumb=waiter
dump=bolt
dump=car
dump=cart
dumping=bucket
dumping=car
dumping=cart
dumping=ground
dumping=reel
dumping=sled
dumping=wagon
dumpling=duck
dumpy=level
dunbird
dunce=table
dun=cow
dunderbolt (a belem-
   nite)
dunderfunk (a kind
   of food)
dunderhead (a dunce)
dun diver
dunfish
dung=bath
dung=beetle

dung=bird
dungchafer (an insect)
dung=fly
dung=fork
dunghill
dunghill=raker
dung=hook
dunghunter (a gull)
dungmere
dung=yard
dunpickle (a buzzard)
dunrobin
dust=ball
dust=bin
dust=brand
dust=brush
dust=cart
dust=chamber
dust=collar
dust=feather
dust=guard
dust=hole
dusting=brush
dusting=colors
dust=louse
dustman
dust=pan
dust=prig
dust=prigging
dust=shot
dust=storm
dust=whirl

dusty=miller (a plant)
Dutchman
Dutchman's=brecches*
Dutchman's=lauda-
   num*
Dutchman's=pipe*
duty=free
D valve
dwelling=house
dwelling=place
dyad=deme
dye=bath
dye=beck
dye=house
dye=kettle
dye=pine
dye=pot
dyer's=broom*
dyer's=greenweed*
dyer's=moss*
dyer's=weed*
dyestone
dyestuff
dye=trial
dye=vat
dyeware
dyeweed
dyewood
dyewood=cutter
dye=works
dykehopper
dynamite=gun

E

eagle=bird
eagle=eyed, etc.
eagle=hawk
eagle=owl
eagle=ray
eaglestone
eagle=vulture
eaglewood
earbob
ear=bone
ear=brisk
ear=brush
ear=cap
ear=cockle
ear=conch
ear=cornet
ear=cough
ear=drop
ear=dropper
ear=drop tree
ear=drum
ear=dust
ear=finger
ear=flap
ear=gland
ear=hole
earing=cringle
ear=kissing
ear=lap
ear=lappet
earl=duck
earlid
ear=lifter
ear=lobe
ear=lock
earmark
earnest=money
ear=net
earning=grass
ear=pendant

earpick
ear=piece
ear=piercer†
ear=pocket
ear=reach
earring
ear=rivet
ear=sand
ear=shell
ear=shot
ear=snail
ear=speculum
ear=splitting
ear=stone
ear=string
ear=syringe
earth=auger
earth=ball
earth=bath
earth=battery
earth=board
earth=borer†
earth=born, etc.
earth=car
earth=chestnut
earth=closet
earth=crab
earth=current
earth=drake
earth=eater†
earthenware
earthfall
earth=fast
earth=flax
earth=flea
earth=fly
earth=foam
earth=gall
earth=hog
earth=house

earth=inductor
earthly=minded
earth=moss
earthnut
earthnut=pea
earth=oil
earth=pea
earth=pig
earth=pit
earth=plate
earth=pulsation
earthquake
earthquake=alarm
earthquake=shadow
earthquake=shock
earth=shine
earth=smoke
earth=star
earth=stopper
earth=table
earth=tilting
earth=tongue
earth=treatment
earth=tremor
earth=wire
earthwolf
earthwork
earthworm
earthworm=oil
ear=trumpet
ear=vesicle
ear=wax
earwig (an insect)
ear=witness
ear=worm
earwort
ease=off
easing=sparrow
easing=swallow
east=about

Easter=flower (a plant)
easter=mackerel
East=Indiaman
East=Indian
eastland
easy chair
easy=going
eating=house
eaves=board
eaves=catch
eaves=drip
eaves=drop, n.
eavesdrop, v.
eavesdropper†
eaves=lath
eaves=swallow
eaves=trough
ebb=anchor
ebb=tide
eboe=light
eboe=torchwood
eboe=tree
écaille=work
eccentric=gear
eccentric=hoop
eccentric=rod
eccentric=strap
eccles=tree
echelon=lens
echo=organ
echo=stop
eddy=water
eddy=wind
edge=bolt
edgebone
edge=coals
edge=cutting
edge=joint
edge=key
edge=mail
edge=mill
edge=moulding
edge=plane
edge=play
edge=rail
edge=roll
edge=setter†
edge=shot
edge=stitch

edge=stone
edge=tool
edge=trimmer†
edge=wheel
edging=iron
edging=machine
edging=saw
edging=shears
edging=tile
eduction=pipe
eduction=port
eduction=valve
eel=basket
eel=buck
eelfare
eel=fly
eel=fork
eel=gig
eel=grass
eel=mother
eel=oil
eel=pot
eel=pout
eel=punt
eel=set
eel=shaped
eel=shark
eel=shear
eelskin
eel=spear
egg=albumin
egg=animal
egg=apparatus
egg=apple
egg=assorter†
egg=bag
egg=bald
egg=basket
egg=beater†
egg=bird
egg=blower†
egg=boiler†
egg=born
egg=carrier†
egg=case
egg=cell
egg=cleavage
egg=cockle
egg=cocoon

egg=cup
egg=dance
egg=detecter†
egg=development
egg=drill
egg=ended
egger=moth
eggfish
egg=flip
egg=forceps
egg=glass
egg=glue
egg=hatching†
egg=hot
egg=laying†
egg=lighter
egg=membrane
egg=mite
egg=nog
egg=parasite
egg=pie
eggplant
egg=pod
egg=pop
egg=pouch
egg=sac
eggs=and=bacon (a
    plant)
eggs=and=collops (a
    plant)
egg sauce
egg=shaped
egg=shell
egg=slice
egg=spoon
egg=squash
egg=sucker†
egg=syringe
egg=tester†
egg=timer†
egg=tongs
egg=tooth
egg=trot
egg=tube
egg=urchin
eggwife
eider=down
eider=duck
eider=goose

eider-yarn
eightfoil
eighth note
eighth rest
eightscore
eis-wool
ejector-condenser
elbow-board
elbow-chair
elbow-cuff
elbow-gauntlet
elbow-grease
elbow-guard
elbow-joint
elbow-piece
elbow-plate
elbow-rail
elbow-room
elbow-scissors
elbow-shaker
elbow-shield
elbow-sleeve
elbow-tongs
elderberry
elder gun
elder-tree
elder wine
elderwort
election-auditor
elephant-apple
elephant-bed
elephant-beetle
elephant-bird
elephant-creeper
elephant-fish
elephant-grass
elephant-leg
elephant-mouse
elephant-seal
elephant's-ear*
elephant's-foot*
elephant's-shrew
elephant's-tusk
elevating-block
elevating-clutch
elevating-screw
elevator-bucket
elevator-engine
elevator-leg

elevator-shaft
eleven-o'clock-lady (a
    plant)
elf-arrow
elf-bolt
elf-child
elf-dart
elf-dock
elf-fire
elf-king
elf-land
elf-lock
elf-locked
elf-queen
elf-shot
elf-stone
elknut (a shrub)
elk-tree
elkwood (a tree)
ellwand
elm-beetle
elm-borer†
elm-butterfly
elm-moth
elm-sawfly
elm-tree
elm-wood
elsewhere
elsewhither
ember-days
ember-eve
ember-fast
ember-goose
embertide
ember-week
embossing-iron
embossing-machine
embossing-press
embroidery-frame
embroidery-needle
embroidery-paste
embryo-sac
emerald-fish
emerald-moth
emery-board
emery-cake
emery-cloth
emery-paper
emery-powder

emery-rifle
emery-stick
emery-stone
emery-wheel
emmer-goose
emmet-hunter†
empty-handed, etc.
enamel-blue .
enamel-cells
enamel-columns
enamel-cuticle
enamel-fibres
enamel-germ
enamelling-furnace
enamelling-lamp
enamel-kiln
enamel-membrane
enamel-organ
enamel-painting†
enamel-paper
enamel-prisms
enamel-rods
end-artery
end-bulb
end-iron
end-man
end-paper
end-piece
end-plate
end-play
end-shake
end-stone
enema-chair
enemy-chit
engine-bearer
engine-counter
engine-driver†
engine-furnace
engine-house
engine-lathe
engineman
engine-plane
engine-room
engine-runner†
engine-shaft
engine-tool
engine-turned
engine-turning
Englishman

Englishwoman
enlarging=hammer
ensign=bearer†
enstatite=diabase
entering=chisel
entering=file
entering=port
entrance=hall
entranceway
envelope=machine
epithelium=cell
epoch=making
equal=aqual
equal=ended
equal=falling
equalizer=spring
equalizing=bar
equalizing=file
equilibrium=scale
equilibrium=valve
erg=ten
ermine=moth
ern=bleater (a snipe)
escalier=lace
escallop=shell
escape=valve
escape=wheel
ess=cock
E string
etch=grain
etching=embroidery
etching=ground
etching=needle
etching=point
etching=varnish
ether=engine
ethyl=blue
ethylene=blue
etter=pike
evaporating=cone
evaporating=dish
evaporating=furnace
evaporating=pan
evaporating=gauge
eve=churr
even=down
evenfall
even=forward
even=handed, etc.

even=hands
evening=song
even=song
ever=bloomer†
ever=during, etc.
everglade
evergreen
everlasting
evermore
everybody
every=day, a.
every one
everything
everywhere
everywhither
evil=disposed, etc.
evil=doer
evil=eel
evil=willing
ewe=cheese
ewe=lease
ewe=neck
ewe=necked
examination=paper
exciseman
exclamation=mark
exclamation=point
exhaust=chamber
exhaust=draught
exhaust=fan
exhaust=nozzle
exhaust=pallet
exhaust=pipe
exhaust=port
exhaust=purifier
exhaust=regulator†
exhaust=steam
exhaust=syringe
exhaust=valve
expansion=cam
expansion=coupling
expansion=curb
expansion=curve
expansion=drum
expansion=engine
expansion=gear
expansion=joint
expansion=valve
express=bullet†

express=car
expression=mark
expression=point
expression=stop
expressman
express=rifle
express=train
express=wagon
extension=pedal
extension table
eye=agate
eye=animalcule
eyebait
eyeball
eye=bar
eyebeam
eye=bolt
eye=bone
eye=bree
eyebright (a plant)
eye=brightening
eyebrow
eye=case
eye=copy
eye=cup
eye=doctor
eye=dotter
eye=drop
eye=eminence
eye=extirpator
eye=flap
eye=forceps
eye=glance
eye=glass
eye=glutting
eyehole
eye=instrument
eyelash
eye=lens
eyelet=hole
eyeletting=machine
eyelet=punch
eyelid
eyelid=dilator†
eye=line
eye=lobe
eye=memory
eye=opener†
eyepiece

eye=pit
eye=point
eye=protector†
eye=reach
eye=salve
eye=servant
eye=server†
eye=service
eye=shade
eyeshot

eyesight
eyesore
eye=sorrow
eye=speck
eye=speculum
eye=splice
eye=spot
eye=spotted
eye=stalk
eyestone

eyestring
eye=sucker
eye=tooth
eye=waiter
eye=wash
eye=water
eye=wink
eye=winker
eye=witness
eyewort

F

fablemonger
face=ache
face=ague
face=card
face=cloth
face=cover
faced=lined
face=flatterer†
face=guard
face=hammer
face=joint
face=lathe
face=mite
face=mould
face=painter†
face=piece
face=plan
face=plate
face=powder
face value
face=wall
face=wheel
facing=brick
facing=machine
facing=sand
factory maund
fag=end
fagot=iron
fagot=vote
fagot=voter
fahl=ore
fail=dike
faint=draw
faint=heart, a.
faint=hearted, etc.
fair=conditioned, fair=
  seeming, fair=spo-
  ken, etc.
fair=ground

fair=hair (a tendon in
  the neck of cattle
  and sheep)
fairies'=horse*
fairies'=table*
fair=leader
fair=maid
fair=maids=of=February
  (a plant)
fair=maids=of=France (a
  plant)
fairway
fair=weather, a.
fairy=bird
fairy=butter
fairy=cups
fairy=fingers
fairy=land
fairylike
fairy=loaf
fairy=martin
fairy=purses
fairy=shrimp
fairy=stone
faith=cure
faith=curer†
faith=doctor
faith=healer†
faithworthy
faking=box
falcon=eyed, etc.
falcon=gentle
faldstool
fall=block
fall=board
fall=cloud
fallen=star (an alga, a
  sea=nettle)
fuller=wire

fallfish
fall=gate
falling=door (a flap=
  door)
falling off
falling out
falling=sickness
falling star
fallow=chat
fallow=crop
fallow deer
fallow=dun
fallow=finch
fall=rope
fall=trap
fall=under
fallway
false=faced, etc.
famble=crop
family name (name
  common to indi-
  viduals of a family)
family=name (name of
  a whole family as
  such, not as indi-
  viduals)
famine=bread
fan=blast
fan=blower
fan=coral
fan=crest
fan=crested, etc.
fan=cricket
fancy=free
fancy=line
fancy=monger
fancy=sick
fancy=store
fancy=work

fanfish
fanfoot
fan-frame
fanging-pipes
fan-governor
fan-jet
fan-lace
fanlight
fanning-machine
fanning-mill
fanning out
fan-palm
fan-shell
fan structure
fantail (a pigeon)
fan-tan
fan tracery
fan-training
fan-veined
fan-ventilator
fan-wheel
fan window
far-away
farcy-bud
far-death
fardel-bound
farding-bag
fare-box
fare-indicator
farewell
fare-wicket
far-fetched, etc.
farina-boiler†
farm-bailiff
farm-building
farmer-general
farm-hand
farmhold
farmhouse
farm-meal
farm-office
farm-place
farmstead
farm-village
farmyard
faro-bank
faro-box
far sight
farthing-bound

fascia-board
fascine-dweller†
fashioning-needle
fashion-monger
fashion-mongering
fashion-monging
fashion-piece
fashion-plate
fashion-timber
fast-day
fasten-een
fasterns-een
fast-handed, etc.
fasting-day
fatback (a fish)
fat-bird (a guachero, a
  sandpiper)
fat-brained, etc.
fat-cell
fate-like
fat-faced
fathead (a fish)
fat-hen (a plant)
father-in-law
fatherland
fatherlasher (a fish)
father-long-legs
father-sick
fathom-line
fathom-wood
fatigue-call
fatigue-cap
fatigue-dress
fatigue-duty
fatigue-party
fat-lean
fat-lute
fatting-knife
faucet-bit
faucet-filter
faucet-joint
faucet-key
faucet-valve
fauld-dike
fault-block
fault-escarpment
faultfinder†
fault-rock
faultworthy

fause-house
favus-cup
fawn-colored, etc.
fearnaught
feast-day
feather-alum
feather-bearer†
feather bed
feather-bed (a bird)
feather-bird
feather-boarding
featherbone
featherbrain (a person)
feather-brained, etc.
feather-cloth
feather-curler†
feather-driver†
feather-edge
feather-fisher†
feather flower
featherfoil (a plant)
feather-grass
featherhead (a person)
feathering-screw
feathering-wheel
feather-joint
feather-maker†
feather-man
feather-moss
feather-ore
feather-palm
feather-poke
feather-renovator†
feather-shot
feather-spray
feather-spring
feather-star
feather-stitch
feathertop (a grass)
feathertop-grass
feather-tract
feather-veined
feather-weight (a
  weight)
featherweight (a per-
  son)
featherwing (a moth)
feather-work
feeble-minded, etc.

feed-apron
feed-bag
feed-cloth
feed-cutter†
feed-door
feed-hand
feed-head
feed-heater†
feeding-bottle
feeding-engine
feeding-ground
feeding-head
feeding-platform
feed-motion
feed-pipe
feed-pump
feed-rack
feed-regulator†
feed-roll
feed-screw
feed-trough
feed-water
feed-wheel
fee-estate
fee-farm
fee-farmer†
fee-fund
fee-grief
feeing-market
felling-axe
felling-machine
felling-saw
fell-lurking
fellow being
fellow citizen
fellow commoner
fellow countryman
fellow-craft
fellow creature
fellow-feel
fellow-feeler†
fellow generator
fellow heir
fellow helper
fellow-like
fellow man
fellow mortal
fellow subject
fellow-wheel

felly-auger
felly-bending†
felly-boring†
felly-coupling
felly-dresser†
felly-machine
felly-plate
felly-sawing†
felonwood (a plant)
felonwort
felt-cloth
felt-grain
felting-machine
feltmaker†
feltwork
femme-de-chambre
fen-boat
fence-jack
fence-lizard
fence-month
fence-play
fence-post
fence-rail
fence-time
fence-viewer†
fencing-gauge
fencing-machine
fencing-nail
fencing-school
fen-cricket
fender-beam
fender-board
fender-bolt
fender-pile
fender-pose
fender-stop
fen-duck
fen-fire
fen-fowl
fen-goose
fen-land
fenman
fennel-flower (a plant)
fennel-water
fen-orchis
fen-thrush
fer-de-lance
fermenting-square
fermenting-vat

ferment-oil
ferment-organism
ferment-secretion
fern-leaf (leaf of a fern)
fernleaf (an alga)
fern-owl
fern-palm
fern-seed
fernshaw
ferry-boat
ferry-bridge
ferryman
ferry-master
fertilization-tube
fertilizer-mill
fertilizer-sower
fescue-grass
fesse-point
festing-penny
festoon-blind
fetch-candle
fetch-light
fête-day
fetish-man
fetish-snake
fetlock-boot
fetlock-joint
fetter-bone
fetter-bush
feu-contract
feu-duty
fever-bark
fever-blister
feverbush (a plant)
fever-heat
fevernut (seed of a
    shrub)
feverroot (an herb)
fever-sore
fever-tree
fevertwig (a vine)
feverweed
feverwort
fibre-cross
fibre-faced
fibre-gun
fibre-plant
fibre-stitch
fibre-tester†

fiddle=beetle
fiddle=block
fiddle=bow
fiddle=come=faddle
fiddle=de=dee
fiddle=faddle
fiddle=faddler
fiddle=fish
fiddle=head
fiddler=crab
fiddle=shaped
fiddlestick
fiddle=string
fiddle=wood (used to make fiddles)
fiddlewood (a tree)
fidging=fain
fid=hammer
fid=hole
field=ale
field=allowance
field=artillery
field=basil
field=battery
field=bean
field=bed
field=bird
field=book
field=bug
field=carriage
field=colors
field=cornet
field=cricket
field=day
field=derrick
field=dog
field=driver
field=duck
field=equipage
fieldfare
field=glass
field=gun
field=gunner
field=hand
field=hospital
field=house
field=ice
field=kirk
field=lark

field=lens
field=lore
field=madder
field=magnet
field=marigold
field=marshal
field=marshalship
field=martin
field=mouse
field=night
field=notes
field=officer
field=park
field=piece
field=plover
field=preacher†
field=roller†
field=room
field=service
field=show
field=sparrow
field=sports
field=staff
field=telegraph
field=titling
field=train
field=trial
field=vole
field=work
field=works
fiendlike
fiery=flare
fiery=footed, etc.
fiery=hot
fiery=new
fiery=short
fife=major
fife=player†
fife=rail
fifty=fold
fig=apple
fig=banana
fig=blue
fig=cake
fig=dust
fig=eater†
figeater (a beetle)
fig=faun
figfeeder (an insect)

fig=gnat
fighting cock
fighting=fish
fighting=sandpiper
fighting=stopper
fig=leaf
fig=marigold
fig=shell
fig=tree
figure=casting
figure=dance
figurehead
figure=maker†
figure=stone
fig=wart
figwort
filbert=gall
filbert=tree
file=blank
file=card
file=carrier†
file=chisel
file=cleaner†
file=closer†
file=cloth
file=cutter†
file=finishing†
file=firing
filefish
file=grinding†
file=guard
file=leader† ·
file=marching
file=mark
file=sharpening†
file=shell
file=stripper†
file=tempering†
filigree=glass
filigree=point
filigree=work
filing=block
filing=board
filing=machine
filings=separator
filler=box
fillet=cutter†
fillet=plane
fill=horse

filling-can
filling-engine
filling-pile
filling-post
filling-thread
filling-timbers
filter-bed
filter-faucet
filter-gallery
filtering-bag
filtering-basin
filtering-box
filtering-cup
filtering-funnel
filtering-hydrant
filtering-paper
filtering-press
filtering-stone
filtering-tank
filter-paper
filter-press
filter-pump
filth-disease
fimble-hemp
finback (a whale)
finback-calf
fin-chain
finch-backed
finch-falcon
finch-tanager
finding-list
finding-store
find-spot
fine-arch
fine-cut, fine-fingered,
  etc.
finedraw, v.
finedrawer†
fine-rolls
finery-furnace
fine-still
fine-stiller†
finetop-grass
finfish
fin-fold
fin-foot (a foot)
finfoot (a bird)
fin-footed, fin-toed, etc.
finger-alphabet

finger-and-toe (a dis-
  ease of turnips)
finger-bar
finger-board
finger-bowl
fingerbreadth
finger-brush
finger-coral
finger-counting†
finger-cymbals
finger-fern
fingerflower (a plant)
finger-glass
finger-grass
finger-grip
finger-guard
finger-hole
finger-key
finger-mark
finger-mirror
finger-nut
finger-plate
finger-point
finger-post
finger-puff
finger-reading†
finger-ring
finger-shell
finger-shield
finger-sponge
finger-stall
finger-steel
finger-tip
fining-forge
fining-pot
fining-roller
finishing-card
finishing-drill
finishing-hammer
finishing-press
finishing-rolls
finishing-tool
finish-turn
finnan-haddock
finner-whale
fin-pike
fin-ray
fin-spine
finweed

fin-whale
fir-apple
fir-cone
fire-alarm
fire-annihilator
fire-ant
firearm
fire-arrow
fireback
fire-backed, etc.
fire-ball
fire-balloon
fire-bar
fire-barrel
fire-basket
fire-bavin
fire-beacon
fire-bell
fire-bill
fire-bird
fire-blast
fire-blight
fireboard
fire-boat
firebody (an ascidian)
fire-boom
fire-bote
fire-box
firebrand
fire-brick
fire-bridge
fire-brigade
fire-brush
fire-bucket
firebug
fire-cage
fire-chamber
fire-clay
fire-cock
fire-company
firecracker
firecrest (a wren)
fire-cross
fire-damp
fire department
fired-off, a.
fire-dog
fire-door
firedrake

fire=dress
fire=eater†
fire=engine
fire=escape
fire=extinguisher†
fire=eye (an ant=thrush)
fire=fan
fire=feeder†
fire=fiend
fire=finch
fire=fishing
fire=flag
fireflare
fireflirt
firefly
fire=fork
fire=gilding
fire=gilt
fire=god
fire=grate
fire=guard
fire=holder†
fire=hole
fire=hook
fire=house
fire=hunt
fire=hunting†
fire=hydrant
fire=insurance
fire=iron
fire=kiln
fire=ladder
fire=leaves
firelight
fire=lighter†
fire=lock (a lock)
firelock (a gun)
fire=mace
fire=main
fireman
fire=marble
fire=master
fire=new
fire=office
fire=opal
fire=ordeal
fire=pan
fire=pike
fire=pink

fireplace
fire=plating
fire=plug
fire=point
fire=policy
fire=pot
fire=proof, a.
fireproof, v.
fire=quarters
fire=raft
fire=raising†
fire=red
fire=regulator†
fire=roll
fire=room
fire=screen
fire=set
fire=setting†
fire=shield
fire=ship
fire=shovel
fireside
fire=silvering†
fire=spirit
fire=spot
fire=steel
fire=stick
fire=stone
fire=stop
fire=surface
fire=swab
firetail (an insect, a
    bird)
fire=telegraph
fire=tower
fire=trap
fire=tree
fire=tube
fire=ward
fire=warden
fire=water
fireweed
fire=wood
fireworks
fire=worm
fire=worship
fire=worshipper†
firing=iron
firing=machine

firing=party
firing=point
firmer=chisel
firm=footed, etc.
firm name
fir=parrot
first=begotten, etc.
first=class
first=foot
first=fruit
first=hand
first=rate
fir=tree
fir=wood
fir=wool
fise=dog
fish=back
fish=backed, etc.
fish=bait
fish=ball
fish=bar
fish=basket
fish=beam
fish=bed
fishberry
fish=block
fish=bolt
fishbone=tree
fish=book
fish=boom
fish=breeder†
fish=cake
fish=can
fish=car
fish=carver†
fish chowder
fish=chum
fish=coop
fish=creel
fish=crow
fish=cultural
fish=culture
fish=culturist
fish=davit
fish=day
fish=driver†
fish=duck
fisher=boat
fisherfolk

fisherman
fish=fag
fish=fall
fish=farm
fish=farmer†
fish=flake
fish=flour
fish=food
fish=fork
fish=freezer†
fish=front
fish=fungus
fish=garth
fish=gig
fish=globe
fish=glue
fish=god
fish=goddess
fish=guano
fish=hawk
fish=hook
fish=husbandry
fishing=banks
fishing=boat
fishing=duck
fishing=eagle
fishing=float
fishing=frog
fishing=ground
fishing=hawk
fishing=line
fishing=net
fishing out
fishing=place
fishing=rod
fishing=room
fishing=smack
fishing=station
fishing=swivel
fishing=tackle
fishing=tube
fish=joint
fish=kettle
fish=killer†
fish=knife
fish=ladder
fish=line
fish=louse
fish=manure

fish=market
fish=maw
fish=meal
fishmonger
fishmoth (an insect)
fish=net
fish of Paradise
fish=oil
fish=owl
fish=packing†
fish=pearl
fish pie
fish=plate
fish=poison
fish=pomace
fish=pond
fish=pool
fish=pot
fish=preserve
fish=prong
fish=pugh
fish=refuse
fish=roe
fish=sauce
fish=scale
fish=scrap
fish=show
fish=skin
fish=slice
fish=slide
fish=smother
fish=sound
fish=spear
fish=stage
fish=store
fish=story
fish-strainer†
fish=tackle
fish=tail (tail of a fish)
fishtail (an insect)
fish=tongue
fish=torpedo
fish=trap
fish-trowel
fish=van
fish=warden
fishway
fish=weir
fishwife

fishwoman
fish=wood
fish=worker†
fish=works
fishworm
fission=fungi
fissure=needle
fissure=vein
fist=ball
fist=law
fist=mate
fitch=brush
fit=rod
fitroot (a plant)
fittie=lan'
fitting=shop
fitweed
five=boater
fivefinger (a plant)
five=fingered, etc.
fivefingers (a starfish)
five=finger=tied
fiveleaf (a plant)
fivemouths (a parasite,
     the tonguelet)
fivepence
fivepenny
fives=court
five=spot
five=square
five=twenty
fixed=eyed
fixing=bath
flag=bearer†
flag=captain
flageolet=tones
flag=feather
flagging=iron
flag-lieutenant
flagman
flag=officer
flagpole
flag=root
flag=share
flag=ship
flag side
flagstaff
flag=station
flagstone

flagworm
flail=stone
flake=feather
flake=room
flake=stand
flake=white
flake=yard
flaking hammer
flame=bearer†
flame=bed
flame=bridge
flame=cell
flame=chamber
flame=color
flame=colored, etc.
flame=engine
flameflower (a plant)
flame=of=the=woods (a plant)
flame=reaction
flame=stop
flame=tree
flamingo=plant
flange=gauge
flange=joint
flange=lip
flange=pipe
flange=rail
flange=turning†
flange=wheel
flanging=machine
flanging=press
flannel cake
flannel=flower (a plant)
flannel=mouthed, etc.
flap=door
flapdragon
flap=eared, etc.
flapjack (griddle=cake)
flap=keeper†
flapper=skate
flaptail (a monkey)
flap=tile
flap=valve
flare=tin
flare=up
flashboard
flash=flue
flash=house

flashing=board
flashing=bottle
flashing=furnace
flashing=point
flash=light
flashman
flash=pan
flash=pipe
flash=point
flash=test
flash=torch
flash=wheel
flask=board
flask=clamp
flask=shaped, etc.
flatbill (a bird)
flatboat
flat=bottomed, etc.
flat car
flat=clam
flatfish
Flathead (an Indian)
flat=house
flat=iron
flatlong
flat=orchil
flat=press, v.
flat=rod
flattening=furnace
flattening=hearth
flattening=mill
flattening=oven
flattening=plate
flattening=stone
flattening=tool
flatter=blind
flatting=coat
flatting=furnace
flatting=hearth
flatting=mill
flatting=plate
flatting=stone
flatting=tool
flat=tool
flattop (an herb)
flat=ware
flatworm
flaughter=spade
flaw=piece

flax=bird
flax=brake
flax=bush
flax=comb
flax=cotton
flax=cutting†
flax=dresser†
flax=mill
flax=plant
flax=puller†
flax=scutcher†
flaxseed
flaxseed=mill
flax=thresher†
flaxweed
flax=wench
fleabane (a plant
flea=beetle
fleabite
fleabitten
flea=glass
flea=louse
fleam=tooth
fleaseed (fleawort)
fleawort
fleece=folder†
fleece=wool
fleet=dike
flect=foot
fleet=footed, etc.
fleet=milk
flesh=axe
flash broth
flesh=brush
flesh=clogged, etc.
flesh=color
flesh=crow
flesh=eater†
flesh=flea
flesh=fly
flesh=fork
flesh=hook
flesh=hoop
fleshing=knife
flesh=juice
flesh=knife
fleshly=minded
flesh=meat
fleshmonger

flesh=pot
flesh=red
flesh=spicule
flesh=tint
flesh=tooth
flesh=worm
flesh=wound
fleur=de=lis
fleur=volant
flier=lathe
flight=arrow
flight=feather
flight=goose
flight=shaft
flight=shooting†
flight=shot
flimmerball (a proto-
    zoan)
flinging=tree
flinking=comb
flint glass
flint=hearted, etc.
flint=knacker†
flint=knapper†
flint=lock (a lock)
flintlock (a gun)
flint=mill
flint=paring
flint=rope
flint=sponge
flintstone
flintware
flintwood
flip=dog
flipflap
flipjack (a flapjack)
flitch=beam
flitterchack (a bird)
flixweed
float=board
float=case
float=copper
float=file
float=gold
float=grass
floating=board
floating=heart
floating=island
floating=lever

floating=plate
floating=screed
float=mineral
float=ore
floatstone
float=valve
flock bed
flock=cutter†
flock=duck
flock=grinding†
flocking=fowl
flocking=machine
flockman
flockmaster
flock=opener†
flock=paper
flock=powder
flock=printing†
floe=berg
floe=ice
floe=rat
flogging=chisel
flogging=hammer
flogmaster
flood=anchor
flood=cock
flood=fence
flood=flanking†
floodgate
flood=mark
flood=tide
floor=chisel
floor=cloth
floor=cramp
floor=frame
floor=guide
floor=hanger
floor=head
floor=hollow
flooring=clamp
floor=light
floor=pan
floor=plan
floor=plate
floor=timber
floor=walker†
flop=damper
flopwing
floridia=green

floridia=red
flosh=hole
flosh=silk
floss=embroidery
floss=hole
floss=silk
floss=yarn
flounder=lantern
flour=barrel
flour=beetle
flour=bolt
flour=box
flour=cooler†
flour=dredge
flour=dredger†
flour=dresser†
flour=emery
flour=gold
flouring=mill
flourishing=thread
flour=mill
flour=mite
flour=packer†
flour=sifter†
flouting=stock
flow=bog
flower=animals
flower=bell
flower=bird
flower=bug
flower clock
flower=cluster
flower=de=luce
flower=fence (a plant)
flower=fly
flower=gentle (a plant)
flower=head
flower=of=an=hour (a
    plant)
flower=pecker (a bird)
flower=piece
flower=pot
flower=pride (a plant)
flower=stalk
flower=water
flower=work
flowery=kirtled
flowing=furnace
flow=moss

flue-boiler
flue-bridge
flue-brush
flue-cinder
flue-cleaner†
flue-hammer
flue-plate
flue-scraper†
flue-stop
flue-surface
flue-work
fluff-gib
fluid-compass
fluid-lens
fluid-meter
fluke-chain
fluke-rope
fluke-spade
fluke-worm
flukewort
flume-car
fluor-spar
flushboard
flush-box
flush-decked, etc.
flushing-box
flushing-rim
flush-pot
flush-tank
flush-wheel
flute-bird
flute-bit
flutemouth (a fish)
flute-organ
flute-pipe
flute-player†
flute-shrike
flute-stop
flute-work
fluting-cylinder
fluting-iron
fluting-lathe
fluting-machine
fluting-plane
fluting-scissors
flutter-wheel
fluxing-bed
fluxion-structure
flux-spoon

fluxweed
fly-agaric
flyaway, a.
flyaway-grass (hair-
    grass)
fly-bait
flybane
fly-bitten
fly-blister
fly-block
flyblow
flyblown
fly-board
flyboat
fly-book
fly-boy
fly-brush
fly-bug
fly-cap
fly-case
fly-caster†
fly-catcher (one who
    catches flies)
flycatcher (special bird-
    name ; compare
    woodpecker)
fly-catching
fly-clip
fly-dressing
fly-drill
fly-dung
fly-dunging†
flyer-lathe
fly-finisher†
flyfish
fly-fisher†
fly-flap
fly-flapper
fly-frame
fly-fringe
fly-gallery
fly-governor
fly-honeysuckle
fly-hook
flying cat
flying dragon
flying-feather
flying fish
flying fox

flying frog
flying gecko
flying gurnard
flying hook
flying lemur
flying lizard
flying-machine
flying marmot
flying phalanger
flying robin
flying shot
flying squid
flying squirrel
flying torch
flying-watchman
fly-leaf
fly-line
fly-maker†
flyman
fly-mixture
fly-net
fly-nut
fly-oil
fly-orchis
fly-paper
fly-penning
fly-poison
fly-powder
fly-press
fly-punching
fly-rail
fly-reed
fly-rod
fly-sheet
fly-shuttle
flysnapper (a bird)
fly-speck
fly-specked
fly-tackle
flytail (a fishing-net)
fly-taker†
fly-tent
fly-tier†
fly-tip
fly-trap
fly-up-the-creek (a
    heron, a person)
fly-water
fly-weevil

fly=wheel
foalfoot (a plant)
foal=teeth
foam=bow
foam=cock
foam=collectoi †
foam=spar
foam=wreath
fob=chain
fob=watch
focusing=cloth
focusing=frame
focusing=glass
fodder=grass
fodder=plant
foeman
fog=alarm
fog=bank
fog=bell
fog=bound
fog=bow
fog=cheese
fog=dog
fog=eater†
fogfruit (a plant)
fog=gun
foggy=bee
fog=horn
fog=ring
fog=signal
fog=smoke
fog=trumpet
fog=whistle
foil=carrier
foil=stone
fold=garth
folding=boards
folding=machine
fold=net
fold=yard
foliage=plant
foliage=tree
folk=free
folk=frith
folkland
folk=lore
folkmoot
folk=psychology
folk=right

folk=song
folk=speech
folk=story
follow=board
follower=plate
following=time
food=fish
food=plant
foodstuff
food=vacuole
food=yolk
foo=foo
fool=born
fool=duck
fool=fangle
foolfish
foolhardy
fool=hen
fool=killer
fool's cap (a cap)
foolscap (paper, a mol-
    lusk)
fool's=coat*
fool's=parsley*
foolstones (an orchid)
fool=trap
foot=artillery
football
foot=band
foot=bank
foot=barracks
foot=base
foot=bath
foot=bellows
foot=bench
foot=blower†
foot=board
footboy
foot=breadth
foot=bridge
foot=brig
foot=cloth
foot=cushion
footfall
foot=fight
foot=folk
foot=gear
foot=grain
foot=guard

foot=halt
foot=hammer
foot=handed
foot=hawker
foot=hedge
foot=hill
foothold
foothook
foot=hot
footing=beam
foot=iron
foot=jaw
foot=joint
foot=key
foot=lathe
foot=level
footlights
foot=line
foot=loose
footman
footman=moth
footmark
foot=muff
foot=note
footpace
foot=pad (a thing for
    padding)
footpad (a person)
foot=page
foot=passenger
foot=pavement
foot=path
foot=picker
foot=plate
foot=plow
foot=poet
foot=post
foot=pound
foot=poundal
foot=press
footprint
foot=race
foot=rail
foot=rest
foot=rope
foot=rot
foot rule
foot=scent
foot=screw

foot=secretion
footset
foot=soldier
foot=sore
foot=space rail
footstalk
footstall
footstep
foot=stick
footstool
foot=stove
foot=stump
foot=ton
foot=tub
foot=tubercle
foot=valve
foot=visc
foot=waling
foot=walk
foot=wall
foot=warmer†
foot=washing†
footway
foot=worn
forage=cap
forage=guard
forage=master
foraging=cap
force=diagram
force=function
forcemeat
force=piece
forceps=candlestick
forceps=tail
force=pump
forcible=feeble
forcing=house
forcing=pit
forcing=pump
fore=and=aft
forearm
forebay
forebeam
forebody
fore=boom
forebrace
forebrain
fore=carriage
forecastle

forecastleman
fore=choir
fore=cited
forecourt
foreday
foredays
fore=deck
fore=door
fore end
forefather
forefinger
fore=bank
fore foot (a foot in front)
forefoot (fore part of foot)
forefront
fore=gaff
fore=gift
foregirth
foreground
forehammer
forehard
forehead
forehead=cloth
forehearth
forehold
forehook
foreland
forelock
forelock=bolt
forelock=hook
fore=looper
foreman
foremast
foremastman
foremother
forename
forenight
forenoon
fore part
fore=part iron
fore=passage
forepeak
fore=piece
foreplan
fore=plane
fore=plate
fore=rake

fore=room
foresail
fore=sheet
foreship
foreshore
foreshot
foreside
foresight
foreskin
foresleeve
fore=staff
fore=stall
fore=starling
forestay
forestaysail
forest=bug
forest=court
forest=fly
forest=folk
forest=lizard
forest=marble
forestone
forest=ox
forest=peat
forest=steading
forest=tree
foresummer
fore teeth
forethought
foretop
foretopgallant
foretopgallantmast
foretopgallantsail
foretopman
foretopmast
foretopmastman
for ever
forewalc
forewind
fore wing
forewoman
foreyard
foreyard=arm
forge=roll
forgeman
forge=scale
forget=me=not (a plant)
forge=train
forge=water

forging=hammer
forging=machine
forging=press
fork=beam
forkbeard (a fish)
fork chuck
forked=beard (a fork-
  beard)
fork head
fork=moss
fork=rest
forks=and=knives (a
  moss)
forktail (a fish, a bird)
fork=tailed
fork wrench
form=board
form=element
form=genus
forming=cylinder
forming=iron
forming=machine
form=species
form=word
fort=adjutant
forte=piano
forthcoming
forthgoing
forth=issuing
forth=pushing
forthputting
forthright
forthwith
fortification=agate
fortnight
fortune=book
fortune=hunter†
fortune=tell
fortune=teller†
forty=five
forty=knot
forty=niner
forty=spot
fossway
foster=babe
foster=brother
foster=child
foster=dam
foster=daughter

foster=earth
foster=father
foster=land
foster=mother
foster=nurse
foster=parent
foster=sister
foster=son
foul=brood (a disease of
  bees)
foul=faced, foul=mouth-
  ed, etc.
foundation=chain
foundation=muslin
foundation=net
foundation=school
foundation=square
foundation=stone
founder=shaft
foundryman
fountain=fish
fountainhead
fountain inkstand
fountain pen
fountain pump
fountain=shell
four=boater
four=cant
four=centred, etc.
four=corners (an old
  game)
fourfold
four=horse
four=in=hand
four=jointer
four=lane=end (a place)
four=o'clock (a plant)
four=part
fourpence
fourpence=halfpenny
fourpenny
four=poster
four=pounder
fourscore
foursquare
fourth=class
fourth=rate
four=way
four=wheeler

fourwings (a bird) ·
fowl=cholera
fowling=net
fowling=piece
foxbane (a plant)
fox=bat
foxberry (a plant)
fox=bolt
fox=brush
fox=case
fox=chase
fox=earth
fox=evil
fox=finch
foxfire
foxfish
foxglove (a plant)
foxglove=pug (a moth)
fox=goose
fox=grape
foxhound
fox=hunt
fox=hunter†
fox=moth
fox=nosed, etc.
fox=shark
fox=sleep
fox=snake
fox=sparrow
fox=squirrel
foxtail (a grass)
foxtail=grass
foxtail=pine
foxtongue (a plant)
fox=trap
fox=trot
Fox=type
fox=wedge
fox=wolf
foxwood
fracture=box
frame=breaker†
frame bridge
frame=diagram
frame=helmet
frame house
frame=house (house to
  do framing in)
frame=knitting

frame=level
frame=saw
frame=timber
frame=work (fancy=
  work done on
  a frame)
framework (a framing
  or skeleton struct-
  ure)
framing=chisel
framing=table
frank=bank
frank=chase
frank=fee
frank=ferm
frank=fold
frank=hearted, etc.
frankincense
frankincense=pine
frank=law
frank=marriage
frank=pledge
frank=service
frank=tenant
frank=tenement
freckle=faced
free=and=easy
free=bench
free=board
free=born, free=footed,
  etc.
free=borough, a.
free=chase
freedman
freedwoman
free=hand
freehold
freeing=stick
free=lance
free=liver†
free love
free=lover
freeman
freemartin
freemason
freemason's=cup*
free=milling
free soil
free=soil, a.

Free=soiler
Free=soilism
freestone (a brown-
  stone, a peach)
free=swimmer†
freethinker†
free trade
free=trade, a.
free=trader
freewarren
free=will, a.
free=willer
freewoman
free=writer
freezing=box
freezing=liquid
freezing=mixture
freezing=point
freight=car
freight=engine
freight=house
freight=locomotive
freight=train
Frenchman
French=tub
Frenchwoman
fresco=painter
fresco=painting
fresh=blown, fresh=col-
  ored, fresh=run, etc.
freshman
fresh=new
fresh=sophomore
fresh=water, a.
freshwoman
fret=saw
fretwork
friar=bird
friar's=cap*
friar's=cowl*
friar's=crown*
friar=skate
friar's=lantern*
friar's=thistle*
friction=balls
friction=brake
friction=breccia
friction=card
friction=clutch

friction=cones
friction=coupling
friction=gear
friction=gearing
friction=match
friction=plate
friction=powder
friction=primer†
friction=sound
friction=tight
friction=tube
friction=wheel
fried=chicken (chicken
  broth)
friendlike
frieze=panel
frieze=rail
friezing=machine
frigate=bird
frigate=built
frigate=mackerel
frigate=pelican
frillback (a pigeon)
frill=lizard
fringe=backed, etc.
fringe=like
fringepod
fringe=tree
frithborg
frithsoken
frithsplot
frithstool
fritting=furnace
frizzing=machine
frizzling=iron
frock coat
frogbit
frog=cheese
frog=clock
frog=crab
frog=eater†
frogfish
frog=fishing†
frog=fly
frogfoot (a plant)
frog=grass
froghopper (an insect)
frogmouth (a bird)
frog=mouthed, etc.

frog=orchis
frog=plate
frog's=bit*
frog=shell
frog's march
frog=spawn
frog=spit
frog=spittle
frogstool (a toadstool)
frontierman
frontiersman
frost=bearer†
frost=bird
frost=bite
frost=blite
frost=bound
frost=butterflies
frostfish
frost=line
frost=mist
frost=nail
frost=nailed, etc.
frostroot (a plant)
frost=smoke
frost=valve
frostweed
frostwork
frostwort
froth=fly
froth=insect
froth=spit
froth=worm
frou=frou
fruit=alcohol
fruit=bat
fruit=bearer†
fruit=bud
fruit=cake
fruit=car
fruit=crow
fruit=culture
fruit=dot
fruit=drier†
fruit=fly
fruit=gatherer†
fruit=house
fruit=jar
fruit=knife
fruit=loft

fruit=picker†
fruit=piece
fruit=pigeon
fruit=press
fruit=stand
fruit=store
fruit=sugar
fruit=tree
fruit=trencher
fruit=worm
fuddlecap (a person)
fudge=wheel
fuel=economizer†
fuel=feeder†
fuel=gas
fugie=warrant
full=armed, full=blown,
    etc.
full=back
full=binding
full=blood
full=bottom
full=brilliant, a.
full=dress, a.
fuller's=herb
fuller's=teazel
f .ller's=thistle
fuller's=weed
full=face
full=hot
fulling=mill
fulling=soap
full=length, a.
fullmouth (a person)
fumewort
fuming=box
fuming=pot
fund=holder†
fund=monger†
funeral=ale
fungus=beetle
fungus=cellulose
fungus=foot
fungus=gnat
fungus=midge
fungus=stone
fungus=tinder
funnel=like
funnel=shaped, etc.

funnel=top
funny=bone
funny man
fur=bearing†
fur=moth
furnace=bar
furnace=bridge
furnace=burning
furnaceman
furniture=plush
furniture=print
furniture=stop (a stop
    in an organ)
furniture=store
furr=chuck
furrow=drain
furrow=faced, etc.
furrowing=machine
furrow=slice
furrow=weed
Furry=day
fur=seal
furzechat
furze=chirper
furze=chitter
furze=hacker
furze=wren
fuse=auger
fusee=engine
fuse=extractor†
fuse=gauge
fuse=hole
fusel=oil
fuse=mallet
fuse=plug
fuse=setter†
fuse=wheel
fuse=wrench
fusil=mortar
fusing=disk
fusing=point
futtock=band
futtock=hoop
futtock=plates
futtock=shrouds
futtock=staff
futtock=stave
futtock=timbers
fuzzball

G

gable=board
gable end
gable=ended, etc.
gable=pole
gable roof (character-
    ized by a gable)
gab=lever
gable=window
gab=lifter†
gadabout (a person)
gad=bush
gadding=car
gadding=machine
gadfly
gad=steel
gad=stick
gad=whip
gaff=hook
gaffsman
gaff=topsail
gag=law
gag=rein
gagroot (a plant)
gag=runner
gain=gear
gaining=machine
gaining=twist
gala=day
gala=dress
galapee=tree
gale=beer
gale=day
galilee=porch
galimeta=wood
gall=apple
gall=beetle
gall=bladder
gall=cyst
gall=duct
gallery=furnace

gallery picture
gallery road
galleta=grass
galley=balk
galley=bird
galley=cabinet
galley=fire
galley=man
galley=news
galley=proof
galley=punt
galley=rack
galley=rest
galley=slave
galley=work
galley=yarn
gall=fly
gall=gnat
gall=insect
gall=louse
gall=maker†
gall=midge
gall=mite
gall=moth
gallnut
galloper=gun
gallou=berry
gallou=bird
gallow=grass
gallows=bird
gallows=bitts
gallows=faced
gallows=frame
gallows=free
gallows=locks
gallows=ripe
gallows=stanchions
gallows=top
gallows=tree
gall=pipe

gall=sickness
gall=stone
gall=wasp
gally=worm
gama=grass
gambet=snipe
gambling=house
gambrel roof
game=bag
game=bird
game=cock
game=egg
game=fish
game=fowl
game=hawk
gamekeeper†
game=law
game=preserve
game=preserver†
gaming=house
gaming=room
gaming=table
gamma=moth
gammoning=hole
gammon=plate
gammon=shackles
gander=party
gander=pull
gander=pulling
gangboard
gang=boring†
gang=by
gang=cask
gang=cultivator†
gang=day
gang=drill
gang=edger
gangflower (a plant)
ganging=line
gauging=plea

ganglion=cell
ganglion=corpuscle
ganglion=globule
gangmaster
gangplank
gang=plow
gang=press
gang=punch
gang=rider
gang=saw
gangsman
gang=there=out
gang=tide
gangway
gangway=ladder
gang=week
gant=line
gape=eyed
gape=gaze
gapemouth (a fish)
gapeseed
gaping=stock
gap=lathe
gap=toothed, etc.
gap=window
garboard=plank
garboard=strake
garde=brace
garde=collet
garde=cou
garde=faude
garden=balm
garden=balsam
garden=beetle
garden=bond
garden=dormouse
garden=engine
garden=bird
gardener's=garters*
garden=flea
garden=gate (a pansy)
garden=glass
garden=house
garden=mite
garden=mould
garden=net
garden=party
garden=plot
garden=pump

garden=snail
garden=spider
garden=squirt
garden=stand
garden=stuff
garden=sweep
garde=nuque
garden=warbler
garde=queue
garde=reine
gare=fowl (a bird)
garfish
garland=flower (a
    plant)
garlic=eater†
garlic=mustard
garlic=shrub
garlicwort
garnetberry
garnet=blende
garnet=hinge
garnet=rock
garnetwork
garnish=bolt
garret=master
garrison=artillery
garter=fish
Garter king
garter=plate
garter=ring
garter=snake
garthman
gas=alarm
gas=analyzer†
gas=apparatus
gas=bag
gas=bath
gas=battery
gas=bellows
gas=black
gas=bleaching
gas=blowpipe
gas=boiler
gas=bracket
gas=buoy ·
gas=burner†
gas=carbon
gas=check
gas=coal

gas company
gas=compressor†
gas=condenser†
gas=drain
gas=drip
gas=engine
gas=engineer
gas=field
gas=fitter†
gas=fixture
gas=flame
gas=furnace
gas=gauge
gas=generator†
gas=globe
gas=governor
gas=gun
gas=heater†
gas=holder†
gas=house
gash=vein
gas=indicator
gas=jet
gasket=iron
gas=lamp
gaslight
gas=lighted
gas=lighting
gas=lime
gas=liquor
gas=machine
gas=main
gas=man
gas=meter
gas=motor
gas=oven
gas=pipe
gas=plant
gas=plate
gas=plot
gas=pore
gas=port
gas=purifier†
gas=range
gas=register
gas=regulator†
gas=retort
gas=ring
gas=sand

gassing=frame
gas=socket
gas=stove
gas=table
gas=tank
gas=tar
gas=trap
gas=tube
gas=valve
gas=washer
gas=water
gas=well
gas=works
gatch=decoration
gatch=work
gate=bill
gate=chamber
gate=channel
gate=end
gate=fine
gate=hook
gate=house
gatekeeper†
gateman
gate=meeting
gate=money
gate=post
gate=road
gate=saw
gate=shutter
gate=tower
gate=valve
gate=vein
gateward
gateway
gathering=board
gathering=coal
gathering=hoop
gathering=iron
gathering=note
gathering=pallet
gathering=peat
gathering=rod
gathering=string
gathering=thread
gaud=day
gaude=lake
gaudy=day
gauge=bar

gauge=block
gauge=box
gauge=cock
gauge=concussion
gauge=door
gauge=glass
gauge=knife
gauge=ladder
gauge=lathe
gauge=pin
gauge=play
gauge=point
gauge=saw
gauge=stuff
gauge=wheel
gauging=caliper
gauging=rod
gauging=rule
gauging=thread
gaum=like
gauntlet=guard
gauntlet=pipe
gauntlet=shield
gauntlet=sword
gauze=dresser†
gauze=tree
gauze=winged, etc.
gavelkind
gavelman
gayfeather (a plant)
gay=you
gazehound
gazing=stock
gear=box
gear=cutter†
gearing=chain
gearing=wheel
gear=wheel
geiger=tree
gem=cutting†
gemel=ring
gemel=window
gem=engraving†
gem=peg
gem=ring
gem=sculpture
gemshorn (an organ=
      stop)
gem=stick

gem=stone
geneat=land
generating=surface
genip=tree
gentian=bitter
gentian=spirit
gentianwort
gentlefolk
gentle=hearted, etc.
gentleman
gentleman=at=arms
gentlemanlike
gentlewoman
genus=name
Georgesman
gerbe=fuse
germ=area
germ=cell
germ=cup
germ-disease
germ=disk
germ=form
germ=gland
germ=history
germ=layer
germ=membrane
germ=plasma
germ=pore
germ=shield
germ=stock
germ=tube
germ=vesicle
gerund=grinder†
gesture=language
gesture=speech
get=nothing
getting=rock
get=up
ghostfish
ghostland
ghost=moth
ghost=plant
ghost=seer†
ghost=show
ghost=soul
ghost=story
ghost=word
giant=kettle
giant=killer†

giant powder
giant=queller†
gibbet=tree
gibble=gabble
gib=cat
gib=fish
gib=keeler†
giblet=check
giblet=cheek
gibstaff
gib=tub
giddyhead (a person)
giddypate (a person)
giff=gaff
gift=enterprise
gift=horse
gift=rope
gigging=machine
gig=lamp
gig=machine
gigman
gig=mill
gig=saddle
gig=saw
gigsman
gig=tree
gilding=press
gilding=size
gilding=tool
gilding=wa
gil=guy
gill=arch
gillaroo=trout
gill=bar
gill=beer
gill=box
gill=breather†
gill=cavity
gill=chamber
gill=cleft
gill=comb
gill=cover
gill=filament
gill=fishing†
gill=flap
gill=flirt
gill=frame
gill=hooter (a barn=owl)
gill=house

gilling=machine
gill=lid
gill=machine
gill=membrane
gill=net
gill=netter†
gill=opening†
gill=plate
gill=plume
gill=raker
gill=sac
gill=slit
gillyflower=apple
gilt=bronze
gilt=edged, etc.
gilthead (a fish)
gimbal=jawed
gimlet=eye
gimlet=eyed
gim=peg
gimp=nail
gin=block
gin fizz
ginger ale
ginger beer
gingerbread
gingerbread=plum
gingerbread=tree
gingerbread=work
ginger=grass
gingernut
ginger=pine
ginger pop
gingersnap
ginger wine
gingerwort
gingko=tree
gin=horse
gin=house
gin=mill
ginny=carriage
gin=palace
gin=pulley
gin=race
gin=ring
gin=shop
gin sling
gin=tackle
gin=wheel

gipsy=herb
gipsy=herring
gipsy=moth
gipsy=winch
gipsywort
gip=tub
girder bridge
girder=tester
girding=beam
girding=hook
girdle=belt
girdle=bone
girdle=knife
girdle=swivel
girdle=wheel
girt=line
giveaway
gizzard=fallen
gizzard=shad
gizzard=trout
glacier=snow
glade=net
glad=eye (a bird)
glamberry
glance=coal
gland=box
gland=cock
glass=argonaut
glass=blower†
glass=cavity
glass=cement
glasschord
glass=cloth
glass coach
glass=coloring†
glass=crab
glass=cutter†
glass=dust
glass=enamel
glass=engraving†
glasseye (a bird, a fish)
glass=eyed, etc.
glass=furnace
glass=gall
glass=gazing
glass=grinder†
glass=hard
glass=house (where
    glass is made)

glassing=jack
glassing=machine
glass=maker†
glassman
glass=metal
glass=mould
glass=mounter†
glass=oven
glass=painter†
glass=paper
glass=pot
glass=press
glass=rolling
glass=rope
glass=shell
glass=shrimp
glass=silvering†
glass=snail
glass=snake
glass=soap
glass=soldering†
glass=spinning†
glass=sponge
glass=stainer†
glass=tinner†
glass=tongs
glassware
glass=welding†
glasswork
glass=worker†
glass=works
glasswort
glaze=kiln
glaze=wheel
glazing=barrel
glazing=machine
glazing=panel
glazing=tool
glazing=wheel
glebe=house
glebe=land
glee=club
gleeman
gleg=hawk
glib=gabbet
gliding=plane
glimmer=gowk
glister=pipe
globe=amaranth

globe=animal
globe cock
globe=daisy
globefish
globeflower (a plant)
globe lightning
globe=ranunculus
globe=runner†
globe=sight
globe=slater†
globe=thistle
globe=trotter†
globe=tube
globe valve
globigerina=mud
globigerina=ooze
globigerina=shells
glory=hole
glory=pea
gloss=buffed
glost=oven
glove=band
glove=buttoner†
glove=calf
glove=clasp
glove=fight
glove=hook
glove=leather
glove=maker†
glove=money
glove=sheep
glove=shield
glove=silver
glove=sponge
glove=stretcher†
glow=lamp
glowworm
glue=boiler
glue=can
glue=drier†
glue=pot
glue=size
glue=stock
gluing=machine
gluing=press
gluten=bread
gluten=casein
gluten=fibrine
glut=herring

glycogen=mass
gnat=hawk
gnat=worm
gnome=owl
goadsman
goad=spur
goaf=flap
go=ahead, a.
go=aheadative
go=aheadativeness
goal=keeper†
goal=post
goat=antelope
goatbeard (a plant)
goatchafer (a beetle)
goatfish
goathead (a bird)
goatherd
goatland
goat=leather
goat=marjoram
goat=milker†
goat=moth
goat=owl
goat's=bane*
goat's=beard*
goat's=foot*
goat's=horn*
goatskin
goat's=rue*
goat's=thorn*
goatstone (a bezoar)
goatsucker (a bird)
goatweed
goatweed=butterfly
gobbin=stitch
gobble=cock
go=between, n.
gob=fire
goblet=cell
goblet=shaped, etc.
gob=line
gobly=gossit
gob=road
gobstick
go=by, n.
go=cart
godchild
goddaughter

go=devil
godfather
God=fearing
God=forsaken
godlike
god=maker†
godmother
go=down
God's acre
godsend
god's=eye*
godson
God=speed.
god=tree
goer=between
goer=by
goffering=iron
goffering=press
goffering=tool
goggle=eye
goggle=eyed
gogglenose
go=harvest
going=barrel
going=fusee
goings=on
going=wheel
goiter=stick
gold=bank
goldbasket (a plant)
gold=bearing†
gold=beater†
gold=blocking†
gold=book (a book of
    gold=leaf)
gold=bound, etc.
goldbreast (a bird)
goldcrest (a bird)
goldcup (a plant)
gold=cushion
gold=digger†
gold=dust (dust of gold)
golddust (a plant)
goldenback (a plover)
goldenbough (mistle-
    toe)
goldenbug (a ladybird)
goldenchain (a plant)
golden=cheeked, etc.

goldenclub (a plant)
goldenear (a moth)
goldeneye (a duck, a
    fish, an insect)
golden=flower (corn=
    marigold)
goldenhead (a widgeon)
goldenknop (a lady-
    bird)
goldenmaid (a fish)
goldenpert (an herb)
goldenrod (a plant)
goldenrod=tree
goldenseal (a plant)
golden=spoon (a tree)
golden=swift (a moth)
gold=fern
gold=field
goldfinch
gold=finder†
goldfinny (a fish)
goldfish
gold=foil
gold=furnace
gold=hammer (a ham-
    mer
goldhammer (a bird)
gold=hunter†
gold=knife
gold=leaf
gold=lily
gold=mine
gold=mining†
gold=mole
gold=note
gold=of=pleasure (a
    plant)
gold=paint
gold=powder
gold=proof
gold=shell
goldsinny (a fish)
gold=size
goldsmith
goldsmith=beetle
goldspink (the gold-
    finch)
gold=stick
goldstone

goldtail (a moth)
goldthread (a plant)
gold=washer†
goldwasp (an insect)
goldworm
golf=club
golfing=ground
goliath=beetle
gombeen=man
gonad=duct
gong=bell
gong=hammer
gong=metal
gong=stand
good=brother (Scotch
    for brother=in=law)
good=by
good=conditioned, etc.
good=day, n.
good=even, n.
good=evening, n.
good=for=little, a.
good=for=nothing, a.
good=for=nothingness
good=Henry (a plant)
good=King=Harry (a
    plant)
good=King=Henry (a
    plant)
goodman
good=morning, n.
good=morrow, n.
good=night, n.
goods=engine
goods=shed
goods=train
goods=truck
goods=wagon
goods=van
goodwife
good will
good=will (of a busi=
    ness)
goody=bread
goody=good
goody=goody
goody=goodyism
goora=nut
goosebeak (a dolphin)

gooseberry
gooseberry=bush
gooseberry=moth
goose=bird
goose=brant
goose=corn
goose=egg
goosefish
gooseflesh
goosefoot (a plant, etc.)
goose=footed, etc.
goosegog (gooseberry)
goose=grass
goose=green
goose=gull
gooseherd
goose=house
goose=mussel
gooseneck
goose=pimples
goose=quill
goose=skin
goose=step
goose=tansy
goosetongue (a plant)
goose=wing
goosey=gander
gopher=man
gopherroot (a shrub)
gopher=snake
gopher=wood (wood)
gopherwood (tree)
gorcock
gor=crow
gorebill (a fish)
gore=strake
gorge=curtain
gorge=hook
gorgon's=head*
gorse=duck
gorsehatch (a bird)
gorsehopper (a bird)
gory=dew
gosling=green
gossipmonger
gouge=bit
gouge=chisel
gouge=furrow
gouge=slip

gourdmouth (a fish)
gourdseed=sucker (a
   fish)
gourd=shaped, etc.
gourd=shell
gourd=tree
gourdworm
gout=stone
goutweed
goutwort
gouty=gall
governor=block
governor=general
governor=generalship
governor=valve
gowkmeat
gownman
gown=piece
gownsman
grab=bag
grab=game
grab=hook
· grab=iron
grab=line
grace=hoop
grace=note
grace=stroke
grading=instrument
grading=plow
grading=scraper †
grading=shovel
graduation=engine
graft=hybrid
graft=hybridization
grafting=chisel
grafting=knife
grafting=saw
grafting=tool
grafting=wax
grain=alcohol
grain=bin
grain=binder†
grain=bruiser†
grain=car
grain=cleaner†
grain=conveyor†
grain=cradle
grain=damper†
grain=door

grain=drier†
grain=farm
grain=fork
grain=gauge
grain=harvester†
grain=huller†
graining=board
graining=colors
graining=plate
graining=tool
grain=leather
grain=meter
grain=mill
grain=moistener†
grain=moth
grain=oil
grain=rake
grain=sacker†
grain=scale
grain=scourer†
grain=screen
grains=drier†
grain=separator†
grain=shovel
grainsman
grain=soap
grain=staff
grain=tester†
grain=tin
grain=tree
grain=weevil
grain=wheel
grama=grass
gram=centimetre
gram=degree
grammar=school
granat=guano
grandchild
granddaughter
grand=ducal
grand duke (a duke)
grand=duke (an owl)
grandfather
grandfather=long=legs
grand=guard (armor)
grandma
grandmamma
grandmother
grandnephew

grandniece
grandpa
grandpapa
grandparent
grand=piece (armor)
grandson
granduncle
granite=axe
granite=porphyry
graniteware
granny=knot
granny's knot
granulating=machine
granule=cells
grape=cure
grape=fern
grapeflower (a plant)
grapefruit (a plant or
  its fruit)
grape=hyacinth
grape=juice
grape=louse
grape=mildew
grape=root
grape=rot
grape=shot
grape=stone
grape=sugar
grape=tree
grape=trellis
grape=vine
grapnel=plant
grapple=plant
grapple=shot
grappling=iron
grappling=line
grappling=tongs
grass=bar
grass=bass
grass=bird
grass=bleaching
grass=character
grasschat (a bird)
grass=cloth
grass=cutter†
grass=drake
grass=embroidery
grassfinch
grass=green

grass=grown
grass=hand
grass=harvester†
grasshopper
grasshopper=beam
grasshopper=engine
grasshopper=lark
grasshopper=sparrow
grasshopper=warbler
grass=land
grass=like
grass=linen
grass=moth
grassnut (a tuberous
  root)
grass=oil
grass=parrakeet
grass=pink
grass=plot
grass=plover
grass=poly
grassquit (a grassfinch)
grass=seed
grass=snake
grass=snipe
grass=spider
grass=sponge
grass=table
grass=tree
grass=vetch
grass=warbler
Grass=week
grass=widow
grass=widower
grass=worm
grass=wrack
grate=bar
grate=room
grate=surface
grave=clothes
grave=digger†
gravel=car
gravel=laspring
gravel=mine
gravel=pit
gravel=plant
gravelroot (a plant)
gravel=stone
grave=robber†

gravestone
graveyard
graving=dock
graving=piece
gravity=battery
gravity=railroad
gravity=solution
gravy=boat
grayback (a person, a
  duck, etc.)
gray=bear (a spider)
graybeard (a person,
  etc.)
graybird
graycoat (a person)
grayfish
gray=fly
grayhead (a person,
  etc.)
graylord (a fish)
graystone
graywacke
gray=washing†
graywether
gray=whaler†
grazing=ground
grease=box
grease=cock
grease=cup
grease=jack
grease=pot
greasewood (a shrub)
great=aunt
greatcoat
great=eyed, etc.
great=grandfather, etc.
great-great=grandson,
  etc.
greathead (a duck)
great=uncle
grebe=cloth
greedy=gut
greedy=guts
gree=gree
greenback (a note, etc.)
greenbane (a fish)
green bass
green=bearded, etc.
greenben (a fish)

greenbird

greenbone (a fish)

greenbrier (a plant)

greenbroom (a plant)

greenchafer (an insect)

green=cod (a fish)

green=corn (string of
 egg=capsules of a
 whelk)

greenfinch

greenfish

greenfly

greengill (an oyster)

greengrocer

greenhead (a plover)

greenheart (a tree)

greenhorn (a person)

greenhouse (house for
 plants)

greening=weed

green=laver (a seaweed)

greenroom (retiring=
 room in a theatre)

green=rot

greensand (a sandstone)

greensauce (a plant)

greenshank (a bird)

greensick

green=sloke (green=
 laver)

green=snake

green=stall

greenstone

greenweed

greenwing (a duck)

greenwithe (an orchid)

greenwood (a forest)

griddle=cake

grief=muscle

grief=shot

griffin=male

griffin=vulture

grim=the=collier (a
 plant

grinding=bed

grinding=bench

grinding=block

grinding=clamp

grinding frame

grinding=lathe

grinding=machine

grinding=mill

grinding=plate

grinding=roll

grinding=slip

grinding=spheres

grinding=tooth

grinding=vat

grinding=wheel

grindlestone

grindstone

grindstone=grit

grinning=muscle

grip=car

gripe=all (a miser)

gripe=penny (a miser)

grip=grass

gripman

gripping=wheel

grip=pulley

gripsack

grist=mill

grit=rock

gritstone

groaning=malt

groceryman

grocery=store

grog=blossom

grogram=yarn

grog=shop

groin=arch

groin=centring

groin=point

groin=rib

gromet wad

groom=grubber

groom=porter

groomsman

groove=fellow

groove=ram

grooving=plane

grosbeak

gross=headed, etc.

grotto=work

ground=angling†

ground=annual

ground=ash

ground=auger

ground=bailiff

ground=bait

ground=beam

ground=beetle

groundberry

ground=bird

ground=cherry

ground=cistus

ground=cloth

ground=cock

ground=cuckoo

ground=cypress

ground=dove

ground=down, n.

ground=fast

ground=feeder

ground=finch

ground=fir

ground=fish

ground floor

ground form

ground=game

ground=gru

ground=gudgeon

ground=hemlock

ground=hog

ground=hold

ground=hornbill

ground=ice

grounding=tool

ground=ivy

ground=joint

ground=joist

ground=keeper†

ground=layer†

ground=line

ground=liverwort

ground=lizard

ground=mail

ground=marker

ground=mass

ground=mould

ground=mullet

ground=nest

ground=net

ground=niche

groundnut

ground=parrakeet

ground=pea

ground=pearl
ground=pig
ground=pigeon
ground=pine
ground=plan
ground=plane
ground=plate
ground=plot
ground=plum
ground=rat
ground=rent
ground=robin
ground=roller†
ground=rope
ground=scraper†
ground=scratcher†
ground=sea
ground=seat
groundsel=tree
ground=shark
groundsill
ground=sloth
ground=sluice
ground=snake
ground=sparrow
ground=squirrel
ground=starling
ground=strake
ground=swell
ground=table
ground=tackle
ground=throw
ground=thrush
ground=timbers
groundways
ground=wheel
groundwork
group=spring
grouse=pigeon
grout=ale
grouthead (a block-
. head)
grout=headed
growing=cell
growing=slide
growth=form
grozing=iron
grub=axe
grubbing=axe

grubbing=hoe
grub=hook
grub=plank
grub=saw
grub=stake
Grub street
grub=time
grubworm
gru=gru
grunting ox
G string
guano=mixer†
guano=sower†
guard=boat
guard=book
guard=brush
guard=cell
guard=chain
guard=chamber
guard=duty
guard=finger
guardfish
guard=flag
guard=house
guardian angel
guardian=cell
guard=irons
guard=lock
guard=mounting
guard=pile
guard=plate
guard=rail
guard=rein
guard=ring
guard=room
guard=ship
guardsman
guard=tent
guelder=rose
guess=rope
guess=warp
guesswork
guest=chamber
guest=fly
guest=moth
guest=room
guest=rope
guide=bar
guide=block

guide=book
guidecraft
guide=eye
guide=feather
guide=flag
guide=pile
guide=post
guide=pulley
guide=rail
guide=roller
guide=ropes
guide=screw
guide=tube
guideway
guide=yoke
guild=ale
guild=brother
guildhall
guild=rent
guilt=sick
Guinea=cloth
guinea=cock
guinea=corn
guinea=edge
guinea=fowl
guinea=goose
guinea=grains
guinea=grass
guinea=green
guinea=hen
Guineaman
guinea=pig
guinea=worm
guitar=player†
guitar=string
gulfweed
gul=gul
gull=billed, etc.
gull=catcher (a bird)
gull=chaser (a bird)
gulleting=file
gulleting=press
gulleting=stick
gullet=larval
gullet=saw
gulley=trap
gullfish
gull=teaser (a bird)
gully=hunter

gullymouth (a pitcher)
gum=animal
gum=boil
gumbo=limbo
gum=cistus
gum=drop
gum dynamite
gum=game
gum=plant
gum=pot
gum=rash
gum resin
gum=stick
gum=top tree
gum=tree
gum=water
gum=wood (wood)
gumwood (a tree)
gun=barrel
gun=battery
gunboat
gun=brig
gun=captain
gun=carriage
guncotton
gun=deck
gun=fire
gun=flint
gun=gear
gun=harpoon
gun=iron
gun=lift
gun=lock

gunmaker†
gunman
gun=metal
gun=money
gunner=fluke
gunnery=lieutenant
gunnery=ship
gunning=boat
gunny bags
gunny=cloth
gun=pendulum
gun=pit
gun=port
gunpowder
gunpowder=engine
gunpowder=hammer
gunpowder=manufac-
    turing†
gunpowder=mill
gunpowder=press
gun=reach
gun=room
gun=searcher†
gunshot
gun=shy
gun=slide
gun=sling
gunsmith
gun=stick
gun=stock
gun=stocker†
gun=tackle
gun=wad

gun=wadding
gun=work
gurry=bait
gurry=butt
gurry=fish
gurry=ground
gurry=shark
guru=nut
gut=formed
gut=length
gut=scraper†
gutta=percha
gutta=putih
gutta=rambong
gutta=shea
gutta=singgarip
gutta=sundek
gutta=taban
gutta=trap
gutter=blood
gutter=boarding
gutter=cock
gutter=flag
gutter=hole
gutter=ledge
gutter=snipe
gutter=spout
gutter=stick
gutter=teetan
gutwort
guy=rope
gypsum=furnace
gyre=carlin

H

habit=cloth
habit=maker†
habit=shirt
hack=barrow
hackberry
hackbolt (a sea=bird)
hack=file
hack=hammer
hacking=seat
hack=iron
hackle=bar
hackle=feather ·
hackle=fly
hackling=machine
hackman
hackney=coach
hackney=coachman
hackneyman
hack=trap
hack=watch
haddock=tea
haft=pipe
hagberry
hagfish
hag=gull
hag=mouth
hag=ridden
hag=staff
hag's=tooth*
hag=taper
hag=tracks
hagweed
hag=worm
ha-ha
hail=fellow
hailstone
hail=storm
hair=bird
hair=bracket
hairbranch=tree

hairbreadth
hair=brush
hair=bulb
haircap=moss
hair=cell
hair=clam
haircloth
hair=compasses
haircup=flower (a plant)
hair=dividers
hair=dress
hair=dresser†
hair=dye
hair=eel
hair=feather
hair=follicle
hair=gland
hair=grass
hair=knob
hair=lace
hair=lichen
hair=line
hair=net
hair=oil
hair=picker†
hairpin
hair=powder
hair=pyrites
hair=quag,
hair=sac
hair=salt
hair's breadth
hair=seal
hair=shaped, etc.
hair=sheath
hair=space
hair=splitter†
hair=spring
hair=star
hairstreak (a butterfly)

hair=stroke
hairtail (a fish)
hair=trigger
hairtrigger=flower (a
    plant)
hair=weaving†
hair=work
hair=worker†
hairworm
hairybait (a worm)
hairycrown (a bird)
hairyhead (a bird)
hakesdame (a fish)
hake's=tooth*
halberd=headed, etc.
halberdman
halberd=weed
half=and=half
half=ape
half=back
half=baked
half=baptize
halfbeak (a fish)
half=belt
half=bent, etc.
halfbill (a bird, a fish)
half=binding
half=blood
half=bloom
half=board
half=boarder
half=boot
half=box
half=breed
half=brilliant
half=brother
half=caponiere
half=caste
half=cent
half=cheek

half=chess
half=cock
half=communion
half=crown
half=curlew
half=deck
half=dime
half distance
half=dollar
half=eagle
half=face
half=facet
half=falconet
half=farthing
half=feather
half=fish
half=floor
half=guinea
half=hatchet
half=heather
half=hitch
half=holiday
half=hose
half=hour
half=hourly
half=kirtle
half=length
half=line
half=lop
half=marrow
half=mask
half=mast
half=measure
half=merlon
half=moon
half=mounting
half=mourning
half note
half=pace
half pay
half=pay, a.
halfpenny
half=pike
half=port
half price
half=price, a. and adv.
half=principal
half=read
half=relief

half rest
half=round
half=royal
half=seas=over
half=shell
half=shift
half=sister
half=snipe
half=sole
half=sovereign
half=spade
half=spear
half step
half=stitch
half=stop
half=stuff
half=suit
half=sword
half=tangent
half=tercte
half=thought
half=throw
half=tide
half=timber
half=timer
half=tint
half=title
half=tone
half=tongue
half=trap
half=travel
half=truth
half=virtue
half=way
half=wit
half=yard
half=yarn
half=year
half=yearly
halibut=broom
halibut=slime
hall Bible
hall=house
hall=mark
Hallowe'en
Hallow=eve
Hallow=fair
Hallowmas
Hallow=tide

hallway
halter=break
halve=net
halving=belt
halyard=rack
ham=beetle
hame=fastener†
hame=lock
hame=ring
hame=strap
ham=knife
hammer=axe
hammer=beam
hammer=blow
hammer=cap
hammer=catcher†
hammer=cloth
hammer=dressed, etc.
hammer=fish
hammer=harden
hammer=head (head of
  a hammer)
hammerhead (a fish,
  bird)
hammer=helve
hammer=joint
hammerman
hammer=mark
hammer=nail
hammer=oyster
hammer=pick
hammer=pike
hammer=scale
hammer=sedge
hammer=shell
hammer=spring
hammer=stone
hammer=tail
hammer=tongs
hammerwort
hammer=wrought
hammock=batten
hammock=cloth
hammock=clues
hammock=nettings
hammock=rack
hamstring
hand=anvil
hand=bag

hand-baggage
handball
hand-barrow
hand-bell
hand-bill (an imple-
 ment)
handbill (a printed cir-
 cular)
handbook
hand-borrow
hand-bow
hand-brace
handbreadth
hand-bridge
hand-buckler
hand-cannon
hand-car
hand-cart
hand-claw
handcuff
hand-director
hand-drop
handfish
hand-flail
hand-float
handflower-tree
hand-fly
hand-footed, etc.
hand-fork
hand-frame
hand-gallop
hand-gear
hand-glass
hand-gout
hand-grenade
hand-grip
hand-gripe
hand-guard
hand-guide
hand-gyve
hand-hammer
hand-harmonica
hand-heat
handhold
hand-hole
hand-book
hand-iron
handkerchief
hand-language

hand-lathe
hand-lead
handle-net
hand-letter
hand-lever
hand-line
handlining
hand-list
handlocked
hand-loom
hand-made
handmaid
handmaiden
handmaid-moth
hand-mill
hand-mirror
hand-mould
hand-money
hand-mortar
hand-orchis
hand-organ
hand-paper
hand-pegger†
hand-plant
hand-planter†
hand-play
hand-plow
hand-post
hand-pot
hand-press
hand-promise
hand-pump
hand-punch
hand-quill
hand-rackle, a.
hand-rail
hand-railing
hand-running
hand-sail
hand-sale
hand-saw
handsaw-fish
hand's breadth
hand-screen
handscrew
hand-shake
hand-shaking†
hand-spear
handspike

handspikeman
handspring
handstaff
hand-strap
hand's turn
hand-target
hand-taut
hand-tennis
hand-tight
hand-to-hand, a.
hand-to-mouth, a.
hand-vise
hand-waled, etc.
hand-warmer†
hand-wheel
handwhile
hand-work
hand-worker†
handworm
handwrist
handwrite
handwriting
hand-wrought
handy-billy
handybook (a hand-
 book)
handy-dandy
handy man
hangbird (an oriole)
hang-choice
hangdog, a.
hanger-board
hanger-on
hanging-bird (an ori-
 ole)
hanging-guard
hanging-machine
hanging-moss
hanging-needle
hanging-pear
hanging-post
hanging-stile
hanging-tie
hanging-tool
hangman
hangnail
hang-nest (a nest)
hangnest (a bird)
hang-net

hang=worm
hauk=worsted
hanky=panky
hanse=house
hansom cab
haphazard
happy=go=lucky
hap=warm
hara=nut
harbinger=of=spring (a
 plant)
harbor=dues
harbor=gasket
harbor=light
harbor=log
harbor=master
harbor=reach
harbor=seal
harbor=watch
hardbake (a sweetmeat)
hardbeam (a tree)
hardbill (a grosbeak)
hard=bitted, etc.
hardening=furnace
hardening=kiln
hardening=machine
hardening=skin
hard=fern
hard finish
hard=fish
hard=grass
hardhack (a shrub)
hardhay (a plant)
hardhead (a coin, a
 fish, etc.
hard metal
hardmouth (a fish)
hard=pan
hard=pear (a tree)
hard=port, a
hard=shell
hardtack (biscuit, a
 duck)
hardtail (a mackerel)
hardware
hardwareman
hard wood (wood)
hard=wood, a.
hardwood (a tree)

hardwood=tree
hardy=shrew
harebrain (a person)
harebrained
hare=eyed, etc.
hare=foot (a foot like a
 hare's)
harefoot (a ptarmigan,
 a plant)
harehound
hare=kangaroo
harelip (a divided lip, a
 fish)
hare's=bane*
hare's=beard*
hare's=colewort*
hare's=ear*
hare's=foot*
hare's=lettuce*
hare's=palace*
hare's=parsley*
hare's=tail*
harestane (a hoarstone)
hare=thistle
haricot=bean
hark=away
harlequin duck
harlequin=flower (a
 plant)
harmala=red
harness=bell
harness=board
harness=cask
harness=clamp
harness=hook
harness=leather
harness=maker†
harness=mounting†
harness=pad
harness=plate
harness=room
harness=saddle
harness=snap
harness=tub
harness=weaver†
harnpan (the brainpan)
harping=iron
harp=lute
harpoon=arrow

harpoon=fork
harpoon=gun
harpoon=rocket
harpoon=shuttle
harp=pedal
harp=player†
harp=seal
harp=shell
harp=shilling
harpsichord=graces
harp=string
harp=style
harp=treadle
harpy=eagle
harpy=footed
harry=gad
harry=gaud
Harry=long=legs
hartberry
hart=crop
hart's=clover*
hartshorn (ammonia, as
 coming from the
 hart's horn)
hartshorn=plantain
hart's=thorn*
hart's=tongue*
hart's=trefoil*
hart's=truffles*
hartwort
harum=scarum
harvest=apple
harvest=bells
harvest=bug
harvest=doll
harvest=feast
harvest=field
harvest=fish
harvest=fly
harvest=goose
harvest=home
harvesting=machine
harvest=lady
harvest=lord
harvest=louse
harvestman (a man, a
 spider)
harvest=mite
harvest=month

harvest=moon
harvest=mouse
harvest=queen
harvest=spider
harvest=tick
has=been, *n.*
haskwort
hasp=lock
hassagay=wood
hassock=filler
hassock=grass
hasting=apple
hasting=pear
hasty=footed, etc.
hasty pudding
hatband
hat=block
hat=body
hat=box
hat=brush
hat=case
hatch=bar
hatch=boat
hatchet=bolt
hatchet=face
hatchet=faced, etc.
hatchet=stake
hatchet=vetch
hatching=box
hatching=jar
hatching=trough
hatch=ladder
hatchway
hat=conformator
hat=die
hat=embossing†
hat=finishing†
hat=fitting†
hat=forming†
hat=fulling†
hat=hardening†
hat=honor
hat=ironing†
hat=maker†
hat=measure
hat=mould
hat=money
hat=napping†
hat=piece

hat=planking
hat=plant
hat=pouncing†
hat=press
hat=protector†
hat=rack
hat=rail
hat=roller†
hat=stand
hat=stiffening
hat=store
hat=stretching†
hat=sweat
hatted=kit
hatti=humayun
hat=tip
hatti=sherif
hattit=kit
hat=tree
hat=ventilator†
hat=weaving†
hat=worship
haulage=clip
haul=seine
hausse=pouch
haute=de=barde
haute=lisse
haute=piece
haut=gout
haven=master
haverbread
havercake
haver=grass
haverstraw
hawbuck (a person)
hawfinch
haw=haw
hawk=bell
hawkbill (a sea=turtle,
 pliers)
hawk=billed, etc.
hawkbit (a plant)
hawk=boy
hawk=eagle
Hawkeye
hawk=fly
hawking=glove
hawk=moth
hawknut (tuber, plant)

hawk=owl
hawk=parrot
hawk's=beard*
hawk's=bill*
hawk's=eye*
hawk=swallow
hawkweed
hawse=bag
hawse=block
hawse=bolster
hawse=buckler
hawse=hole
hawse=hook
hawse=piece
hawse=pipe
hawse=plug
hawser=laid
hawse=timber
hawse=wood
hawsing=iron
hawsing=mallet
hawthorn
hawthorn=grosbeak
hawthorn=tree
hay=asthma
hay=bacillus
hay=band
hay=bird
hay=cap
hay=car
hay=cart
haycock
hay=cold
hay=cutter†
hay=elevator†
hay=fever
hay=field
hay=fork
hay=hook
hay=jack
hay=knife
hay=loader†
hay=loft
haymaiden (ground=
 ivy)
haymaids (ground=ivy)
haymaker†
hay=market
haymow

hay=plant	head=cracker	head=ring
hay=press	head=cringle	head=rope
hay=rack	head=dress	head=sails
hayrake	head=earing	headshake
hayrick	headfast	head=sheets
hay=scent	headfish	head=shield
hay=seed (seed)	head=frame	head=sill
hayseed (a plant, a per-	head=gate	head=silver
son)	head-gear	head=skin
hay=spreader†	head=guide	headsman
haystack	head-house	head=spade
haystacker†	head-hunter†	headspring
haysuck (a bird)	heading=chisel	head=stall
haysucker (a bird)	heading=circler	head=station
hay=tea	heading=course	head=stick
hay=tedder	heading=joint	head=stock
haythorn	heading=knife	headstone
hay=tit	heading=machine	head=stool
hay=unloader†	heading=tool	headstrong
hazard=table	head=kerchief	head=sword
hazel=crottles	head=kidney	head=tabling
hazel=earth	head=knee	head=timber
hazel=grouse	head=knot	head=tire
hazel=hen	headland	head=tone
hazelnut	headledge	head=turner†
hazel=oil	headlight	head=valve
hazel=rag	head=line	head=veil
hazel=raw	head=lining	head=voice
hazel=tree	headlong	head=wark
hazelwort	head=louse	headway
headache	head man	head=word
headache=tree	head=marl	head=work
headache=weed	head master	head=worker†
head=and=head, a., adv.	head=money	head=yard
head=band	head=mould	healall
head=bay	head=moulding	heal=dog
head=betony	head=netting	healing=herb
head=block	head=note	healing=pyx
headboard	head=oil	health=guard
headboom	head=penny	health=lift
headborough	head=piece	health officer
head=case	head=plate	heap=cloud
head=cell	head=post	heap=keeper†
head=chair	head=pump	hearing=trumpet
headcheese	headquarters	hearse=cloth
head=chute	headrace	hearse=like
head=cloth	head=rail	heartache
head=coal	head=reach	heart=beat
head=court	head=rest	heart=bird

heart-block
heart-blood
heart-bond
heartbreak
heartbreaking†
heartbroken
heartburn
heartburning
heartburnt
heart-cam
heart-clot
heart-clover
heart-cockle
heart-disease
heart-case
heart-casing
heart-eating
heart-failure
heartfelt
heart-free
hearth-brush
hearth-cinder
hearth-cricket
heart-heaviness
heart-heavy
hearth-ends
hearth-money
hearth-penny
hearth-plate
hearth-rug
hearthstead
hearthstone
hearth-tax
heartleaf (a plant)
heart-liverleaf
heart-net
heart-of-the-earth (a
; plant
'heart-pea
heartquake
heartrending
heart-robbing
heart-rot
heart-scald
heart's case (ease of
 heart)
heartscase (a plant)
heartseed (a plant)
heart-seine

heart-service
heartshake
heart-shaped
heart-shell
heart-sick
heart-sickening
heart-sinking
heart-snakeroot
heart-sore
heart-spoon
heart-steel
heart-stirring
heartstrings
heart-struck
heart-swelling
heart-throb
heart-trefoil
heart-urchin
heart-wheel
heart-whole
heart-wood
heart-yarn
heat-apoplexy
heat-economizer†
heat-engine
heater-car
heater-plate
heater-shaped
heat-factor
heat-fever
heat-focus
heath-bell (the flower
 of heath)
heathberry
heath-bird
heath-clad
heath-cock
heath-corn
heathcup (a plant)
heath-cypress
heath-egger
heather-bell
heather-bleat
heather-bleater
heather-claw
heather-grass
heather-lintie
heather-peeper
heather-wool

heath-fowl
heath-grass
heath-hen
heath-honeysuckle
heath-pea
heath-peat
heath-poult
heath-pout
heath-snail
heath-throstle
heathwort
heating-apparatus
heating-back
heating-chamber
heating-oven
heating-pan
heating-stove
heating-surface
heating-tube
heat-pimple
heat-potential
heat-regulator†
heat-spectrum
heat-spot
heat-unit
heaven-born, etc.
heaven-bright
heavenly-minded
heaven-tree
heave-offering
heave-shoulder
heave-thigh
heaving-days
heaving-line
heavy-armed, etc.
heavy-pine
heavy-spar
heavy-stone
heavyweight (a person)
Hebrew-marked
he-cabbagetree
heckberry
heck-box
heckle-cell
he-clam
heddle-eye
heddle-hook
heddle-yarn
hedge-accentor

hedge=bedstraw
hedgebells (a plant)
hedgeberry
hedge=bill
hedge=binding
hedge=bindweed
hedge=bird
hedge=born
hedge=bote
hedge=carpenter
hedge=chafer
hedge=chanter
hedge=chicken
hedge=clipper†
hedge=garlic
hedgehog
hedgehog=cactus
hedgehog=fruit
hedgehog=grass
hedgehog=parsley
hedgehog=plant
hedgehog=rat
hedgehog=thistle
hedge=hyssop
hedge=jug
hedge=knife
hedge=laurel
hedgemaids (ground=
  ivy)
hedge=marriage
hedge=mike
hedge=mushroom
hedge=mustard
hedge=nettle
hedge=parsley
hedge=parson
hedge=peak
hedge=pink
hedge=plant
hedge=planter†
hedge=priest
hedge=rhyme
hedge=row
hedge=school
hedge=schoolmaster
hedge=scissors
hedge=shrew
hedge=sparrow
hedge=speak

hedge=spick
hedge=spurgie
hedge=taper
hedge=thorn
hedge=vine
hedge=violet
hedge=warbler
hedging=bill
hedging=glove
hedging=tools
heel=ball
heel=blank
heel=block
heel=bone
heel=breasting†
heel=burnishing†
heel=calk
heel=chain
heel=cutter†
heeling=error
heel=iron
heel=jigger
heel=joint
heel=knee
heel=lift
heel=machine
heel=pad
heel=path
heel=piece
heelpiece, v.
heel=plate
heel=post
heel=ring
heel=rope
heel=seat
heel=shave
heel=tap
heeltap, v.
heel=tip
heel=tool
heel=tree
heel=trimmer†
hegberry
height=board
height=staff
heir=apparency
heir apparent
heir=land
heirloom

he=jalap
hellbender
hell=bent, etc.
hell=black
hell=broth
hell=cat
hell=diver
hell=driver
hell=fire
hell=gate
hellgrammite=fly
hell=hag
hell=hound
hell=kite
hell=rake
helm=bar
helm=cloud
helmet=beetle
helmet=bird
helmet=cockatoo
helmet=crab
helmet=crest
helmet=flower (a plant)
helmet=quail
helmet=shaped, etc.
helmet=shell
helm=guard
helm=port
helmsman
help=ale
helpmate
helpmeet
helpworthy
helter=skelter
helter=skelteriness
helve=hammer
hemlock=dropwort
hemlock=parsley
hemlock=pitch
hemlock=spruce
hemp=agrimony
hemp=brake
hemp=bray
hemp=bush
hemp=harvester†
hemp=nettle
hemp=palm
hemp=plant
hemp=resin

hemp-seed
hemp-tree
hempweed
hempwort
hemstitch
hen-and-chickens (a plant)
henbane
henbill (a bird)
hen-billed, etc.
henbit (a plant)
hen-blindness
hen-buckie
hen-cavey
henceforth
henceforward
henchman
hen-clam
hen-coil
hen-coop
hen-curlew
henfish
hen-hawk
hen-house
hen-huzzy
hen-mould
hen-paidle
henpeck
henpecked
hen-plant
hen-roost
hen's-bill*
hen's-foot*
henware
henwife
henwoman
he goat, etc.
he-oak
hep-bramble
hep-brier
herald-crab
herald-moth
herbage-plant
herb-bane
herb-barbara
herb-bennet
herb-carpenter
herb-christopher
herb-doctor

herb-frankincense
herb-gerard
herb-grace
herb-ivy
herb-lily
herb-louisa
herb-margaret
herb-of-grace
herb-paris
herb-peter
herb-repentance
herb-robert
herb-sophia
herb-trinity
herb-truelove
herb-twopence
herb-william
herbwoman
Hercules-beetle
Hercules'-club*
herd-book
herdboy
herd-grass
herding-ground
herd's-grass*
herdsman
herdswoman
hereabout
hereabouts
hereafter
hereat
hereaway
here-being
hereby
herefor
herefrom
herein
hereinafter
hereinbefore
hereinto
hereof
hereon
hereright
hereto
heretofore
hereunder
hereunto
hereupon
herewith

hermit-bird
hermit-crab
hermit-crow
hermit-thrush
hermit-warbler
hernant-seeds
heron's-bill*
hero-worship
hero-worshipper†
herring-bank
herring-bone
herring-buss
herring-cobs
herring-cod
herring-curer†
herring-driver†
herring-fishery
herring-gull
herring-hake
herring-hog
herring-king
herring mountain
herring-pike
herring-pond
herring-spink
herring-work
herself
herst-pan
hewhole (woodpecker)
hey-go-mad
hick-joint
hickory-acacia
hickory-elm
hickory-eucalyptus
hickory-girdler
hickoryhead (a duck)
hickory-nut
hickory-pine
hickory-shad
hickory shirt
hidden-eyed, etc.
hide-and-seek
hide-blown
hidebound
hide-handler†
hide-mill
hide-rope
hide-scraper†
hide-shaving†

hide-stretcher†
hide-worker†
hiding-place
hiera-picra
higgledy-piggledy
higglehaggle
high-backed
highbinder
high-blest, high-
blooded, etc.
high-boy
High-church
High-churchism
High-churchman
high-cockalorum
high-cross
high-day
high-dilutionist
high-flier†
high-flown
high-go
highholder (a wood-
pecker)
highhole (a wood-
pecker)
high-hook
highland
Highlandman
high-line (a fisherman)
high-liner (a fisherman)
high-low
high-low-jack
high-mallow
high-pressure, a.
high priest
high-priesthood
high-priestly
high-priestship
high-proof
high-reaching
highroad
high-sounding
high-stepper†
high-street
high-taper
high-top (an apple)
highty-tighty
highway
highwayman

hill-ant
hillberry
hill-bird
hill-country
hill-digger†
hill-fever
hill-folk
hill-fort
hill-francolin
hillman
hill-mina
hill-oat
hillock-tree
hill-partridge
hill-plover
hillside
hillside-plow
hill-site
hill-sparrow
hill-star
hill-tit
hilltop
hillwort
himself
hinau-tree
hindberry
hindbrain
hinder-end
hinder-night
hind-foremost
hindgut
hindhand
hindhead
hindsight
hinge-band
hinge-joint
hinge-line
hinge-pillar
hinge-pin
hinge-tooth
hinging-post
hip-bath
hip-belt
hipberry
hip-bone
hipbrier (a plant)
hip-girdle
hip-gout
hip-hop

hip-joint
hip-knob
hip-lock
hip-moulding
hippety-hoppety
hippo-sandal
hip-rafter
hip-roof
hiprose (a plant)
hip-shot
hip-strap
hip-tile
hip-tree
hip-tub
hipwort
history-painting
history-piece
hitching-bar
hitching-clamp
hitching-post
hitherto
hit-off
hit-or-miss, a., adv.
hity-tity
hive-bee
hive-nest
hive-vine
hoar frost
hoarhound
hoarstone
hob-a-nob
hob-and-nob
hobble-bobble
hobble-bush
hobby-horse
hobbyhorsical
hobby-owl
hoblike
hob-nail
hobnail-liver
hob-or-nob
hobthrush (a hobgob-
lin)
hobthrush-louse
hock-cart
hockelty-card
hockey-cake
hockey-load
hock-glass

hocus=pocus
hod=carrier†
hodden=gray
hodding=spade
hoddy=peak
hod=elevator†
hodgepodge
hodge=pudding
hodman
hoe=cake
hoe=down
hoeing=machine
hoe=plow
hog=ape
hog=apple
hog=back (a back)
hogback (a fish or
    other thing shaped
    like the back of a
    hog)
hog=backed, etc.
hog=bean
hog=bed
hog=brace
hog=caterpillar
hog=chain
hog=cherry
hogchoker (a fish)
hog=cholera
hog=colt
hog=constable
hog=cote
hog=deer
hog=elevator
hog=fennel
hogfish
hog=fleece
hog=frame
hogger=pipe
hogging=frame
hog=gum
hogherd
hog=hook
hog=in=armor
hog=louse
hog=mace
hog=mane
hog=meat
hogmolly

hog=money
hog=monkey
hog=mullet
hognose=snake
hognut
hog=peanut
hog=pen
hog=plum
hog=rat
hog=reeve
hog=ring
hog=ringer
hog=rubber
hog's=back*
hog's=bane*
hog's=bean*
hog's=bread*
hog=scalding†
hog=score
hog's=fennel*
hog's=garlic*
hog's=haw*
hogshead
hog=shearing
hogskin
hog=snake
hog's=pudding*
hogsty
hog=succory
hogsucker (a fish)
hog=wallow
hogwash
hogweed
hogwort
hoist=bridge
hoisting=apparatus
hoisting=crab
hoisting=engine
hoisting=jack
hoisting=machine
hoisting=tackle
hoistway
hoity=toity
hoky=poky
holdback (that which
    holds something
    back, restraint)
hold=beam
holder=forth

holdfast (that which
    holds something
    fast)
hold=gang
holding=ground
hole=and=corner, a.
hole=board
hole=dove
hole=stitch
holewort
holing=axe
holing=pick
hollie=point
hollie=stitch
hollow=billed, etc.
hollowhead (a plover)
hollow=horn (a disease
    of cattle)
hollowing=knife
hollowing=plane
hollow=plane
hollowroot (a plant)
hollowstock (a plant)
hollowwort
holly=fern
hollyhock=rose
hollyhock=tree
holly=laurel
holly=oak
holly=rose
holly=tree
holm=cock
holm=oak
holm=screech
holm=thrush
holus=bolus
holy=cruel
Holy=Ghost pear
Holy=Ghost plant
holy=hay
holy=herb
holystone
homage=jury
home=born, etc.
home=brew
homecome
home=coming
home=keeping†
homelike

home rule
home=ruler
homesick
homespun
homestall
homestead
homeward=bound
homewort
homing=mill
honest=hearted
honestone
honewort
honey=ant
honey=badger
honey=bag
honey=balm
honey=basket
honey=bear
honey=bearer†
honey=bee
honeyberry
honey=bird
honey=blob
honey=bloom
honeybread (a tree)
honey=brown
honey=buzzard
honey=cell
honeycomb
honey=creeper
honey=crock
honeydew
honey=eater†
honey=flower (a plant)
honey=garlic
honey=guide
honey=locust
honey=lotus
honey=mesquit
honeymoon
honey=moth
honey=mouthed, etc.
honey=pod
honey=pot
honey=pots
honey=ratel
honey=stalk
honey=stomach
honeystone

honey=strainer†
honey=sucker†
honeysuckle
honeysuckle=apple
honeysuckle=clover
honeysuckle=tree
honey=sugar
honey=sweet, a.
honeysweet (a plant)
honey=tube
honeyware (a plant)
honeywort
honor=court
honor=man
honor=point
hood=cap
hood=cover
hood=end
hood=gastrula
hoodie=crow
hooding=end
hood=jelly
hoodman=blind
hood=mould
hood=moulding
hood=sheaf
hood=shy
hood top
hoodwink
hoodwort
hoof=bound, etc.
hoof=cushion
hoofing=place
hoof=mark
hoof=pad
hoof=paring†
hoof=pick
hoof=spreader†
hook and eye
hooka=stand
hook=beaked, etc.
hook=bill (bill with a
    hook)
hookbill (a salmon)
hook=block
hock=bolt
hook=bone
hook=climber†
hooking=frame

hook=ladder
hook=land
hook=money
hook=motion
hook=net
hook=pin
hook=plate
hook=rope
hook=scarf
hook=squid
hook=sucker†
hook=swivel
hooktip (a moth)
hook=tool
hookweed
hook=wrench
hoop=ash
hoop=bee
hoop=bending†
hoop=coiling†
hoop=cramp
hoop=crimping†
hoop=cutting†
hoop=dressing†
hoop=driver†
hoop iron
hoopkoop-plant
hoop=lock
hoop=net
hoop=petticoat
hoop=pine
hoop=planing†
hoop=pole
hoop=punching†
hoop=racking†
hoop=riving†
hoop=sawing†
hoop=shaving†
hoop=shell
hoop=skirt
hoop=snake
hoop=splaying†
hoop=splitting†
hoop=tree
hooting-owl
hoot=owl
hoot=toot
hop=back
hopbine

hop=bush
hop=clover
hop-cushion
hop=dog
hop=drier†
hop=factor
hop=feeder†
hop=flea
hop=fly
hop=frame
hop=frogfly
hop=frothfly
hop=garden
hop=hornbeam
hop=jack
hop=kiln
hop=marjoram
hop=medick
hop=mildew
hop=oil
hop=o'=my=thumb
hopper=boy
hopper=cake
hopper car
hopper closet
hopper=cock
hopper=hood
hop=pest
hop=picker†
hop pillow
hopping=dick
hopping-john
hop=pocket
hop=pole
hop=press
hop=raising†
hop=sacking†
hop=scotch
hop=setter†
hop=tree
hop=trefoil
hop=vine
hop=yard
horizon=glasses
horn=band
horn=bar
hornbeak (a fish)
hornbeam (a tree)
horn=beech

hornbill (a bird)
hornbill=cuckoo
horn=blower†
hornbook
horn=bug
horn=card
horn=coot
horn=core
horn=cuirass
horn=distemper
horn=drum
horn=eel
hornet=clearwing
hornet=fly
hornet=moth
hornfinch
hornfish
horn=footed
horn=lead
horn=machine
horn=mad
horn=madness
horn mail
horn=maker†
horn=mercury
horn=mullet
horn of plenty (a cor-
   nucopia)
horn=of=plenty (a plant)
horn=owl
hornpie (a bird)
horn=pike
hornpipe
horn=pith
hornplant
horn=plate
horn=player†
horn=pock
horn=poppy
horn=pout
horn=pox
horn=press
horn=presser†
horn=quicksilver
horn=shavings
horn=shoot
horn=silver
hornsman (an adder)
hornsnake

hornstone
horn swivel
horntail (an insect)
horn=tip
hornweed
hornwork
hornwort
hornwrack
horny=fisted, etc.
hornyhead (a fish)
horny=hoolet
hornywink (a bird)
horror=stricken
horror=struck
horse=aloes
horse=ant
horse=arm
horse=armor
horse=artillery
horseback
horse=balm
horsebane
horse=bean
horse=beech
horse=blob
horse=block
horse=boat
horse=boot
horse=bot
horse=box
horse=boy
horse=bramble
horse=breaker†
horsebrier (a plant)
horse=brush
horse=cadger
horse=cane
horse=capper†
horse=car
horse=cassia
horse=chanter
horse=chestnut
horse=clipper†
horse=cloth
horse=collar
horse=coper
horse=crab
horse=crevalle
horse=cucumber

horse-daisy
horse-dealer†
horse-doctor
horse-drench
horse-eating†
horse-elder
horse-emmet
horse-eye
horse-faced
horse-fair
horse-fettler†
horsefinch
horsefish
horseflea-weed
horse-flesh
horseflower (a plant)
horse-fly
horsefly-weed
horsefoot (a plant, a
   crab)
horsefoot crab
horsefoot-snipe
horse-furniture
horse-gear
horse-gentian
horse-gin
horse-ginseng
horse-godmother
horse-gogs
horse-gowan
horse-gram
horse-guards
horsehair
horsehair-lichen
horsehair-worm
horse-halter
horsehead (a fish, a
   duck)
horseheal (a plant)
horse-hitching†
horse-hoe
horse-holder†
horsehoof (a plant)
horse-hook
horse-iron
horse-jag
horse-jockey
horse-jug
horse-knacker†

horse-knob
horse-knop
horse-lark
horse-latitudes
horse-laugh
horse-leech
horseleek (a plant)
horse-litter
horse-load
horse-lot
horse-mackerel
horseman
horse-marine
horse-masher
horsemaster
horse-match
horse-mill
horsemint
horse-musher
horse-mushroom
horse-mussel
horse-nail
horse-net
horse-nettle
horse-parsley
horse-path
horse-pick
horse-piece
horse-pile
horse-pipe
horse-pistol
horse-play
horse-plum
horse-pond, n.
horsepond, v.
horse-poppy
horse-post
horse-power
horsepox
horse-purslane
horse-race
horse-racer†
horse-rack
horseradish
horseradish-tree
horse-railroad
horse-rake
horse-rider†
horse-rough

horse-run
horse-sense
horseshoe
horseshoe-anvil
horseshoe bat
horseshoe-blank
horseshoe crab
horseshoe-head
horseshoe-kidney
horseshoe-machine
horseshoe-nail
horseshoe vetch
horse-shovel
horse-smatch
horse-soldier
horse-sorrel
horse-sponge
horse-stealing†
horse-stinger†
horse-sugar
horsetail
horsetail lichen
horsetail-tree
horse-thief
horse-thistle
horse-thrush
horse-thyme
horse-tick
horsetongue (a plant)
horse-trainer†
horse-tree
horse-trick
horse-vetch
horse-violet
horseway
horseweed
horsewell-grass
horse-whim
horsewhip
horse-winkle
horsewoman
horsewood (a tree)
horse-worm
horse-wrangler†
horsing-block
horsing-iron
horst-beech
hose-bib
hose-bridge

hose=carriage
hose=carrier†
hose=cart
hose=clamp
hose company
hose=coupling
hose=fittings
hose=hook
hose=in=hose
hose=jumper†
hoseman
hose=nipple
hose=pipe
hose=protector†
hose=reel
hose=screw
hose=shield
hose=union
hose=wrench
hospital=fever
hospital ship
hot=air, a.
hot=and=hot
hotbed
hot=blooded, etc.
hot=chisel
hotchpot
hotchpotch
hotel car
hot=flue
hotfoot, adv.
hothead (a person)
hothouse
hot=plate
hot=pot
hot=press
hot=saw
hot=short
hot=shot (a foolish fel-
    low, as making hot
    shots)
hotskull (a person)
hotspur (a person)
Hottentot's=bread*
Hottentot's=head*
Hottentot's=tea*
hot=wall
hot=well
houndfish

hound=plate
hound's=berry*
hound=shark
hound's=tongue*
hound's=tree*
hour=bell
hour=circle
hour=glass
hour=hand
hour=line
hour=plate
house=agent
house=ball
house=bell
house=boat
house=bote
housebreaker†
house=builder†
house=car
house=cricket
house=dog
house=duty
house=engine
house=factor
housefather
house=finch
house=flag
house=fly
house=fungus
household
householder
housekeep
housekeeper†
house=lamp
houseleek (a plant)
houseleek=tree
house=line
houseling=cloth
house=lot
housemaid
house=martin
house=master (master
    or head of a house-
    hold)
house master (school-
    master residing in
    the schoolhouse)
housemate
housemonger

housemother
house=mover†
house=painter†
house physician
house=pigeon
house=place
house=proud
house=raising†
house=room
house=shrew
house=snake
house=sparrow
house=spider
housestead
house steward
house surgeon
house=swallow
house=tax
housetop
house=urn
housewarm
housewarming†
housewife
housewright
housing=box
housing=cloth
housing=frame
hout=tout
hover=hawk
howdy=do
however
howsoever
hubble=bubble
hubbleshow
hub=borer†
hub=centring†
hub=lathe
hub=mortising†
hub=turning†
huckberry
huckie=buckie
hucklebacked
huckleberry
huckle=bone
huck=muck
hugger=mugger
huia=bird
huller=gin
hull=gull

hulling=machine
human=heartedness
humankind
humblebee
humble=mouthed, etc.
humble=pie
humble=plant
humbuzz
hum=cup
humdudgeon
hummelling=ma-
   chine
humming=bird
humpback
humpty=dumpty
humus=plant
hunchback
hundred=court
hundred=eyes
hundred=legs
hundredman
hundred=penny
hundredweight
hunger=bitten, etc.
hunger=flower (a
   plant)
hunger=grass
hunger=rot
hungerweed
hunky=dory
hunt=counter
hunting=box

hunting=cap
hunting=case
hunting=coat
hunting=cog
hunting=crop
hunting=dog
hunting=field
hunting=ground
hunting=horn
hunting=jug
hunting=knife
hunting=leopard
hunting=seat
hunting=shirt
hunting=skiff
hunting=song
hunting=spider
hunting=sword
hunting=tide
hunting=watch
hunting=whip
hunt=sergeant
huntsman
huntsman's=cup*
huntsman's=horn*
hunt's=up*
huon=pine
hurdleman
hurdle=nail
hurdle=race
hurdy=gurdy
hurlbone

hurly=burly,
hurlygush
hurly=hacket
hurlyhawkie
hurly=house
hurricane=deck
hurry=burry
hurry=scurry
hurse=skin
hurst=beech
hurtleberry
hurtsickle
husband=land
husbandman
hush=bagaty
hush=money
hush=paddle
husk=hackler†
husking=bee
husking=glove
husking=peg
husking=pin
hustle=cap
hut=urn
hydrocarbon=burner†
hydrocarbon=furnace
hydrocarbon=stove
hyena=dog
hymn=book
hymn=singing†
hymn=tune
hymn=writer†

I

I beam
ice-anchor
ice-apron
ice arrow
ice-auger
ice-axe
ice-bag
ice-banner
ice-beam
ice-bearer†
ice-belt
iceberg
ice-bird
ice-blink
ice-boat
ice-bone
ice-bound
ice-box
ice-breaker†
ice-brook
ice-built
ice-calk
ice-calorimeter
ice-canoe
ice-cap
ice-carriage
ice-chair
ice-chest
ice-chisel
ice-claw
ice-closet
ice-cold
ice-cream
ice-creeper†
ice-crusher†
ice-cutter†
ice-drift
ice-drops
ice-elevator†
ice-escape

ice-fall
ice-feathers
ice-fern
ice-field
ice-fishing
ice-float
ice-floe
ice-foot
ice-fork
ice-fox
ice-glass
ice-gull
ice-hill
ice-hook
ice-house
ice-indicator
iceleaf (a plant)
ice-ledge
ice-leveller†
ice-locomotive
ice-loon
ice-machine
ice-making†
ice-mallet
iceman
ice-mark
ice-marker†
ice-master
ice-mountain
ice-pack
ice-pail
ice-paper
ice-pick
ice-pit
ice-pitcher
ice-plane
ice-plant
ice-plow
ice-poultice
ice-preserver†

ice-quake
ice-river
ice-safe
ice-sandal
ice-saw
ice-scraper
ice-screw
ice-sheet
ice-ship
ice-spade
ice-spar
ice-stream
ice-table
ice-tongs
ice-tools
ice-wagon
ice-wall
ice-water
ice-whale
ice-wool
icework
ice-worn
ice-yacht
ice-yachting
ice-yachtsman
ichneumon-fly
icy-pearled
ideal-real
ideal-realism
idle-moss
idle-wheel
idol-fire
idol-shell
idol-worship
I iron
ill-advised, etc.
illawarra-palm
ill-deedie
ill-footing
Illinois-nut

ill=treat, v.
ill treatment
illupi=oil
ill will
ill=willer†
ill=willy
ill=wisher†
image=breaker†
image=mug
image=worship
immersion=lens
imou=pine
imposing=stone
imposing=table
imp=pole
impregnating=tube
improving-furnace
in=and=in
inasmuch
inbearing
inboard
inbond, a.
inborn
inbreaking
inburst
incast
incense=boat
incense=breathing†
incense=burner†
incense=cedar
incense=cup
incense=tree
inch board
inch=pound
inch stuff
inchworm
in=circle
income
incomer†
in=conic
increase=twist
in=cubic
incut
index=correction
index=digit
index=error
index=finger
index=gauge
index=glass

index=law
index=machine
Indiaman
Indian=arrow (a plant)
Indian=cup (a plant)
Indian=eye (a plant)
Indian=heart (a plant)
Indian=pipe (a plant)
Indian=poke (a plant)
Indian=root (a plant)
Indian=sal (a plant)
Indian=saul (a plant)
Indian's=dream*
Indian=shoe (a plant)
Indian=shot (a plant)
india=rubber
indicator=card
indicator=diagram
indigo=berry
indigo=bird
indigo blue
indigo=broom
indigo brown
indigo carmine
indigo=copper
indigo extract
indigo=finch
indigo=mill
indigo=plant
indigo red
indigo=snake
indigo=weed
indigo white
indraught
indraw
indrawn
induction=balance
induction=bridge
induction=coil
induction=machine
induction=pipe
induction=port
induction=valve
induct=pipe
indwelling†
ineunt=point
infant=class
infant=school
infantryman

infield, a.
in=field
influence=machine
ingather
ingathering
ingle=cheek
ingle=nook
ingleside
ingoing
ingot=iron
ingot=mould
ingrowing†
ingrowth
in=hexagon
injection=cock
injection=condenser
injection=engine
injection=pipe
injection=syringe
injection=valve
injection=wate⁻
injector=valve
ink=bag
ink=ball
ink=bench
inkberry
inkberry-weed
ink=block
ink=bottle
ink=brayer†
ink=cup
ink=cylinder
ink=duct
ink=eraser†
inkfish
ink=fountain
ink=gland
inkholder†
inkhorn
inking=apparatus
inking=ball
inking=pad
inking=roller
inking=table
inking=trough
ink=knife
ink=mushroom
in=kneed
inknut

ink=pad
ink=pencil
ink=plant
ink=powder
ink=roller
inkroot
ink=sac
inkshed
ink=slice
ink=slinger
inkstand
inkstone
ink=surface
ink=table
ink=well
inkwood
ink=writer†
inland
inlaying=saw
inlet
inlook
in=lot
inmate
inmeat
innholder†
innkeeper†
in=over
in=parabola
in=patient
in=pensioner
in=pentahedron
in=polygon
inpour
inpouring
input
in=quadric
in=quadrilateral
inquisitor=general
inroad
inrush
insect=destroyer†
insect=fungi
insect=gun
insect=net
insect=powder
insect=trap
inset
inshore
inside

insight
in=sole
inspection=car
inspector=general
in=square
instead
instep=stretcher
intagliotype
interfering=strap
intake
intakeholder
intaker
into
in=triangle
invalid=bed
invalid=chair
invert=sugar
invoice=book
inwall, n.
inwheel, n.
I rail
Irish=American
Irishman
Irishwort
iris=root
iris=swallow
iron age
iron=alum
ironbark (a tree)
ironbark=tree
iron=black
iron=bound, etc.
iron cement
iron=chamber
iron=clad, a.
ironclad, n.
iron=clay
iron=cloth
iron cross
iron crown
iron=flint
iron=founder†
iron=foundry
iron=furnace
iron=glance
iron=grass
iron=gray
iron=gumtree
ironhead (a duck)

ironheads (a plant)
iron horse
ironing=board
ironing=box
ironing=cloth
ironing=lathe
ironing=machine
iron=iodide
iron lacquer
iron=line
iron=liquor
ironman
ironmaster
iron=mould
ironmonger
iron=oak
iron=ochre
iron=red
iron=rust
iron=sand
iron=saw
iron=scale
iron=shrub
iron=sick
ironsides (a person)
ironsmith
iron=stain
ironstone
iron=strap
iron=tree
ironware
ironweed
ironwood (a tree)
ironwork
iron=worker†
iron=works
ironwort
iron=yellow
isabella=wood
isabel=yellow
isinglass=stone
islesman
issue=pea
istle=grass
itaka=wood
ita=palm
itching=berry
itch=insect
itch=mite

itchweed
ivorybill (a wood-
    pecker)
ivory=billed, etc.
ivory=black
ivory=brown
ivory=gull
ivory=gum
ivory lines
ivorynut

ivory=palm
ivory=paper
ivory=paste
ivory=porcelain
ivory=shell
ivory spaces
ivory=tree
ivorytype
ivory=white
ivory=yellow

ivy=bindweed
ivy=bush
ivy=gum
ivy=leaf
ivy=mantled
ivy=owl
ivy=tod
ivy=tree
ivywort
ixia=lily

J

jaal=goat
jabbering crow
jack=adams (a fool)
jackadandy
Jack=a=green
jackal=buzzard
jackalegs (a knife, a man)
Jack=a=Lent
jackals=kost
jackanape
jackanapes
jack=ape
jack=arch
jackass
jackass=brig
jackass=deer
jackass=fish
jackass=penguin
jackass=rabbit
jack=at=the=hedge (a plant)
jack=back
jack=baker
jack=bird
jack=block
jack=boot
jack=by=the=hedge (a plant)
jack=chain
jack=crosstree
jack=curlew
jackdaw
jack=engine
jackfish
jack=fishing†
jack=flag
jack=frame
jack=friar
jack=fruit

jack=hare
jack=hern
jack=hole
jack=hunting†
jack=in=a=bottle
jack=in=a=box
jacking=machine
jack=in=the=box
jack=in=the=bush
jack=in=the=pulpit
jack=jump=about
jack=knife
jack=ladder
jack=lamp
jack=lantern
jack=light
jackman
jack=nasty
jack=oak
Jack=o'=lantern
Jack=o'=Lent
jack=pin
jack=pit
jack=plane
jack=pot
jack=pudding
jack=rabbit
jack=rafter
jack=rib
jack=roll
jack=salmon
jack=saw
jack=screw
jack=sinker
jacksmith
jack=snipe
Jackson's=broom*
jack=spaniard
jack=spinner†
jack=staff

jack=stay
jackstone
jackstraw
jack=timber
jack=towel
jack=tree
jackweight
jack=wood
jacobæa=lily
Jacob's=chariot*
Jacob's=ladder*
Jacob's=rod*
Jacob's=staff*
Jacob's=sword*
jadding=pick
jade=green
jaggery=palm
jagging=board
jagging=iron
jailbird (a person)
jail=delivery
jail=fever
jail=house
jail=keeper†
jalap=plant
jamb=lining
jamb=post
jamb=shaft
jamb=stone
jamesweed
jameswort
jam=nut
jam=weld
janca=tree
jane=of=apes
Janus=cloth
Janus=cord
Janus=faced
Janus=headed
jar=fly

jarnut
jar=owl
jasmine=tree
jasper=dip
jasper=opal
jasper=ware
jasper=wash
jasp=opal
jatropha=oil
jaundice=berry
jaundice=tree
jaunting=car
javanee=seeds
javelin=bat
javelin=man
javelin=snake
jaw=bit
jaw=bolt
jaw=bone
jaw=box
jaw=breaker†
jaw=chuck
jawfall
jawfallen
jaw=foot
jaw=footed
jaw=hole
jawing=tackle
jaw=jerk
jaw=lever
jaw=mouthed
jaw=rope
jawsmith
jaw=spring
jaw=tackle
jaw=tooth
jaw=wedge
jay=bird
jay=cuckoo
jayhawker
jay=pie
jay=piet
jay=teal
jay=thrush
jayweed
jean=cherry
jedding=axe.
Jehoiada=box
jelly=bag

jellyfish
jelly=lichen
jelly=plant
Jenny ass
Jenny crudle
jenny=spinner†
Jenny wren
jerboa=mouse
jerkin=head
jerry=builder†
jerry=built
jerry=shop
jest=book
jesting=beam
jesting=stock
jest=monger
jestword
jet=ant
jet=black
jet=break
jet=glass
jet=pump
Jew=baiter†
jew=bush
Jew=crow
jewel=block
jewel=case
jewel=drawer
jewel=house
jewel=like
jewel=office
jewel=setter†
jewel=stand
jewelweed
jewfish
Jews'=apple*
Jew's=ear*
jews'=harp*
Jews'=mallow*
Jews'=manna*
Jews'=myrtle*
Jews'=stone*
Jews'=thorn*
Jew=stone
jib=boom
jib=door
jib=frame
jib=hank
jib=head

jib=iron
jiblet=check
jiblet=cheek
jib=lot
jib=netting
jib=o'=jib
jib=sheet
jib=stay
jib=topsail
jig=clog
jigger=knife
jigger=mast
jigger=pump
jigging=machine
jig=given
jig=maker†
jig=mould
jig=pin
jig=saw
jimber=jaw
jimber=jawed
Jim=crow
Jim=crow's=nose (a
     plant)
jimson=weed
jingle=jangle
jingle=shell
jink=game
jobbing=man
job=master
job=office
job=printer†
Job's=tears*
job=type
job=watch
job-work
jockey=box
jockey=club
jockey=gear
jockey=grass
jockey=jurnal
jockey=pad
jockey=pulley
jockey=sleeve
jockey=stick
jockey=wheel
jockey=whip
joe=ben
Joe=Millerism

Joe-Millerize
joepye-weed
joewood
jogging-cart
joggle-beam
joggle-joint
joggle-piece
joggle-post
joggle-truss
jogglework
joggling-table
jog-trot
john-apple
John-Bullism
John-crow (a buzzard)
John-crow's-nose (a
  plant)
John-dory
John-go-to-bed-at-
  noon (a plant)
johnny-cake
johnny-cocks
johnny-cranes
Johnny-jump-up (a
  plant)
Johnny-verde (a fish)
john-paw
John's-wood*
John's-wort*
john-to-whit (a bird)
joint-chair
joint-coupling
joint-end
jointer-plane
joint-evil
joint-file
joint-fir
joint-grass
joint-hinge
jointing-machine
jointing-plane
jointing-rule
joint-oil
joint-pipe
joint-pliers
joint-racking
joint-ring
joint-rod
joint-saw

joint-snake
joint-splice
joint-stock
joint-stool
joint-strip
joint-test
jointweed
joint-wire
jointworm
jokesmith
jolly-boat
jolt-head (a head)
jolthead (a person)
Joseph-and-Mary (a
  plant)
Joseph's-coat*
Joseph's-flower*
Joshua-tree
joss-block
joss-house
jossing-block
joss-paper
joss-pidgin
joss-stick
joukery-pawkery
journal-bearing
journal-book
journal-box
journal-brass
journal-packing
journeyman
journey-ring
journey-weight
journey-work
Jove's-fruit*
Jove's-nuts*
joy-bells
juba-patting
Juba's-brush*
Juba's-bush*
Judas-colored
Judas-cup
Judas-ear
judas-hole
Judas-light
Judas-tree
judge-advocate
judgment-cap
judgment-day

judgment-hall
judgment-note
judgment-seat
jug-fishing
jumble-bead
jumpabout (a plant)
jump-coupling
jumping bean
jumping-betty
jumping bug
jumping deer
jumping hare
jumping mouse
jumping mullet
jumping rat
jumping seed
jumping shrew
jumping spider
jump-joint
jump-ring
jump-rocks
jump-seat
jump-up-and-kiss-me
  (a plant)
jump-up-Johnny (a
  plant)
jump-weld
junction-box
junction-plate
junction-rails
June-berry
June-bug
jungle-bear
jungle-bendy
jungle-cat
jungle-cock
jungle-fever
jungle-fowl
jungle-ghau
jungle-nail
jungle-ox
jungle-sheep
junior-right
juniper-oil
juniper-resin
junk-bottle
junk-dealer†
junkman
junk-ring

junk=shop	Jupiter's=nut*	jury=rig
junk=strap	Jupiter's=staff*	jury=rigged
junk=vat	jurema=bark	jury=room
junk=wad	jury=box	jury=rudder
Juno's=rose*	jury=duty	jurywoman
Juno's=tears*	jury=leg	just=borne
Jupiter's=beard*	jury=list	juste=au=corps
Jupiter's=distaff*	juryman	justice=broker
Jupiter's=eye*	jury=mast	justicing=room
Jupiter's=flower*	jury=process	justifying=stick

K

kadi=kana
kadle=dock
Kafir=boom
Kafir=bread
Kafir=corn
Kafir's=tree*
Kafir=tea
kain=fowl
kain=hen
kaladana=seed
kale=bell
kale=blade
kale=brose
kale=pot
kale=runt
kalestock
kale=turnip
kalewife
kale=worm
kangaroo=apple
kangaroo=bear
kangaroo=beetle
kangaroo=dog
kangaroo=grape
kangaroo=grass
kangaroo=hare
·· kangaroo=hound
kangaroo=mouse
kangaroo=rat
kangaroo=thorn
kangaroo=vine
karamani=resin
karat=seed
karat=tree
katydid
kauri=gum
kauri=pine
kauri=resin
kawa=kawa
ka=wattie

keb=ewe
keckle=meckle
kedge=anchor
kedge=rope
keeping=glass
keel=block
keel=compelling
keeler=tub
keelhaul
keelman
keel=moulding
keel=petals
keelrake
keel=shaped
keelvat
keena=nut
keena=oil
keen=witted
keeping=room
keepsake
keepworthy
kei=apple
kekune=oil
kelp=fish
kelp=goose
kelp=pigeon
kelp=whaling
kelpwort
keora=oil
kerfing=machine
kerite=wire
kermes=berry
kermes=insect
kermes=mineral
kermes=oak
kern=baby
kern=cut
kern=dollie
kernel=substance
kernelwort

kern=supper
ket=crow
kettle=bail
kettle=case
kettle=de=benders
kettle=dock
kettle=drum (a drum)
kettledrum (an enter-
    tainment)
kettle=drummer†
kettle=hole
kettleman
kettle=moraine
kettle=pin
kettle=smock
kettle=stitch
kevel=head
key=action
key=basket
key=bed
keyboard
key=bolt
key=bone
key=bugle
key=chain
key=chord
key=color
key=coupler†
key=desk
key=drop
key=fastener†
key=file
key=fruit
key=grooving†
key=guard
key=harp
key=head
keyhole
keyhole=guard
keyhole=limpet

keyhole=protector†
keyhole=saw
key=note
key=pattern
key=piece
key=pin
key=pipe
key=plate
key=point
key=ring
key=seat
key=signature
keystone
key=stop
key=tail
key=tone
key=trumpet
key=valve
keyway
key=word
khatzum=oil
kiabooca=wood
kibble=chain
kick=off
kickup
kidnap
kidney=bean
kidney=cotton
kidney=form
kidney=link
kidney ore
kidney potato
kidneyroot (a plant)
kidney=shaped
kidney=stone
kidney=vetch
kidneywort
kidsman
kie=kie
killbuck (a butcher)
killcalf (a person)
killcow (a person)
kill=cu
killdevil (a person,
    bait)
killhog (a trap)
killing=time
killjoy (one who kills
    joy)

killman (a kilnman)
kiln=dried
kiln=hole
kiln=house
kilnman
kindergarten
kind=hearted, etc.
kindling=coal
kindling=wood
kindly=savin
king=apple
king=at=arms
king=auk
king=bird
king=bolt
king=crab
kingcraft
king=crow
kingcup (a plant)
king=devil
king=duck
king=eider
king=fern
kingfish
kingfisher (a bird)
king=gutter
king=hake
kinghunter (a bird)
king=killer†
kingmaker†
king=mullet
kingnut
king=ortolan
king=penguin
king=piece
king=pin
king=pine
king=plant
king=post
king=rail
king=rod
king=roller
king=salmon
king's=clover*
king's=cushion*·
king's=feather*
king's=fisher*
king's=flower*
king's=hood*

Kingsman
king=snake
king's=piece*
king's=spear*
king=table
king=truss
king=tyrant
king=vulture
kingwood
kinsman
kinswoman
kip=leather
kip=shop
kipskin
kirkmaster
kirkyard
kirschwasser
kiskitomas=nut
kissing=comfit
kissing=crust
kissing=hand
kissing=muscle
kiss=me (a plant)
kit=cat
kitcat=roll
kitchen=fare
kitchen=fee
kitchen=garden
kitchen=knave
kitchen=maid
kitchen=midden
kitchen=mort
kitchen=physic
kitchen=stuff
kitchen=wench
kite=eagle
kite=falcon
kite=flying†
kitefoot
kite=key
kite=stick
kite=string
kite=tail
kite=tailed
kite=wind
kit=fox
kitten=shark
kittly=benders
kitty=coot

kitty=cornered
kitty=key
kiwi=kiwi
ki=yi
knapping=hammer
knapping=machine
knapsack
knapweed
knave bairn
knave's=mustard*
kneading=machine
kneading=trough
knee=bone
knee=boss
knee=breeches
knee=brush
knee=cap (a covering
   for the garments
   at the knee)
kneecap (the kneepan)
knee=cop
knee=cords
knee=crooking
knee=deep
knee=guard
knee=gusset
knee=high
kneeholly (a plant)
kneeholm (a plant)
kneehulver (a plant)
knee=iron
knee=jerk
knee=joint
knee=jointed
knee=kick
kneepan
knee=piece
knee=pine
knee=plate
knee=rafter
knee=reflex
knee roof

kneestead
knee=stop
knee=strap
kneestring
knee=swell
knee=timber
knee=tribute
knee=worship
knickknack
knicky=knackers
knife=bar
knife=basket
knife=bayonet
knife=blade
knife=board
knife=box
knife=boy
knife=cleaner†
knife=dagger
knife=edge
knife=edged
knife=file
knife=grass
knife=grinder†
knife=guard
knife=handle
knife=lanyard
knife=money
knife=polisher†
knife=rest
knife=sharpener†
knife=tool
knife=tray
knight errant
knight=errantry
knight=erratic
knight=head
knighthood errant
knight=service
knight's=spur*
knight's=wort*
knitting=burr

knitting=case
knitting=gauge
knitting=machine
knitting=needle
knitting=pin
knitting=sheath
knitting=stick
knitting=work
knob=fronted, etc.
knob=latch
knobstick
knobweed
knobwood (a shrub)
knock=down
knocker=off
knocking=bucker
knocking=trough
knock=knee
knock=kneed
knock=off
knock=out, a.
knockout, n.
knockstone
knopweed
knot=grass
knotting=needle
knotweed
knot=wood
knotwork
knotwort
knoutberry
know=all
knowledge=box
know=nothing
Know=nothingism
knuckle=bow
knuckle=duster
knuckle=guard
knuckle=joint
knuckle=shield
knuckle=timber
koft=work

L

labelling=machine
label=machine
laboratory forge
laboratory furnace
labor market
labor=pains
labor=saving†
labor=time
labor=union
labor=yard
lac=dye
lacebark (a tree)
lacebark=pine
lace=boot
lace border (made of lace)
lace=border (on lace)
laceborder (a moth)
lace=coral
lace=embossing†
lace=fern
lace=fly
lace=frame
lace=leather
lace=lizard
lace=making†
laceman
lace=mender†
lace=paper
·lace=piece
lace=pillow
lace=runner†
lace=tree
lace=winged
lace=woman
lacing=cutter
lac=insect
lackall
lackbeard (a person)
lackbrain (a person)

lackey=moth
lack=Latin
lack=linen
lack=lustre
lack=thought
lac=lake
lac=painted
lacquering=stove
lacquer=tree
lacquer=ware
lacrosse=stick
lac=work
ladder=braid
ladder=carriage
ladder=dredge
ladderman
ladder=shell
ladder=sollar
ladder=stitch
ladderway
ladder=work
lademan
lade=pail
lading=hole
ladle=board
ladle=furnace
ladle=shell
ladlewood (a tree or its wood)
lad's=love*
ladybird (an insect, a duck)
ladybug (an insect)
lady=cat (a catfish)
lady=chair
ladycloak (an insect)
lady=cockle
lady=court
ladycow (an insect)
lady=crab

Lady=day
lady=fern
ladyfinger (a plant, etc.)
ladyfish
lady=fluke
ladyfly (an insect)
lady=hen
lady=key
lady=killer†
ladylike
lady=love
lady's=bedstraw*
lady's=bower*
lady's=comb*
lady's=cushion*
lady's=delight*
lady's=eardrops*
lady's=finger*
lady's=glove*
lady's=gown*
lady's=hair*
lady's=maid*
lady's=mantle*
lady's=seal*
lady's=slipper*
lady's=smock*
lady's=thistle*
lady's=thumb*
lady's=tresses*
lagam=balsam
lag=bellied
lager=beer
lag=goose
lag-link
lag=machine
lagoon whaling
lag=screw
laisser=faire
lake=dweller†

lake-fever
lake-fly
lake-herring
lake-lawyer
lake-shad
lake-sturgeon
lake-trout
lakeweed
lake-whiting
laking-place
lamb-ale
lambkill (a plant)
lamblike
lambskin
lamb's-lettuce*
lamb's-quarters*
lamb's-tongue*
lamb's wool
lamb's-wool (a drink)
lamellar-stellate
lameskirting
laminating-machine
laminating-roller
Lammas-day
lammas-land
Lammas-tide
lampblack
lampblack-furnace
lamp-bracket
lamp-burner†
lamp-canopy
lamp-case
lamp-cement
lamp-chimney
lamp-cone
lamper-eel
lamp-elevator†
lampflower (a plant)
lamp-fly
lamp-furnace
lamp-glass
lamp-globe
lamp-hanger†
lamp-head
lamp-holder†
lamp-hole
lamp-hoop
lamp-iron
lamp-jack

lamplight
lamplighter†
lamp-making†
lamp-pendant
lamp-plug
lamp-post
lamp-protector†
lamp-pruner†
lamp-shade
lamp-shell
lamp-stand
lamp-store
lamp-stove
lamp-wick (a wick)
lampwick (a plant)
lance-bucket
lance-corporal
lance-fly
lance-head
lance-hook
lance-leafed
lance-linear
lance-oval
lance-plate
lancepod (a plant)
lance-rest
lance-sergeant
lance-shaped, etc.
lance-snake
lancet-arch
lancet-fish
lance-throw
lancet-pointed, etc.
lancet window
lancewood (a tree)
land-bank
land-beetle
land-blink
land-breeze
land-bug
land-carriage
land-cod
land-compass
land-crab
land-crake
land-cress
land-crocodile
land-daw
land-dog

land-drainage
land-drake
landfall
land-floe
land-flood
land-grabber†
landgrave
landholder†
land-hunger
land-hungry
land-ice
landing-bar
landing-net
landing-place
landing-stage
landing-strake
landing-surveyor
landing-waiter
land-jobber†
landlady
land-leaguer
land-leech
landlocked
landloper
landlord
landman
landmark
land-marker†
land-measure
land-measurer†
land-office
land-otter
landowner
land-owning
land-parer†
land-pike
land-pilot
land-pirate
land-plaster
land-poor
land-rail
landreeve
land-rent
land-roll
land-roller†
landscape
landscape-gardening†
landscape-mirror
landscape-painter†

land=scrip
land=scurvy
land=shark
land=shell
landshut
land=sick
land=side
land=slater
landslide
landslip
landsman
land=snail
land=spout
land=spring
land=steward
land=tax
land=tenure
land=tie
land=tortoise
land=turn
land=turtle
land=urchin
land=waiter
land=warrant
land=wash
land=wind
landworker†
lane=route
lang=kale
lang=settle
language=lesson
language=master
lantern=bellows
lantern=carrier†
lantern=fish
lanternflower (a plant)
lantern=fly
lantern=gurnard
lantern=jack
lantern=jawed, etc.
lantern=jaws
lantern=keg
lantern=light
lantern=pinion
lantern=pump
lantern=shell
lantern=sprat
lantern=tower
lantern=wheel

lap=bander†
lap=board
lap=dog
lap=dovetail
lap=eared, etc.
lap=frame
lap=joint
lap=machine
lapper=milk
lappet=end
lappet=frame
lappet=head
lappet=moth
lappet=weaving
lapping=engine
lapping=machine
lap=plate
lapp=owl
lap=ring
lap=roller
lap=scale
lap=shaver
lap=sided
lap=stone
lapstreak
lap=table
lap=tea
lap=weld, n.
lapweld, v.
lapwing (a bird)
lapwork
larch=bark
larch=tree
lard=boiler†
lard=cooler†
larder=beetle
larding=needle
larding=pin
lard=oil
lard=press
lard=renderer†
lardstone
lard=tank
large=acred, etc.
lark=bunting
lark=finch
lark=heeled, etc.
lark=plover
lark's=heel*

lark=sparrow
larkspur
lark=worm
laserwort
lash=comb
lashing=eye
lashing=ring
lashing=string
lash=rail
lash=lorn
lasso=cell
last=court
last=finishing†
last=holder†
lasting=awl
lasting=jack
lasting=machine
lasting=pincers
lasting=tool
last=lathe
last=making†
last=turning†
latch=closer†
latch=key
latch=lifter†
latch=lock
latch=pan
latch=string
lateral=temporal
lath=brick
lath=coop
lath=cutter†
lathe=bearer
lathe=bed
lathe=carrier†
lathe=centre
lathe=chuck
lathe=cords
lathe=dog
lathe drill
lathe=head
lathe=hoist
lathe=saw
lathe=tool
lath=hammer
lathing=clamp
lathing=hammer
lath=mill
lath=nail

lath=pot
lath=sawing†
latigo=strap
latten=brass
latter=day, *a.*
latter=kin
lattermath
latter=mint
lattice blind
lattice braid
lattice bridge
lattice girder
latticeleaf (a plant)
lattice=moss
lattice=plant
lattice truss
lattice window
latticework
laughing=bird
laughing crow
laughing dove
laughing=gas
laughing goose
laughing gull
laughing hyena
laughing=jackass
laughing=muscle
laughing=stock
laughing thrush
laughworthy
launch=engine
launching=tube
launching=ways
launchways
laundrymaid
laundryman
laundry=stove
laurel=bottle
laurel=cherry
laurel=oak
laurel=oil
laurel=shrub
laurel=tree
laurel=water
lave=eared
lave=lugged
lavender=cotton
lavender=drop
lavender=oil

lavender=thrift
lavender=water
laver=bread
laver=pot
laverwort
law=abiding
law=binding
law=blank
law=book
lawbreaker†
law=burrows
law=calf
law=court
law=day
lawgiver†
lawk=a=day
law=list
law=lord
lawmaker†
lawmonger
lawn=mower†
lawn=roller†
lawn=sprinkler†
lawn=tennis
law=officer
law=piece
law=sheep
law=stationer
lawsuit
law=writer†
lay=cap
lay=day
layer=board
layer=boarding
layer=on
layer=out
layer=over
layer=up
lay=figure
laying=down
laying=hook
laying=in
laying=machine
laying=on
laying=press
laying=top
layman
layout
lay=race

lay=rod
lazar=house
lazar=like
lazarman
lazulite=blue
lazyback
lazy=bed
lazyboard
lazybones (a person)
lazyboots (a person)
lazy=jack
lazy=pinion
lazy=tongs
leaching=vat
leach=line
leach=trough
leach=tub
lead=arming
lead=ash
leadback (a bird)
lead=bath
lead=colic
lead=color
lead=colored, etc.
lead=cutter†
lead=eater†
lead=encephalopathy
leaden=gray
leader=boy
leader=furrow
leader=hook
leader=writer†
lead=furnace
lead=glance
lead=glaze
lead=gray
leading=block
leading=buoy
leading=hose
leading=in
leading=rod
leading=screw
leading=spring
leading=staff
leading=strings
leading=wheel
leading=wires
lead=lap
lead=line

lead=lustre
lead=mill
lead=mule
lead=nail
lead=ochre
lead=paralysis
lead=pencil
lead=plant
lead plaster
lead=poisoning
lead=pot
lead=screw
lead=shaving
lead=sinkers
leadsman
lead soap
lead=spar
lead=tracery
lead=tree
lead=vitriol
lead=water
lead=works
leadwort
leaf=bearing†
leaf=beetle
leaf=blade
leaf=blight
leaf=bridge
leaf=bud
leaf=bug
leaf=butterfly
leaf=carrier†
leaf=climber†
leaf=comb
leaf=crumpler†
leafcup (a plant)
leaf=cutter†
leaf=feeder†
leaf=finch
leaf=folder†
leaf=footed, etc.
leaf=gilding†
leaf gold
leaf=hopper
leaf=insect
leaf lard
leaf=lichen
leaf=louse
leaf metal

leaf=miner†
leaf=mould
leaf=netting
leafnose (a bat)
leaf=roller†
leaf=rust
leaf=sheath
leaf=sight
leaf silver
leaf=silvering†
leaf=spot
leaf=spring
leafstalk
leaf=tier
leaf tobacco
leaf=trace
leaf=turner†
leaf=valve
leafwork
leak=alarm
leak=indicator†
leak=signal
lean=faced, etc.
leaning=knife
leaning=note
lean=to
leap=frog
leaping=fish
leap=ore
leap=year
lear=board
lea=rod
leasehold
leascholder†
leasemonger
lease=pin
lease=rod
leasing=maker†
leather=awl
leatherback (a turtle, a
　duck)
leather=backed, etc.
leather=beetle
leather=board
leather=boarding
leather=brown
leather=buffing†
leather=carp
leather=chamfering†

leather=cloth
leathercoat (an apple,
　etc.)
leather=corrugating†
leather=creasing†
leather=cutting†
leather=dicing†
leather=dresser†
leather=embossing†
leather=finishing†
leather=fleshing†
leatherflower (a plant)
leather=fluting†
leather=glassing†
leather=gluing†
leather=gouge
leather=graining†
leather=grinder†
leather=hammering†
leatherhead (a person,
　a bird)
leather=jack
leather=jacket
leather=knife
leather=lap
leatherleaf (a plant)
leather=paper
leather=plant
leather=polisher†
leather=pressing†
leather=punch
leather=punching†
leather=quilting†
leather=raising†
leather=reducing†
leather=rolling†
leather=rounding†
leather=scalloping†
leather=scarfing†
leather=scouring†
leather=seat
leatherside (a fish)
leather=skin
leather=skiving†
leather=slitting†
leather=softener†
leather=sorting†
leather=splitting†
leather=stamp

leather-stretcher†
leather-striping†
leather-stripping†
leather-stuffer†
leather-tapering†
leather-turtle
leatherwood (a shrub)
leave-looker
leave-taking
leaving-shop
lecture-day
lecture-room
Leda-clay
ledger-bait
ledger-blade
ledger-book
ledgment-table
ledon-gum
lee-board
lee-bow, v.
leechcraft
leech-eater (a plover)
leech-fee
leech-gaiters
leech-line
leech-rope
lee-clue
lee-gauge
leek-green
leer-pan
leerspool
leet-man
leeway
left-handed, etc.
left-hander
left-handiness
left-off
legacy-hunter†
legal-tender, a.
leg-bail
leg-band
leg-bone
leg-boot
leg-by
leg-harness
leg-iron
leg-lock
leg-muff
leg-rest

leg-shield
lemon-balm
lemon-bird
lemon-cadmium
lemon-color
lemon-colored, etc.
lemon-dab
lemon-drop
lemon-fish
lemon-grass
lemon-juice
lemon-kali
lemon-sole
lemon-squash
lemon-squeezer†
lemon thyme
lemon verbena
lemon walnut
lemonweed
lemon-yellow
lengthening-bar
lengthening-piece
lengthening-rod
lens-cap
lens-holder†
lenten-crab
lentil-shell
Lent-lily
Lent-rose
leopard-cat
leopard-fish
leopard-flower (a plant)
leopard-frog
leopard-lily
leopard-moth
leopard's-bane*
leopard-seal
leopard-tortoise
leopardwood (a tree)
leper-house
lese-majesty
let-alone
let-off
letter-balance
letter-board
letter-book
letter-box
letter-carrier†
letter-case

letter-clip
letter-cutter†
letter-drop
letter-file
letter-founder†
letter-foundry
letter-head
letter-heading
lettering-box
lettering-tool
letterleaf (an orchid)
letter-lichen
letter-lock
letter-name
letter-office
letter-ornament
letter-paper
letter-perfect
letter-plant
letter-press (press to
   copy letters)
letterpress (printed
   matter),
letter-punch
letter-rack
letter-scale
letter-stamp
letter-winged
letterwood (a tree)
letter-writer†
lettuce-bird
lettuce-opium
lettuce-saxifrage
leucite-basalt
level-dyeing
level-headed, etc.
levelling-block
levelling-instrument
levelling-plow
levelling-pole
levelling-rod
levelling-screw
levelling-staff
levelling-stand
lever-board
lever-brace
lever-compressor
lever-drill
lever-engine

lever=escapement
leveret=skin
lever=faucet
lever=frame
lever=hoist
lever=jack
lever=press
lever=punch
lever=valve
leverwood (a plant)
levigating=machine
levigating=mill
lewis=bolt
lewis=hole
ley=pewter
liberty=book
liberty=cap
liberty=man
liberty=pole
library=keeper†
licca=tree
license=tax
lichen=starch
lich=fowl
lich=gate
lich=owl
lichroad
lichway
lichwort
licker=in
licker=up
lickety=cut
lickety=split
lick=pan
lickpenny
lickplatter
lickspittle
licorice=mass
licorice=paste
licorice=vetch
licoriceweed
lid=cells
lid=closer
lidflower (a tree or
    shrub)
lic=a=bed
liegeman
liege=poustie
lien=holder†

lieutenant=colonel
lieutenant=commander
lieutenant=general
lieutenant=governor
lieutenant=governor-
    ship
life=arrow
life=belt
life=blood
life=boat
life=breath
life=buoy
life=car
life=cord
life=cycle
life=drop
life=estate
life=everlasting (a
    plant)
life=giving
life=guard
life=history
life=hold
life=insurance
life=interest
life=land
lifelike
life=line
lifelong
life=mortar
life=office
life=peer
life=peerage
life=plant
life=preserver†
life=raft
life=rate
life=rendering
life=rent
life=renter†
life=rentrix
life=rocket
liferoot (a plant)
life=saving†
life's=blood*
life=shot
life=signal
life=size
life=spot

lifespring
lifestring
life=table
life=tenant
lifetime
life=weary
life=work
lift=bridge
lift=gate
lift=hammer
lifting=apparatus
lifting=bar
lifting=blade
lifting=bridge
lifting=day
lifting=dog
lifting=gate
lifting=gear
lifting=hitch
lifting=jack
lifting=machine
lifting=piece
lifting=pump
lifting=rod
lifting=screw
lifting=set
lifting=tongs
lifting=wire
lift=latch
lift=lock
lift=pump
lift=tenter
lift=wall
ligature=carrier
light=apostrophe
light=armed, etc.
light=ball
light=barrel
light=boat
light=box
lightbrain (a person)
light=course
light=dues (paid for
    light)
light=elasticity
light=equation
lighterman
lighter=screw
lighter=staff

light=foot
light=horse
light=horseman
lighthouse
lighthouseman
light=iron
light=keeper†
light=maker†
light=moderator
light=money
lightning=arrester
lightning=bug
lightning=conductor
lightning=discharger
lightning=print
lightning=proof
lightning=protector
lightning=rod
lightning=tube
light=organ
light=room
light=ship
light=tight
light=vessel
light=wave
lightweight (that which
    has light weight)
lightwood
lignum=aloes
lignum=vitæ
like=minded, etc.
lilac=gray
lilac=mildew
lilac=rust
lilacthroat (a bird)
lily=beetle
lily=encrinite
lily=faced, etc.
lily=hyacinth
lily=iron
lilyliver (a person)
lily=of=the=valley
lily=pad
lily=star
lily=white
lima=wood
limb=bearing
limber=board
limber=box

limber=chain
limber=chest
limber=hole
limber=strake
limb=girdle
limb=guard
limb=root
limeball
limeball-light
lime=boil
lime=burner†
lime=bush
lime=catcher†
lime=cracker
lime=feldspar
lime=floor
lime=juice
lime=juicer
lime=kiln
lime=light
lime=machine
lime ointment
lime=pit
lime=powder
lime punch
lime=rod
lime=sink
lime=sour
lime=spreader†
limestone
limestone=meter
lime=tree
lime=twig, n.
limetwig, v.
lime=vial
lime=wash, n.
limewash, v.
lime=water
limit=gauge
limit=point
linch=hoop
linchpin
linden=tree
line=and=line
linear=acute
linear=ensate
linear=lanceolate
linear=oblong
line=conch

line=coördinate
line=density
line=engraving†
line=equation
line=fish
line=fisherman
line=fishing†
line=integral
lineman
linen-draper
linen=muslin
linen=panel
linen=prover†
linen=scroll
line=pin
line=riding†
line=rocket
linesman
line=squall
line=storm
line=wire
lingberry (a plant,
    berry of the ling)
ling=bird
ling=pink
lingthorn (a starfish)
lining=brush
lining=felt
lining=nail
lining=paper
lining=strip
link=block
linkboy
link=lever
linkman
link=motion
link=rooming
linkwork
linnet=finch
linnet=hole
linseed
linseed=cake
linseed=meal
linseed=mill
linseed=oil
linsey=woolsey
lint=doctor
lint=white, a.
lintwhite (a linnet)

linty=white
lion=ant
lion=dog
lion=dragon
lionheart (a person)
lion=hearted, etc.
lion=hunter†
lion=leopard
lion=like
lion=lizard
lion=monkey
lion's=ear*
lion's=foot*
lion's=heart*
lion's=leaf*
lion's=mouth*
lion's=tail*
lion's=tooth*
lion's=turnip*
lip=bit
lip=born, etc.
lip=cell
lip=comfort
lip=comforter†
lip=devotion
lip=fern
lip=fish
lip=good
lip=head
lip=homage
lip=hook
lip=labor
lip=laborious
lip=language
lip=ornament
lip=plate
lip=protector†
lip=reading
lip=righteousness
lip=salve
lip=service
lip=spine
lip=tooth
lip=wisdom
lip=wise
lip=work
lip=working
liquation=furnace
liquation=hearth

liqueur=cup
liqueur=glass
liquid=refrigerator
liquor=bottle
liquor=cock
liquor=dealer†
liquor=gauge
liquor=pump
liquor=saloon
liquor=seller†
liquor=store
liquor=thief
listing=plow
list=mill
list=pan
list=pot
list=wheel
listwork
litany=desk
litany=stool
lit=house
littlebeak (a mollusk=
      like animal)
little=ease (that which
      gives little ease)
little=endian
little=gude
little=worth
live=box
live=centre
live=for=ever (a plant)
live=head
livelong
live=oak
liver=color
liver=colored, etc.
liver=complaint
liver=fluke
liverleaf (a plant)
liver=ore
liver=pyrites
liver=spots
liverstone
liver=wing
liverwort
livery=coat
livery=collar
livery=colors
livery company

livery=cupboard
livery=fish
livery=gown
liveryman
livery=office
livery=servant
livery=stable
live=spindle
live=well
living=chamber
living=room
lizard=bait
lizard=fish
lizard=seeker†
lizard's=tail*
lizard=stone
lizard's=tongue*
lizardtail (a plant)
lizard=tailed, etc.
loading=bar
loading=funnel
loading=machine
loading=plug
loading=tongs
loading=tray
load=line
load=penny
loaf sugar
loam=beater†
loam=board
loam=cake
loam=mould
loam=moulding†
loam=plate
loam=work
loan=office
loan=word
lobby=member
lobe=berry
lobefoot (a bird)
lobe=footed, etc.
lobe=plate
loblolly=bay
loblolly=boy
loblolly=pine
loblolly=sweetwood
loblolly=tree
lobster=car
lobster=chum

lobster=claw (claw of a
   lobster)
lobster=claws (an alga)
lobster=crawl
lobster=louse
lobsterman
lobster=moth
lobster=pot
lobster=tail
lobster=tailed
lobtail, v.
lobworm
loch=moulinet
lock=band
lock=bay
lock=bolt
lock=bond
lock=box
lock=chain
lock=chamber
lock=cock
lock=cramp
lock=down
locker=up
lockfast
lock=faucet
lock=gate
lock=hatch
lock=hole
lock=hook
lock=house
locking=pallet
locking=plate
lockjaw
lock=keeper†
lock=lanyard
lockman
lock=nail
lock=nut
lockout
lock=paddle
lock=piece
lock=plate
lock=pulley
lock=rail
lockrand
lock=saw
lock=sill
locksman

locksmith
lock=spit
lock=spitting†
lock=step
lock=stitch
lock=string
lock=tool
lock=tortoise
lockup
lock=weir
lockwork
loco=disease
locomotive=balance
locomotive car
locomotive=pump
loco=plant
loco=weed
locum=tenency
locum=tenens
locust=bean
locust=berry
locust=bird
locust=borer†
locust=eater†
locust=shrimp
locust=tree
lodestar
lodestone
lodestuff
lodge=gate
lodging=car
lodging=house
lodging=knee
lodh=bark
log=beam
log=board
log=book
log=butter
log cabin
log=chip
log=cock
logfish
log=frame
loggerhead (a block-
   head, a turtle, etc.)
loggerheat (a mass of
   iron)
logging=axe
logging=bee

logging=camp
logging=head
logging rock
log=glass
loghead (a blockhead)
log=headed, etc.
log house
logic=chopping†
log=line
logman
log=measurer†
log=perch
log=reel
logroll
log=roller†
log=scale
log=slate
log=turner†
logwood
logwood black
logwood blue
loin=cloth
loll=poop
lollybanger
lomi=lomi
London=pride (a plant)
London=rocket (a plant)
London=tuft (a plant)
long=arc, a.
longbeak (a snipe)
longbeard (a man, etc.)
longbill (a bird)
long=boat
longbow
long=breathed, etc.
long coats
long=ears (a donkey, an
   owl)
long=field (a fielder in
   cricket)
long=glass (an aleyard)
longhand (writing)
longhorn (a moth, an
   insect)
long=legs (an insect)
long=moss (a plant)
longneck (a duck)
longnose (a garfish)
long=off

long-on
long primer
long-purples
long-range, a.
long-rest (in music)
long-ruffer
long-settle
longshanks (a person, a bird)
long shawl
longshore
longshoreman
long-short
loug slide
long-slip (a fielder in cricket)
longspur (a bird)
long-staple, a.
long-stitch
long-stop (a fielder in cricket)
longstop, v.
long-sufferance
long-suffering
long-tail, a.
longtail (an animal)
long-take (a number of herrings)
longtongue (a bird, a person)
long-wall, a.
longworm (a certain long worm)
lookdown (a fish)
looker-on
looking for
looking-glass
lookout (a looking, a person, a place)
lookout-basket
loo-mask
loom-card
loom-comb
loom-figured, etc.
loom-harness
loom-picture
loom-sheeting
loop-bolt
loop-head

loop-holder†
loophole
looping-snail
looping-worm
looplight
loop-test
loopwork
loopworm
loop-yoke
loose-bodied, etc.
loose-box (a stable)
loose-house (a stable)
loose-kirtle (a woman)
loosening-bar
loosestrife (a plant)
loose-work
loo-table
lop-eared, etc.
lopez-root
lopping-axe
lopping-shears
lopseed (a plant)
lopsided
loptail, v.
lop-wood
lord-lieutenancy
lord-lieutenant
lordlike
lords-and-ladies (a plant, a duck)
lordwood (a tree)
losh-hide
lote-bush
lote-fruit
lote-tree
lot-tree
lotus-berry
lotus-eater†
lotus-tree
loud-lunged, etc.
lounging-room
loup-cervier
loup-garou
louping-ill
loup-the-dike
louseberry (a tree)
louse-bur
louse-fly
louse-herb

lousewort
lousybill (a curlew)
louver-board
louver-window
love-affair
love-apple
love-bird
love-broker
love-charm
love-child
love-dart
love-favor
love-feast
loveflower (a plant)
love-grass
love-in-a-mist (a plant)
love-in-a-puzzle (a plant)
love-in-idleness (a plant)
love-knot
love-letter
love-lies-bleeding (a plant)
love-lock
love-lorn
love-lornness
love-making†
loveman
love-match
love-parrakeet
love-parrot
love-plant
love-potion
love-ribbon
love-scene
love-shaft
love-sick
love-song
love-spell
love-suit
love-tap
love-token
love-tree
love-trout
love-worth
loveworthy
loving-cup
loving-kindness

lowbell
' =boy
   =rch, a.
   =y
low=dilutionist
low=down, a.
low=downer
lower=case, a.
Low=German, a.
lowland
low=line
low=lived, etc.
low=pressure, a.
low=warp, a.
low=worm
lozenge=coach
lozenge=fret
lozenge=goad
lozenge=graver†
lozenge=machine
lozenge=moulding
lozenge=shaped
lozenge=spur
lozenge=tool
lubber=cock
lubber=grasshopper
lubberhead (a person)
lubber=hole
lubber=line
lubberwort
lubricant=tester
lubricating=oil
luck=penny
lucky=bag
lucky=dad
lucky=daddie
lucky=hands
lucky=minnie

lucky=proach (a fish)
lucky=stone (an ear=
   stone of a fish)
luffer=board
luffer=boarding
luff=hook
luff=tackle
lug=a=leaf (a fish)
lugbait (a worm)
lug=bolt
lug=foresail
luggage=saddle
luggage=van
lug=mark
lug=perch
lug=sail
lugworm
lukewarm
lumber=car
lumber=drier†
lumber=kiln
lumberman
lumber=measure
lumber=port
lumber=room
lumber=wagon
lumber=yard
lum=head a (chimney=
   top)
lumpfish
lump=sucker (a lump-
   fish)
lump sugar
lumpy=jaw
luna=moth
luna=silkworm
lunch=counter
luncheon=bar

lung fever
lung=fish
lungflower (a plant)
lung=grown, etc.
lung=lichen
lung=moss
lung=strongle
lung=tester†
lung=worm
lungwort
lurch=line
lurking=place
lust=breathed, etc.
lustre=ware
lustre=wash
lying=down (confine-
   ment)
lying=in (confinement)
lying to
lyme=grass
lymph=cell
lymph=channel
lymph=corpuscle
lymph=heart
lymph=sac
lymph=sinus
lymph=space
lymph=vessel
lynch=law
lynx=eyed
lyra=way
lyre=bat
lyre=bird
lyreman (an insect)
lyre=pheasant
lyretail (a lyre=bird)
lyre=tailed
lyre=turtle

M

ma'am-school
macaco-worm
macaw-bush
macaw-palm
macaw-tree
mace-ale
mace-bearer†
mace-cup
mace-reed
machine-bolt
machine-boy
machine gun
machine-head
machine-made
machine-man
machine-minder†
machine-oven
machine ruler
machine-shop
machine tool
machine-twist
machine-work
mackerel-bait
mackerel-boat
mackerel-bob
mackerel-cock
mackerel-gaff
mackerel-guide
mackerel-gull
mackerel-latch
mackerel-midge
mackerel-mint
mackerel-pike
mackerel-plow
mackerel-scad
mackerel-scales
mackerel-scout
mackerel-shark
mackerel sky
mad-apple

madbrain
mad-brained, etc.
madcap
madder-bloom
madder brown
madder carmine
madder red
madder-print
madderwort
mad-doctor
Madeira-vine
Madeira-wood
madel-paroowa
madhouse
madman
madnep
madpash
madstone
madu-nut
madweed
madwort
mafurra-tree
magazine battery
magazine gun
magazine rifle
magazine stove
maggot-eater (a bird)
maggot-snipe
mag-loon
magma-basalt
magnesium-lamp
magneto-bell
magnifying-glass
magnifying-lens
magnum-bonum
magpie-diver
magpie-finch
magpie-maki
magpie-moth
magpie-robin

magpie-shrike
mahogany-birch
mahogany-brown
mahogany-color
mahogany-gum
mahogany-tree
mahwa-butter
mahwa-oil
mahwa-tree
maid child
maidenhair (a fern)
maidenhair-grass
maidenhair-tree
maidenlike
maiden-meek, a.
maiden-nut
maiden-pink
maiden-plum
maiden's-blush*
maiden's-honesty*
maiden-skate
maiden-tongued, etc,
maid-of-the-meadow (a
    plant)
maid-pale
maid servant
mail-bag
mail-box
mail-car
mail-carrier†
mail-cart
mail-catcher†
mail-cheeked, etc.
mail-coach
mail-coif
mailed-checks (fishes)
mail-guard
mail-hood
mail-hose
mailing-machine

mailing-table
mail-master
mail-matter
mail-net
mail-pouch
mail-quilt
mail-route
mail-sack
mail-shell
mail-stage
mail-train
main-beam
main-boom
main-brace
main-chocks
main-couple
main-de-fer
main-hatch
main-hold
mainland
main-link
mainmast
mainmastman
main-pendant
main-pin
main-post
main-rigging
mainroyal
mainroyalmast
mainsail
main-sheet
mainspring
mainstay
mainstaysail
main-tack
maintaining-wheel
maintop
maintopgallantmast
maintopmast
maintopsail
maintopsail-yard
main-wales
main-yard
maize-bird
maize-eater (a bird)
maize-oil
maize-smut
maize-thief (a bird)
majoe-bitter

major-general
major-generalship
makebate (a person, a
    plant)
make-believe
makegame (a person)
make-hawk
makepeace (a person)
make-ready, n.
maker-up
makeshift
make-up
makeweight
making-felt
making-iron
making-off
male-fern
male-spirited, etc.
malletflower (a plant)
mallow-rose
mallowwort
malmstone
malt-barn
malt-drier†
malt-dust
malt-extract
malt-floor
malt-horse
malt-house
malt-kiln
malt-mad
maltman
maltmaster
malt-mill
malt-rake
malt-screen
malt-surrogate
malt tea
malt-turner†
mammee-apple
mammee-sapota
man-ape
man-at-arms
man-bound
man-car
man child
mandate-bread
mandelstone
mandolin-player†

mandrel-collar
mandrel-frame
mandrel-lathe
mandrel-nose
mandrel-screw
man-eater†
mane-comb
man-engine
mane-sheet
man-fungus
manganese-glaze
mange-insect
mangel-wurzel
mange-mite
manger-board
mangle-bark
mangle-rack
mangle-wheel
mango-bird
mango-fish
mango-hummer (bird)
mangold-wurzel
mango-tree
mangrove-bark
mangrove-cuckoo
mangrove-hen
mangrove-snapper   (a
    fish)
manhandle
man-hater†
manhole
manhole-cover
manifold-paper
manifold-writer†
manjack (a tree)
mankind
manlike
man-made
man midwife
man milliner
manna-ash
manna-croup
manna-grass
manna-gumtree
manna-lichen
manna-seeds
manners-bit
man-of-the-earth (a po-
    tato-vine)

man=of=war
man=orchis
manor=house
manor=seat
man=pleaser†
man=power
manroot (a morning=
   glory)
man=rope
man servant
mansion=house
manslaughter
manslayer†
manstealer†
man=sty
mantelboard
mantel=clock
mantelpiece
mantel=set
mantel=shelf
manteltree
mantis=crab
mantis=shrimp
mantle=animal
mantle=breathing†
mantle=cell
man=trap
mantua=maker†
manual=key
manure=desiccator†
manure=distributer†
manure=drag
manure=drill
manure=fork
manure=hook
manure=loader†
manure=spreader†
manway
man=worship
manworthy
Manxman
Manxwoman
many=folded, etc.
manyplies
manyroot (a plant)
map=drawing
map=holder†
maple=borer†
maple=cup

maple=disease
maple=honey
maple=molasses
maple=sugar
maple=syrup
maple=tree
map=lichen
map=measurer†
map=mounter†
map=projection
map=study
map=turtle
marabou=feathers
marabou=stork
marble=breasted, etc.
marble=constant
marble=cutter†
marble=handsaw
marblehead (a petrel)
marble=paste
marble=polisher†
marble=rubber†
marble=saw
marble=scourer†
marble silk
marble=thrush
marblewood (a tree)
marble=worker†
marchland
march=line
March=mad
marchman
march=movement
march=time
march=treason
march=ward
mare's nest
mare's-tail*
margaret=grunt
margate=fish
margin=draft
margin=line
margin=tailed
marigold=finch
marigold window
mariposa=lily
marish=beetle
mark=boat
market=basket

market=bell
market=court
market=cross
market=day
market=fish
market=garden
market=gardener†
market=house
market=Jew
market=lead
market=maid
marketman
market=master
market=place
market=pot
market=town
marking=gauge
marking=ink
marking=iron
marking=machine
marking=nut
marking=plow
markman
markmote
marksman
markswoman
mark=tooth
markworthy
marlberry
marlborough=wheel
marl brick
marl=grass
marlinespike
marling=hitch
marl=pit
marl=slate
marl stock
marlstone
marmalade=plum
marmalade=tree
marmala=water
marmot=squirrel
marplot (a person)
marrow=bone
marrow=cells
marrowfat (a pea)
marrow pudding
marrow=spoon
marrow squash

marshalman
marsh=beetle
marsh=bellflower
marsh=blackbird
marshbunker
marsh=buttercup
marsh=cinquefoil
marsh=cross
marsh=diver
marsh=elder
marsh=fern
marsh=fever
marshfish
marsh=fivefinger
marsh=flower
marsh=gas
. marsh=goose
marsh=grass
marsh=harrier
marsh=hawk
marsh=hen
marsh=land
marshmallow (a plant,
    etc.)
marsh=marigold
marsh=miasma
marsh=nut
marsh=parsley
marsh=peep
marsh=pennywort
marsh=pestle
marsh=plover
marsh=pullet
marsh=quail
marsh=ringlet
marsh=robin
marsh=rosemary
marsh=samphire]
marsh=shrew
marsh=snipe
marsh=tackey
marsh=tea
marsh=tern
marsh=tit
marsh=trefoil
marsh=watercress
marshwort
marsh=wren
martel-de=fer

marteline=chisel
martext (a person)
martin=snipe
martin=swallow
Martling=men
marvel=monger
marvel=of=Peru (a
    plant)
mary=sole
mash=cooler†
mashing=tub
mash-machine
mash=pulper†
mash=tub
mash=tun
mash=vat
mash=wort
mask=ball
mask=crab
maskflower (a plant)
masking=piece
mason=bee
mason=shell
mason=spider
mason=swallow
mason=wasp
masonwork
masoola=boat
mass=bell
mass=book
mass=centre
mass=day
massé=shot
mass=house
massing=chalice
mass=meeting
mass=penny
mass=priest
mass=vector
mass=velocity
mast=bass
mast=carline
mast=coat
master-at=arms
master carpenter
master=joint
master=key
master=lode
masterpiece

master printer
master=sinew
mastersinger
master=spring
master=stroke
master=touch
master=wheel
masterwork
masterwort
masthead
mast=hoop
mast=house
mastic=cement
mastic=cloth
mastic=herb
mastic=tree
mastiff=bat
masting=house
masting=shears
mast=maker†
mastman
mast=pocket
mast=prop
mast=rope
mast=scraper†
mast=step
mast=tackle
mast=tree
mast=trunk
mat=boat
mat=braid
match=board
match=boarding
match=box
match=cord
match=dipping†
matcher=head
match=gearing
match=hook
matching=machine
matching=plane
match=joint
match=line
match=lock (a lock)
matchlock (a musket
matchlockman
match=making†
match=pipe
match=plane

match-planing†
match-plate
match-pot
match-rifle
match-rifling†
match-safe
match-shooting†
match-splint
match-staff
match-terms
match-tub
match-wheel
match-wood
mat-grass
mating-time
matrimony-vine
matting-boat
matting-loom
matting-punch
matting-tool
mattress-boat
matweed
matwork
maudlin-drunk
maudlin-fair
maul-in-goal
maul-oak
maulstick
Mauritius-weed
mavis-skate
mawmouth (a bass)
mawseed (poppy-seed)
mawskin (rennet)
maw-worm
maxim-monger
May-apple
maybe
May-beetle
May-bird
May-blob
May-bloom
May-blossom
May-bug
May-bush
May-chafer
May-cherry
maycock (a plover)
maycock-fluke
May-curlew

May-day
May-dew
may-drink
Mayfish
Mayflower (a plant)
May-fly
May-fowl
May-game
May-garland
mayhap
May-haw
May-hill
May-lady
May-lily
May-lord
May-morn
May-pole
may-pop (a plant)
May queen
may-skate
may-sucker (a fish)
May-time
mayweed
maywort
mazard-bowl
mazarine-blue
mazer-tree
mazer-wood
meadow-beauty
meadow-bird
meadow-bright
meadow-brown
meadow-campion
meadow-clapper
meadow-clover
meadow-crake
meadow-cress
meadow-drake
meadow-fern
meadow-fescue
meadow-foxtail
meadow-gallinule
meadow-gowan
meadow-grass
meadow-hen
meadow-land
meadow-lark
meadow-mouse
meadow-mussel

meadow-ore
meadow-parsnip
meadow-pea
meadow-pine
meadow-pink
meadow-pipit
meadow-queen
meadow-rue
meadow-saffron
meadow-sage
meadow-saxifrage
meadow-snipe
meadowsweet
meadow-titling
meadowwort
meal-arc
meal-beetle
mealberry
meal bread
meal-cooler
mealie-field
mealing-stone
mealman
mealmonger
meal-moth
meal-mouthed
meal-offering
meal-time
meal-tub
meal-worm
mealy-bird
mealy-mouthed, etc.
mealy-tree
meander-line
mean-spirited, etc.
meantime
meanwhile
measle-worm
measure-moth
measuring-chain
measuring-faucet
measuring-funnel
measuring-glass
measuring-line
measuring-machine
measuring-pump
measuring-tape
measuring-wheel
measuring-worm

meat=chopper†
meat=crusher†
meat=earth
meat=fly
meat=hammer
meat=hunter
meat=maggot
meat=mangler†
meat=offering
meat pie
meatrife, a.
meat=safe
meat=saw
meat=screen
meat=spit
meat=tea
meat=tub
meatus=knife
medal=cup
medallion carpet
medallion pattern
medal=machine
medal=tankard
median=ventral
medicine=bag
medicine=chest
medicine=man
medicine=pannier
medicine=seal
medicine=spoon
medicine=stamp
medicine=stone
medium=sized, etc.
medlar=tree
medlar=wood
medusa=bell
medusa=bud
Medusa's=head*
meek=eyed, etc.
meeting=house
meeting=post
meeting=seed
melancholy=thistle
mela=rosa
melic=grass
mell=doll
mell=supper
melon=blubber
melon=cactus

melon=caterpillar
melon=hole
melon=oil
melon=seed
melon=shaped, etc.
melon=shell
melon=thick
melon=thistle
melon=tree
melon=worm
melting=chamber
melting=furnace
melting=pan
melting=point
melting=pot
membrane-bone
membrane=suture
membrane=winged
memorandum=book
memorial=stone
mem=sahib
menhaden=fishery
mentum=tooth
mercury=cup
mercury=furnace
mercury=gatherer†
mercury=goosefoot
mercury=holder†
Mercury's=violet*
mercy=seat
mercy=stroke ˉ
mere=stake
merestead
merestone
mere=tree
meridian=circle
meridian=mark
Merlin's=grass*
mermaid
mermaiden
mermaid=fish
mermaid's=egg*
mermaid's=glove*
mermaid's=hair*
mermaid's=head*
mermaid's=purse*
mermaid=weed
merman
merry=andrew

merry=go=down
merry=go=round
merrymake
merrymaking
merry night
merrythought
merrywing (a duck)
merveil=du=jour (a
    moth)
merwoman
meshing=net
mesh=stick
mesh structure
meshwork
mesitine=spar
mesquit=bean
mesquit=grass
mesquit=gum
mesquit=tree
messan=dog
mess=chest
mess=cloth
mess=deck
messenger=at=arms
mess=gear
mess=kettle
mess=kit
mess=locker
messmaking
messmate
messmate=gum
messmate=tree
mess=table
mess=traps
metal=bath
metal=bending†
metal casting (a piece
    of metal cast into
    shape)
metal=casting†
metal=gauge
metal=plane
metal=saw
metal=wheel
metal=work
meteor=cloud
meteor=dust
meter=prover†
meter=wheel

metestick
metewand
methinks
methylamine
methyl-blue
methylconine
methylene-blue
methyl-salicylic
methyl-violet
mew-gull
mezza-majolica
mezzo-rilievo
miana-bug
mica-powder
mica-schist
mica-slate
micrometer-balance
micrometer-screw
microscope-lamp
Midas's-ear*
midbody
midbrain
mid-couples
midday
midday-flower
midden-crow
middenstead
middle-aged, etc.
middle-class, a.
middle earth
middleman
middle-rate
middle-sized
middle-spear
middle-stead
middleweight (that
    which is of middle
    weight)
middlings-purifier†
midethmoid
midfeather
mid-gut
mid-heaven
mid-hour
mid-impediment
midland
midlayer
midleg
Mid-Lent

mid-main
mid-morn
mid-morrow
midnight
mid-noon
mid-ocean
mid-off
mid-on
mid-parent
mid-parentage
midrib
mid-sea
midship
midshipman
midshipmite
midships
midstream
mid-styled
midsummer
midsummer-men (a
    plant)
mid-superior
midvein
mid-watch
midway
midwicket
midwife
midwinter
migration station
migration-wave
mildew-bronze
mild-spoken, etc.
mile-post
mile-stone
milk-abscess
milk-and-water, a.
milk-blotch
milk-can
milk-car
milk-cooler†
milk-crust
milk-cure
milk-dentition
milk-duct
milk-factory
milk-fever
milkfish
milk-gauge
milk-glass

milk-globule
milk-hedge
milk-house
milking-shield
milking-stool
milking-time
milking-tube
milk-kinship
milk-ky
milk-leg
milk-livered, etc.
milkmaid
milkman
milk-meat
milk-mirror
milk-mite
milk-molar
milk-nurse
milk-pail
milk-pan
milk-pap
milk-parsley
milk-pea
milk-plasma
milk-porridge
milk-pump
milk punch
milk-quartz
milk-rack
milk-scab
milk shake
milk-sick
milk-sickness
milk-snake
milksop
milkstone
milk-sugar
milk-tester†
milk-thistle
milk-thrush
milk-tie
milk-tooth
milk-tree
milk-tube
milk-vat
milk-vessel
milk-vetch
milk-walk
milk-warm

milkweed
milk=white
milkwoman
milkwood (a tree)
milkwort
milky=tailed, etc.
mill=bar
millboard
millboard=cutter†
mill=cake
mill=cinder
mill=dam
mill=driver†
miller's=dog*
miller's=thumb*
millet=grass
mill=eye
mill=feeder†
mill=file
mill=furnace
mill=gang
mill=hand
mill=head
mill=holm
mill=hopper
mill=hopper alarm
mill=horse
milling=cutter
milling=machine
milling=tool
mill=jade
millman
mill=money
mill=owner†
mill=pick
mill=pond
mill=pool
mill=post
mill=race
mill=ream
mill=rine
mill=rolls
mill=round
mill=rynd
mill=saw
mill=scale
mill=sixpence
mill=skate
mill=spindle

millstone
millstone=balance
millstone=bridge
millstone=curb
millstone=dress
millstone=dresser†
millstone=driver†
millstone=feed
millstone grit
millstone=hammer
millstone=pick
millstone=regulator†
millstone=spindle
millstone=ventilator†
mill=tail
mill=ward
millweir
mill=wheel
mill=work
millwright
miltwaste (a fern)
mimic=beetle
mim=mouthed
mimosa=bark
mina=bird
mince=meat
mince pie
mincing=horse
mincing=knife
mincing=spade
mind=cure
mind=curer†
mind=day
mind=healer†
minding=school
mind=reader†
mind=stuff
mind=transference
mine=captain
mine=chamber
mine=dial
mineral=dresser†
mineral=holder†
mingle=mangle
minifer=pin
minim rest
mining=camp
mining=district
mining=machine

mining=pump
mining=region
mining=tool
minion=like
minne=drinking
minnesinger
minnow=harness
minstrel=squire
mintbush (a plant)
mint=drop
mint julep
mint=mark
mintmaster
mint sauce
mint=stick
mint=tree
mint=warden
minute=book
minute=clock
minute=hand
minute=glass
minute=jack
minute=jumper
minuteman
minute=watch
minute=wheel
minx=otter
miracle=monger
miracle=play
miracle=worker†
mire=crow
mire=drum
mire=duck
miriti=palm
mirror=black
mirror=carp
mirror=galvanometer
mirror=script
mirror=writer†
mischief=maker†
mischief=night
missel=tree
mission=rooms
mission school
Miss Nancy
Miss=Nancyism
missoy=bark
mist=bow
mist=colored, etc.

mistflower (a plant)
mistlethrush
mistletoe=bough
mistlike
mist=rick
mist=tree
mitch=board
mitis=casting
mitis=green
mitre=block
mitre=board
mitre=box
mitre=cut
mitre=dovetail
mitre=drain
mitreflower (a plant)
mitre=gauge
mitring=machine
mitre=iron
mitre=jack
mitre=joint
mitre=mushroom
mitre=plane
mitre=post
mitre=shaped, etc.
mitre=shell
mitre=sill
mitre=square
mitre=valve
mitre=wheel
mitrewort
mixing=machine
mixing=sieve
mixture=stop
mixty=maxty
mizzenmast
mizzen=rigging
mizzensail
moat=hen
mob=law
mob=master
mobsman
mob=story
moccasin=flower (a
    plant)
moccasin=plant
moccasin=snake
mock=apple
mock=bird

mockernut
mock=heroic
mocking=bird
mocking=wren
mock=orange
mock=shadow
mock=thrush
mock=turtle
mock=velvet
mode=book
modelling=board
modelling=clay
modelling=loft
modelling=plane
modelling=stand
modelling=tools
model=wood
moderator=lamp
mohair=shell
moist=eyed
molasses=gate
mole=bat
mole=but
mole=cast
mole=catcher†
mole=cricket
mole=eyed, etc.
mole=hill
mole=hole
mole=plant
mole=plow
mole=rat
mole=shrew
moleskin
mole=spade
mole=track
mole=tree
moll=hern
moll=washer
moll=wire
mollycoddle
momie=cloth
monad=deme
money=bag
moneybags (a wealthy
    person)
money=bill
money=box
money=broker

money=changer†
money=corn
money=cowry
money=dealer†
money=drawer
money=dropper†
moneyflower (a plant)
money=grubber†
money=jobber†
money=land
money=lender†
money=maker†
money market
money matter
money=monger
money=mongering
money=order
money=pot
money=scrivener
money=spider
money=spinner
money's worth
money=taker†
moneywort
mongrel=skate
monitor=lizard
monitor=roof
monk=bat
monk=bird
monkey=apple
monkey=bag
monkey=block
monkey=board
monkey=boat
monkey=bread
monkey=cup
monkey=engine
monkeyflower (a plant)
monkey=gaff
monkey=grass
monkey=hammer
monkey=jacket
monkey=pot
monkey=press
monkey=pump
monkey=puzzle
monkey=rail
monkey's=face*
monkey=shine

monkey-spar
monkey-tail (tail of a
   monkey)
monkeytail (a lever, a
   rope)
monkey-wheel
monkey-wrench
monkfish
monk-seal
monk-seam
monk's-gun*
monk's-harquebus*
monk's-hood*
monk's-rhubarb*
monk's-seam*
mont-de-piété
monte-bank
montero-cap
moodooga-oil
moody-hearted, etc.
moonbeam
moonbill (a duck)
moon-blasted, etc.
moon-blind
moon-blink
moon-box
moon-calf
moon-creeper (a plant)
moon-culminating
moon-culminations
moon-daisy
moon-dial
moon-eye (an eye)
mooneye (a fish)
moon-face
moon-fern
moonfish
moonflaw
moonflower (a plant)
moonglade
moon-knife
moonlight
moonlit
moon-madness
moon-month
moon-penny
moon-plant
moon-raker†
moonrise

moon-sail
moonseed (a plant)
moonset
moonshine
moonstone
moonstricken
moonstruck
moon-trefoil
moonwort
moon-year
moor-ball
moorband
moorberry
moor-blackbird
moor-bred
moor-buzzard
moor-coal
moor-cock
moor-coot
Moor dance
moor-fowl
moor-game
moor-grass
moor-hawk
moor-heath
moor-hen
moor-ill
mooring-bend
mooring-bitts
mooring-block
mooring-bridle
mooring-chocks
mooring-pall
mooring-post
mooring-shackle
mooring-stump
mooring-swivel
moorland
Moorman
moor-monkey
moorpan
moor-peat
moorstone
moor-tit
moor-whin
moorwort
moose-bird
moose-call
moose-deer

moose-elm
moosewood (a tree)
moose-yard
mootchie-wood
moot-hill
mopboard
mope-eyed, etc.
mop-fair
mop-head (a head)
mophead (a person)
mop-headed, etc.
mop-nail
mopstick
mopsy-eyed
mop-wringer
morass-weed
more-hough
moreover
more-pork
morning-cap
morningflower (a
   plant)
morning-gift
morning-glory
morning-gown
morning-land
morning-room
morning-sphinx
morning-star (weapon)
morning-tide
morocco-head
morocco-jaw
morris-dance
morris-dancer†
morsing-horn
mortar-battery
mortar-bed
mortar-board
mortar-boat
mortar-carriage
mortar-mill
mortar-vessel
mortar-wagon
mortcloth
mort-de-chien
mortgage-deed
mortier-à-cire
mortise-block
mortise-bolt

mortise-chisel
mortise-corner
mortise-gauge
mortise-joint
mortise-lock
mortise-wheel
mortising-machine
mort-safe
moses-boat
mosquito-bar
mosquito-canopy
mosquito-curtain
mosquito-hawk
mosquito-net
mosquito-netting
moss-agate
moss-alcohol
moss-animal
moss-animalcule
mossback (a fish, a
　person)
moss-bass
mossberry
moss-box
mossbunker
moss-campion
moss-capped, etc.
moss-cheeper
moss-coral
moss-crops
moss-duck
moss-hags
mosshead (a duck)
moss-locust
moss-owl
moss-pink
moss-polyp
moss-rake
moss-rose
moss-rush
moss-trooper†
moss-wood
moth-blight
moth-cicada
moth-eaten
mother-cask
mother-cell
mother-cloves
mother country

Mother Hubbard
mother-in-law
motherland
mother-liquor
mother-lode
mother-love
mother-lye
mother-maid
mother-naked
mother of-coal
mother-of-pearl
mother-of-thousands
　(ivy)
mother-of-thyme
mother-of-vinegar
mother queen
mother-spot
mother tongue
mother-vessel
mother-water
mother-wit
motherwort
moth-gnat
moth-hawk
moth-hunter†
moth-mullein
moth-orchid
moth-patch
moth-plant
moth-sphinx
moth-trap
motion-bar
motion-distortion
motion-indicator
motley-minded, etc.
motor-car
mottle-faced, etc.
motto-kiss
mould-blacking†
mould-board
mould-box
mould-candle
mould-cistern
mould-facing
moulding-apparatus
moulding-bed
moulding-board
moulding-box
moulding-crane

moulding-cutter†
moulding-file
moulding-flask
moulding-frame
moulding-hole
moulding-loam
moulding-machine
moulding-mill
moulding-plane
moulding-plow
moulding-sand
moulding-saw
moulding-table
mould-loft
mould-stone
mould-turner†
mouldy-hill
mouldy-rat
mound-bird
mound-builder†
mound-maker†
mountain-artillery
mountain-ash
mountain-avens
mountain-balm
mountain-beauty
mountain-beaver
mountain-blackbird
mountain-blue
mountain-bramble
mountain-cat
mountain-chain
mountain-cock
mountain-cork
mountain-cowslip
mountain-crab
mountain-cranberry
mountain-cross
mountain-curassow
mountain-damson
mountain-deer
mountain-dew
mountain-duck
mountain-ebony
mountain-fern
mountain-fever
mountain-finch
mountain-flax
mountain-fringe

mountain=grape
mountain=green
mountain=guava
mountain=hare
mountain=holly
mountain=howitzer
mountain=laurel
mountain=leather
mountain=licorice
mountain=linnet
mountain=lion
mountain=lover
mountain=magnolia
mountain=mahoe
mountain=mahogany
mountain=man
mountain=mango
mountain=maple
mountain=meal
mountain=milk
mountain=mint
mountain=parsley
mountain=pepper
mountain=pine
mountain=plum
mountain=pride
mountain=rhubarb
mountain=rice
mountain=rose
mountain=sandwort
mountain=sheep
mountain=soap
mountain=sorrel
mountain=sparrow
mountain=spinach
mountain=sweet
mountain=tallow
mountain=tea
mountain=tobacco
mountain=witch
mountain=wood
mounting=block
mounting=stand
mount=needlework
mournful=widow (a
   plant)
mourning=bride (a
   plant)
mourning brooch

mourning cloak
mourning coach
mourning=dove
mourning livery
mourning=piece
mourning ring
mourning stuff
mourning=widow (a
   plant)
mouse=barley
mouse=bird
mouse=bur
mouse=buttock
mouse=chop
mouse=color
mouse=colored
mouse=deer
mouse=dun
mouse=ear
mousefish¦
mouse=grass
mouse=hawk
mouse=hole
mouse=hound
mouse=hunt
mouse=lemur
mouse=mill
mouse=owl
mouse=pea
mouse=piece
mouse=roller
mouse=sight
mousetail (a plant)
mousetail=grass
mouse=thorn
mouse=trap
mousing=hook
mousseline=de=laine
mousseline=glass
moustache=cup
mouth=arm
mouth=blower
mouth=case
mouth=filling
mouth=foot
mouth=footed
mouth=friend
mouth=gauge
mouth=glass

mouth=glue
mouth=honor
mouthing=machine
mouth=made
mouth=organ
mouth=part
mouthpiece
mouth=pipe
mouth=ring
mouthroot (a plant)
mouth=speculum
movement=cure
moving=plant
mowing=machine
mow=land
mow=lot
mow=yard
M roof
M teeth
mucilage=bottle
mucilage=brush
mucilage=canal
mucilage=cell
mucilage=reservoir
mucilage=slit
muck=bar
muck=fork
muck=heap
muck=hill
muckle=hammer
muck=midden
muck=pit
muck=rake
muck=rolls
muck=sweat
muck=thrift
muck=worm (a worm)
muckworm (a person)
muco=pus
mud=bank
mud=bass
mud=bath
mud=bit
mud=boat
mud=burrower
mud=cat
mud=cock
mud=cone
mud=coot

mud-crab
mud-dauber
mud-devil
mud-dipper
muddlehead (a person)
muddle-headed, etc.
mud-drag
mud-dredger†
mud-drum
muddy-brained, etc.
muddy-breast (plover)
mud-eel
mudfish
mud-flat
mud-frog
mud-goose
mud-hen
mud-hole
mud-hook
mud-laff
mud-lamprey
mud-lark
mud-lava
mud-minnow
mud-pattens
mud-plantain
mud-plover
mud-plug
mud-puppy
mud-rake
mud-scow
mud-shad
mudsill
mud-snail
mud-snipe
mudstone
mud-sucker
mud-swallow
mud-teal
mud-terrapin
mud-tortoise
mud-turtle
mud-valve
mud-volcano
mud-walled
mud-wasp
mudweed
mud-worm
mudwort

muff-dog
muff-glass
muffin-cap
muffin-man
muffin-ring
muffle-furnace
mufflejaw (a fish)
muffle-painting
mug-house
mug-hunter†
mugweed
mugwort
muir-duck
muir-ill
muir-poot
mulberry-faced
mulberry-germ
mulberry-juice
mulberry-mass
mulberry-rash
mulberry-silkworm
mulberry-tree
mule-armadillo
mule canary
mule-chair
mule-deer
mule-doubler†
mule-driver†
mulekiller (a scorpion)
mule-skinner†
mule-spinner†
mule-twist
mulewort
muley-axle
muley-head
muley-saw
mulga-grass
mullein-pink
mullein-shark
mullet-hawk
mullet-smelt
mullet-sucker
mull-madder
mull-muslin
multiple poinding
multiplying-lens
multiplying-machine
multiplying-wheel
mumble-the-peg

mumbo-jumbo
mummy-case
mummy-cloth
mummy-wheat
mumping-day
muniment-house
muniment-room
murumuru-palm
muruxi-bark
muscle-band
musclebill (a duck)
muscle-case
muscle-casket
muscle-cell
muscle-clot
muscle-column
muscle-compartment
muscle-corpuscle
muscle-current
muscle-nucleus
muscle-plasm
muscle-plate
muscle-plum
muscle-prism
muscle-reading†
muscle-rod
muscle-serum
muscle-sugar
mushroom-hitches
mushroom-spawn
mushroom-stone
mushroom-strainer†
mushroom-sugar
music-book
music-box
music-cabinet
music-case
music-chair
music-clamp
music-club
music-demy
music-desk
music-engraver†
music-folio
music-hall
music-holder†
music-house
music-loft
music-mad

music=master
music=mistress
music=paper
music=pen
music=printing†
music=rack
music=recorder†
music=roll
music=school
music=shell
music=smith
music=stand
music=stool
music=type
music=wire
music=writer†
musk=bag
musk=ball
musk=beaver
musk=beetle
musk=cake
musk=cat
musk=cattle
musk=cavy
musk=deer
musk=duck
musket=lock
musket=proof
musket=rest
musket=shot
muskflower (a plant)
musk=gland
musk=hyacinth
muskit=grass
muskmallow
muskmelon
musk=mole

musk=okra
musk=orchis
musk=ox
musk=pear
musk=plant
musk=plum
muskrat
musk=root (the root of
a plant)
muskroot (a plant)
musk=rose
musk=seed
musk=sheep
musk=shrew
musk=thistle
musk=tortoise
musk=tree
musk=turtle
musk=weasel
muskwood (a tree)
musky=mole
muslin=de=laine
muslin=glass
muslin=kale
musquash=root
mussel=band
mussel=bed
mussel=bind
mussel=digger†
mussel=duck
mussel=eater†
mussel=pecker
mussel=shell
mustard=leaf
mustard=paper
mustard plaster
mustard=pot

mustard poultice
mustard=seed
mustard=shrub
mustard=spoon
mustard=token
muster=book
muster=day
muster=file
muster=master
muster=roll
mutation=stop
mutton=bird
mutton=chop
mutton=fish
mutton=fist
mutton=ham
muttonhead (a person)
mutton=headed, etc.
mutton=legger
mutton=thumper†
muzzle=bag
muzzle=cap
muzzle=energy
muzzle=lashing
muzzle=loader†
muzzle=sight
muzzle=strap
muzzle=velocity
myriad=minded
myrrh=oil
myrrh=plaster
myrrh=seed
myrtle=berry
myrtle=bird
myrtle=green
myrtle=wax
myth=history

N

nadir-basin
nail-ball
nail-bone
nailbourne
nail-brush
nail-driver†
nail-extractor†
nail-fiddle
nail-file
nail-hammer
nail-head
nail-headed, etc.
nailing-machine
nail-machine
nail-maker†
nail-plate
nail-rod
nail-rolling†
nail-scissors
nail-selector†
nailwort
naked-eyed, etc.
naked-lady (a plant)
nakedwood (a tree
namby-pamby
name-board
name-day
name-father
name-plate
name-saint
namesake
name-son
nancy-pretty
nannyberry
nanny-goat
nap-at-noon (a plant)
nape-crest
napha-water
napier-cloth
napkin-ring

nap-meter
napping-machine
nap-warp
narras-plant
narrow-gauge, a.
narrow-minded, etc.
narrow-work
naseberry-bat
nassfish
native-born, etc.
natterjack-toad
natty-boxes
natural-born, etc.
nature-deity
nature-god
nature-myth
nature-print
nature-printing
nature-spirit
nature-worship
nautch-girl
nautilus-cup
nave-box
nave-hold
navel-gall
navel-hole
navel-hood
navel-ill
navel-string
navelwort
nave-shaped, etc.
navy-agent
navy-bill
navy-list
navy-register
navy-yard
near-by, a.
near-dweller
near-hand, a.
near horse

near-legged, etc.
near-point
near side
neat-handed, etc.
neatherd
neat-land
nebbuk-tree
neb-neb
neck-band
neck-bearing
neck-beef
neck-bone
neck-break
neck-cell
neck-chain
neck-cloth
neck-guard
neck-hackle
neck-handkerchief
necklace
necklace-moss
necklace-poplar
necklace-shaped, etc.
necklace-tree
neck-mould
neck-moulding
neck-piece
neck-ring
neck-strap
necktie
neck-twine
neckwear
neckweed
neck-yoke
nectar-bird
nectar-gland
need-be
needle-annunciator
needle-bar
needle-beam

needle=bearer†
needle=board
needle=book
needle=bug
needle=carrier†
needle=case
needle=clerk
needle=file
needle=fish
needle=forceps
needle=gun
needle=holder†
needle=hook
needle=house
needle=instrument
needle=loom
needle=making†
needleman
needle=ore
needle=papering†
needle=pointed, etc.
needle=setter†
needle=sharpener†
needle=shell
needle=spar
needle=stone
needletail (a bird)
needle=telegraph
needle test
needle=threader†
needlewoman
needlework
needle=woven
needle=wrapper†
needle=zeolite
neem=bark
neem=oil
ne'er=be=lickit
ne'er=do=good
ne'er=do=weel
negative=bath
negative=rack
negro=bug
negro=head
negro's=head*
nephelin=basalt
nephelin=rock
nephelin=tephrite
nerve=aura

nerve=broach
nerve=canal
nerve=capping
nerve=cell
nerve=centre
nerve=collar
nerve=cord ,
nerve=corpuscle
nerve=drill
nerve=ending
nerve=fibre
nerve=fibril
nerve=fibrilla
nerve=force
nerve=hill
nerve=hillock
nerve=motion
nerve=needle
nerve=obtundent
nerve=paste
nerve=path
nerve=pentagon
nerve=plate
nerve=ring
nerve=rudiment
nerve=shaken
nerve=storm
nerve=stretching
nerve=substance
nerve=tire
nerve=tissue
nerve=track
nerve=tube
nerve=tuft
nerve=tunic
nerve=twig
nerve=wave
nerve=winged
nest=egg
nest=pan
nest=spring
net=berth
net=braider†
net=fern
net=fish
net=fisherman
net=fishery
net=fishing†
nether=formed

nether=vert
net=loom
net=mackerel
net=maker†
net=masonry
net=mender†
net structure
netted=carpet (a moth)
netted=veined
netting=machine
netting=needle
nettle=bird
nettle=blight
nettle=butterfly
nettle=cell
nettle=cloth
nettle=creeper
nettle=fever
nettle=fish
nettle=geranium
nettle=leaf
nettle=monger
nettle=rash
nettle=springe
nettle=stuff
nettle=tap
nettle=thread
nettle=tree
nettlewort
net=veined
network
nevermore
never=strike
nevertheless
new=born
new=come
newcomer
new=create
New=Englander
newfangle
newfangled
new=fashion
new=fashioned, etc.
New=light
New=Mexican
new=model, v.
New=Platonist
new=sad
news=agent

newsboy
news=house
news=ink
newsman
newsmonger
news=pamphlet
newspaper
newspaper=clamp
newspaper=file
news=room
news=stand
news=vender†
news=writer†
news=yacht
New=year
New=Yorker
next=ways
nib=nib
nick=eared
nickel=bloom
nickel=glance
nickel=green
nickel=ochre
nickel=plated
nickel=plating†
nickel=silver
nicker=nuts
nicker=pecker
nicker=tree
nicking=buddle
nicking=file
nicking=saw
nickname
nick=stick
niddle=noddle
niello=work
niepa=bark
nigger=fish
niggerhair (a seaweed)
niggerhead (tobacco, a
    rock)
nigger=killer†
night=ape
night=bat
night=bell
night=bird
night=blindness
night=blooming†
night=bolt

night=born
night=brawler†
night=breeze
night=butterfly
nightcap
night=cart
night=chair
night=charm
nightchurr
nightclothes
night=cloud
night=comer
night=crow
night=dew
night=doctor
night=dog
night=dress
night=eyed, etc.
nightfall
night=faring
night=feeder†
night=fire
night=fish
night=fishery
night=flier†
nightflower (a plant)
night=fly
night=foe
night=fossicker†
night=foundered
night=glass
nightgown
night=hag
night=hawk
night=heron
night=house
nightjar
night=key
night=lamp
night=latch
night=light
night=line
night=liner
night=long
night=magistrate
night=man
nightmare
night=monkey
night=moth

night=owl
night=palsy
night=parrot
night=partridge
night=peck
night=piece
night=porter
night=raven
night=robe
night=school
night=season
nightshade (a plant)
nightshirt
night=shoot
night=side
night=sight
night=singer†
night=soil
night=sparrow
night=spell
night=steed
night=stool
night=swallow
night=sweat
night=taper
night=terrors
night=time
night=tripping†
night=waker†
night=walk
night=walker†
night=wanderer†
night=warbling†
night=watch
night=watcher†
night=watchman
night=witch
night=work
night=yard
nilly=willy
nimble=fingered, etc.
nimble=Will (grass)
nimini=pimini
ninebark (a shrub)
nine=eyed, etc.
nine=eyes (a fish)
nine=holes (a game, a
    fish)
nine=killer (a bird)

nine-murder
ninepegs
ninepence
ninepins
ninety-knot
ninnyhammer
niopo-snuff
niopo-tree
niota-bark
nipcheese (a person)
nipper-crab
nipper-gauge
nipper-men
nipperty-tipperty
nipping-claws
nipple-cactus
nipple-line
nipple-piece
nipple-pin
nipple-seat
nipple-shield
nipplewort
nipple-wrench
nitre-bush
nitre-cake
nit-grass
nitta-tree
no-account, a.
noble-ending
noble-finch
nobleman
noble-minded, etc.
noblewoman
nobody
nob-thatcher
nocking-point
noddy-tern
node-and-flecnode
node-and-spinode
node-couple
node-cusp
node-plane
node-triplet
nogging-piece
nohow
noil-yarn
noli-me-tangere
no-man's-land
nonce-word

none-so-pretty (a plant)
none-sparing
nonesuch
nonsense-name
nonsense-verses
noodle-soup
noonday
noonflower (a plant)
noon-mark
Norseman
North-American
North-Carolinian
north-cock (a bird)
northeast, etc.
north-northeast
north-northwest
northwest, etc.
nose-ape
nose-bag
nose-band
nose-bit
nosebleed
nose-brain
noseburn (a tree)
nosefish
nose-flute
nose-fly
nosegay
nosegay-tree
nose-glasses
nose-hole
nose-horn
nose-key
nose-leaf
nose-led
nose-ornament
nose-piece
nose-pipe
nose-ring
nosing-motion
nosing-plane
notch-block
notch-board
notch-eared
notching-adze
notching-machine
notchweed
notchwing (a moth)
note-book

note-paper
noteworthy
nothing-gift
notice-board
notion-counter
not-self
not-wheat
notwithstanding
November-moth
nowadays
noway
noways
nowhere
nowhither
nowise
nozzle-block
nozzle-clock
nozzle-mouth
nozzle-plate
nulla-nulla
null-line
numbering-machine
numbering-press
numbering-stamp
numbfish
numskull (a person)
nun-bird
nun-buoy
nun's-cloth*
nun's-collar*
nun's-cotton*
nun's-thread*
nun's-veiling*
nur-and-spell
nurling-tool
nurse-child
nurse-frog
nurse-hound
nurse-keeper
nurse-maid
nurse-name
nurse-pond
nursery-maid
nurse-shark
nursing-bottle
nursing-lamp
nut-bone
nutbreaker (a bird)
nut-brown

nutcake
nut coal
nut=cracker†
nutcracker (a bird)
nut=fastening†
nutgall
nutgrass
nuthacker (a bird)
nuthatch (a bird)
nut=hole
nut=hook
nutjobber (a bird)
nut=lock
nut=machine

nutmeal
nutmeg=bird
nutmeg=butter
nutmeg=flower (a plant)
nutmeg=grater
nutmeg=hickory
nutmeg=liver
nutmeg=oil
nutmeg=pigeon
nutmeg=tree
nutmeg=wood
nut=oil
nutpecker (a bird)
nut=pick

nut=pine
nut=planer†
nut=roaster†
nut=rush
nut=sedge
nutshell
nut=tapper†
nutta=tree
nut=topper†
nut=tree
nut=weevil
nut=wrench
N=way
nymph=like

O

oak-apple
oak-ba⁻k
oak-barren
oak-beauty
oak-beetle
oak-chestnut
oak-feeding
oak-fern
oak-fig
oak-frog
oak-gall
oak-hooktip
oak-lappet
oak-leather
oak-lungs
oak-opening
oak-paper
oak-pest
oak-plum
oak-potato
oak-spangle
oak-tangle
oak-tanned, etc.
oak-tree
oak-wart
oak-web
oarfish
oar-footed, etc.
oarlap
oar-lock
oar-propeller
oarsman
oar-swivel
oast-house
oat-cake
oat-flight
oat-fowl
oat-grass
oath-bound
oath-breaking†

oath-rite
oat-malt
oatmeal
oat-mill
oatseed-bird
obi-woman
object-finder†
object-glass
object-lesson
object-object
object-soul
object-staff
object-teaching†
oblique-angled
oblong-ellipsoid
oblong-lanceolate
oblong-ovate
obovate-clavate
obovate-cuneate
obovate-oblong
observation-car
obstacle-race
obtuse-angled
obtuse-angular
obtuse-ellipsoid
obverse-lunate
octave-flute
octave-stop
octavo-post
octo-bass
ocuba-wax
odd-come-short
odd-come-shortly
odd-ends
Odd-fellow
odd-looking
odd-mark
odd-pinnate
oddy-doddy
ode-factor

od-force
œil-de-bœuf
œil-de-perdrix
ofbit
off-and-on, a.
off-bear
off-bearer†
offcast
off-come
off-corn .
offcut
offering-sheet
off-flow
offhand
off horse
office-bearer†
office-book
office-holder†
office-seeker†
off-reckoning
offsaddle
offscouring
offscum
offset
offset-glass
offset-pipe
offset-sheet
offset-staff
offsetting-blanket
offshoot
offshore, adv.
off side
off-side, adv.
offspring
offtake
often-bearing
oftentimes
ofttimes
ogee-plane
ohm-ammeter

oil=bag
oil=beetle
oil=bird
oil=bottle
oil=box
oil=bush
oil=cake
oil=can
oil=car
oil=cellar
oilcloth
oil=cock
oil=collar
oil=cup
oil=derrick
oil=distributer†
oil=dregs
oil=dried
oil=drop
oil=extracting†
oil=factory
oil=filter
oil=fuel
oil=gauge
oil=gas
oil=gilding†
oil=gland
oil=green
oil=hole
oil=jack
oilman
oil=mill
oil=nut
oil=painting†
oil=palm
oil=plant
oil=press
oil=pump
oil=refining†
oil=ring
oil=rubber
oil=safe
oil=sand
oil=seed
oil=shale
oil=shark
oilskin
oil=smeller†
oil=spring

oil=still
oil=stock
oilstone
oilstone=powder
oilstone=slips
oil=stove
oil=tank
oil=tawing
oil=temper
oil=tempered
oil=tempering†
oil=tester†
oil=tight
oil=tree
oil=tube
oilway
oil=well
oily=grain
ointment=syringe
old=ewe (a fish)
old=faced, etc.
old=fogyish
old=fogyism
old=gentlemanly
old=grain
old=light
old=line
old maid
old=maid (a plant, a
    clam)
old=maidhood
old=maidish
old=maidism
old=man (a tree)
old=man's=beard (a
    plant)
old=man's=eyebrow (a
    plant)
old=man's=head (a
    plant)
old=school, a.
old=sightedness
old=squaw (a duck)
old=time, a.
old=timer
oldwife (a duck, a
    fish)
old=witch grass
old=womanish

old=woman's=bitter (a
    plant)
oleander=fern
oleo=oil
oliveback (a thrush)
olive=backed
olivebark=tree
olive=branch
olive=green
olive=nut
olive=oil
olive=ore
olive=plum
olive=shell
olive=tree
olive=tyrant
olive=wood
olivewort
olive=yard
olivin=diabase
olivin=gabbro
olivin=norite
olivin=rock
omander=wood
omnibus=box
omnium=gatherum
oncome
on=coming
one-and=thirty
one=berry
one=blade (a plant)
one=cross
one=eyed, etc.
one=horse, a.
one=leaf (a plant)
oneself (an erroneous
    form often used)
one's self
onfall
onga=onga
ongoing
on=hanger†
onion=couch
onion=eyed, etc.
onion=fish
onion=fly
onion=grass
onion=maggot
onion=shell

onion=skin
onion=smut
onlooker†
onshore, *adv.*
onstead
opal=blue
opal=jasper
open=air
openbill (a stork)
open=breasted, etc.
open=cast
open=dot
opening=bit
opening=knife
opening=machine
open=steek
open=tide
openwork
opera=cloak
opera=dancer
opera=girls
opera=glass
opera=hat
opera=house
opera=season
opera=singer
operating=table
opera=troupe
opium=eater†
opium=habit
opium liniment
opium plaster
opium=poppy
opossum=mouse
opossum=shrew
opossum=shrimp
opus=number
orange=bird
orange=blossom
orange=butter
orange=colored
orange=crowned
orange=dog
orange=flower
orange=grass
orange=juice
orangeleaf (a shrub)
orange=legged
orange=lily

orange=list
Orangeman
orange=musk
orange=oil
orange=pea
orange=peel
orange=pekoe
orange=pippin
orangeroot (a plant)
orange=scale
orange=seed
orange=skin
orange=spoon
orange=tawny
orange=thorn
orangetip (a butterfly)
orange=wife
orange=woman
orang=utan
orbfish
orbit=sweeper†
orb=like
orb=weaver
orchard=clam
orchard=grass
orchard=house
orchard=oriole
orchella=weed
orchilla=weed
ordcal=root
ordeal=tree
order=book
order=class
ordnance office
ordnance officer
ordnance sergeant
ore=concentrator†
ore=crusher†
ore=deposit
ore=hearth
ore=roasting †
ore=separator†
ore=smelting†
ore=stamp
ore=washer†
oreweed
orewood
organ=albumin
organ=bench

organ=blower†
organ=builder†
organ=coupler
organ=fish
organ=grinder†
organ gun
organ=harmonium
organ=ling
organ=loft
organ=piano
organ=pipe
organ=player†
organ=point
organ=rest
organ=screen
organ=seat
organ=stop
oriole=tanager
orizaba=root
orlop=deck
ormolu=varnish
orphan asylum
orphrey=work
orris=pea
orris=root
osier=ait
osier=bed
osier=holt
osier=peeler†
ostrich=board
ostrich=egg
ostrich=farm
ostrich=farming†
ostrich=feather
ostrich=fern
ostrich=plume
otherwhere
otherwhile
otherwhiles
other=world
otherworldliness
otherworldly
otoba=butter
otter=canoe
otter=dog
otter=hound
otter=pike
otter=shell
otter=shrew

otter-spear
ouabe-oil
ounce land
ouster-le-main
out-and-out
out-and-outer
outask
out-at-elbows
outbalance
outbar
outbargain
outbid
outblown
outblush
outbluster
outboard
outbond
outborn
out-bound
outbowed
outbrag
outbrave
outbrazen
outbreak
outbreaker†
outbreathe
outbring
outbud
outbuilding
outburn
outburst
outburst-bank
outcarry
outcast
outcaste
outcatch
outchase
outclearance
outclimb
outcome
outcompass
out-court
outcreep
outcrier
outcrop
outcry
out-cut
outdare
outdistance

outdo
outdoor
outdoors
out-edge
out'ace
outfall
out-field
out-fielder
outfit
outfitter†
outflank
outfling
outflow
outflush
outfrown
outgeneral
outglare
outgo
outgoer
outgoing
outground
outgrow
outgrowth
outguard
outhaul
outhauler
out-herod
outhouse
outkeeper
outlabor
outland
outlash
outlast
outlay
outlayer
outleap
outlearn
outlet
outlie
outlier†
outline
outlive
out-lodging
outlook
outlooker†
outman
outmanœuvre
outmantle
outmarch

outmatch
outmate
outmove
outname
outnoise
out-nook
outnumber
out-of-door
out-of-doors
out-of-fashion, a.
out-of-the-way, a.
out-oven
out-over
outpace
outparagon
out-parish
outpart
out-patient
out-pensioner
out-picket
outplay
outpoint
outpoise
outporch
outport
outpost
outpour
outpouring
outpower
outpray
outprize
output
outrake
outrange
outrank
outray
outreach
outreason
outreckon
outreign
outride
outrider
outrigger
outrigger-hoist
outright
outrival
outroad
outroar
outromance

outroom	outstrip	ovate=oblong
outrun	outsucken	ovate=rotundate
outrush	outsum	ovate=subulate
outsail	outswear	ovate=ventricose
out=sale	outswell	ovato=acuminate
outscold	outsyllable	ovato=ellipsoidal
outscorn	out=talk	ovato=oblong
outscouring	out=tongue	oven=bird
outsell	out=top	oven=builder†
outsentry	out=travel	oven=cake
out=servant	out=turn	oven=coke
outset	outvalue	oven=tit
outsetter†	outvenom	oven=wood
out=settlement	outvie	overalls
outsettler	outvillain	over=anxiety
outshine	outvoice	over=anxious
outshoot	outvote	over=anxiously
outshot	outwait	overarch
outside	outwake	overawe
outside=car (a jaunting= car)	outwalk	overawning
	outwall	overbalance
outsider	out=ward (a ward in a wing of a hospital)	overbear
outsight		overbearing
outsit	outward=bound	overbid
outskirt	outward=sainted	overblow
outsleep	outwash	overblowing
outslide	outwatch	overblown
outsoar	outway	overboard
outsole	outwear	overbowed
outspan	outweary	overbrim
outsparkle	outweed	over=brimmed
outspeak	outweep	overbrood
outspeckle (Scotch, a spectacle)	outweigh	overbrow
	outwell	overbuild
outspeed	outwelling	overburden
outspend	outwind	overburn
outspent	outwing	overbusy
outspin	outwit	overbuy
outspoken	outwith	overcanopy
outsport	outwoman	overcare
outspread	outwork	overcast
outstand	outworker	overcasting
outstare	outwrest	overcharge
outstay	outwrite	over=chord
outstep	oval=lanceolate	overclimb
out=street	ovate=acuminate	over=cloth
outstretch	ovate=cylindraceous	overcloud
outstride	ovate=deltoid	overcloy
outstrike	ovate=lanceolate	overcoat

overcoating
overcolor
overcome
over=confidence
over=confident
over=confidently
overcount
overcover
overcrow
overcrowd
overcup=oak
over=curious
overcurtain
overdare
overdaring
overdark
overdate
over=development
over=diligent
over=discharge
overdo
overdoer
overdose
overdraft
overdraw
overdraw=check
overdredge
overdress
overdrink
overdrive
overdrop
overdry
overdue
overdye
overeat
over=entreat
overestimate
overexcite
over=exertion
over=exposure
over=exquisite
overfare
overfawn
overfeed
overfill
over=fired
overfish
overflood
overflourish

overflow
overflow=basin
overflow=bug
overflow=gauge
overflow meeting
overflush
overflux
overfly
overfold
over=fond
over=fondly
over=force
over=forward
overfreight
over=fruitful
overfull
overgarment
over=gaze
overgild
overgird
overgive
overglance
overglaze
overglide
overgloom
overgo
overgorge
overgrace
overgrain
overgrainer
overgreat
overgreedy
overgreen
overground, a.
overgrow
overgrown
overgrowth
over=hair
overhand
overhanded
overhandle
overhang
overhaste
over=hastily
over=hastiness
overhaul
overhead
overhear
overheat

overheating=pipe
over=hours
overhouse
over=inform
overissue
overjoy
overjump
over=kind
over=king
overknowing
overlabor
overlactation
overlade
overlaid
overland
overlap
overlap=joint
overlaunch
overlay
overleaf
overleap
over=learnedness
over=learning
overleaven
overlie
overlive
overliver
overload
overload=magnet
overload=switch
overlock
overlook
overlord
overlove
overman
overmantel
overmarch
overmask
overmast
overmaster
overmatch
overmeasure
overmickle
over=modest
overmount
overmuch
overmultiply
overmultitude
overname

overneat
overnice
overnoise
overpart
overpass
overpay
overpayment
overpeople
overpersuade
overpick=loom
overpicture
overplant
over=plate
overplus
overply
overpoise
overpopulate
overpopulation
overpost
overpower
overpraise
overpreach
overpress
overpressure
overprize
over=produce
over=production
overproof
over=purchase
overrack
overrake
overrank
overrate
overreach
overread
overreckon
over=refine
over=refinement
overrent
override
over=righteous
overripe
overripen
overroast
overrule
overruler
overrun
overrunner
oversail

oversay
overscent
overscore
over=scrupulous
over=scrupulousness
over=scutched
oversea
overseam
overseaming
oversee
overseer
oversell
overset
oversew
overshade
overshadow
overshake
overshave
overshine
overshirt
overshoot
overshot
overside
oversight
oversightedness
oversize
overskip
overskirt
overslaugh
oversleep
overslip
oversman
oversnow
oversoon
oversorrow
over=soul
oversow
overspan
oversparred
overspeak
overspent
overspread
overspring
overstain
overstand
overstare
overstate
overstatement
overstay

overstep
overstock
overstore
overstory
overstrain
overstream
overstretch
overstrew
overstride
overstrike
overstring
overstrow
overstrung
overstudied
overstudy
oversup
oversupply
overswarming
oversway
overswell
overtake
overtalk
overtask
overtax
overtcemed
overthrow
overthrust
overthwart
overtilt
overtime
overtire
overtitle
overtoil
overtoise
overtone
overtop
overtower
overtrade
overtrip
overtrust
overturn
overtwine
overuse
overvaluation
overvalue
overvault
overveil
overview
over=violent

overvote	ox=acid	oyster=boat
overwalk	ox=antelope	oyster=bottom
overwatch	ox=balm	oyster=brood
overwear	oxberry	oyster=catcher†
overweary	oxbiter (a bird)	oyster=crab
overweather	ox=bow	oyster=cracker
overween	ox=brake	oyster=culture
overweening	ox=cheek	oyster=culturist
overweigh	oxeye (a plant)	oyster=dredge
overweight	ox=eyed, etc.	oyster=farm
overwell	ox=fence	oyster=farming†
overwhelm	ox=fly	oyster=field
overwhile	ox=foot	oyster=fish
overwind	ox=gall	oyster=fishery
overwing	ox=goad	oyster=fishing†
overwise	ox=head	oyster=fork
overwoody	oxheal (a plant)	oyster=gauge
overword	oxheart (a cherry)	oyster=grass
overwork	ox=hide	oyster=green
overworry	oxhoof (a leaf)	oyster=hammer
overwrest	ox=horn	oyster=keg
overwrestle	oxidizing=furnace	oyster=knife
overwrite	ox=land	oysterman
overwrought	oxlip (a primrose)	oyster=mushroom
overyear	oxman	oyster=opener†
ovolo=plane	ox=mushroom	oyster=park
ovum=cycle	oxpecker (a bird)	oyster pie
ovum=product	ox=ray	oyster=plant
owl=butterfly	ox=reim	oyster=plover
owlet=moth	ox=shoe	oyster=rake
owl=eyed, etc.	ox=sole	oyster=reef
owl=gnat	ox=stall	oyster=rock
owl=head	ox=team	oyster=shell
owl=light	ox=tongue (a tongue)	oyster=shop
owl=monkey	oxtongue (a plant)	oyster=sign
owl=moth	ox=yoke	oyster stew
owl=parrot	oyster=bank	oyster=tongs
owl=swallow	oyster=bar	oyster=wife
owl=train	oyster=bay	oyster=woman
own=form	oyster=bed	ozone=box
own=root	oyster=bird	ozone=paper

P

pace-aisle
pace-board
pace-eggs
pace-maker†
packaging-machine
packall (a basket)
pack-animal
pack-cinch
pack-cloth
pack-duck
packet-boat
packet-day
packet-note
packet-ship
packet-vessel
packhorse
pack-house
pack-ice
packing-awl
packing-block
packing-bolt
packing-box
packing-case
packing-cell
packing-crib
packing-expander
packing-gland
packing-leather
packing-needle
packing-nut
packing-officer
packing-paper
packing-press
packing-ring
packing-shed
packing-sheet
packing-stick
pack-load
packman
packmoth

pack-mule
packneedle
pack-rat
pack-road
pack-saddle
packsheet
packstaff
packthread
pack-train
pack-wall
packware
packwax
packway
pad-bracket
pad-clinking
pad-cloth
pad-crimp
padding-flue
padding-ken
padding-machine
paddle-beam
paddle-board
paddle-boat
paddle-box
paddlecock
paddle-crab
paddle-end
paddle-fish
paddle-hole
paddle-row
paddle-shaft
paddle-sloop
paddle-staff
paddle-tumble
paddle-wheel
paddlewood (a tree)
paddling-crab
paddock-pipe
paddock-rud
paddock-stone

paddockstool (a toad-
   stool)
paddy-bird
paddy-field
paddy-melon
paddy-pounder
paddywhack .
pad-elephant
pad-hook
padlock
pad-nag
padow-pipe
pad-saddle
pad-screw
pad-top
pad-trace
pad-tree
page-cord
page-gauge
paging-machine
pagoda-stone
pagoda-tree
pail-brush
pail-handle
pail-lathe
pail-machine
pail-nail
pail-stake
painstaking†
painsworthy
paint-box
paint-bridge
paint-brush
paint-burner†
paint-can
painted-cup (a plant)
painted-lady (a butter
   fly, a plant)
painter-stainer
paint-frame

paint=mill
paint=mixer†
paint=remover†
paint=room
paintroot (a plant)
paint=strake
paintwork
pairing=time
pair=toed
palace=car
palace=court
palanquin=bearer†
palate=myograph
palebelly (a young
plover)
palebreast (a young
plover)
palebuck (an antelope)
paleface (a white man)
pale=faced, etc.
palette=knife
palier=glissant
paling=board
palisade=cell
palisade=parenchyma
palisade=tissue
palisade=worm
palkee=gharee
pall=bearer†
pallet=arbor
pallet=box
pallet=eye
pallet=leather
pallet=moulding
pallet=tail
pall=mall
palmbark=tree
palm=barley
palm=bird
palm=butter
palm=cabbage
palm=cat
palm=color
palm=crab
palm=cross
palmer=worm
palm=fibre
palm=honey
palm=house

palm=kale
palm=leaf
palm=lily
palm=marten
palm=oil
palm=sugar
palm=tree
palm=veined
palm=viper
palm=warbler
palm=wasp
palm=wax
palm wine
palm=worm
palmyra=palm
palmyra=tree
palmyra=wood
palo=blanco
palsywort
pamban=manche
pameroon=bark
pampas=cat
pampas=deer
pampas=grass
pampas=rice
pancake
pancake=turner†
pan=cover
pancreas=ptyalin
pandle=whew
panel door
panel=furring
panel=game
panel=house
panel=picture
panel=plane
panel=planer†
panel=rail
panel=raiser†
panel=saw
panel=strip
panel=thief
panel=truss
panel=wheel
panel=working†
pan=fish (any fish for
the pan)
panfish (the king=
crab)

pan=handle (handle of
a pan)
panhandle (strip of
land)
pan=ice
panic=grass
panic=monger
panic=stricken
panic=struck
pan=man
pannier=man
panning=machine
Pan=pipe
pan=pudding
pan=rock
panther=lily
panther=moth
panther=wood
pantile=lathe
pantile=shop
papaw=tree
pap=boat
paperbark (a tree)
paperbark=tree
paper=birch
paper box (made of
paper)
paper=box (to hold
paper)
paper=case
paper=chase
paper=clamp
paper=clip
paper=cloth
paper=coal
paper=coloring†
paper=cutter†
paper=day
paper=enamel
paper=enamelling†
paper=faced
paper=feeder†
paper=file
paper=folder†
paper=gauge
paper=glosser†
paper=hanger†
paper=holder†
paper=hornet

paper=knife
paper=machine
paper=maker†
paper=marbler†
paper=mill
paper=moulding†
paper=mulberry
paper=muslin
paper=nautilus
paper=office
paper=perforating†
paper=polishing†
paper=pulp
paper=punch
paper=reed
paper=ruler†
paper=rush
paper=sailor
paper=shell
paper=size
paper=spar
paper=splitting†
paper=stainer†
paper=stock
paper=tester†
paper=tree
paper=washing†
paper=weight
papier=mâché
papillate=scabrous
papmeat
papmouth (a person)
papooseroot (a plant)
pap=pox
pap=spoon
parachute=light
parade=ground
parade=rest
parade=wall
paradise=bird
paradise=stock
paradise=tree
paraffin=butter
paraffin=oil
paraffin=scales
paragonite=schist
Pará=nut
parasol=ant
parasol=fir

parasol=handle
parcelling=machine
parcel=lift
parcel=maker†
parcel=office
parcel=paper
parcel=post
parcel=van
parchment=beaver
parchment=lace
parchment=skin
pardon=bell
pardon=chair
pardon=screen
pardon=stall
parent=cell
parent=form
parent=kernel
parge=board
paring=chisel
paring=iron
paring=knife
paring=machine
paring=plow
paring=scissors
paring=spade
park=keeper†
parkleaves (a plant)
parliament=cake
Parliament roll
parlor=boarder
parlor=car
parlor=organ
parlor=skate
parole=arrest
parrel=rope
parrel=truck
parr=marks
parrotbeak (a plant)
parrot=bill
parrot=bullfinch
parrot=coal
parrot=crossbill
parrot=finch
parrot=fish
parrot=flower (a plant)
parrot=green
parrot=greenfinch
parrot=lawyer

parrot's=bill*
parrotweed
parrot=wrasse
parsley=camphor
parsley=fern
parsley=haw
parsley=piert
parsnip=chervil
parson=bird
parson=gull
parting=cup
parting=glass
parting=line
parting=rail
parting=sand
parting=shard
parting=strip
parting=tool
part=music
part=owner
partridgeberry
partridge=hawk
partridge=pea
partridge=wood
part=singing
part=song
part=writing
party=coated, etc.
party=color
party=gold
party=jury
party=list
party man
party wall
pasch=egg
pasqueflower (a plant)
passage=board
passage=money
passageway
pass=book
pass=box
pass=by
pass=check
passenger=car
passenger=elevator
passenger=engine
passenger=locomotive
passenger=pigeon
passenger=ship

passenger=train
passe=partout
passer=by
pass=guard
pass=holder†
passing=bell
passing=braid
passing=discord
passing=measure
passing=note
passing=place
passing=tone
passion=flower (a plant)
passion=music
passion=oratorio
passion=play
Passion=tide
passion=vine
pass-key
passman
passmaster
Passover
pass=parole
passport
pass=shooting
pass=ticket
password
passwort
pasteboard
pasteboard=cutter†
paste=down
paste=eel
paste=maker†
paste=point
paste=pot
pastern=bone
pastern=joint
paste=rock
paste=wash
pastil=paper
past=perfect
pastry=cook
pastry=man
pasture=grass
pasture=land
pat=a=cake
patch=box
patchhead
patch=polled

patchwork
patent=right
patent=rolls
pathfinder†
path=maker†
patrolman
patrol=wagon
pattern=book
pattern=box
pattern=card
pattern=chain
pattern=cylinder
pattern=drawer†
pattern=maker†
pattern=moulder†
pattern=reader†
pattern=shop
pattern=wheel
patter=song
patty=cake
patty=pan
paunch=mat
pavement epithclium
pavement=pipe
pavement=rammer†
paving=beetle
paving=machine
paving=stone
paving=tile
pawl=bitt
pawl=post
pawl=press
pawl=rim
pawnbroker†
pawncock
pawnshop
pawn=ticket
paw=paw
paw=waw
pax=board
pay=bill
pay=car
pay=clerk
pay=corps
pay=day
pay=director
pay=inspector
pay=list
paymaster

paymistress
pay=office
pay=roll
pea=bean
pea=beetle
peaberry
peabird
pea=bluff
pea=bone
pea=bug
pea=bush
peace=breaker†
peace=maker†
peace=offering
peace=officer
peace party
peace=pipe
pea=chafer
peach=black
peach=blight
peach=blister
peach=blossom
peachblow (a potato)
peach=borer†
peach=brake
peach brandy
peach=color
peach=colored, etc.
peach=down
peach=house
pea=chick
pea=chicken
peach=myrtle
peach=oak
peach=palm
peach=parer†
peach=stone
peach=stoner†
peach=tree
peach=water
peach=wood
peach=worm
peachwort
peach=yellows
pea=clam
pea coal
pea=coat
peacock
peacock=bittern

peacock=blue
peacock=butterfly
peacock=fish
peacock=flower (a
  plant)
peacock=hatter
peacock iris
peacock=pheasant
peacock's=tail*
pea=cod
pea=comb
pea=crab
pea=dove
pea=dropper
pea=finch
pea=flower (a flower)
peaflower (a plant)
peafowl
pea=green
pea=grit
pea=gun
peahen
pea=jacket
peak=arch
peak=cleat
peak=crest
peak=downhaul
peak=halyards
peak=purchase
pealip (a fish)
peal=ringer†
pea=maggot
pea=measle
pea=moth
peanut
peanut=digger†
peanut=picker†
pea=ore
pea=pheasant
pea=pod
pea=rake
pear=blight
pear=encrinite
pea=rifle
pea=rise
pearlash
pearl=barley
pearl=bearing†
pearl=berry

pearl=bird
pearl=blue
pearl=bush
pearl=disease
pearl=divert
pearl=edge
pearl=eye
pearl=eyed, etc.
pearl=fishery
pearl=fishing†
pearl=fruit
pearl=grain
pearl=grass
pearl=gray
pearl=hen
pearling=mill
pearl=lashing
pearl=mica
pearl=moss
pearl=moth
pearl=mussel
pearl=nautilus
pearl=opal
pear=louse
pearl=oyster
pearl=plant
pearl=powder
pearl=purl
pearl=sago
pearl=shell
pearlside (a fish)
pearlsides (a fish)
pearl=sinter
pearl=skipper (a butter-
  fly)
pearl=spar
pearl=stitch
pearlstone
pearl=tea
pearl=tie
pearl=tumor
pearlweed
pearl=white
pearl=winning†
pearlwort
pearmonger
pea=roe
pear=shaped, etc.
pear=shell

pear=slug
pear=tree
pear=withe
peascod=doublet
pease=crow
pease=hook
pease=meal
pease porridge
pease pudding
pease soup
peaseweep (a bird)
pea=shell
pea=sheller†
pea=shooter†
pea soup
pea=spawn
peastone
peat=bed
peat=bog
peat=burning†
peat=charcoal
peat=coal
peat=coke
peat=cutter†
peat=gas
peat=hagg
peat=machine
peat=moor
peat=moss
pea=tree
peat=reck
peat=soil
peat=spade
pea=vine
pea=weevil
pebble=dashing†
pebble=leather
pebble=paving†
pebble=powder
pebble=stone
pebbleware
pebbling=machine
pecan=nut
pecking=bag
pedal=point
peddler's=basket*
pedestal=box
pedestal=cover
pedicel=cell

peek=a=boo
peel=axe
peel=end
peel=house
peeling=axe
peeling=iron
peel=tower
peen=hammer
peep=bo
peep=eye
peep=hole
Peep=o'=day Boy
peep=show
peep=sight
peg=cutter†
peg=fiched
peg=float
pegging=awl
pegging=jack
pegging=machine
pegging=rammer
peggy=chaw
peggy=cutthroat
peg=joint
peg=ladder
peg=leg
peg=striker†
peg=strip
peg=tankard
peg=top
pelican=fish
pelican=flower
pelican's=foot*
pelican's=head*
pellet=powder
pell=mell
pelt=rot
pelt=wool
penang=lawyer
pen=case
pence=table
pencil=blue
pencil=case
pencil=cedar
pencil=compass
pencil=drawing
pencil=flower
pencil=making†
pencil=sharpener†

pencil=sketch
pencil=tree
pencil=vase
peu=cutter†
pendant=tackle
pen=driver†
pendulum=hausse
pendulum=level
pendulum=pump
pendulum=spindle
pendulum=wheel
pendulum=wire
pen=feather
penfish
penfold
pen=gossip
penguin=duck
penguin=rookery
pen=gun
penholder
pen=holding
pen=maker†
penman
pen=master
penny=a=liner
penny=a=linerism
penny=bird
penny=cress
penny=dog
penny=fee
penny=flower (a plant)
penny=gaff
penny=grass
penny=land
penny=mail
penny=pies
penny=purse
penny=rent
penny=room
pennyrot (a plant)
pennyroyal
pennyweight
penny=wisdom
penny=wise
pennywort
pennyworth
pen=rack
pen=sack
pensioning warrant

pension=writ
penthouse
pen=tray
pent=roof
pen=trough
pent=stock
pen=wiper†
penwoman
pepper=and=salt, a.
pepper=and=salt (a
    plant)
pepper=bottle
pepper=box
pepper=bush
pepper=cake
pepper=caster
peppercorn
pepper=cress
pepper=crop
pepper=dulse
pepper=elder
pepper=gingerbread
peppergrass (a plant)
pepper=mill
peppermint
peppermint=camphor
peppermint=drop
peppermint=tree
pepper=moth
pepper=plant
pepper=pod
pepper=pot
pepper=rod
pepperroot (a plant)
pepper=sauce
pepper=saxifrage
pepper=shrub
pepper=tree
pepper=vine
pepper=water
pepperwood (a tree)
pepperwort
perch=iron
perch=loop
perch=pest
perch=plate
perch=pole
perch=stay
percussion=bullet

percussion=cap
percussion=fuse
percussion=grinder†
percussion=gun
percussion=hammer
percussion=lock
percussion=match
percussion=powder
percussion=primer†
percussion=stop
percussion=table
perfecting machine
perfecting press
perforating=machine
perfume=burner†
perfume=fountain
perfume=set
permutation=lock
perspective=glass
perspective=instrument
pestilence=weed
pestilence=wort
pestle=pie
peter=boat
Peter=pence
pething=pole
petit=baume
petition=crown
petit=maître
petroleum=burner†
petroleum=car
petroleum=ether
petroleum=filter
petroleum=furnace
petroleum=still
petroleum=stove
petticoat=affair
petticoat=breeches
petticoat=pensioner
petticoat=pipe
petticoat=trousers
petty=morrel
petty=rice
petty=whin
pew=chair
pew=gaff
pewholder†
pew=opener†
pew=rent

pewter=mill
pewterwort
pheasant=cuckoo
pheasant=duck
pheasant=finch
pheasant's=eye*
pheasant=shell
pheasant=tail
pheasant=wood
phloem=sheath
phlox=worm
phœnix=stone
phonograph=grapho-
      phone
phosphor=bronze
phosphor=copper
phosphorus=box
phrase=book
phraseman
phrase=mark
phrasemonger
physic=nut
pia=matral
piano=case
piano=cover
pianoforte
pianoforte=player†
piano=maker†
piano=music
piano=player†
piano=school
piano=stool
piano=tuner†
piano=violin
pibble=pabble
pickaback
pickapack
pickaxe
pickback
pickcheese (a bird, a
      fruit)
picker=bar
picker=bend
pickerel=weed
picker=motion
picker=staff
picket=clamp
picket fence
picket=guard

picket=line
picket=machine
picket=pin
picket=pointer†
picket=rope
pickettail (a duck)
picking=peg
picking=stick
pickle=cured
· pickle=herring
pickle=worm
pickman
pick=mattock
pickmaw (a gull)
pickmire (a gull)
pick=mirk
pick=over
pickpack
pickpocket (a person)
pick=pointed, etc.
pickpurse (a person)
pick=rake
picktooth (a plant)
pick=up
pickwick (that with
      which to pick
      wicks)
picot=ribbon
picqué=work
picture=board
picture=book
picture=frame
picture=gallery
picture=lens
picture=moulding
picture=mosaic
picture=nail
picture=plane
picture=rod
picture=writing
pie=baker†
piece=broker
piece=dyed, etc.
piece=goods
piece=liquor
piece=master
piecemeal
piece=mould
piece=work

piece=worker
pie=crust
pied=billed
pied=fort
pied=winged
pie=eater†
pie=finch
pie=mag
pie=making†
pieman
pie=nanny
piend=check
piend=rafter
pie=plant
pier=arch
piercing=drill
piercing=file
piercing=saw
pier=glass
pier=table
pig=bed
pig=boiling†
pig=cote
pig=deer
pigeonberry (a plant)
pigeon=breast
pigeon=breasted, etc.
pigeon=cherry
pigeon=express
pigeon=fancier†
pigeonfoot (a plant)
pigeon=goose
pigeon=grass
pigeon=hawk
pigeonhole
pigeon=house
pigeon=match
pigeon=pair
pigeon=pea
pigeon=plum
pigeon's=blood*
pigeon's=grass*
pigeontail (a duck)
pigeon=tremex
pigeon=wing (a wing)
pigeonwing (figurative)
pigeonwood (a tree)
pigeon=woodpecker
pig=eyed, etc. ·

pigfish
pigfoot (a fish)
pig=hole
pig iron
pig lead
pigment=cell
pigment=granule
pigment=molecule
pigment=printing
pigment=spot
pig metal
pignut
pig=pen
pig=rat
pigroot (a plant)
pig's=face*
pigskin
pig=sticker†
pigsty
pig's=wash*
pig's=wrack*
pigtail
pika=squirrel
pike=fork
pike=head (head of a pike)
pikehead (a fish)
pike=headed, etc.
pike=keeper
pikeman
pike=perch
pike=pole
pikestaff
pike=sucker
piketail (a duck)
pile=beam
pile bridge
pile=builder†
pile=cap
pile=clamp
pile dam
pile=driver†
pile dwelling
pile=engine
pile=hoop
pile pier
pile=plank
pile=saw
pile=shoe

pile=start
pile=warp
pile=weaving†
pile=wire
pilework
pile=worm
pile=worn
pilewort
pilgrim=bottle
piling=iron
pillar=block
pillar=box
pillar=brick
pillar=compasses
pillar=file
pillar=lip
pillar=plait
pillar=saint
pill=beetle
pill=box
pill=bug
pill=coater†
pillcorn
pill=milleped
pillow-bar
pillow=bear
pillow=beer
pillow=block
pillow=case
pillow=cup
pillow=lace
pillow=linen
pillow=pipe
pillow=sham
pillow=slip
pillow=word
pill=tile
pill=willet
pill=worm
pillwort
pilori=rat
pilot balloon
pilot=bird
pilot=boat
pilot=bread
pilot=cloth
pilot=engine
pilot=fish
pilot=flag

pilot-house
pilot-jack
pilot-jacket
pilot-light
pilot-snake
pilotweed
pilot-whale
pimple-metal
pimple-mite
pimp-like
piña-cloth
pinafore
pinaster-pine
pinball-sight
pin-block
pinborer (a beetle)
pin-bush
pincase
pince-nez
pinchback (a person)
pinch-bar
pinch-cock
pin-cherry
pinchfist (a person)
pinchgut (a person)
pinching-bar
pinching-bug
pinching-nut
pinching-pin
pinching-tongs
pinchpenny (a person)
pinch-plane
pinch-point
pinch-spotted
pin-clover
pin-connection
pin-cop
pine-pine
pincushion
pin-drill
pindust
pineapple
pineapple-cloth
pineapple-flower
pine-barren
pine-beauty
pine-beetle
pine-blight
pine-bullfinch

pine-carpet (a moth)
pine-chafer (a beetle)
pine-clad
pine-cloth
pine-cone
pine-drops
pine-finch
pine-grosbeak
pine-grouse
pine-gum
pine-house
pine-kernel
pine-knot
pine-linnet
pine-lizard
pine-marten
pine-mast
pinemaw (a gull)
pine-mouse
pine-needle
pine-nut
pine-oil
pine-sap
pine-siskin
pine-snake
pine-stove
pine-thistle
pine-tree
pine-warbler
pineweed
pine-weevil
pine-wool
pine-worm
pin-eyed, etc.
pin-feather
pin-feathered
pin-fire
pinfish
pin-flat
pinfold
pin-grass
pin-head
pin-head sight
pinhold
pinhole
pinion-bone
pinion-file
pinion-gauge
pinion-jack

pinion-wire
pin-joint
pinkcheek (a fish)
pinkeye (a disease)
pink-eyed, etc.
pinking-iron
pink-needle
pinkroot (a plant)
pink-saucer (one that
    makes things pink)
pinkster-flower (a
    plant)
pink-stern
pinkweed
pinkwood (a tree)
pinky-built
pin-lock
pin-machine
pin-maker†
pin-mark
pin-mill
pin-money
pinnacle-work
pinna-wool
pin-oak
pinpatch (a periwinkle)
pin-pillow
pin-point
pin-pool
pin-poppet
pin-rack
pin-rail
pin-rib
pin-rod
pin-switch
pin-tail, a.
pintail (a duck, a
    grouse)
pintle-hook
pin-tongs
pin-tool
pint pot
pint-pot (a person)
pint stoup
pin-vise
pinwheel
pin-winged
pinwork
pinworm

pious-minded, etc.
pipe-bender†
pipe-box
pipe-case
pipe-clamp
pipe-clay
pipe-clearer†
pipe-connection
pipe-coupling
pipe-covering†
pipe-cutter†
pipe-dance
pipe-die
pipe-driver†
pipefish
pipe-fitter†
pipe-fittings
pipe-foot
pipe-grab
pipe-grip
pipe-joint
pipe-key
pipe-layer†
pipe-lee
pipe-line
pipe-loop
pipe-metal
pipe-moulding†
pipemouth (a fish)
pipe-mouthed, etc.
pipe-office
pipe-organ
pipe-oven
pipe-plug
pipe-prover†
pipe-rack
pipe-reducer†
pipe-roll
pipe-slotting†
pipe-socketting†
piper-urchin
pipe-screwing
pipe-staple
pipe-stay
pipe-stem
pipe-stick
pipe-stone
pipe-stop
pipe-threading

pipe-tongs
pipe-tree
pipe-twister†
pipe-union
pipe-vein
pipe-vine
pipe-vise
pipe-wine
pipewood (a tree)
pipework
pipewort
pipe-wrench
piping crow
piping guan
piping hare
piping-iron
piping plover
pipit-lark
pippin-face
pippin-faced, etc.
piqué-work
piquia-oil
pirate-fish
pirate-perch
piri-jiri
pirlie-pig
pirogue-rig
pish-pash
pishymew (a gull)
pistachio-green
pistachio-nut
pistachio-tree
pistacite-rock
pistol-cane
pistol-carbine
pistol-crack
pistol-grip
pistol-pipe
pistol-router†
pistol-shaped, etc.
pistol-shot
pistol-split
piston-bellows
piston-head
piston-knob
piston-packing
piston-pump
piston-rod
piston-sleeve

piston-spring
piston-valve
piston-wheel
piston-whistle
pita-fibre
pitahaya-woodpecker
pitapat
pita-wood
pit-bottom
pitch-and-toss
pitch-black
pitch-blende
pitch-block
pitch-board
pitch-boat
pitch-chain
pitch-circle
pitch-coal
pitch-dark
pitcher-mould
pitcher-moulding
pitcher-nose
pitcher-plant
pitcher-shaped, etc.
pitcher-vase
pitch-faced, etc.
pitch-farthing
pitchfork
pitching-machine
pitching-pence
pitching-piece
pitching-stable
pitching-temperature
pitching-tool
pitching-yeast
pitch-kettle
pitch-kettled
pitch-ladle
pitch-line
pitch-mineral
pitch-opal
pitch-ore
pitch-pine
pitch-pipe
pitch-plaster
pitch-point
pitch-polisher†
pitch-pot
pitchstone

pitch-tankard
pitch-tree
pitch-wheel
pitch-work
pit-coal
pit-cock
pit-crater
pit-eye
pitfall
pit-fish
pit-frame
pit-game
pit-guide
pith-ball
pit-head
pit-headed, etc.
pith-paper
pith-tree
pith-work
pit-kiln
pitman
pitman-box
pitman-coupling
pitman-head
pitman-press
pit-martin
pit-mirk
pitpan
pit-saw
pit-sawyer
pit-viper
pit-wood
pit-work
pivot-bolt
pivot-bridge
pivot-broach
pivot-drill
pivot-file
pivot-gearing
pivot-gun
pivot-joint
pivot-lathe
pivot-man
pivot-pin
pivot-polisher†
pivot-span
pivot-tooth
pix-jury
pixy-led

pixy-puff
pixy-purse
pixy-seat
pixy-stool
pixy-wheel
pizan-collar
place-brick
place-broker†
place-hunter†
placeman
placemonger
place-name
place-proud
placket-hole
plack-pie
plague-mark
plague-sore
plague-spot
plainbacks (bombazet)
plain-chant
plain-clay
plain-dealer†
plain-edge, a.
plain-hearted, etc.
plain-pug
plain-singing
plainsman
plain-song
plain-wanderer
plain-wave
plain-work
plaiting-machine
plait-work
plane-bit
plane-guide
plane-iron
plane-plane, a.
plane-polarized
planer-bar
planer-centre
planer-chuck
planer-head
planer-tree
planer-vise
plane-sailing
plane-stock
plane-table
plane-tabler†
planet-gearing

plane-tree
planet-stricken
planet-struck
planet-wheel
planing-machine
planing-mill
planishing-hammer
planishing-iron
planishing-roller
planishing-stake
plank-hook
planking-clamp
planking-machine
planking-screw
plank-sheer
plantain-cutter†
plantain-eater†
plantain-lily
plantain-tree
plant-animal
plantation-mill
plant-bug
plant-cane
plant-cutter†
plant-disease
plant-eating†
plant-feeder†
plant-food
planting-ground
plant-louse
plant-marker†
plant-movement
plant-of-gluttony
plant-organ
plashing-tool
plash-wheel
plasterbill (a duck)
plastering-machine
plaster-mill
plaster-spatula
plaster-stone
plastron-de-fer
plate armor
plate-basket
plate-bender†
plate-black
plate-bone
plate-box
plate-brass

plate=bulb
plate=culture
plate=engraving†
plate=frame
plate=gauge
plate girder
plate glass
plate=hat
plate=hoist
plate=holder†
plate iron
plate=key
plate=layer†
plate=leather
plate=machine
plate mail
plate=mark
plate matter
plate metal
plate=mill
plate=paper
plate=piece
plate=planing†
plate=powder
plate=press
plate=printer†
plate=rack
plate=rail
plate=railway
plate=roller†
plate=shears
plate=tracery
plate=vise
plate=warmer†
plate=wheel
platform bridge
platform car
platform carriage
platform crane
platform scales
platform spring
plating=hammer
platinum=black
platinum=lamp
play=acting
play=actor
play=actorism
playbill
play=book

play=day
playfellow
playgame
playgoer†
playground
playhouse
playing=card
playing=passage
play=maker†
playmate
play=right
playroom
plaything
playtime
playwright
play=writer†
pleading=place
pleasant=spirited, etc.
pleasure=ground
pleasure=house
pleasure=train
pleasure=trip
pledge=cup
pledge=ring
plerome=sheath
pleugh=paidle
pleurisy=root
plotting=machine
plotting=scale
plout=net
plover=quail
plover=snipe
plow=beam
plow=bolt
plow=bote
plowboy
plow=clevis
plow=gang
plow=gate
plow=handle
plow=head
plowing=machine
plow=iron
plow=knife
plowland
plowman
plow=point
plow=press
plow=service

plowshare
plowshare=bone
plow=shoe
plow=silver
plow=sock
plow=staff
plow=star
plow=stilt
plow=swain
plow=tail
plow=team
plow=tree
plow=truck
plow=wise
plow=witcher
plowwright
plug=arbor
plug=basin
plug=bayonet
plugboard (a switch-
    board)
plug=cock
plug=finisher†
plugging=forceps
plug hat
plug=hole
plug=joggle
plug=machine
plug=rod
plug=switch
plug=tap
plug=tree
plug=ugly
plug=valve
plumb=bob
plumber=block
plum=bird
plumb=joint
plumb=level
plumb=line
plum=broth
plumb=rule
plum=budder†
plum=cake
plum=color
plum=colored, etc.
plum=curculio
plum duff
plume=alum

plume-bird
plume-holder†
plume-maker†
plume-moth
plume-nutmeg
plume-plucked, etc.
plum-fir
plum-gouger
plum-juice
plum-juniper
plum-loaf
plummer-block
plummer-box
plummet-level
plum-moth
plump-faced, etc.
plum-pig
plum-pit
plum porridge
plum pudding
plum-puddinger
plum-tree
plum-weevil
plunge-bath
plunge-battery
plunge-pole
plunger-bucket
plunger-case
plunger-lift
plunger-piston
plunger-pump
plunging-siphon
plush-copper
plush-stitch
plush velvet
plush velveteen
pock-broken
pocket-book (a book)
pocketbook (a pouch or
    case, also money or
    resources)
pocket-dial
pocket-drop
pocket edition
pocket-flap
pocket-gopher
pocket-hammer
pocket-handkerchief
pocket-judgment

pocket-knife
pocket-lid
pocket-money
pocket-mouse
pocket-net
pocket-piece
pocket-pistol
pocket-rat
pocket-relay
pocket-sheriff
pock-house
pock-mark
pock-marked, etc.
pock-bitten
pock-pudding
pockwood (a tree)
pod-auger
pod-bit
pod-fern
pod-gaper (a mollusk)
pod-lover
pod-pepper
pod-shell
pod-shrimp
pod-thistle
pod-ware
poe-bird
poet-musician
pogy-catcher†
pogy-gull
pointblank
point-circle
point-coördinate
point-equation
pointer dog
point-finder†
point-hole
pointing-machine
pointing-stock
point-lace
point-pair
point-paper
point-rail
pointsman
point-sphere
point-tool
poison-ash
poison-bag
poison-bay

poisonberry
poisonbulb (an herb)
poison-cup
poison-dogwood
poison-elder
poison-fang
poison-gland
poison-hemlock
poison-ivy
poison-nut
poison-oak
poison-organ
poison-pea
poison-plant
poison-sac
poison-sumac
poison-tooth
poison-tower
poison-tree
poison-vine
poisonwood (a tree)
poke-bag
pokeberry
poke bonnet
poke-milkweed
poke-net
pokeroot (a plant, its
    root)
poker-painting
poker-picture
poker-player†
poke-stick
pokeweed
polar-bilocular
polarization-micro-
    scope
polar-plant
polder-land
poleaxe
pole-bean
pole-brackets
pole-burn
polecat
polecatweed
pole-chain
pole-changer†
pole-crab
pole-dab
pole-foot

pole-hammer
pole-head
pole-hook
pole-horse
pole-lathe
pole-mast
pole-net
po'e pad
pole-piece
pole-plate
pole-prop
pole-rack
pole-rush
pole-sling
pole-staff
pole-star
pole-strap
pole-tip
pole-torpedo
pole-vault
pole-vaulting
polewig (a fish)
policeman
police nippers
policy-book
policy-holder†
policy-shop
policy-slip
polishing-bed
polishing-block
polishing-cask
polishing-disk
polishing-hammer
polishing-iron
polishing-jack
polishing-machine
polishing-mill
polishing-paste
polishing-powder
polishing-slate
polishing-snake
polishing-stone
polishing-tin
polishing-wheel
polish-powder
polka-dot
polka gauze
polka-jacket
poll-adze

poll-book
poll-clerk
pollen-brush
pollen-catarrh
pollen-cell
pollen-chamber
pollen-fever
pollen-gland
pollen-grain
pollen-mass
pollen-paste
pollen-sac
pollen-spore
pollen-tube
poll-evil
polling-booth
polling-place
polling-sheriff
polling-station
poll-mad
pollman
poll-pick
poll-suffrage
poll-tax
polt-foot
polyp-colony
polyp-stem
polyp-stock
polystome-fluke
pomme-blanche
pompano-shell
pond-apple
pond-carp
pond-dogwood
pond-fish
pond-hen
pond-lily
pond-mullet
pond-mussel
pond-perch
pond-pickerel
pond-pine
pond-scum
pond-shrimp
pond-snail
pond-spice
pond-turtle
pondweed
pontoon bridge

pontoon-train
pont-volant
ponty-sticker
pony engine
pony-saw
pony-truck
pooh-pooh
pool-ball
pool-player†
pool-room
pool-rush
pool-seller†
pool-snipe
pool-ticket
poona-wood
poonay-oil
poondy-oil
poonga-oil
poon-oil
poonseed-oil
poon-spar
poon-wood
poop-cabin
poop-lantern
poor-box
poor-farm
poorhouse
poor-lights
poor-man-of-mutton
    (Scotch name for
    cold mutton)
poormaster
poor-rate
poor-spirited, etc.
poorwill (a bird)
pop-corn
pop-dock
pope-Joan
pope's-eye*
pope's-head*
pope's-nose*
pop-eyed, etc.
pop-eyes
pop-gun
poplar-birch
poplar-borer (a beetle)
poplar-buds
poplar-dagger (a moth)
poplar-girdler (a beetle)

poplar-gray
poplar-kitten
poplar-leaf
poplar-lutestring
poplar-root
poplar-spinner
poplar-tree
poplar-twig
poppet-head
poppet-valve
popping-crease
poppy-bed
poppy-bee
poppy-bud
poppy-flower
poppy-head
poppy-leaf
poppy-mallow
poppy-oil
poppy-seed
poppy-stem
pop-shop
porcelain-cement
porcelain-clay
porcelain-color
porcelain-crab
porcelain-furnace
porcelain-gilding†
porcelain-jasper
porcelain-lace
porcelain-oven
porcelain-paper
porcupine-crab
porcupine-disease
porcupine-fish
porcupine-grass
porcupine-quill
porcupine-wood
pork-butcher
pork-chop
pork-eater†
pork pie
pork-pit
pork sausage
porkwood (a tree)
porphyry-moth
porphyry-shell
porpoise-oil
porpoise-skin

port-bar
port-bit
port-caustic
port-crayon
porte-acid
porte-bonheur
porte-cochère
porte-drapeau
port-electric, a.
porte-lumière
porte-monnaie
porter-house (a house)
porterhouse steak
port-face
port-fire
port-flange
port-hole
port-hook
port-lanyard
portlast
port-lid
port-lifter†
portman
portman-note
port-mote
port-pendant
portrait-lens
portrait-painter†
portrait-stone
portreeve
port-rope
port-rule
port-sale
port-sash
port-sill
port-stopper†
port-tackle
port-tackle man
port-town
portway
port wine
posing-apparatus
position-finder†
position-micrometer
posset-ale
posset-cup
posset-pot
possum-oak
post-adjutant

postage-stamp
postal card
post-angel
post-bag
post-bill
post bird
post-book
post-box
postboy
post-butt
post-captain
post-card
post-cedar
post-chaise
post-chariot
post-coach
post-day
post-disseizin
post-disseizor
post-drill
post-driver†
postern-door
postern-gate
post-free
post-hackney
post-haste
post-holder†
post-hole
post-horn
post-horse
post-house
postilion-basque
postilion-belt
posting-house
posting-inn
post-jack
post-line
postman
postmark
postmaster
postmaster-general
postmaster-generalship
post-mill
postmistress
post-morning
post-night
post-note
post-oak
post-office

post=paid
post=pocket
post=rider†
post=road
post=stamp
post-time
post-town
post=trader†
posture=maker†
post=wagon
post=windlass
posy=ring
potation-penny
potato=beetle
potato=bing
potato=blight
potato=bread
potato=bug
potato=digger†
potato=disease
potato=eel
potato=fern
potato=fungus
potato=grant
potato=hook
potato=masher†
potato=mould
potato=murrain
potato=oat
potato=oil
potato=onion
potato=pen
potato=peeler†
potato=plant
potato=planter†
potato=rot
potato=scoop
potato=separator†
potato=skin
potato=spirit
potato=starch
potato=sugar
potato=vine
potato=washer†
pot=barley
pot=bellied, etc.
pot=belly (a belly)
potbelly (a person, a
    fish)

pot=boiler
pot=boiling
pot=boy
pot=cake
pot=celt
pot-cheese
potcher=engine
potching=engine
potching=machine
pot=claw
pot-clep
pot=companion
potence=file
pot-eye
pot-fish
pot=fisher†
pot=fisherman
pot=hanger
pot=hat
pothead (a person)
pot=hellion
pot=helmet
pot=herb
pot=hole
pot=hook (a hook)
pothook (a character)
pot=house
pot=hunter†
pot=knight
pot=lace
pot=lead
pot=lid
pot=liquor
pot=luck
pot=man
pot=marigold
pot=metal
pot=miser
pot=paper
potpie
pot=plant
pot=plate
potrack
pot=roast
pot=setting†
potshell
potsherd
pot=shop
pot=shot

pot=stick
pot=still
potstone
potter=wasp
pottery=gauge
pottery=kiln
pottery=painting†
pottery=printing†
pottery=tissue
pottery=tree
pottery=ware
potting=cask
potting=house
potting=stick
pottle=bellied, etc.
pottle=deep
pottle=draught
pot=tree
pot=valiant
pot=valiantry
pot=wabbler†
pot=waller
pot=walloper†
pot=wheel
potwork
pot=works
pot=wrestler†
pouch=bone
pouchet=box
pouchgill (a fish)
pouch=gilled
pouch=hook
pouch=maker†
pouch=mouse
pouch=toad
poult=de=soie
poult=foot
poultice=boot
poultice=shoe
poultry=farm
poultry=feeder†
poultry=house
poultry=yard
pounce=bag
pounce=box
pounce=paper
pouncet=box
pounce=tree
pouncing=machine

pound-boat	powder-room	praise-meeting
pound-breach	powder-scuttle	praiseworthy
pound-cake	powder-shoot	prattlebox (a person)
pound-foolish	power-capstan	prayer-bead
pounding-barrel	power-hammer	prayer-book
pounding-machine	power-house	prayer-carpet
pound-keeper†	power-lathe	prayer-cure
poundman	power-loom	prayer-meeting
poundmaster	power-machine	prayer-mill
pound-net	power-press	prayer-monger
pound-rate	power-user	prayer-rug
pound-scoop	pox-stone	prayer-stick
pound weight	poy-bird	prayer-thong
poundwort	practice-ship	prayer-wheel
pouring-gate	prad-holder†	praying-desk
pouring-hole	prairie-alligator	praying-insect
pouring-stick	prairie-apple	praying-machine
pousse-café	prairie-bean	praying-mantis
pout-net	prairie-bird	praying-wheel
poverty-grass	prairie-bitters	preacher-in-the-pulpit
poverty-plant	prairie-brant	(a plant)
poverty-stricken	prairie-burdock	preaching-cross
poverty-struck	prairie-chicken	prescription-glass
poverty-weed	prairie-clover	presence-chamber
powder-blower	prairie-cocktail	presence-room
powder-box	prairie-dock	present-perfect
powder-cart	prairie-dog	preserve-jar
powder-chamber	prairie-falcon	press-agent
powder-chest	prairie-fly	press-beam
powder-division	prairie-fox	press-bed
powder-down	prairie-goose	press-blanket
powder-flag	prairie-grass	press-blocks
powder-flask	prairie-hawk	press-boards
powder-gun	prairie hen	press-boy
powder-horn	prairie-marmot	press-cake .
powder-hose	prairie-mole	presser-bar
powdering-gown	prairie-oyster	presser-flyer
powdering-mill	prairie-pigeon	presser-foot
powdering-tub	prairie-plover	presser-frame
powder-magazine	prairie-plow	press-gang
powder-man	prairie-rattler	press-girthing
powder-mill	prairie-rattlesnake	pressing-bag
powder-mine	prairie-rose	pressing-board
powder-mixer†	prairie-schooner	pressing-iron
powder-monkey	prairie-snipe	pressing-plate
powder-paper	prairie-squirrel	pressing-roller
powder-post	prairie turnip	press-key
powder-prover†	prairie-warbler	pressman
powder-puff	prairie-wolf	press-mark

press=master
press=money
press=pack
press=pile
press=pin
press=plate
press=printing
press=proof
pressroom
press=stone
pressure=bar
pressure=blower
pressure=figure
pressure=filter
pressure=forging
pressure=frame
pressure=gauge
pressure=note
pressure=register
pressure=screw
pressure=spot
pressure=tone
presswork
press=yeast
prest=money
pretty=grass (a plant)
prettypretty
pretty=spoken, etc.
price=current
price=list
price=tag
prick=eared, etc.
pricking=note
pricking=wheel
prickleback (a fish)
prickle=cell
prickle=fish
prickle=layer
prickle=yellow
pricklouse (a tailor)
prickly=ash
pricklyback (a fish)
prickly=broom
prickly=cedar
prickly=grass
prickly=pear
prickly=pole
prickly=spined, etc.
prickly=withe

prick=me=dainty
prick=post
prick=punch
prickshot
prick=spur
prick=the=garter
prick=the=louse (a
   tailor)
pricktimber (a tree)
prick=wheel
prickwood (a tree)
pride=gavel
pride=of=Barbados (a
   plant)
pride=of=China (a plant)
pride=of=Columbia (a
   plant)
pride=of=India (a plant)
pride=of=London (a
   plant)
pride=of=Ohio (a plant)
prie=dieu
priest=cap
priestcraft
priestfish
priest=ill
priest=monk
priestridden
priest's=crown*
prima=vista
primer=pouch
primer=seizin
prime=staff
priming=horn
priming=iron
priming=machine
priming=powder
priming=tube
priming=wire
primrose=peerless
primrose=willow
prince's=feather*
prince's=pine*
princewood
prinkum=prankum
prinpriddle (a titmouse)
print=broker
print=cloth
print=cutter†

print=field
print=holder†
printing=body
printing=frame
printing=house
printing=ink
printing=machine
printing=office
printing=paper
printing=press
printing=telegraph
printing=type
printing=wheel
print=room
print=seller†
print=shop
print=works
prism=train
prison=bars
prison=base
prison=breach
prison=breaking†
prison=fever
prison ship
prison=van
prittle=prattle
privat=docent
privateersman
privet=hawkmoth
privy=fly
prize=bolt
prize=court
prize=fight
prize=fighter†
prize=list
prizeman
prize=master
prize=money
prize=ring
probate=duty
probe=pointed
probe=scissors
probe=syringe
probing=awl
proboscis=monkey
proboscis=rat
procession=flower
process=server†
produce=broker

produce exchange
produce-merchant
profile-board
profile-cutter†
profile-paper
profile-piece
profiling-machine
profit-sharing†
promise-breach
promise-breaker†
promise-crammed, etc.
prompt-book
prompt-centre
prompt-note
prompt-side
prongbuck (an antelope)
prong-chuck
prongdoe (female of the prongbuck)
prong-hoe
pronghorn (the prongbuck)
proof-armor
proof-galley
proof-glass
proof-house
proof-leaf
proof-mark
proof-paper
proof-plane
proof-press
proof-print
proof-printer†
proof-reader†
proof-sheet
proof-spirit
proof-staff
proof-stick
proof-text
propagating-bench
propagating-box
propagating-glass
propagating-house
propeller-engine
propeller-mower
propeller-pump
propeller-shaft
propeller-well

propeller-wheel
property-man
property-master
property-plot
property-room
property tax
prophecy-monger
prophetflower (a plant)
prop-joint
prop-stay
prop-wood
prose-man
prose-writer†
protocol-book
proto-compound
protracting-bevel
prott-goose
proud-hearted, etc.
proving-ground
proving-hut
proving-machine
proving-press
proving-pump
provision-car
provision-dealer†
provision-merchant
proxy-wedded, etc.
prune-purple
prune-tree
pruning-chisel
pruning-hook
pruning-knife
pruning-saw
pruning-shears
pruning-tools
psalm-book
psalm-melodicon
psalm-singing†
psalm-tone
public-hearted, etc
puckball
pudding-bag
pudding-cloth
pudding-faced, etc
pudding-fish
pudding-grass
puddinghead (a person)
pudding-pie
pudding-sleeve

pudding-stone
pudding-time
pudding-wife
puddle-ball
puddle-bar
puddle-duck
puddle-poet
puddle-rolls
puddling-furnace
puddling-machine
puddling-rolls
puff-adder
puffball
puff-bird
puff-box
puffer-pipe
puff-fish
puffing adder
puffing pig
puff-netting
puff-paste
pug-dog
pug-faced, etc.
pug-mill
pug-nose (a nose)
pugnose (an eel)
pug-piles
pug-piling
puka-puka
pukeweed
puking-fever
pulas-oil
pulas-tree
pulk-hole
pullback, n.
pull-cock
pull-devil
pull-down
pulley-block
pulley-box
pulley-check
pulley-clutch
pulley-drum
pulley-frame
pulley-mortise
pulley-sheave
pulley-shell
pulley-stand
pulley-stone

pulley-wheel
pulling-jack
pulling-out
pull-iron
pull-off
pull-over
pull-piece
pull-pipes
pull-to
pulp-boiler†
pulp-cavity
pulp-colors
pulp-digester†
pulp-dresser†
pulp-engine
pulp-grinder†
pulping-machine
pulp-machine
pulp-meter
pulp-mill
pulp-strainer†
pulp-washer†
pulque brandy
pulse-beat
pulse-curve
pulse-glass
pulse-rate
pulse-warmer†
pulse-wave
pulverizing-mill
pulza-oil
pumice-stone
pumie-stone
pump-barrel
pump-bit
pump-bob
pump-bolt
pump-box
pump-brake
pump-cart
pump-chain
pump-cistern
pump-coat
pump-dale
pump-gear
pump-handle
pump-head
pump-hood
pump-house

pumping-engine
pumping-haft
pump-kettle
pumpkinhead (a per-
    son)
pumpkin-plant
pumpkin-seed (a seed)
pumpkinseed (a fish,
    etc.)
pumpkin-vine
pump-lug
pump-piston
pump-plunger
pump-room
pump-scraper†
pump-spear
pump-staff
pump-stock
pump-stopper
pump-thunder
pump-well
puna-wind
punch-bowl
punch-check
punch-cutter†
punch-glass
punch-house
punching-bag
punching-bear
punching-machine
punching-press
punch-jug
punch-ladle
punch-pliers
punch-prop
punctate-striate
punctate-sulcate
punk-oak
punt-fishing†
punt-gun
puntsman
punty-rod
pupil-teacher
puppetman
puppetmaster
puppet-play
puppet-player
puppet-show
puppet-valve

puppy-dog
puppy-fish
puppy-headed, etc.
purchase-block
purchase-fall
purchase-money
purchase-shears
purge-cock
purging-agaric
purging-cassia
purging-cock
purging-flax
purging-nut
purification-flower
purl-goods
purl-house
purlin-post
purlman
purple-egg (sea-urchin)
purple-fish
purpleheart (a tree, its
    wood)
purpleclip (an orchid)
purple-marbled, etc.
purplewood (a tree, its
    wood)
purplewort
purple-wreath (a plant)
purpose-like
purre-maw
purse-bearer†
purse-boat
purse-clasp
purse-crab
purse-crew
purse-cutter†
purse-davit
purse-gang
purse-gill
purse-gilled, etc.
purse-leech
purse-line
purse-mouth
purse-net
pursenet-fish
purse-pride
purse-proud
purse-ring
purse-rope

purse=seine
purse=seiner†
purse=silk
purse=snap
purse=spider
purse=strings
purse=taking†
purse=twist
purse=weight
pursing=block
pursing=gear
pursing=line
purslane=tree
purslane=worm
push=button
push=car
push=hoe
push=hole

pushing=jack
push=pick
push=pin
puss=clover
puss=gentleman
puss=moth
pusstail (a grass)
pussy=cat
pussy=willow
putlog
putlog=hole
put=off
put=pin
putting=green
putting=stone
putty=eye
putty=faced, etc.
putty=knife

putty=powder
puttyroot
putty=work
put=up
puzzle=cup
puzzlehead (a person)
puzzle=headed, etc.
puzzle=jug
puzzle=lock
puzzle=monkey
puzzle=peg
puzzle=ring
pye=powder
pygmyweed
pyramid=shell
pyx=cloth
pyx=kerchief
pyx=veil

Q

qua-bird
quack-grass
quacksalver
quadrant-compass
quail-call
quail-dove
quail-mutton
quail-pigeon
quail-pipe
quail-snipe
quake-grass
quaker-bird
Quaker-color
quaker-grass
quaker-moth
quaketail (a bird)
quaking-grass
quality-binding
quamash-rat
quantity-culture
quantity-fuse
quarrel-pane
quarrel-picker†
quarry-faced, etc.
quarry-hawk
quarrying-machine
quarryman
quarry-slave
quarry-stone
quarry-water
quarter-angled, etc.
quarter-aspect
quarter-back
quarter-badge
quarter-bend
quarter-bill
quarter-bitts
quarter-blanket
quarter-blocks
quarter-board

quarter-boat
quarter-boot
quarter-boys
quarter-bred
quarter-cask
quarter-cast
quarter-cloth
quarter-day
quarter-deck
quarter-decker
quarter-evil
quarter-face
quarter-fast
quarter-fishes
quarter-franc
quarter-gallery
quarter-grain
quarter-guard
quarter-gunner
quarter-hollow
quarter-horse
quarter-ill
quartering-belt
quartering-block
quartering-hammer
quartering-machine
quarter-iron
quarterland
quarter-light
quarter-line
quartermaster
quartermaster-general
quartermaster-sergeant
quarter-netting
quartern-loaf
quarter-noble
quarter note
quarter-pace
quarter-partition
quarter-pieces

quarter plate
quarter-point
quarter-rail
quarter rest
quarter-round
quarter-saver
quarter-seal
quarter-section
quarter-sessions
quarter-sights
quarter-sling .
quarter-square
quarter-staff
quarter-stanchion
quarter-stuff
quarter-tackle
quarter-timber
quarter-tone
quarter-trap
quarter-turn
quarter-undulation
quarter-vine
quarter-waiter
quarter-watch
quarter-wind
quarter-yard
quartz-crusher†
quartz-liquefier†
quartz-mill
quartz-porphyry
quartz-reef
quartz-rock
quartz-sinter
quartz-trachyte
quartz-vein
quashy-quasher
quassia-tree
quaver rest
quay-berth
queen-apple

queen bee
queen=cell
queen=conch
queencraft
Queen=day
queen dowager
queenfish
queen=gold
queen=lily
queen mother
queen=of=the=meadows
   (a plant)
queen=of=the=prairie (a
   plant)
queen=post
queen's=arm*
queen's=delight*
queen's=flower*
queen's=lily*
queen's=metal*
queen's=pigeon*
queen's=root*
queen=stitch
queen's=ware*
queen's=yellow*
queen=truss
queez=madam
quenching=tub
quercitron=bark

quercitron=oak
quernstone
quick=beam
quick=eyed, etc.
quick=grass
quickhatch
quick=hedge
quick=in=hand
quicklime
quick=march
quick=match
quicksand
quickset
quicksilver
quicksilver=furnace
quickstep
quickwood (hawthorn)
quick=work (part of
   a ship)
quieting=chamber
quillai=bark
quillback (a fish)
quill=bit
quill=coverts
quill=driver†
quill=feather
quill nib
quill pen
quilltail (a duck)

quill=turn
quill=work
quillwort
quilting=bee
quilting=cotton
quilting=frame
quince=essence
quince=juice
quince=seed
quince=tree
quince wine
quink=goose
quinsy=berry
quinsywort
quintuple=nerved, etc.
quirk=float
quirking=plane
quitch=grass
quitclaim
quitclaimance
quit=rent
quiver=tree
quiz=class
quiz=master
quizzing=glass
quoin=post
quoit=player†
quotation=mark
quoteworthy

R

rabbet=joint
rabbet=plane
rabbet=saw
rabbetting=machine
rabbitberry
rabbit=brush
rabbitear (an oyster)
rabbit=eared, etc.
rabbit=fish
rabbit=hutch
rabbit=moth
rabbit=rat
rabbitroot (a plant)
rabbit=spout
rabbit=squirrel
rabbit=warren
rabble=fish
raccoonberry
raccoon=dog
raccoon=oyster
raccoon=perch
race=card
race=cloth
race=course
race=cup
race=ginger
race=ground
race=horse
race=knife
race=meeting
race=plate
race=saddle
race=track
raceway
racing=bell
racing=bit
racing=calendar
rackabones (a lean person or animal)
rackapelt (a person)

rackarock (an explosive)
rack=bar
rack=block
rack=calipers
rack=car
rack=compass
racket=court
racket=ground
rackettail (a bird)
racket=tailed, etc.
rack=hook
racking=can
racking=cock
racking=crook
racking=faucet
racking=pump
racking=table
rack=pin
rack=rail
rack=railway
rack=rent
rack=renter†
rack=saw
rack=stick
ruck=tail
rackwork
raddle=hedge
radiate=veined, etc.
radius=bar
radius=rod
radius=saw
raffle=net
raffling=net
raff=merchant
raft=breasted, etc.
raft=dog
raft=duck
rafter=bird
rafting=dog

raft=like
raft=merchant
raft=port
raft=rope
raftsman
ragabash
ragamuffin
rag=bolt
rag=bush
rag=cutting†
rag=dust
rag=duster†
rag=engine
rag=fair
ragged=lady (a plant)
ragged=robin (a plant)
ragged=sailor (a plant)
ragged=school
ragged=staff (an animalcule)
ragging=frame
ragging=hammer
rag=knife
rag=looper†
ragman
ragpicker†
rag=shop
rag=sorter†
ragstone
rag=tag
rag=turnsol
ragweed
rag=wheel
rag=wool
rag=work
ragworm
ragwort
rail=bender†
rail=bird
rail=bittern

rail=board
rail=borer
rail=brace
rail=chair
rail=clamp
rail=coupling†
rail=drilling
rail=guard
railing=post
rail=jack
rail=joint
rail=key
rail=post
rail=punch
railroad
railroad=car
railroad company
railroad=worm
rail=saw
rail=snipe
rail=splitter†
rail=straightening†
railway
railway=carriage
railway=chair
railway company
railway crossing
railway=frog
railway=slide
railway=stitch
railway=switch
railway=tie
railway=train
rainball
rainband
rainbird
rainbow
rainbow=agate
rainbow darter
rainbow=fish
rainbow-hued, etc.
rainbow quartz
rainbow trout
rainbow=worm
rainbow wrasse
rain=box
rain=chamber
rain=chart
rain=cloud

rain=crow
rain=doctor
rain=door
rain=drop
rainfall
rainfall=chart
rain=fowl
rain=gauge
rain=goose
rain=maker†
rain=map
rain=paddock
rain=pie
rainpour
rain=print
rain=proof
rain=quail
rain=storm
rain=tight
rain=tree
rain=wash
rain=water
raising=bee
raising=board
raising=gig
raising=hammer
raising=knife
raising=piece
raising=plate
raisin=seed
raisin=tree
raisin wine
rake=dredge
rake=head
rakehell, a. and n.
rake=vein
raking=piece
rallying=point
ram=bow
ram=cat
ram=goat
ram=head
ram=headed, etc.
ramie=fibre
ramie=plant
ram=line
rampart=grenade
rampart=slope
rampsman

ram=riding
ramrod
ramrod=bayonet
ramshackle
ram's=head*
ram's=horn*
ramskin
ram=stag
ram=stam
ranch=house
ranchman
randall=grass
randan=gig
randing=machine
randing=tool
randle=balk
randle=bar
randle=tree
range=finder†
range=heads
range=lights
range=stove
range=table
ranging=rod
rank=axis
rank=curve
rank=plane
rank=point
rank=radiant
rank=scented, etc.
rank=surface
rannel=balk
ransom=bill
ransom=free
rantle=tree
ran=tree
rape=butterfly
rape=cake
rape=oil
rape=seed
rape=wine
rap=full
rapier=fish
rarebit
rarce=show
`rareripe
rascal=like
rasing=iron
rasing=knife

raspberry
raspberry-borer
raspberry-bush
rasp-house
rasping-machine
rasping-mill
rasp-palm
rasp-pod
rasp-punch
ratan cane
ratany-root
rat-catcher†
ratchet-brace
ratchet-burner
ratchet-coupling
ratchet-drill
ratchet-jack
ratchet-lever
ratchet-pedal
ratchet-post
ratchet-punch
ratchet-rifling
ratchet-wheel
ratchet-wrench
rate-book
ratepayer†
rate-tithe
ratfish
rat-goose
rat-hare
rat-hole
rating-instrument
ration-money
rat-kangaroo
ratline-stuff
rat-mole
rat-pit
rat-poison
ratsbane
rat-snake
rat's-tail*
rat-tail (a tail)
rattail (fish, horse,
   plant)
rat-tailed, etc.
rat-terrier
rattlebags (an herb)
rattle-barrel
rattle-box (a toy)

rattlebox (a plant)
rattlebrain (a person)
rattle-brained, etc.
rattlebush (a plant)
rattlecap (a person)
rattlehead (a person)
rattlepate (a person)
rattleskull (a person)
rattlesnake
rattlesnake-fern
rattlesnake-grass
rattlesnake-herb
rattlesnake-master
rattlesnake-plantain
rattlesnake-root
rattlesnake-weed
rattletrap (a shaky
   object)
rattleweed
rattlewing (a duck)
rattlewort
rat-trap
rave-hook
ravel-bread
ravelling-engine
raven-cockatoo
raven's-duck*
ravenstone (a gallows)
ravine-deer
raw-boned, etc.
rawhead (a bugbear)
rawhide
raw-port
raw-pot
ray-floret
ray-flower
ray-grass
ray-oil
razorback (a fish, a
   hog)
razor-backed, etc.
razorbill (a bird)
razor-blade (blade of a
   razor)
razorblade (an oyster)
razor-clam
razor-fish
razor-grass
razor-grinder†

razor-hone
razor-paper
razor-paste
razor-shell
razor-stone
razor-strop
reaching-post
reach-me-down, a.
reaction-period
reaction-time
reaction-wheel
reading-book
reading-boy
reading-desk
reading-glass
reading-lamp
reading-matter
reading-pew
reading-room
reading-stand
reading-table
ready-made
ready-man
ready-pole
ready-reckoner
real-school
reamer-bit
reaming-iron
ream-kit
reap-hook
reaping-hook
reaping-machine
rear-admiral
rear-guard
rearhorse
rearing-bit
rearing-box
reason-piece
rebolting-machine
receipt-book
receiving-house
receiving-magnet
receiving-office
receiving-ship
receiving-tomb
receiving-vault
reception-room
recitation-room
reciting-note

reckoning=book
reckoning=penny
reclamation=plow
reclining=board
reclining=chair
recoil=check
recoil=escapement
recoil=pallet
recoil=wave
record=office
recreation=ground
recruiting=ground
recruiting=party
recruiting=sergeant
redback (a bird)
red=backed, etc.
red bass
redbeard (a red sponge)
redbelly (a terrapin, etc.)
redberry (a plant)
redbird
redbreast (a bird)
redbuck (an antelope)
redbud (a tree)
redbug (an insect)
redcap (a finch, a hen)
red=carpet (a moth)
red=chestnut (a moth)
redcoat (a person)
red cod
red=cross, a.
red cusk
red dace
redding=comb
redding=straik
reddleman
red=dog (flour)
red drum
redecraft
rededge (a mollusk)
redeye (a fish)
red fender
red fighter
redfin (a fish)
redfish
red=green
red=gum (a disease, a tree)

red=hand
redhead (a person, a duck, etc.)
redhorn (an insect)
red=horse (a fish)
red=hot
redknees (a plant)
red=lac (a tree)
redlegs (a bird, a plant)
red=letter, a.
redman (a fish)
red metal
red=morocco (a plant)
red=mouth, a.
redmouth (a fish)
red oak
red=paidle
redpoll (a bird)
redribbon (a fish)
red=robin (a fungus)
redroot (a plant)
redsear, v.
redseed (small crustaceans)
redshank (a bird, a person)
redshanks (a plant)
redshare, v.
red=short
red=shortness
redsides (a fish)
redskin (a person)
red spider
red=staff (a straight=edge)
redstart (a bird)
redstreak (an apple, cider)
red=tail, a.
redtail (a buzzard)
red=tape, a.
red=tapery
red=tapism
red=tapist
red thrush
redtop (a grass)
red=tubs (a gurnard)
reducing=coupling
reducing=furnace

reducing=press
reducing=scale
reducing=T
reducing=valve
reduction=compasses
reduction=formula
reduction=works
red=underwing (a moth)
redware (a seaweed)
red=wat, a.
red=water (a disease of cattle)
red=water tree
redweed
red=whelk
redwing (a bird)
red=withe
redwood (a tree)
reedbird
reedbuck
reed=bunting
reed=grass
reed=instrument
reed=knife
reed=mace
reed=mote
reed=moth
reed=motion
reed=organ
reed=palm
reed=pheasant
reed=pipe
reed=pit
reed=plane
reed=sparrow
reed=stop
reed=thrush
reed=tussock
reed=wainscot
reed=warbler
reed=work
reed=wren
reef=band
reef=builder†
reef=cringle
reef=earing
reef=goose
reefing=beckets

reefing-jacket
reefing-point
reef-jig
reef-jigger
reef-knot
reef-line
reef-oyster
reef-pendant
reef-point
reef-sponge
reef-squid
reef-tackle
reel-band
reel-bed
reel-check
reel-click
reel-cotton
reel-holder†
reeling-machine
reel-keeper†
reel-line
reel-oven
reel-seat
reel-stand
reeming-beetle
reeming-iron
refining-furnace
refining-hearth
reflux-valve
refrigerating-chamber
refrigerating-machine
refrigerator-car
regard-ring
regenerator-furnace
regent-bird
regent-oriole
register-grate
register-office
register-plate
register-point
registrar-general
reglet-plane
regulating-screw
regulating-valve
regulator-box
regulator-cock
regulator-cover
regulator-lever
regulator-shaft

reheating-furnace
reindeer-lichen
reindeer-moss
reinforce-band
reinforce-rings
rein-holder†
rein-hook
rein-orchis
rein-slide
reinsman
rein-snap
release-spring
relic-knife
relic-monger
relief-engraving†
relief-map
relief-perspective
relief-valve
relief-work
relieving-tackle
relishing-machine
remainder-man
rendering-pan
rendering-tank
rendle-balk
rendrock
rennet-bag
rennet-ferment
rennet-whey
rennet-wine
rent-arrear
rent-charge
rent-day
renter-warden
rent-free
rent-roll
rent-seck
rent-service
repair-shop
replacing-switch
repressing-machine
repressing-press
request-note
request programme
requiem-mass
rerebrace
rere-brake
resawing-machine
rescue-grass

resin-bush
resin-cell
resin-duct
resin-flux
resin-gland
resin-passage
resin-tube
resistance-box
resistance-coil
resist-work
resonance-box
resorcinol-phthalein
responde-book
restaurant-car
rest-cure
rest-harrow
resting-cell
resting-owing
resting-place
resting-sporangium
resting-spore
resting-stage
resting-state
result-fee
resurrection-man
resurrection-plant
retain-wall
reticulate-veined
retort-holder
retort-house
retort-scaler
retouching-desk
retouching-easel
retouching-frame
retouching-table
return-alkali
return-ball
return-bead
return-bend
return cargo
return check
return-crease
return-day
returning-board
returning-officer
return match
return-piece
return-shock
return tag

return ticket	ribbon=stamp	richel=bird
return=valve	ribbon=tree	rich=left
revenue=officer	ribbon=wave	rickrack
reversing=cylinder	ribbonweed	rick=stand
reversing=gear	ribbon=wire	rickyard
reversing=layer	ribbonwood (a tree)	riddle=cake
reversing=lever	ribbonworm	riddle=like
reversing=machine	rib=faced, etc.	ride=officer
reversing=motion	rib=grass	rider=roll
reversing=shaft	rib=like	ridge=band
reversing=valve	rib=piece	ridge=beam
rhea=fibre	rib=roast	ridge=drill
rhea=grass	rib=roaster†	ridge=fillet
Rhein=berry	rib=stitch	ridge=harrow
rhinoceros=auk	rib=vaulting	ridge=hoe
rhinoceros=beetle	ribwort	ridge=piece
rhinoceros=bird	rice=bird	ridge=plate
rhinoceros=bush	rice=bunting	ridge=plow
rhinoceros=chameleon	rice=corn	ridge=pole
rhinoceros=hornbill	rice=drill	ridge=roof
rhinoceros=tick	rice=dust	ridge=rope
rhodes=wood	rice=embroidery	ridge=stay
rhodium=gold	rice=field	ridge=tile
rhodium=wood	rice=flour	ridging=grass
rhomb=solid	riceflower (a plant)	ridging=plow
rhomb=spar	rice=glue	riding=bitts
rhubarb=root	rice=grain	riding=boot
rhumb=line	rice=hen	riding=day
rhumb=sailing	rice=huller†	riding=glove
rib=band	rice=meal	riding=graith
rib=baste	rice=milk	riding=habit
ribbing=nail	rice=mill	riding=hood
ribble=rabble	rice=paper	riding=light
ribbon=bordering	rice=plantation	riding=master
ribbon=brake	rice=planter†	riding=robe
rib=bone	rice=pounder†	riding=rod
ribbon=fish	rice pudding	riding=sail
ribbon=grass	rice=rat	riding=school
ribbon gurnard	rice=shell	riding=skirt
ribbon iron	rice soup	riding=suit
ribbon=line	rice=sower†	riding=whip
ribbon=loom	rice=stitch	riesel=iron
Ribbonman	rice=stone .	riffle=bars
ribbon=map	rice=sugar	riffraff
ribbon=pattern	rice=tenrec	rifle=ball
ribbon=register	rice=troopial	rifle=bird
ribbon=saw	rice=water	rifle=corps
ribbon=seal	rice=weevil	rifleman
ribbon=snake	rice wine	rifleman=bird

rifle-pit
rifle-range
rifle-shell
rifle-shot
rifling-machine
rifling-tool
rigging-cutter†
rigging-loft
rigging-screws
rigging-tree
right-about
right-angled, right-
   drawn, etc.
right-edge
right-hand, a.
right-hander
right-whaler†
rig-out
rill-mark
rime-frost
rime-frosted
rime-letter
rim-fire
rim-line
rim-lock
rim-planer†
rim-rock
rim-saw
rim-stock
rinderpest
rind-gall
rind-grafting†
rind-layer
ring armature
ring armor
ring-banded, etc.
ring-bark
ring-barker†
ringbill (a duck)
ring-bird
ring-bit
ring-blackbird
ring-bolt
ring-bone (bony callus)
ringbone (a disease)
ring-boot
ring-brooch
ring-bunting
ring-bush

ring-canal
ring-carrier
ring-chuck
ring-cross
ring-dial
ring-dog
ring-dotterel
ring-dove
ring-dropper†
ringed-arm (an echino-
   derm)
ringed-carpet (a moth)
ring fence
ring-finger
ringfish
ring-fowl
ring-frame
ring-gauge
ring-handle
ring-head
ring-hedge
ringing-engine
ringing out
ring-joint
ring-keeper†
ringleader
ringlestone
ring-lock
ring-locket
ring mail
ring-mallet
ringman
ringmaster
ring-money
ring-mule
ringneck (a plover, a
   duck)
ring-net
ring-ouzel
ring-parrot
ring-perch
ring-plain
ring-plover
ring-rope
ringsail
ring-saw
ring-small
ring-snake
ring-sparrow

ring-spinner
ring-stand
ring-stopper
ringtail (a bird, a sail)
ring-throstle
ring-thrush
ring-time
ring-tongue
ring-top
ring tumbler
ring valve
ring-vortex
ring-wad
ring-wall
ringwork
ringworm
ringworm-root
ringworm-shrub
rinsing-machine
rin-thereout
rip-fishing
ripping-bed
ripping-chisel
ripping-iron
ripping-saw
ripple-barrel
ripple-grass
ripple-mark
ripple-marked
ripsack
rip-saw
rise-bush
rise-dike
riser-pipe
rise-wood
rising-anvil
rising-line
rising-main
rising-rod
rising-seat
rising-square
rising-wood
ritt-master
rival-hating
river-bank
river-bass
river-bed
river-birch
river-bottom

river=bullhead
river=carp
river=chub
river=crab
river=craft
river=crawfish
river=dolphin
river=dragon
river=driver
river=duck
river=flat
river=god
riverhead
river=hog
river=horse
river=jack
river=lamprey
river=limpet
river=man
river=meadow
river=mussel
river=otter
river=perch
river=pie
river=plain
river=shrew
riverside
river=snail
river=swallow
river=terrace
river=tortoise
river=turtle
river=wall
river=water
riverweed
river=weight
river=wolf
rivet=clipper†
rivet=cutter†
rivet=hearth
rivet=joint
rivet=knob
rivet=machine
rivetting=bur
rivetting=forge
rivetting=hammer
rivetting=machine
rivetting=plates
rivetting=set

rivetting=tools
riving=knife
riving=machine
rivulet=tree
rix=dollar
roach=backed, etc.
roach=dace
road=agent
road=bed
road=book
road=car
road=drift
road=harrow
road=level
road=leveller†
road=locomotive
road=machine
road=maker†
roadman
road=measurer†
road=metal
road=plow
road=roller†
road=runner†
road=scraper†
roadside
roadsman
roadstead
road=steamer
road=sulky
road=surveyor
roadway
roadweed
road=work
roadworthy
roan=tree
roast=bitter
roaster=slag
roasting=bed
roasting=cylinder
roasting=ear
roasting=furnace
roasting=jack
roasting=kiln
roasting=oven
· roast=stall
rob=altar
robber=crab
robber=fly

robber-gull
robe=de=chambre
robe=maker†
robin=accentor
robin=breast
robin=dipper
robing=room
robin redbreast
robin ruddock
robin=run=in=the=hedge
(a plant)
robin=sandpiper
robin=snipe
robin's=plantain*
robin's=rye*
robin=wheat
roching=cask
rock alum
rock=alyssum
rock=badger
rock=barnacle
rock=basin
rock=bass
rock=beauty
rock=bird
rock=blackbird
rock=borer
rock=bound
rock=brake
rock=breaker†
rock=butter :
rock=candy
rock=cavy
rock=cist
rock=cod
rock=cook
rock=cork
rock=crab
rock=cress
rock=crowned, etc.
rock=crusher†
rock=crystal
Rock day
rock=demon
rock=dolphin
rock=dove
rock=drill
rock=drilling†
rock=duck

rock=eel
rock=elm
rocker=cam
rocker=shaft
rocker=sleeve
rocket=bird
rocket=case
rocket=drift
rocket=harpoon
rocket=larkspur
rock=falcon
rock=fever
rock=fire
rockfish
rock=flint
rock=flour
rock=gas
rock=goat
rock=goose
rock=hair (a lichen)
rock=harmonicon
rock=hawk
rock=head
rock=hopper†
rocking=bar
rocking=beam
rocking=chair
rocking=horse
rocking pier
rocking shaft
rocking=tree
rock=kangaroo
rock=kelp
rock=knotweed
rock=lark
rock=leather
rock=lever
rock=lily
rock=limpet
rock=lintie
rock=lobster
rock=lychnis
rock=manikin
rock=maple
rock=meal
rock=milk
rock=moss
rock=mouse
rock=nosing

rock=oil
rock=ousel
rock=oyster
rock=parrakeet
rock=pigeon
rock=pipit
rock=plant
rock=plover
rock=ptarmigan
rock=pulverizer†
rock=punch
rock=rabbit
rock=rat
rock=rose
rock=ruby
rock=salmon
rock salt
rock=samphire
rock=scorpion
rock=seal
rock=serpent
rock=shaft
rock=shell .
rock=shrike
rock=slater
rock=snake
rock=snipe
rock=soap
rock=sparrow
rock=staff
rock=starling
rock=sturgeon
rock=sucker
rock=swallow
rock=swift
rock=tar
rock=temple
rock=thrush
rock=tools
rock=tripe
rock=trout
rock=turquoise
rock=violet
rock=warbler
rock=water
rockweed
rock=winkle
rock=wood
rockwork

rock=wren
rod=bacterium
rod=bayonet
rod=chisel
rod=coupling
roddin=tree
rod=end
rod=fish
rod=fisher†
rod=fructification
rod=granule
rod=holder†
rod=iron
rod=line
rod=machine
rodman
rod=planer†
rod=ring
rodsman
rodwood (a shrub or
    tree)
roebuck (a deer)
roebuck=berry
roe=deer
roe=fish
roe=stone
rogation=flower (a
    plant)
rogue=house
roll=about
roll=boiling
roll=box
roll=call
roll=cumulus
roller=bar
roller=barrow
roller=bearing
roller=bird
roller=board
roller=bowl
roller=box
roller=composition
roller=die
roller=flag
roller=forks
roller=gin
roller=grip
roller=lift
roller=mill

roller=mould
roller=skate
roller=stock
roller=stop
roller=towel
rollyway
rolling=barrel
rolling=chock
rolling=cleat
rolling=dam
rolling=frame
rolling=machine
rolling=mill
rolling=pin
rolling=plant
rolling=press
rolling=rope
rolling=stock
rolling=tackle
roll=joint
roll=lathe
roll=moulding
roll=top
roll=train
roll=up
rollway
roly=poly
rood=arch
rood=altar
rood=beam
rood=free
rood=loft
rood=screen
rood=spire
rood=steeple
rood=tower
roof=cell
roof=gradation
roof=guard
roofing=felt
roofing=machine
roofing=paper
roofing=slate
roof=like
roof=nucleus
roof=plate
roof=rat
roof=shaped, etc.
roof=staging

roof=stay
rooftree
roof=truss
room=keeper†
roommate
room=paper
room=ridden
roomstead
roosa=oil
roost=cock
root=alcohol
root=bark
root=barnacle
root beer
root=book
root=borer†
root=bound
root=breaker†
root=bruiser†
root=built
root=cap
root=cellar
root=drop
root=digger†
root=eater†
rootfast
root-fibril
root-footed, etc.
root=forceps
root=form
root=grafting
root=grinder†
root=hair
root house (made of
    roots)
root=house (to store
    roots)
root=knot
root=leaf
root=loop
root=louse
root=parasite
root=pressure
root=pulper†
root=sheath
rootstock
root=tree
root=vole
root=washer†

root=wood
root=zone
rooye=bok
rope=band
ropebark (a shrub)
rope=clamp
rope=clutch
rope=cord
rope=dancer†
rope=drilling†
rope=elevator
rope=end
rope=grass
rope=house
rope=machine
rope=maker†
rope=pattern
rope=porter
rope=pull
rope=pulling†
rope=pump
rope=railway
rope=ripe
rope=roll
rope=runner†
rope's=end, v.
rope=shaped, etc.
rope=socket
rope=spinner†
rope=stitch
rope=trick
ropewalk
rope=walker†
ropeway
rope=winch
ropework
rope=yarn
roping=needle
roping=palm
roquet croquet
rosary=plant
rosary=shell
rose=acacia
rose=aniline
rose=aphis
rose=apple
rose=back
rose=bay
roseberry

rose=bit
rose=blanket
rosebone (a fish)
rose=box
rose=breasted, etc.
rosebud
rose=bug
rose burner
rose=bush
rose=camphor
rose=campion
rose=carnation
rose=catarrh
rose=chafer
rose=cold
rose=color
rose=comb
rose=copper
rose=cross
rose=cut
rose=drop
rose=ear
rose=encrinite
rose=engine
rose=festival
rose=fever
rosefish
rose=fly
rose=flycatcher
rose=gall
rose=geranium
rose=haw
rose=house
rose=knot
rose=lashing
rose=lathe
rose=leaf
rose=lip
rosella=fibre
rose=mallow
rose=maloes
rosemary=moorwort
rosemary=pine
rose moulding
rose=money
rose=nail
rose=noble
rose=of=heaven (a plant)
rose=oil

rose=ouzel
rose=parrakeet
rose=pink
rose=point
rose=quartz
rose=rash
rose=red
roseroot (a plant)
rose=rowel
rose=ryal
rose=sawfly
rose=slug
rose=steel
rose=tanager
rose=tangle
rose=topaz
rose=tree
rosetta=wood
rosette burner
rosette=cell
rosette=copper
rosette=cutter†
rosette=plate
rose=vinegar
rose=water
rose=willow
rose window
rosewood
rosewood=oil
rose=worm
rosewort
rose=yard
rosin=oil
rosin=plant
rosin soap
rosin=tin
rosinweed
rossing=machine
rosy=bosomed, etc.
rosy=drop (a disease)
rosy=footman (a moth)
rosy=marsh (a moth)
rosy=rustic (a moth)
rosy=wave (a moth)
rotate=plane
rotating=ring
rotation=area
rote=song
rot=grass

rotgut
rother=beast
rothermuck
rother=nail
rother=soil
rot=steep
rotten=egg, v.
rottenstone
rotund=ovate
rotund=pointed
rouelle=guard
rouge=berry
rouge=dish
rouge=et=noir
rouge=plant
rouge=pot
rouge=powder
rough=backed, etc.
rough=bore, v.
rough=cast, v.
rough=caster†
rough=clad
rough=cull, v.
rough=dab, v.
rough=draft, v.
rough=draw, v.
rough=dry
rough=grind, v.
roughhead (a lizard, a
 fish)
rough=hew, v.
rough=hewer†
rough=hound
roughing=drill
roughing=hole
roughing=lathe
roughing=mill
roughing=rolls
roughleg (a hawk)
rough=perfect
rough=rider
rough=scuff
rough=setter
roughshod
rough=slant, v.
rough=spun
rough=string, v.
rough stuff
roughtail (a snake)

rough=tree
roughwing (a moth, a
  bird)
rough=work, v.
rounce=handle
roundabout
round=all
round=arched, etc.
round=arm, a.
round=bend, a.
roundfish
roundhand
Roundhead
roundhouse
rounding=adze
rounding=gauge
rounding=jack
rounding=machine
rounding=out
rounding=plane
rounding=tool
round=iron
roundmouth (a fish)
roundsman
roundstone (cobble-
  stone)
round=up
roundworm
roun=tree
rout=cake
router=gauge
router=out
router=plane
router=saw
route=step
routing=machine
routing=tool
rove=beetle
rover=beetle
roving=frame
roving=head
roving=machine
roving=plate
roving=reel
rowan=berry
rowan=tree
rowboat
row=cloth
rowel=head

rowelling=needle
rowelling=scissors
rowel=spur
rowet=work
rowing=feather
rowing=gear
rowlock
row=marker
row=port
royalmast
royal=yard
rubber=file
rubber=gauge
rubber=knife
rubber=mould
rubber=saw
rubber=tree
rubber=vine
rubbing=batten
rubbing=bed
rubbing=block
rubbing=machine
rubbing=punch
rubbing=post
rubbing=stone
rubbish=heap
rubbish=pulley
rubble=ice
rubble=stone
rubble=walling
rubblework
rub=iron
rübsen=cake
rubstone
ruby=blende
ruby=copper
ruby=crowned, etc.
ruby=mica
rubytail (a wasp)
ruby=tiger (a moth)
rubywood (a tree)
rudder=band
rudder=brace
rudder=brake
rudder=breeching
rudder=case
rudder=chain
rudder=chock
rudder=coat

rudder=duck
rudder=feather
rudder=fish
rudder=hanger
rudder=head
rudder=hole
rudder=iron
rudder=nail
rudder=pendant
rudder=perch
rudder=port
rudder=post
rudder=stock
rudder=tackle
rudder=trunk
rudder=wheel
ruddleman
ruddy=rudder (a fish)
rude=growing, etc.
rudge=wash
rue=anemone
rue=bargain
rue=fern
ruewort
ruff=band
ruff=cuff
ruff=wheel
ruffy=tuffy
rug=gowned, etc.
ruin=agate
ruin=marble
rule=case
rule=cutter†
rule=driller†
rule=joint
rule=staff
rule=work
ruling=engine
ruling=machine
ruling=pen
rum=barge
rumblegumption
rumble=tumble
rum=blossom
rum=bud
rum=cherry
rum=hole
rump=bone
rump=fed

rump=post
rump=steak
rumseller†
rumshop
rum shrub
rumswizzle
runabout
runagate
runaway
runch=balls
runecraft
runesmith
rune=stone
run=fish
rung=head
run=lace
run=man
runner=ball
runner=stick
runner=tackle
running=gear
running=rein
running=roll

running=string
running=thrush
running=trap
run=out
runrig
run=up
runway
rusa=oil
ruset=offal
rush=bearing
rush=bottomed, etc.
rush=broom
rush candle
rush=daffodil
rush=grass
rush=grown
rush=holder†
rushlight
rush=like
rush=lily
rush=line
rush=nut
rush=stand

rush=stick
rush=toad
rushy=fringed
russel=cord
rust=ball
rust=colored, etc.
rust=fungus
rustic=work
rust=joint
rust=mite
rust=proof
rust=red
rustyback (a fern)
rusty=crowned, etc.
rut=time
rutting=time
rutton=root
rye=grass
rye=moth
rye=straw
rye whiskey
rye=wolf
rye=worm

S

Sabbath=breaker†
Sabbath=school
sabrebill (a bird)
sabre=billed, etc.
sabre-fish
sabretooth (a fish)
sabrewing (a bird)
sabicu=wood
sable=fish
sable=stoled, etc.
sabrina=work
sachet=powder
sack=barrow
sack=bearer†
sack=cloth
sack=coat
sack=doodle
sack=emptier†
sack=filter
sack=hoist
sack=holder†
sacking=bottomed
sack=lifter†
sack=moth
sack=packer†
sackpipe (a bagpipe)
sack=posset
sack=pot
sack=race
sack=tree
sack=winged
sad=colored, etc.
saddleback (an oyster, a gull, etc.)
saddle=backed, etc.
saddle=bag
saddle=bar
saddle=blanket
saddle=bow
saddle=bracket

saddle=clip
saddle=cloth
saddle=fast
saddle=feathers
saddle=gall
saddle=girth
saddle=graft
saddle=hackle
saddle=harness
saddle=hill
saddle=hook
saddle=horse
saddle=joint
saddle=leaf
saddle=leather
saddle=nail
saddle=plate
saddle=quern
saddle=rail
saddler=corporal
saddle=reed
saddlerock (an oyster)
saddle=roof
saddler=sergeant
saddle=rug
saddlescaling
saddle=shell
saddle=sick
saddle=stone
saddletree (frame of a saddle, a plant)
sad=iron
sad=tree
safe=alarm
safe=conduct
safe=deposit
safed=siris
safe=edged, etc.
safeguard
safe=keeping

safe=lock
safe=pledge
safety=arch
safety=beam
safety=belt
safety bicycle
safety=bolt
safety=bridle
safety=buoy
safety=cage
safety=car
safety=catch
safety=chain
safety=disk
safety=door
safety=funnel
safety=fuse
safety=grate
safety=hanger
safety=hatch
safety=hoist
safety=hook
safety=ink
safety=lamp
safety=link
safety-lintel
safety=lock
safety=loop
safety=match
safety=paper
safety=pin
safety=plug
safety=rail
safety=razor
safety=rein
safety=stop
safety=strap
safety=switch
safety=tackle
safety=tube

safety=valve
safflower=oil
saffron=crocus
saffron=thistle
saffronwood (a tree)
sage=apple
sage=brush
sage=bush
sage=cock
sage=green
sage=grouse
sage=hare
sage=hen
sage=rabbit
sage=rose
sage=sparrow
sage=thrasher
sage=tree
sage=willow
sagewood (sage=brush)
sagger=house
sago=palm
sago=plan
sago=spleen
saiga=antelope
sailboat
sail=borne
sail=burton
sail=cloth
sail=clutch
sail=cover
sailfish
sail=fluke
sail=gang
sail=hook
sail=hoop
sailing=directions
sailing=fish
sailing=gang
sailing=ice
sailing=master
sailing=orders
sail=lizard
sail=loft
sailmaker†
sail=needle
sailor=fish
sailorman
sailor=plant

sailor's=choice*
sailor's=purse*
sail=room
sail=trimmer†
sail=wheel
sail=yard
saintlike
saint=seeming
salad=burnet
salad=fork
salad=oil
salad=plate
salad=rocket
salad=spoon
salal=berry
sal=dammer
sale=pond
salesgirl
saleslady
salesman
salesroom
saleswoman
salework
salinometer=pot
saliva=ejector
saliva=pump
sallee=man
sallow=kitten
sallow=moth
asllow=thorn
sally=lunn
sallyman
sallypicker (a bird)
sallyport
sally=wood
salmon=belly
salmon=berry
salmon=color
salmon=colored, etc.
salmon=disease
salmon=fishery
salmon=fishing†
salmon=fly
salmon=fry
salmon=killer†
salmon=ladder
salmon=leap
salmon=louse
salmon=peal

salmon=peel
salmon=pink
salmon=pool
salmon=spear
salmon=spring
salmon=stair
salmon=tackle
salmon=trout
salmon=twine
salmon=weir
saloon=car
saloon=keeper†
saloon=bush
sal=soda
salt=barrow
salt=bearer†
salt=block
salt=box
salt=burned, etc.
salt=bush
salt=cake
salt-cat
saltcellar
salt=cote
salt=duty
salt=foot
salt=furnace
salt=gauge
salt=garden
salt=glaze
salt=grass
salt=group
salt=holder†
salt=horse
salting=box
salting=house
salting=point
salt=lick
salt=marsh
saltmaster
salt=mill
salt=mine
salt=money
salt=pan
salt=pit
salt=raker†
salt=rheum
salt=rising
salt=spoon

salt-spring
salt-stand
salt-tree
salt-water, *a.*
salt-works
saltwort
salve-bougie
salve-bug
salver-shaped
samel-brick
sampfen-wood
sample-card
sample-cutter†
sample-room
sample-scale
sample-spigot
sampling-tube
samson-post
Sancho-Pedro (a game)
sandal-tree
sandalwood
sandalwood-bark
sandara-tree
sand-badger
sand-bag
sandbag, *v.*
sand-ball
sand-band
sand-bank
sand-bath
sand-bear
sand-bearings
sand-bed
sand-beetle
sand-bellows
sand-bird
sand-blackberry
sand-blast
sand-blind
sand-blower†
sand-board
sand-box
sand-brake
sand-bug
sand-bur
sand-burned, etc.
sand-canal
sand-cherry
sand-clam

sand-club
sand-cock
sand-collar
sand-corn
sand-crab
sand-crack
sand-cricket
sand-crusher
sand-cusk
sand-dab
sand-dart
sand-darter
sand-diver
sand-dollar
sand-drier†
sand-drift
sand-dune
sand-eel
sand-ejector†
sandel-brick
sand-fence
sandfish
sand-flag
sand-flaw
sand-flea
sand-flood
sand-flounder
sand-fluke
sand-fly
sand-gall
sand-gaper
sand-glass
sand-grass
sand-grouse
sand-guard
sand-heat
sand-hill
sand-hiller
sand-holder†
sandhopper (an insect)
sand-hornet
sanding-plate
sand-jack
sand-jet
sand-lance
sand-lark
sand-leek
sand-lizard
sand-lob

sand-lot
sandman
sand-martin
sand-mason
sand-mole
sand-monitor
sand-mouse
sand-myrtle
sand-natter
sandnecker (a fish)
sand-oyster
sandpaper
sandpaper-tree
sand-partridge
sandpeep (a bird)
sand-perch
sand-picture
sand-pigeon
sand-pike
sand-pillar
sand-pine
sand-pipe
sandpiper (a bird)
sand-pit
sand-plover
sand-prey
sand-pride
sand-pulverizer†
sand-pump
sand-rat
sand-reed
sand-reel
sand-ridge
sandrock
sandrunner (a bird)
sand-saucer
sand-scoop
sand-screen
sandscrew
sand-shark
sand-shot
sand-shrimp
sand-sifter†
sand-skink
sand-skipper
sand-smelt
sand-snake
sand-snipe
sand-sole

sandspout	sapsago	satin=damask
sand=spurry	sap=shield	satin=de-laine
sand=star	sapskull	satinet=loom
sandstay	sap=spile	satin=finish
sandstone	sap=spout	satinflower (a plant)
sand=storm	sapsucker	satin=foulard
sandsucker (a fish)	sap=sucking	satin=grackle
sand=swallow	sap=tube	satining=machine
sand=thrower†	sapucaia=nut	satinleaf (a plant)
sand=trap	sapucaia=oil	satin=lisse
sand=tube	sap=wood	satin=loom
sand=viper	sardine=tongs	satin=moth
sand=washer†	sargassum=shell	satin=paper
sand=wasp	sash=bar	satin=sheeting
sandweed	sash=boring	satin=spar
sandweld	sash=chisel	satin=sparrow
sand=whirl	sash=clamp	satin=stitch
sandwich=man	sash=door	satin=stone
sand=wind	sash=fastener†	satin=striped, etc.
sandworm	sash=fillister	satin Sultan
sandwort	sash=frame	satin Surah
sandy=carpet (a moth)	sash=gate	satin Turk
sang=de-bœuf	sash=line	satin=wave (a moth)
sang=froid	sash=lock	satin=weave
sang=school	sash=moulding	satinwood (a tree)
sanjak=bey	sash=mortising†	satrap=crowned, etc
sans=appel	sash=planing	satyr-pug
sans=serif	sash=pulley	sauba=ant
sapan=wood	sash=rail	sauce=alone
sap=ball	sash=saw	sauce=boat
sap=beetle	sash=sluice	saucebox (a person)
sap=boiler†	sash=sticking†	sauce=crayon
sap=bucket	sash=supporter†	sauce=dish
sap=cavity	sash=tenoning	saucepan
sap=color	sash=tool	saucepan=fish
sap=fagot	sash=window	saucer=eye
sap=fork	sassafras=bark	saucer=eyed, etc.
sap=green	sassafras=nut	sauce=tureen
saphead (a person)	sassafras=oil	saucy=bark
sap=headed	sassafras=pith	sauerkraut
sapi=utan	sassafras=root	saul=tree
sapling=cup	sassy=bark	sausage=cutter†
sapling=tankard	satan=shrimp	sausage=filler†
sapodilla=plum	satellite=sphinx	sausage=grinder†
sapphirewing (a bird)	satellite vein	sausage=machine
sap=pine	satin=bird	sausage=meat
sapping=machine	satin=bush	sausage=poisoning
sap=roller	satin=carpet (a moth)	sausage=roll
sap=rot	satin=cloth	sausage=stuffer†

savanna-blackbird
savanna-finch
savanna-flower (a
    plant)
savanna-sparrow
savanna-wattle
save-all
savings-bank
savoir-faire
savoir-vivre
saw-arbor
sawarra-nut
saw-back (a gauge for
    the back of a saw)
sawback (a larva)
saw-backed, etc.
saw-bearing
sawbelly (a herring)
saw-bench
sawbill (a bird)
saw-block
sawbones (a person)
sawbuck
saw-clamp
saw-doctor
sawdust
sawdust-carrier†
saw-file
saw-filing
sawfish
saw-fly
saw-frame
saw-gauge
saw-gate
saw-gin
saw-grass
saw-grinding†
saw-guide
saw-gummer†
saw-handle
saw-hanging
sawhorn (an insect)
saw-horse
sawing-block
sawing-machine
saw-jointer†
saw-jumper†
saw-like
sawlog

saw-mandrel
sawmill
sawmill-gate
saw-pad
saw-palmetto
saw-pit
saw-sash
saw-set
saw-setting†
saw-sharpener†
saw-spindle
saw-swage
saw-table
saw-tempering†
saw-tooth
saw-toothing†
saw-upsetter†
saw-vise
saw-whet
saw-whetter†
sawwort
saw-wrack
saw-wrest
saxhorn
sax-tuba
sax-valve
say-so
S brake
scabbard-fish
scabbard-plane
scabbling-hammer
scab-fungus
scab-mite
scabwort
scaff-net
scaffold-bracket
scaffolding-pole
scuff-raff
scaldberry
scaldfish
scald-head
scaldweed
scale armor
scaleback (a marine
    worm)
scale-backed, etc.
scale-beam
scale-bearer†
scale-board

scale-borer†
scale-bug
scale-carp
scale-degree
scale-dove
scale-drake
scale-duck
scale-feather
scale-fern
scale-fish
scalefoot (a fish)
scale-ground
scale-hair
scale-insect
scale-louse
scale-micrometer
scale-moss
scale pattern
scale-pattern, a.
scale-pipette
scale-quail
scale-shell
scale-stone
scaletail (an animal)
scalework
scaleworm
scaling-bar
scaling-furnace
scaling-hammer
scaling-knife
scaling-ladder
scaling-machine
scallop-crab
scalloped-hazel (moth)
scalloped-hooktip (a
    moth)
scalloped-oak (a moth)
scalloping-tool
scalloping-moth
scallop-net
scallop-shell
scalping-knife
scalping-tuft
scalp-lock
scaly-winged, etc.
scandal-bearer†
scandalmonger
scant-of-grace (a
    person)

scapegallows (a per=
son)
scapegoat (a person)
scapegrace (a person)
scape=wheel
scap=net
scappling=hammer!
scarebabe (a bugbear)
scarecrow (a figure
to scare crows,
a person)
scarf=bolt
scarfing=frame
scarfing=machine
scarf=joint
scarf=loom
scarf=pin
scarf=ring
scarf=skin
scarf=weld
scarious=bracted
scarlet=faced, etc.
scarletseed (a tree)
scarlet=tiger (a moth)
scar=limestone
scarn=bee
scart=free
scatchmouth (a bit
for bridles)
scathold
scatland
scatterbrain (a person)
scatter=brained, etc.
scattergood (a person)
scaup=duck
scavenger=beetle
scavenger=crab
scene=dock
scene=man
scene=painter†
scene=plot
scenery=groove
scene=shifter†
scent=bag
scent=bottle
scent=box
scent=gland
scent=holder†
scent=organ

scent=pore
scen.=vase
scent=vesicle
scentwood (a shrub)
schaum=earth
scherben=cobalt
schiller=spar
S chisel
schizopod stage
school board
school=book
schoolboy
school=bred, etc.
school committee
schoolcraft
school=dame
school=days
school district
school doctor
schoolfellow
school=fish
schoolgirl
schoolhouse
school=inspector
schoolma'am
schoolmaid
schoolman
schoolmaster
schoolmate
school=miss
schoolmistress
school=name
school=pence
schoolroom (a room)
school=room (room in
general for schools)
school=ship
school=taught
school=teacher†
school=time
school=whale
schooner=smack
scissorbill (a bird)
scissor=bird
scissors=grinder†
scissortail (a bird)
scissor=tailed
scissor=tooth
scolex form

scoop=net
scoop=wheel
scops=owl
scorched=carpet (a
moth)
scorched=wing (a moth)
scoring=engine
scoring=machine
scorpion=broom
scorpion=bug
scorpion=dagger
scorpion=fish
scorpion=fly
scorpion=grass
scorpion=lobster
scorpion=oil
scorpion=plant
scorpion=senna
scorpion=shell
scorpion=spider
scorpion's=tail*
scorpion=thorn
scorpionwort
Scotch=amulet (a moth)
Scotch=and=English (a
game)
Scotch=cap (a berry)
scotch=collops
scotch=hop
Scotchman (a native of
Scotland)
scotchman (a canvas
wrapping)
scoter=duck
scot=free
Scotsman
scourge=stick
scouring=ball
scouring=barrel
scouring=basin
scouring=drops
scouring=machine
scouring=rush
scouring=stock
scouring=table
scout=master
scouty=aulin
scow=house
scrag=necked, etc.

scrag-whale
scrap-book
scrap-cake
scrap-cinders
scrape-good
scrape-penny
scraper-bar
scraper-machine
scrap-forging
scrap-heap
scrap-house
scraping-ground
scraping-plane
scrap-iron
scrap-metal
scraping-machine
scratch-awl
scratchback
scratch-brush
scratch-coat
scratch-comma
scratch-cradle
scratcher-up
scratch-figure
scratch-finish
scratch-grass
scratch-pan
scratchweed
scratch-wig
scratchwork
screech-cock
screech-hawk
screech-martin
screech-owl
screech-thrush
screed-coat
screening-machine
screw-alley
screw-auger
screw-bean
screw-bell
screw-blank
screw-blast
screw-bolt
screw-box
screw-burner
screw-caliper
screw-cap
screw-clamp

screw-collar
screw-coupling
screw-cut
screw-cutter†
screw-die
screw-dock
screw-dog
screw-dollar
screw-driver†
screwed-work
screw-elevator
screw-eye
screw-feed
screw-fish
screw-forceps
screw-gauge
screw-gear
screw-head
screw-hoist
screw-hook
screwing-engine
screwing-machine
screwing-stock
screwing-table
screw-jack
screw-key
screw-lock
screw-machine
screw-making†
screw-mandrel
screw-medal
screw-moulding
screw-nail
screw-neck
screw-pile
screw-pillar
screw-pin
screw-pine
screw-plate
screw-pod
screw-post
screw-press
screw propeller
screw-punch
screw-quoin
screw-rod
screw rudder
screw-shackle
screw-shell

screw-spike
screw stair
screw-stem
screw-stock
screwstone
screw-table
screw-tap
screw-thread
screw-threading†
screw-tool
screw-tree
screw-valve
screw ventilator
screw-well
screw-wheel
screw-wire
screw-worm
screw-wrench
scribble-scrabble
scribbling-engine
scribbling-machine
scribe-awl
scribing-awl
scribing-block
scribing-compass
scribing-iron
scrimping-bar
scrimp-rail
scrip-company
scrip-holder†
Scripture-reader†
scripturewort
scrive-board
scroll-bone
scroll-chuck
scroll-gear
scroll-head
scroll-lathe
scroll-saw
scroll-wheel
scrollwork
scrubbing-board
scrubbing-brush
scrubbing-machine
scrub-bird
scrub-boxwood
scrub-broom
scrub-cattle
scrub-gang

scrub=grass	sea=bank	sea=carnation
scrub=oak	sea=bar	sea=cat
scrub=pine	sea=barley	sea=caterpillar
scrub=rider	sea=barrow	sea=catfish
scrub=robin	sea=basket	sea=catgut
scrubstone	sea=bass	sea=cauliflower
scrub=turkey	sea=bat	sea=centiped
scrubwood (a tree)	sea=bean	sea=change
scruthing=bag	sea=bear	sea=chart
scudding=stone	sea=beard	sea=chestnut
scuffle=harrow	sea=beast	sea=chickweed
scuffle=hoe	sea=beat	sea=clam
sculping=knife	sea=beaten, etc.	sea=cloth
sculpture=copier†	sea=beaver	seacoast
scupper=hole	sea=beet	sea=cob
scupper=hose	sea=bells	sea=cock
scupper=leather	sea=belt	sea=cockroach
scupper=nail	seaberry	sea=cocoanut
scupper=plug	sea=bindweed	sea=colander
scupper=shoot	sea=bird	sea=colewort
scupper=valve	sea=biscuit	sea=compass
scurf=skin	sea=blite	sea=cook
scurvy=grass	sea=blubber	sea=coot
scutch=blade	seaboard	sea=cormorant
scutch=grass	sea=boat	sea=corn
scutching=machine	sea=bordering	sea=cow
scutching=mill	sea=bottle	sea=crab
scutching=shaft	sea=bow	sea=craft
scutching=stock	sea=boy	sea=crawfish
scutching=sword	sea=brant	sea=crawler
scuttle=butt	sea=breach	sea=crow
scuttle=cask	sea=bream	sea=cucumber
scuttlefish	sea=breeze	sea=cudweed
scythe=fastening†	sea=brief	sea=cunny
scytheman	sea=bristle	sea=cushion
scythe=snath	sea=buckthorn	sea=dace
scythe=stone	sea=bug	sea=daffodil
scythe=whet	sea=bugloss	sea=daisy
sea=acorn	sea=bumblebee	sea=devil
sea=adder	sea=bun	sea=dog
sea=anchor	sea=burdock	sea=dotterel
sea=anemone	sea=butterfly	sea=dove
sea=angel	sea=cabbage	sea=dragon
sea=ape	sea=cactus	sea=drake
sea=apple	sea=calf	sea=duck
sea=apron	sea=campion	sea=eagle
sea=arrow	sea=canary	sea=ear
sea=ash	sea=cap	sea=eel
sea=asparagus	sea=captain	sea=egg

sea-elephant
sea-eringo
sea-fan
seafarer†
sea-feather
sea-fennel
sea-fern
sea-fight
sea-fir
sea-fire
sea-fish
sea-flea
sea-flier
sea-flower
sea-foam
sea-fog
sea-folk
sea-fowl
sea-fox
sea-front
sea-froth
sea-furbelow
sea-gauge
sea-gasket
sea-gates
sea-gherkin
sea-gilliflower
sea-ginger
sea-girdle
sea-god
sea-goddess
seagoing
sea-goose
sea-goosefoot
sea-gourd
sea-grape
sea-grass
sea-green
sea-gudgeon
sea-gull
sea-haar
sea-hair
sea-hanger
sea-hare
sea-hawk
sea-heath
sea-hedgehog
sea-hen
sea-hog

sea-holly
sea-holm
sea-honeycomb
sea-horse
sea-hound
sea-hulver
sea-island
sea-jelly
sea-kale
sea-kelp
sea-kemp
sea-kidney
sea-king
sea-kittie
sea-lace
sea-lamprey
sea-lark
sea-lavender
sea-lawyer
seal-bag
seal-bird
seal-brown
seal-club
sea-leech
sea-legs
sea-lemon
seal-engraving†
sea-lentil
sea-leopard
sea-letter
sea-lettuce
sea-level
seal-fishery
sealflower (a plant)
seal-hook
sea-light
sea-lily
sea-line
sealing-press
sealing-wax
sea-lintie
sea-lion
sea-lizard
seal-lance
seal-lock
seal-loach
sea-longworm
sea-louse
seal-pipe

seal-press
seal-ring
seal-rookery
sealskin
sea-luce
sea-lungs
sea-lungwort
sealwort
sea-magpie
sea-mall
sea-mallow
seaman
seaman-gunn
sea-mantis
sea-marge
sea-mark
sea-mat
sea-matweed
seam-blast
sea-melon
sea-mew
seam-hammer
sea-mile
sea-milkwort
seaming-lace
seaming-machine
seaming-tool
sea-mink
seam-lace
sea-monk
sea-monster
sea-mouse
seam-presser†
seam-rent
seam-roller†
seam-rubber
seam-set
sea-mud
sea-mussel
sea-necklace
sea-needle
sea-nest
sea-nettle
sea-nurse
sea-nymph
sea-oak
see-onion
sea-ooze
sea-orach

sea=orange	sea=rat	sea=spider
sea=orb	sea=raven	sea=spleenwort
sea=otter	search=light	sea=squid
sea=owl	search=party	sea=squirt
sea=ox	search=warrant	sea=staff
sea=oxeye	sea=reach	sea=star
sea=pad	sea=reed	sea=starwort
sea=panther	sea=reeve	sea=stick
sea=parrot	searing=iron	sea=stickleback
sea=parsnip	sea=risk	sea=stock
sea=partridge	sea=robber	sea=strawberry
sea=pass	sea=robin	sea=sunflower
sea=pay	sea=rocket	sea=surgeon
sea=pea	sea=rod	sea=swallow
sea=peach	sea=roll	sea=swine
sea=pear	sea=room	sea=tang
sea=pen	sea=rose	sea=tangle
sea=perch	sea=rosemary	seat=back
sea=pert	sea=rover†	seat=earth
sea=pheasant	sear=spring	sea=tench
sea=pie	sea=ruff	sea=term
sea=piece	sea=ruffle	seat=fastener†
sea=piet	sea=run	sea=thong
sea=pig	sea=running†	sea=thorn
sea=pigeon	sea=salmon	sea=thrift
sea=pike	sea=salt	sea=titling
sea=pilot	sea=sandwort	seat=lock
sea=pimpernel	sea=saurian	sea=toad
sea=pincushion	seascape	sea=tortoise
sea=pink	sea=scorpion	sea=toss
sea=plant	sea=scurf	seat=rail
sea=plantain	sea=sedge	sea=trout
sea=plover	sea=serpent	sea=trumpet
sea=poacher	sea=service	seat=stand
sea=poker	sea=shark	seat=stone
sea=pool	sea=shell	sea=turn
sea=poppy	seashore	sea=turtle
sea=porcupine	sea=shrimp	seat=worm
sea=pork	sea=shrub	sea=umbrella
seaport	seasick	sea=unicorn
sea=potato	seaside	sea=urchin
sea=pudding	sea=skimmer	sea=vampire
sea=pumpkin	sea=slater	sea=view
sea=purse	sea=sleeve	sea=wall
sea=purslane	sea=slug	sea=wand
sea=pye	sea=snail	seaware (a seaweed)
sea=quail	sea=snake	sea=washbells
sea=radish	sea=snipe	sea=water
sea=ragwort	seasoning=tub	sea=wax

seaway
seaweed
sea=whip
sea=whipcord
sea=whiplash
sea=whistle
sea=wife
sea=willow
sea=wind
sea=wing
sea=withwind
sea=wold
sea=wolf
sea=woodcock
sea=woodlouse
sea=worm
sea=wormwood
sea=worn
seaworthy
sea=wrack
Se=Baptist
second=adventist
second=class, a.
second=cut
second=hand
second=mark
second=rate, a.
second=sighted, etc.
seconds=pendulum
secretary=bird
secret=false
section=beam
section=cutter†
section=liner†
section=plane
sector=cylinder
sector=gear
sector=wheel
sedan=chair
sedge=bird
sedge=flat
sedge=hen
sedge=marine
sedge=warbler
sedge=wren
sediment=collector
see=bright
seed=bag
seed=basket

seed=bed
seed=bird
seed=box
seed=bud
seed=cake
seed=coat
seed=cod
seed=coral
seed=corn
seed=crusher†
seed=down
seed=drill
seed=eater†
seed=embroidery
seed=field
seed=finch
seed=fish
seed=gall
seed=garden
seed=grain
seeding=machine
seeding=plow
seed=lac
seed=leaf
seed=leap
seed=lip
seed=lobe
seed•oil
seed=oyster
seed=pearl
seed=planter†
seed=plat
seed=plot
seed=sheet
seedsman
seed=sower†
seed=stalk
seed=tick
seed=time
seed=vessel
seed=weevil
seed=wool
seedy=toe
seek=no=further (an
 apple)
seesaw
segment=gear
segment=rack
segment=saw

segment=shell
segment=valve
segment=wheel
segra=seed
seine=boat
seine=captain
seine=crew
seine=engine
seine=fisher†
seine=gang
seine=ground
seine=hauler†
seine=man
seine=needle
seine=roller†
seining=ground
seizing=stuff
selectman
selen=sulphur
selen=tellurium
self=abandonment
self=abasement
self=absorbed, etc.
self=abuse
self=accusation
self=accusatory
self=activity
self=assertion
self=assertive
self=assertiveness
self=assumption
self=baptizer†
self=binder†
self=bow
self=command
self=complacency
self=complacent
self=conceit
self=condemnation
self=confidence
self=confident
self=congratulation
self=conjugate
self=conscious
self=consistency
self=consistent
self=contempt
self=content
self=contradiction

self=contradictory
self=control
self=conviction
self=correspondence
self=creation
self=criticism
self=culture
self=deceit
self=deceiver†
self=deception
self=defence
self=defensive
self=delation
self=delusion
self=denial
self=dependence
self=dependent
self=depending
self=depreciation
self=depreciative
self=despair
self=destruction
self=destructive
self=determination
self=development
self=devotement
self=devotion
self=disparagement
self=dispraise
self=distrust
self=elective
self=enjoyment
self=esteem
self=estimation
self=evidence
self=evident
self=evolution
self=exaltation
self=examinant
self=examination
self=example
self=existence
self=existent
self=explanatory
self=explication
self=feeder†
self=fertility
self=fertilization
self=flattery

self=forgetful
self=glorious
self=government
self=gratulation
self=heal
self=help
self=importance
self=important
self=impotent
self=induction
self=inductive
self=indulgence
self=indulgent
self=infection
self=interest
self=involution
self=justification
self=knowledge
self=life
self=love
self=luminous
self=mastery
self=motion
self=murder
self=murderer†
self=offence
self=opinion
self=partiality
self=perception
self=pious
self=pity
self=pollution
self=possession
self=praise
self=preservation
self=preservative
self=pride
self=profit
self=protection
self=raker
self=realization
self=reciprocal
self=regard
self=regulative
self=relation
self=reliance
self=reliant
self=renunciation
self=repellency

self=repression
self=reproach
self=reproof
self=repugnant
self=respect
self=restraint
self=reverence
self-reverent
self=righteous
self=sacrifice
selfsame
self=satisfaction
self=scorn
self=seeker†
self=slaughter
self=sterile
self=sterility
self=substantial
self=sufficience
self=sufficiency
self=sufficient
self=suggestion
self=support
self=surrender
self=sustenance
self=sustentation
self-torture
self-trust
self=view
self=violence
self=will
self=worship
self=worshipper†
self=wrong
semaphore=plant
semen=multiplex
senate=chamber
senate=house
senna=tree
sense=body
sense=capsule
sense=cavity
sense=cell
sense=centre
sense=element
sense=epithelium
sense=filament
sense=impression
sense=organ

sense-perception
sense-rhythm
sense-seta
sense-skeleton
sensitive-plant
sentinel-crab
sentry-board
sentry-box
separating-disk
separating-funnel
separating-sieve
separating-weir
sergeant-fish
sergeant-major
serge-blue
sericite-gneiss
sericite-schist
serpentary-root
Serpent-bearer
serpent-boat
serpent-charmer†
serpent-cucumber
serpent-deity
serpent-eagle
serpent-eater†
serpent-fish
serpent-god
serpent-grass
serpent-like
serpent-lizard
serpent-moss
serpent-poison
serpent-star
serpent-stone
serpent's-tongue*
serpent-turtle
serpent-withe
serpentwood (a shrub)
serpolet-oil
servant-girl
servant-maid
servant-man
servant's call
service-berry
service-book
service-box
service-cleaner
service-cock
service-line

service-magazine
service-pipe
service-tree
serving-board
serving-maid
serving-mallet
serving-man
sesame-oil
sessile-eyed
setback
set-bolt
set-down
set-fair
set-foil
set-gun
set-hammer
set-in
set-net
set-off
seton-needle
set-out
set-pin
set-pot
set-ring
set-screw
set-stitched, etc.
setter-grass
setterwort
setting-back
setting-board
setting-box
setting-circle
setting-coat
setting-dog
setting-fid
setting-gauge
setting-machine
setting-needle
setting-pole
setting-punch
setting-rule
setting-stick
setting-sun (a mollusk)
settling-day
set-to
set-trap
set-up
set-work
sevenfold

seven-gilled, etc.
sevengills (a shark)
sevenholes (a lamprey)
sevennight
seven-point
seven-shooter†
seventh-chord (chord
  of the seventh)
seven-thirty
seven-up
sewage-fungus
sewage-grass
sewer-basin
sewer-gas
sewer-hunter†
sewerman
sewer-trap
sewer-rat
sewing-bench
sewing-bird
sewing-circle
sewing-clamp
sewing-cotton
sewing-horse
sewing-machine
sewing-materials
sewing-needle
sewing-press
sewing-silk
sewing-table
sexton-beetle
sey-pollack
shabby-genteel
shackbag (a person)
shack-bait
shack-bolt
shack-fisherman
shack-fishing†
shackle-bar
shackle-bolt
shackle-bone
shackle-crow
shackle-flap
shackle-jack
shackle-joint
shackle-pin
shackle-punch
shack-lock
shad-bellied, etc.

shadbird	shake=down, n.	sharpnails (a fish)
shad=blossom	shake=fork	sharp=saw (a saw=
shadbush (a plant)	shake=up, n.	sharpener)
shadefish	shake=willy	shorpshooter†
shade=hook	shaking=frame	sharptail (a bird)
shade-tree	shaking=machine	shatterbrain (a person)
shadflower (a plant)	Shaking=quaker	shatter=brained, etc.
shad=fly	shaking=shoe	shave=grass
shad=frog	shaking=table	shave=hook
shad=hatcher†	shale=oil	shaveweed
shading=pen	shallow-brained, etc.	shaving=basin
shadow=bird	sham=Abraham	shaving-brush
shadow=figure	shamalo=grass	shaving=cup
shadow=stitch	shamefaced	shaving=horse
shadow=test	shamefast	shaving=machine
shadow=vane	shameflower (a plant)	shavings=conductor
shad=salmon	shame=proof	shaving=tub
shad=seine	shame=reel	shaw=fowl
shad=spirit	shamrock=pea	shawl=loom
shad=splash	shank=cutter†	shawl=mantle
shad=waiter	shank=iron	shawl=material
shad=wash	shank=laster	shawl=pattern
shad=working†	shank=painter	shawl=pin
shaft=alley	shank=shell	shawl=strap
shaft=bearing	shank=spring	shawl=waistcoat
shaft=bender†	shank=wheel	shaya=root
shaft=coupling	shanty=man	shea=butter
shaft=drill	shaper=plate	sheaf=binder†
shaft=eye	shaper=vise	shealing=hill
shaft=furnace	shapesmith	shearbill (a bird)
shaft=horse	shaping=machine	shear=grass
shafting=box	shard=beetle	shearhog (a sheared
shafting=hanger	share=beam	sheep)
shaft=jack	share=bone	shear=hooks
shaft=line	share=broker	shearing=machine
shaft=loop	shareholder†	shearing=stress
shaft=monture	share=line	shearing=table
shaft=pipe	share=list	shear=legs
shaft=spot	sharesman	shearman
shaft=straightener†	sharewort	shears=moth
shaft=stripe	shark=moth	shear=steel
shaft=tackle	shark=mouthed, etc,	shear=structure
shaft=tip	shark=oil	sheartail (a bird, a
shaft=tug	shark=ray	moth)
shaft=tunnel	shark's=mouth*	shearwater (a bird)
shagbark (a tree)	sharp=cedar	sheatfish
shag=dog	sharp=cut	sheathbill (a bird)
shag=eared, etc.	sharp=eyed, etc.	sheath=billed, etc.
shake=bag	sharpfin (a fish)	sheathclaw (a lizard)

sheathfish
sheathing-metal
sheathing-nail
sheathing-paper
sheath-knife
shea-tree
sheave-hole
she-balsam
shedding-motion
shed-line
shed-roof
sheep-backs
sheepberry (a tree, its fruit)
sheep-biting
sheep-bot
sheep-cote
sheep-dip
sheep-dipping
sheep-dog
sheep-faced, etc.
sheep-farmer†
sheepfold
sheephead (a fish)
sheep-holder†
sheep-hook
sheep-laurel
sheep-louse
sheepman
sheep-market
sheepmaster
sheep-pen
sheep-pest
sheep-pick
sheep-plant
sheep-poison
sheep-pox
sheep-rack
sheep-range
sheep-rot
sheep-run
sheep's-bane*
sheep's-beard*
sheep's-bit*
sheep's-eye*
sheep's-fescue*
sheep's-foot*
sheep-shank
sheepshead (a fish)

sheep-shearer†
sheep-shears
sheep-silver
sheepskin
sheep-sorrel
sheep's-parsley*
sheep-split
sheep's-scabious*
sheep's-silver*
sheep-station
sheep-stealer†
sheepswool (a sponge)
sheep-tick
sheepwalk
sheep-walker
sheep-wash
sheep-whistling
sheep-worn
sheer-batten
sheer-hooks
sheer-hulk
sheer-lashing
sheer-leg
sheer-mould
sheer-pole
sheer-strake
sheet-anchor
sheet-bend
sheet-cable
sheet-calender
sheet copper
sheet-delivery
sheet glass
sheeting-machine
sheeting-pile
sheet iron
sheet lead
sheet lightning
sheet metal
sheet-metal, a.
sheet-mineral
sheet-pile
sheet-work
sheldapple (a bird)
sheld-fowl
shelf-bracket
shell-apple
shell-auger
shellback (a sailor)

shell-bank
shellbark (a tree)
shell-bit
shell-blow
shell-board
shell-boat
shell-box
shell button
shell-cracker
shell-crest
shell-dillisk
shell-dove
shell-eater
shell-fire
shell-fish
shellflower (a plant)
shell-follicle
shell-gauge
shell-gland
shell-grinder
shell-gun
shellhead (an insect)
shell-heap
shell-hook
shell-ibis
shell-ice
shell-jacket
shell-lime
shell-limestone
shellman
shell-marble
shell-marl
shell-meat
shell-mound
shell-ornament
shell-parrakeet
shell-parrot
shell-proof
shell-pump
shell-quail
shell-reducer†
shell-room
shell-sac
shell-sand
shell-snail
shellwork
shell-worm
shelter-tent
she-oak

shepherd=bird
shepherd=dog
shepherd's=bag*
shepherd's=club*
shepherd's=cress*
shepherd's=joy*
shepherd's=knot*
shepherd's=myrtle*
shepherd's=needle*
shepherd=spider
shepherd's=pouch*
shepherd's=purse*
shepherd's=rod*
shepherd's=staff*
she=pine
sheriff=clerk
sheriff=officer
sherry cobbler
sherry=vallies
she=sole
shield=animalcule
shield=backed, etc.
shield=bearing†
shield=beetle
shield=belt
shield=bone
shield=brooch
shield=budding
shield=bug
shield=centiped
shield=crab
shield=dagger
shield=drake
shield=duck
shield=fern
shield=gilled
shield=lantern
shield=louse
shield=plate
shield=reptile
shield=ship
shield=slater
shieldtail (a snake)
shield=toad
shield=urchin
shifter=bar
shifting=boards
shilly=shallier
shilly=shally

shin=bone
shin=boot
shingle=jointing†
shingle=machine
shingle=mill
shingle=nail
shingle=oak
shingle=planing†
shingle=riving†
shingle=roofed
shingle=saw
shingle=trap
shingle=tree
shinglewood (a tree)
shingling=bracket
shingling=gauge
shingling=hammer
shingling=hatchet
shingling=mill
shingling=tongs
shinleaf (a plant)
shin=piece
shinplaster
ship=biscuit
ship=board (a board)
shipboard (the con=
    taining space
    of a ship)
ship=boat
ship=borer
ship=borne
ship=boy
ship=breaker†
ship=broker
ship=builder†
ship=canal
ship=captain
ship=carpenter
ship=carver†
ship=chandler
ship=chandlery
ship=deliverer†
ship=fever
ship=holder†
ship=jack
ship=keeper†
ship=letter
ship=load
shipman

shipmaster
shipmate
ship=money
ship=owner†
ship=pendulum
shipping=agent
shipping=articles
shipping=bill
shipping=clerk
shipping=master
shipping=note
shipping=office
ship=plate
ship=pound
ship=propeller†
ship=railway
ship=rigged
ship=scraper†
ship=stayer
shipway
ship=worm
shipwreck
shipwright
ship=writ
shipyard
shire=clerk
shire=day
shire=gemot
shire=ground
shire=host
shire=land
shireman
shire=moot
shire=town
shirt=bosom
shirt=button (a button)
shirtbutton (a plant)
shirt=collar
shirt=frame
shirt=frill
shirt=front
shirt=maker†
shirt=sleeve
shirt=store
shirt=tail
shirt=waist
shishwork
shittah=tree
shittim=wood

shiver=spar
shoal=alarm
shoal=duck
shoal=indicator
shoal=mark
shock=dog
shock=head
shock=headed, etc.
shoddy=machine
shoddy=mill
shode=pit
shode=stone
shoebeak (a bird)
shoebill (a bird)
shoe=billed, etc.
shoeblack
shoeblack=plant
shoe=blacking
shoe=block
shoe=bolt
shoe=boy
shoe=brush
shoe=buckle
shoe=button
shoe=distender†
shoe=embossing†
shoe=eyeletting† .
shoe=fastener†
shoeflower (a plant)
shoe=hammer
shoe=heel
shoe=horn
shoeing=hammer
shoeing=horn
shoe=jack
shoe=key
shoe=knife
shoe=lace
shoe=latchet
shoe=leather
shoemaker†
shoemaker's=bark*
shoepack
shoe=pad
shoe=peg
shoe=pocket
shoe=rose
shoe=sewing†
shoe=shave

shoe=sole
shoe=stirrup
shoe=stone
shoe=strap
shoe=stretcher†
shoe=string
shoe=thread
shoe=tie
shoe=valve
shoe=worker†
shoot=board
shooter=sun
shooting=board
shooting=box
shooting=coat
shooting=gallery
shooting=iron
shooting=jacket
shooting=needle
shooting=plane
shooting=range
shooting star (a star)
shooting=star (a plant)
shooting=stick
shop=bell
shop=bill
shop=board
shop=book
shop=boy
shop=girl
shopholder†
shopkeeper†
shoplifter†
shoplike
shopmaid
shopman
shopmate
shop=thief
shop=walker†
shop=woman
shop=worn
shore=anchor
shore=beetle
shore=bird
shore=cliff
shore=crab
shore=grass
shore=hopper
shore=jumper

shore=land
shore=lark
shore=line
shoreman
shore=oil
shore=pipit
shore=plover
shore=service
shore=shooting
shoresman
shore=snipe
shore=teetan
shore=wainscot
shoreweed
shore=whaling
short=armed, etc.
short=axe
short=bread
shortcake
short=circuit, v. or a.
short=coarse (a grade
  of wool)
short=coming
shorthand
shorthead (a whale)
shorthorn (a bovine)
shortneck (a sand-
  piper)
short=staple, a.
short=stop
shorttail (a snake)
shot=belt
shot=borer
shot=box
shot=bush
shot=cartridge
shot=compressor†
shot=corn
shot=crossbow
shot=flagon
shot=free
shot=gauge
shot=garland
shot=glass
shot=gromet
shot=gun
shot=hole
shot=ice
shot=line

shot-locker
shot-metal
shot-pepper
shot-plug
shot-pouch
shot-proof
shot-prop
shot-rack
shot-sorter†
shot-star
shot-table
shot-tower
shot-window
shoulder-angle
shoulder-belt
shoulder-blade
shoulder-block
shoulder-bone
shoulder-brace
shoulder-brooch
shoulder-callosity
shoulder-cap
shoulder-cover
shoulder-girdle
shoulder-guard
shoulder-hitter†
shouldering-file
shoulder-joint
shoulder-knot
shoulder-knotted, etc.
shoulder-lobe
shoulder-moth
shoulder-note
shoulder-piece
shoulder-pole
shoulder-screw
shoulder-shield
shoulder-slip
shoulder-strap
shoulder-tippet
shoulder-washer
shoulder-wrench
shovelbill (a duck)
shovelboard (a game)
shovel-fish
shovel-footed, etc.
shovel-hat
shovelhead (a sturgeon,
 a shark)

shovelling-flat
shovelnose (a sturgeon,
 a shark)
shovel-plow
show-bill
show-box
showbread
show-card
show-case
show-end
shower-bath
show-glass
showing off
showman
show-place
show-room (room for a
 show)
showroom (a room for
 show of wares)
show-stone
show-up, n.
show-window
show-yard
shread-head
shred-cock
shredding-knife
shred-pie
shrew-ash
shrew-footed, etc.
shrew-mole
shrew-mouse
shrew-struck
shriek-owl
shrift-father
shrike-crow
shrill-edged, etc.
shrimp-chaff
shrimp-net
shrinkage-crack
shrinkage-rule
shrinking-head
shroud-bridle
shrouding-gear
shroud-knot
shroud-laid
shroud-plate
shroud-rope
shroud-stopper
shroud-truck

shrove-cake
shroving-time
shrub-shilling
shrub-snail
shrub-yellowroot
shuck-bottom
shuck-bottomed, etc.
shuffleboard (a game)
shuffle-cap
shuffle-scale
shufflewing (a bird)
shuffling-plates
shunt-gun
shunting-engine
shunt-off, n.
shunt-out, n.
shut-down, n.
shut-off, n.
shutter-dam
shutter-eye
shutter-fastening†
shutter-hook
shutter-lift
shutter-lock
shutter-screw
shutting-post
shuttle-binder
shuttle-board
shuttle-box
shuttle-check
shuttlecock
shuttle-crab
shuttle-lever
shuttle-motion
shuttle-race
shuttle-shaped, etc.
shuttle-shell
shuttle-train
shuttle-winder†
shuttle-wit
sick-bay
sick-bed
sick-berth
sick-brained, etc.
sick-call
sick-flag
sick-headache
sick-leave
sicklebill (a bird)

sickle=billed, etc.
sickle=feather
sickle=head
sickleheal (a plant)
sickleman
sicklepod (a plant)
sicklewced
sicklewort
sick=list
sick=report
sick=room
side=arms
side=axe
side=bar
side=beam
sideboard
side=bone
side=box
side=boy
side=chain
side=chapel
side=comb
side=cousin
side=cover
side=cutting
side=dish
side=drum
side=file
side=fin
side=flap
side=fly
side=guide
side=hatchet
side=head
side=hill
side=hook
side=hunt
side=keelson
side=light
side=line
sideliner (a snake)
side=lock
sidelong
side=mark
side=meat
side=note
side=piece
side=piercing†
side=pipe

side=plane
side=plate
side=pond
side=post
side=rail
side=reflector
side=rib
side=rod
side=round
side=saddle
sidesaddle=flower
side=screw
side=scription
side=seat
side=show
side=slip
sidesman
side=snipe
side=space
side=splitting
side=step
side=stick
side=stitch
side=strap
side=stroke
side=table
side=taking
side=tool
side=track
side=transit
side=tree
side view
sidewalk
side=walker†
sideway
side=wheel
side=wheeler
side=whisker
side=winch
side=wind
sidewinder (a snake)
side=wings
side=wipe
sidewiper (a snake
siding=hook
siding=machine
siege=basket
siege=battery
siege=cap

siege=gun
siege=piece
siege=train
siege=works
sieve=beaked, etc.
sievebeaks (ducks,
   geese)
sieve=cell
sieve=disk
sieve-hypha
sieve-like
sieve-plate
sieve=pore
sieve=tissue
sieve=tube
sieve=vessel
sifting=machine
sight=bar
sight draft
sight=feed
sight=hole
sighting=notch
sighting=shot
sight=opening
sight=pouch
sight=reader†
sightseeing†
sight=seeker†
sight=shot
sight=singing†
sightsman
sight=vane
sightworthy
signal=apparatus
signal=book
signal=box
signal=chest
signal=code
signal=fire
signal=flag
signal=gun
signal=halyard
signal=lamp
signal=lantern
signal=light
signalman
signal=officer
signal=order
signal=post

signal=rocket
signal=service
signal=tower
signature=line
signature=mark
sign=board
signet=ring
sign=painter†
sign=post
sign=symbol
silk=bunting (a bird)
silk=cleaning†
silk=cotton
silk=culture
silk=doubling†
silk=dresser†
silk=factory
silk=figured, etc.
silkflower (a tree)
silk=fowl
silk=gelatine
silk=gland
silk=glue
silk=grass
silk=grower†
silk=hen
silk=loom
silkman
silk=manufacture
silk=mercer
silk=mill
silk=moth
silk=printing†
silk=reel
silk=shag
silk=sizing†
silk=sorting†
silk=spider
silk=spinner†
silk=stretching†
silktail (a bird)
silk=thrower†
silk=throwster
silk=tree
silk=twisting†
silk=vine
silk=weaver†
silkweed
silk=winder†

silkwood (a moss, a
  shrub)
silkworm
silkworm=culture
silky=wainscot (a moth)
silky=wave (a moth)
sill=dressing
siller=fish
siller=fluke
sill=step
silverback (a bird)
silver=barred, etc.
silver bass
silver=bath
silver=beater†
silverbell (a shrub or
  tree)
silverbell=tree
silverberry
silverbill (a bird)
silver=black
silver=boom
silver=bracts
silverbush (a shrub)
silverchain (a tree)
silver=cloud (a moth)
silver=duckwing
silver=eel
silvereye (a bird)
silver=fern
silverfin (a minnow)
silverfish
silver=foil
silver=gilt
silver=glance
silver=grain
silver=grass
silver=gray
si.ver=ground, a.
silverhead (a plant)
silver=king
silver=leaf (silver=foil)
silverleaf (a plant)
silver=mill
silver=moth
silver=owl
silver=paper
silver=plater†
silver=printing†

silver=shell
silversides (a fish)
silversmith
silver=solder
silverspot (a butterfly)
silver=sprig (a rabbit=
  pelt)
silver=stick (a person)
silvertail (a fish)
silver=thistle
silvertongue (sparrow)
silver=top (a disease of
  grass)
silver=tree
silver=vine
silverware
silverweed
silver=white
silver=witch
silverwood (a tree)
silverwork
simbling=cake
simile=mark
simitar=pod
simitar=shaped
simitar=tree
simon=pure
simple=faced, etc.
simpler's=joy*
sin=born, sin=bred, etc.
sine=complement
sine=integral
sinew=shrunk
singeing=lamp
singeing=machine
singing bird
singing=book
singing=flame
singing=gallery
singing=hinny
singing man
singing=master
singing=muscle
singing=school
singing voice
singing woman
single=acting, single=
  banked, etc.
single=bar

single-fire, a.
single-foot (a gait of horses)
single-footer
single-loader†
single-stick
single-taxism
singlethorn (a fish)
singletree (a swingle-tree)
singsing
singsong
singspiel
sink-dirt
sinker-bar
sinker-wheel
sinkfield
sink-hole
sinking-fund
sinking-head
sinking-pump
sinking-ripe
sink-pipe
sink-plug
sink-room
sink-stone
sink-trap
sin-offering
sin-sick
sinuate-dentate
sinuate-lobate
sinuate-undulate
siphon barometer
siphon-bottle
siphon condenser
siphon-cup
siphon-filling†
siphon-gauge
siphon-mouthed, etc.
siphon pipe
siphon pump
siphon recorder
siphon-shell
siphon-slide
siphon-tube
siphon-worm
sirdar-bearer
siskin-green
sister-block

sister-hook
sister-in-law
sister ship
sit-sicker
sitting-room
siva-snake
six-banded, etc.
sixfold
six-footer
six-hour
sixpence
sixpenny
six-point
six-shooter
six-spot
sixteenth note
sixteenth rest
sixty-fourth
sixty-fourth note
size-cue
size-roll
size-stick
size-time
sizing-apparatus
sizing-cistern
sizing-machine
S joint
skate-barrow
skate-grinder†
skate-sucker
skating-rink
skean-dhu
skeelduck
skeelgoose
skee-race
skeer-devil
skee-runner†
skeg-shore
skein-screw
skein-setter†
skeleton-face
skeleton-fibre (of a sponge)
skeleton-screw
skeleton-shrimp
skeleton-spicule
skelp-bender†
sketch-block
sketch-book

sketching-block
sketch-map
skew-bald
skewer-machine
skewer-wood
skew-gee
skew-symmetrical
skid-pan
skiff-handed, etc.
skill-facet
skilty-boots
skimback (a fish)
skimble-scamble
skim-colter
skim-milk
skimming-dish
skimming-gate
skim-net
skimping-roller
skin-area
skin-boat
skin-bone
skin-bound, etc.
skin-coat
skin-deep
skin-eater†
skinflint (a person)
skin-friction
skin game
skin-graft
skin-grafting
skin-house
skin-merchant
skinning-apparatus
skinning-table
skin-planting
skin-sensory
skin-tight
skin-tissue
skin-wool
skip-hegrie
skipjack (a person, a fish, etc.)
skip-mackerel
skipper-bird
skipping-rope
skipping-teach
skip-rope
skip-shaft

skip-wheel
skirmish-drill
skirmish-line
skirt-braid
skirt-dancing†
skirt-furrow
skirting-board
skitter-brained
skitter-wit
skittle-alley
skittle-ball
skittle-dog
skittle-frame
skittle-ground
skittle-pin
skittle-pot
skiver-wood
skiving-knife
skiving-machine
skua-gull
skulking-place
skull-cap (a cap for the
    scull)
skullcap (cap of the
    skull, a plant, etc.)
skull-fish
skull-roof
skull-shell
skunkbill (a duck)
skunk-bird
skunk-blackbird
skunk-cabbage
skunk-farm
skunkhead (a duck)
skunk-porpoise
skunktop (a duck)
skunkweed
sky-blue
sky-born, sky-colored,
    etc.
sky-color
sky-drain
skyflower (a plant)
sky-gazer†
sky-high
skylark
skylight
sky-line
sky-parlor

sky-pipit
sky-rocket
skysail
skyscape
sky-scraper†
slabbing-gang
slabbing-machine
slabbing-saw
slab-board
slab-grinder†
slab-line
slab-sided, etc.
slabstone
slack-backed, etc.
slack-bake, v.
slack-jaw
slack-water, a.
slag-brick
slag-car
slag-furnace
slag-hearth
slag-shingle
slag-wool
slake-kale
slake-trough
slam-bang
slang-whang
slang-whanger
slap-bang
slap-dash
slapjack (a pancake)
slap-sided, etc.
slap-up
slash-pine
slat-bar
slat-crimper†
slate-axe
slate-bevelling†
slate-black
slate-blue
slate-clay
slate-coal
slate-colored, etc.
slate-cutter†
slate-frame
slate-gray
slate-making†
slate-peg
slate-pencil

slate-saw
slate-spar
slate-trimming†
slat-iron
slat-machine
slat-plane
slat-tenoning†
slaughter-house
slaughter-weapon
slave-baron
slave-born, etc.
slave-coffle
slave-driver†
slave-fork
slaveholder†
slave-hunter†
slave-making†
slave-ship
slave-trade
slave-trader†
sleave-silk
sled-brake
sledge-chair
sledge-dog
sledge-hammer
sled-knee
sledman
sled-runner
sleek-headed
slecking-glass
sleep-at-noon (a plant)
sleep-drunk, a.
sleeper-shark
sleeping-bag
sleeping-car
sleeping-carriage
sleeping-draught
sleeping-dropsy
sleeping-room
sleeping-sickness
sleeping-table
sleep-waker†
sleep-walker†
sleepyhead (a person,
    a duck)
sleepy-seeds
sleet-bush
sleet-squash
sleeve-axle

sleeve-board
sleeve-button
sleeve-coupling
sleevefish
sleeve-knot
sleeve-link
sleeve-nut
sleeve-waistcoat
sleeve-weight
sleigh-bell
sleigh-ride
slender-beaked, etc.
slender-grass
sleuth-dog
sleuth-hound
slice-bar
slice-galley
slicing-machine
slick-chisel
slickensides
slide-action
slide-bar
slide-box
slide-case
slide-culture
slide-head
slide-knife
slide-knot
slide-lathe
slide-rail
slide-rest
slide-rod
slider-pump
slide-rule
slide-trombone
slide-trumpet
slide-valve
slideway
sliding-balk
sliding-band
sliding-box
sliding-gauge
sliding-gunter
sliding keel
sliding-nippers
sliding-plank
sliding-relish
slime-eel
slime-fungus

slime-gland
slime-mould
slime-pit
slime-separator†
slime-sponge
sling-band
sling-bone
sling-bullet
sling-cart
sling-dog
sling-piece
sling-stone
sling-wagon
slink-butcher
slink-skin
slip-board
slip-carriage
slip-chase
slip-cleavage
slip-cover
slip-decoration
slip-dock
slip-galley
slip-hook
slip-house
slip-kiln
slip-knot
slip-link
slipper-animalcule
slipper-bath
slipper-drag
slipper-flower (a plant)
slipper-limpet
slipper-plant
slipper-shell
slipper-spurge
slipperwort
slipperyback (a lizard)
slippery-elm
slipping-piece
slipping-plane
slip-rails
slip-rope
slip-shackle
slip-shave
slipshod
slip-slop
slip-stitch
slip-stopper†

slip-strainer†
slipway
slit-shell
slitting-disk
slitting-file
slitting-gauge
slitting-machine
slitting-mill
slitting-plane
slitting-roller
slitting-saw
slitting-shears
sliver-box
slivering-knife
slivering-machine
slob-ice
slocking-stone
slogwood (a tree)
sloop-smack
sloop-yacht
slop-basin
slop-book
slop-bowl
slop-bucket
slop-chest
slop-dash
slope-level
slop-hopper
slop-jar
slop-moulding
slop-pail
slop-room
slopseller†
slop-shop
slop-work
slop-worker†
slosh-wheel
sloth-animalcule
sloth-bear
sloth-monkey
sloth-hound
slotting-auger
slotting-machine
slouch-hat
slovenwood (a tree)
slowback (a person)
slow-gaited, etc.
slow-hound
slow-match

slow=sure	smashing=press	smoke=stone
slow=up	smash=up	smoke=tight
slowworm	smear=case	smoke=tree
slubbing=billy	smear=dab	smoke=washer
slubbing=machine	smee=duck	smokewood (a plant)
sludge=door	smell=feast	smoking=cap
sludge=hole	smelling=bottle	smoking=car
slue=rope	smelling=salts	smoking=carriage
slugabed (a person)	smell=trap	smoking=duck
slug=caterpillar	smelting=furnace	smoking=jacket
slug=fly	smelting=house	smoking=lamp
slugging=match	smelting=works	smoking=pipe
slug=horn	smiddum=tails	smoking=room
slug=shaped, etc.	smiling=muscle	smoking=tobacco
slug=snail	smithwork	smooth=bore, a.
slug=worm	smithy=coal	smoothbore (a gun)
sluice=fork	smiting=line	smooth=bored, etc.
sluice=gate	smock=faced, etc.	smooth=dab
sluice=valve	smock=frock	smoothing=box
sluiceway	smock=linen	smoothing=iron
slump=work	smock=mill	smoothing=mill
slung=shot	smock=race	smoothing=plane
slur=bar	smock=racing†	smoothing=stone
slur=bow	smoke=arch	smooth=sayer†
slush=barrel	smoke=ball	smoothsides (a fish)
slush=bucket	smoke=bell	smother=fly
slush=fund	smoke=black	smother=kiln
slush=horn	smoke=board	smug=boat
slush=pot	smoke=box	smug=faced, etc.
sly=boots	smoke=brown	smut=ball
sly=bream	smoke=bush	smut=fungus
smack=fisherman	smoke=condenser†	smut=machine
smackman	smoke=consumer†	smut=mill
smacksman	smoke=dry	smutty=nosed, etc.
smack=smooth	smoke=gray	snaffle=bit
small arms	smoke=house	snag=boat
small beer	smoke=jack	snagbush (the black-
small=clothes	smoke=money	thorn)
small=dot (lace)	smoke=painted, etc.	snag=chamber
smallfish	smoke=painting†	snaggle=tooth
small=headed, etc.	smoke=penny	snaggle=toothed
smallmouth (a fish)	smoke=pipe	snag=tooth
small pica	smoke=plant	snailbore (a gastropod)
smallpox	smoke=quartz	snail=borer
smart=grass	smoke=rocket	snail=clover
smart=money	smoke=sail	snailfish
smart=ticket	smoke=shade	snailflower (a plant)
smartweed	smoke=silver	snail=like
smashing=machine	smoke=stack	snail=pace

snail-paced, etc.
snail-park
snail-plant
snail-shell
snail-slow
snail-trefoil
snail-water
snail-wheel
snake-bird
snake-boat
snake-box
snake-buzzard
snake-cane
snake-charmer†
snake-coralline
snake-crane
snake-cucumber
snake-doctor
snake-eater†
snake-eel
snake-feeder†
snake-fern
snakefish
snake-fly
snake-gourd
snakehead (a plant, a
   fish, etc.)
snake-headed, etc.
snake-killer†
snake-leaves
snakelike
snake-line
snake-lizard
snake-moss
snakemouth (an orchis)
snakeneck (a bird)
snakenut (a tree)
snakenut-tree
snake-piece
snakepipe (a plant)
snake-rat
snakeroot (a plant)
snake's-beard*
snake's-egg*
snake's-head*
snake-shell
snakeskin
snakeskin-snail
snake's-mouth*

snake's-tail*
snakestone
snake's-tongue*
snakeweed
snakewood (a tree)
snakeworm
snaky-headed, etc.
snap-action
snap-apple
snap-back
snap-beetle
snap-block
snap-bolt
snap-bug
snap-cap
snap-cracker
snapdragon
snap-flask
snap-head
snap-hook
snap-jack
snap-link
snap-lock
snap-machine
snap-mackerel
snapper-back
snapping-beetle
snapping-bug
snapping-cracker
snapping mackerel
snapping-tongs
snapping-tool
snapping turtle
snap-shooter†
snap-tool
snapweed
snapwort
snare-drum
snare-head
snarling-iron
snarling-muscle
snarling-tool
snatch-block
snatch-cleat
snatching-roller
sneak-boat
sneak-box
sneak-shooting
sneak-thief

sneck-drawer†
sneck-drawn
sneck-posset
sneering-match
sneering-muscle
sneeshing-mull
sneeze-horn
sneezeweed
sneezewood (a tree)
sneezewort
sneezing-powder
snell-loop
snifting-valve
snig-eel
snipe-bill
snipe-eel
snipefish
snipe-fly
snipe-hawk
snipe-like
snipe's-head*
snipper-snapper
snip-snap
snivel-nose
snore-hole
snore-piece
snout-beetle
snout-butterfly
snout-mite
snout-moth
snout-ring
snow-apple
snowball
snowball-tree
snowbank
snowberry
snowbird
snow-blind
snow-blink
snow-boot
snow-bound, etc.
snow-box
snowbreak (a thaw)
snow-broth
snow-bunting
snowbush (a shrub)
snowcap (a bird)
snow-chukor
snow-cock

snow=drift
snowdrop (a plant, its
flower)
snowdrop=tree
snow=eater†
snow=eyes
snowfall
snow=field
snow=finch
snowflake
snow=flange
snow=flea
snowfleck
snowflight
snow=flood
snowflower (a plant)
snow=fly
snowfowl
snow=gauge
snow=gem
snow=glory
snow=gnat
snow=goggle
snow=goose
snow=grouse
snow=ice
snow=in=harvest (a
plant)
snow=insect
snow=in=summer (a
plant)
snow=knife
snow=leopard
snow=light
snowlike
snow=line
snow=mouse
snow=on=the=mountain
(a plant)
snow=owl
snow=partridge
snow=pear
snow=pheasant
snow=pigeon
snow=planer†
snow=plant
snow=plow
snow=probe
snow=scraper†

snow=shed
snow=shoe
snow=shoer†
snow=shovel
snow=skate
snowslide
snowslip
snow=snake
snow=sparrow
snow=squall
snow=storm
snow=sweeper†
snow=track
snow=water
snow=white
snow=wreath
snubbing=line
snubbing=post
snub=cube
snub=dodecahedron
snubnose (a mollusk)
snub=nosed, etc.
snub=post
snuff=bottle
snuff=box
snuff=color
snuff=dipper†
snuff=dish
snuffer=dish
snuffer=pan
snuffer=tray
snuff=headed, etc.
snuffing pig
snuff=maker†
snuffman
snuff=mill
snuff=rasp
snuff=spoon
snuff=taker†
soak=barrel
soak=hole
soaking=pit
so=and=so
soap=apple
soap=ashes
soap=balls
soapbark (a tree)
soapbark=tree
soap=barring†

soap=beck
soapberry
soap=boiler†
soap=bubble
soap=bulb
soap=cerate
soap=coil
soap=crutch
soap=crutching†
soap=cutting†
soap=earth
soap=engine
soap=fat
soapfish
soap=frame
soap=glue
soap=house
soap=kettle
soap liniment
soap=lock
soap=maker†
soap=mill
soapnut (a plant)
soap=pan
soap=plant
soap plaster
soap=pod
soaproot (a plant)
soap=slabbing†
soapstone
soap=suds
soap=tree
soapweed
soapwood (a tree)
soap=works
soapwort
soapwort=gentian
sober=blooded, etc.
so=called, a.
social=democratic
socket=bayonet
socket=bolt
socket=caster
socket=celt
socket=chisel
socket=drill
socket=joint
socket=pipe
socket=pole

socket-washer
socket-wrench
sockhead (a person)
soda-alum
soda-apparatus
soda-ash
soda-ball
soda-biscuit
soda-cracker
soda-feldspar
soda-fountain
soda-furnace
soda-lime
soda-lye
soda-mesotype
soda-mint
soda-paper
soda-plant
soda-salt
soda-waste
soda-water
sod-burning†
sod-cutter†
sodding-implements
sodding-mallet
sodding-spade
sod-oil
Sodom-apple
sod-plow
sod-worm
sofa-arm
sofa-back
sofa-bed
sofa-bedstead
sofa-cover
sofa-leg
sofa-pillow
soft-bodied, etc.
softening-iron
softening-machine
soft-grass
softhorn (a person)
soft-sawder
soft-shell
softsoap, v.
soft-solid
soft-tack
softwood (a tree)
soi-disant

soil-bound
soil-branch
soil-cap
soil-cup
soil-pipe
soil-pulverizer†
soke-reeve
solan-goose
solder-casting†
soldering-block
soldering-bolt
soldering-frame
soldering-furnace
soldering-iron
soldering-machine
soldering-nipple
soldering-pot
soldering-tongs
soldering-tool
soldering-union
solder-machine
solder-mould
soldier-ant
soldier-beetle
soldier-bug
soldier-bush
soldier-crab
soldier-fish
soldier-fly
soldierlike
soldier-moth
soldier-orchis
soldier's-herb*
soldierwood (a shrub)
sole-beating†
sole-channel
sole-channelling†
sole-cutting†
sole-finishing†
solefish
sole-fleuk
sole-leather
sole-moulding†
solen-ark
sole-piece
sole-plate
sole-reflex
sole-rounding†
sole-tile

sol-fa
sol-faing
sol-faist
solicitor-general
solid-drawn, etc.
sol-lunar
Solomon's-seal*
somebody
somegate
somehow
something
sometime, adv.
sometimes
someway, adv.
somewhat
somewhen
somewhere
somewhile
somewhither
song-bird
song-book
songcraft
songman
song-muscle
song-music
song-sparrow
song-thrush
son-in-law
sonnet-writer†
soola-clover
soot-dew
sootflake
soothfast
soothsay
soothsayer†
soot-wart
sora-rail
sorb-tree
sore-eyed, etc.
sore-falcon
sorehead (a person)
sorghum-mill
sorghum-stripper†
sorrel-tree
sorrel-vine
sorrow-stricken
sorting-box
sorting-machine

souari=nut
soughing=tile
soul=blind
soul=deaf
soul=fearing, etc.
soul=sick
soul=sleeper
soul=stuff
soundboard
sound=boarding
sound=body (a reso-
    nance=box)
sound=bone (a fish=
    bone)
sound=bow (the edge
    of a bell)
sound=box (a reso-
    nance=box)
sound=chest (a reso-
    nance=box)
sound=deafness
sounder=magnet
sound=figures
sound=hole
sounding=apparatus
sounding=board
sounding=bottle
sounding=lead
sounding=line
sounding=machine
sounding=post
sounding=rod
sound=line
sound=post
sound=proof
sound=radiometer
sound=register
sound=shadow
sound=wave
soup=kitchen
soup=maigre
soup=meat
soup=plate
soup=ticket
sour=eyed, etc.
sour=gourd (a tree)
sour=grass
sour=gum (a tree)
souring=vessel

sour=sop
sour=tree
sourwood (a tree)
South=African
South=American
South=Caroliniau
Southdown
southeast
southernwood (a tree)
southland
south=seeking
south=southerly
southwest
sowback (a ridge of
    sand)
sowbane (a plant)
sow=belly
sowbread (a plant)
sow=bug
sow=drunk
sow=fennel
sow=gelder
sowing=machine
sow=thistle
soy=bean
soy=pea
space=box
space=coördinate
space=curvature
space=homology
space=line
space=mark
space=perception
space=relation
space=rule
space=writing†
spacing=lace
spade=bayonet
spade=farm
spadefish
spade=foot, a.
spadefoot (a toad)
spade=footed, etc.
spade=graft
spade=guinea
spade=gun
spade=handle
spade=husbandry
spade=iron

spade=rack
spading=machine
spae=book
spaeman
spaewife
spake=net
spalding=knife
spalling=floor
spalling=hammer
span=beam
span=block
span=dogs
spandrel=wall
span=fire new
spangling=machine
Spanish=flag (a fish)
spanker=eel
spanker=gaff
spanker=mast
span=lashing
span=long
span=new
span=piece
span=roof
span=saw
span=shackle
spanworm
spar=buoy
spar=deck
spar=dust
spare=built, etc.
sparerib
spark=arrester†
spark=coil
spark=condenser†
spark=consumer†
sparked=back, a.
sparkleberry
spark=netting
sparling=fowl
spar=maker†
sparrow=bill
sparrow=grass
sparrow=hawk
sparrow=owl
sparrow=tail (a tail)
sparrowtail (something
    like a sparrow's
    tail)

sparrowwort
spart=grass
spar=torpedo
spatch=cock
spatterdash
spatter=dock
spatterwork
spattling=machine
spawn=brick
spawn=eater†
spawn=fungus
spawn=hatcher†
spawning=bed
spawning=ground
spawning=screen
spawning=season
spawn=rising
speaking=machine
speaking=trumpet
speaking=tube
speaking voice
speal=bone
spear=billed
spear=dog
spearfish
spearflower (a plant)
spear=foot
spear=grass
spear=hand
spear=head
spear=hook
spear=javelin
spear=leaved, etc.
spear=lily
spearman
spearmint
spear=nail
spear=plate
spear=thistle
spear=widgeon
spearwood (a tree)
spearwort
species=cover
species=cycle
species=monger
species=paper
species=sheet
speck-block
speck=fall

speckle=bellied, etc.
specklebelly (a goose,
    a duck, a trout)
speck=moth
spectacle=furnace
spectacle=gauge
spectacle=glass
spectacle=maker†
spectacle=ornament
spectre=bar
spectre=candle
spectre=crab
spectre=insect
spectre=lemur
spectre=shrimp
speculum=forceps
speculum=metal
speech=centre
speech=crier
speech=day
speechmake
speechmaker†
speech=reading†
speed=cone
speed=gauge
speed=indicator†
speed=measurer†
speed=multiplier†
speed=pulley
speed=recorder†
speed=riggers
speed=sight
speedway
speedwell
speedy=cut (an injury
    to a horse's knee)
spek=boom
spellbind, v.
spellbinder
spell=bone
spellbound
spelling=bee
spelling=book
spelling=match
spell=stopped
spell=work
spencer=gaff
spend=all
spending=money

spendthrift
spermaceti=oil
spermaceti=whale
sperm=ball
sperm=blastoderm
sperm=blastula
sperm=cell
sperm=kernel
sperm=morula
sperm=nucleus
sperm=oil
sperm=rope
sperm=whale
sphere=crystals
sphere=yeast
sphex=fly
sphinx=moth
spice=apple
spiceberry
spice=box
spicebush (a shrub)
spice=cake
spice=mill
spice=nut
spice=shop
spice=tree
spicewood (a shrub)
spick=and=span
spick=and=span new
spick=span new
spicula=forceps
spicule=sheath
spider=ant
spider=band
spider=bug
spider=catcher†
spider=cells
spider=cot
spider=crab
spider=diver
spider=eater†
spiderflower (a plant)
spider=fly
spider=helmet
spider=hunter†
spider=legs
spider=line
spider=mite
spider=monkey

spider=net
spider=orchis
spider=shell
spider=stitch
spider=wasp
spider=web
spider=wheel
spiderwork
spiderwort
spiegel=iron
spigot=joint
spigot=pot
spikebill (a duck)
spike=extractor†
spikefish
spike=grass
spike=horn (a horn)
spikehorn (a deer)
spike=lavender
spike=machine
spike=nail
spikenard=tree
spikenose (a fish)
spike=oil
spike=plank
spike=rush
spike=shell
spike=tackle
spiketail (a duck)
spike=tailed, etc.
spike=team
spike=borer†
spike=hole
spill=case
spill=channel
spillet=fishing†
spilliard=fishing†
spilling=line
spill=stream
spill=trough
spillway
spindle=cataract
spindle=cell
spindle=celled, etc.
spindle=lathe
spindle=legs (legs)
spindlelegs (a person)
spindle=shanked, etc.
spindle=shanks (legs)

spindleshanks (a per-
    son)
spindle=shell
spindle=step
spindle=stromb
spindletail (a duck)
spindle=tree
spindle=valve
spindle=whorl
spindleworm
spine=armed, etc.
spineback (a fish)
spine=bearer†
spinebelly (a fish)
spinebill (a bird)
spinefoot (a lizard)
spinetail (a bird)
spinning=frame
spinning=head
spinning=jack
spinning=jenny
spinning=machine
spinning=mill
spinning=mite
spinning=organ
spinning=roller
spinning=spider
spinning=wart
spinning=wheel
spinode=curve
spinode=torse
spintext (a person)
spiny=finned, etc.
spiraltail (a bird)
spire=bearer†
spire=light
spire=steeple
spirit=back
spirit=blue
spirit=brown
spirit=butterfly
spirit=duck
spirit=gum
spirit=lamp
spiritleaf (a plant)
spirit=level
spirit=merchant
spirit=meter
spirit=rapper†

spirit=room
spirit=stirring
spiritweed
spirit=world
spitball
spitbox
spit=bug
spitchcock
spit=curl
spit=deep
spitfire
spit=poison
spit=rack
spit=sticker†
spitting=snake
spittle=fly
spittle=insect
spittle=of=the=stars (a
    plant)
spit=venom
spitz=dog
spitzflute
spitzkasten
splash=board
splash=wing
splatterdash
splatter=faced
splay=foot (a foot)
splayfoot (a deformity)
splay=footed, etc.
splay=mouth
spleen=pulp
spleen=stone
spleenwort
splice=grafting†
splice=piece
splicing=fid
splicing=hammer
splicing=shackle
splining=machine
splint armor
splint bandage
splint=bone
sptint=bottomed, etc.
splint=box
splint=coal
splinter=bar
splinter=bone
splinter=netting

splinter=proof
splint=machine
splint=plane
split=back, *a.*
splitbeak (a bird)
split=bottomed, etc.
split=brilliant
splitfeet (animals)
splitfoot (Satan)
split=harness
splitmouth (a fish)
split=new
splittail (a fish, a duck)
splitting=knife
splitting=machine
splitting=saw
spogel=seed
spoil=bank
spoil=five
spoil=paper
spoilsman
spoilsmonger
spoil=sport
spoke=auger
spoke=bone
spoke=driving†
spoke=gauge
spoke=lathe
spoke=planing†
spoke=pointer†
spoke=polishing†
spoke=setter†
spoke=shave
spoke=sizing†
spokesman
spoke=tenoning†
spoke=throating†
spoke=turning†
spoke=trimmer†
spoking=machine
sponge=animalcule
sponge=bar
sponge=cake
sponge=cover
sponge=crab
sponge=cucumber
sponge=cup
sponge=diving†
sponge=farmer†

sponge=fisher†
sponge=fishery
sponge=glass
sponge=gourd
sponge=hock
sponge=moth
sponge=spicule
sponge=tongs
sponge=tree
spongewood (a plant)
sponging=house
spongy=pubescent
spongy=villous
spool=cotton
spool=holder†
spooling=machine
spooling=wheel
spool=labelling
spoolstand
spoon=bait
spoonbeak (a bird)
spoonbill (a bird)
spoon=billed, etc.
spoon=bit
spoon=chisel
spoon=drift
spoon=fashion
spoonflower (a plant)
spoon=gouge
spoon=holder
spoon=hook
spoon=meat
spoon=net
spoon=saw
spoon=shaped, etc.
spoontail (a crustacean)
spoon=victuals
spoonwood (a tree)
spoonworm
spore=capsule
spore=case
spore=cell
spore=formation
spore=group
spore=plasm
spore=sac
sporting=book
sporting=house
sportsman

sportsmanlike
sportswoman
spot=ball
spot=lens
spotneck (a bird)
spotrump (a bird)
spot=stitch
spotted bass
spotted=tree
spoutfish
spout=hole
spout=shell
sprag=road
sprat=barley
sprat=borer†
sprat=day
sprat=loon
sprat=mew
spray=board
spray=drain
spraying=machine
spray=instrument
spray=nozzle
spread=eagle
spread=eagleism
spreading=adder
spreading=board
spreading=frame
spreading=furnace
spreading=hammer
spreading=machine
spreading=oven
spreading=plate
spreettail (a duck)
sprig=bolt
sprig=crystal
sprigtail (a duck, a
    grouse)
sprig=tailed, etc.
spring=back
spring balance
spring=band
spring=bar
spring=beam
spring=beauty
spring bed
spring=beetle
spring=bell
spring=block

spring=board
spring=box
spring=buck
spring carriage
spring cart
spring=flood
spring=fly
spring=forelock
spring=gun
spring=haas
spring=halt
spring=hammer
spring=hanger
spring=head
spring=hook
spring=house
springing=beetle
springing=course
springing=hairs
springing=line
springing=tool
springing=wall
spring=jack
spring=latch
spring=ligament
springlike
spring=line
spring=lock
spring mattress
spring=net
spring=oyster
spring=padlock
spring=pawl
spring=plank
spring=pole
spring punch
spring searcher
spring=shackle
spring=stay
spring=stud
springtail (an insect)
spring=tailed
spring=tide (a tide)
springtide (time)
springtime
spring tool
spring trap
spring valve
spring wagon

spring=water
spring=weir
springworm
springwort
sprink=buck
sprint=race
sprint=runner†
spritsail
sprittail (a duck)
sprocket=wheel
sprout=cell
sprout=chain
sprout=gemma
sprout=germination
spruce beer
spruce=duff
spruce=fir
spruce=grouse
spruce=gum
spruce=ochre
spruce=partridge
spruce=pine
sprue=hole
spun=out, a.
spun=yarn
spur=bunting
spurflower (a plant)
spur=fowl
spur=gall
spur=gally
spur=gear
spur=gearing
spurge=creeper
spurge=flax
spurge=laurel
spurge=nettle
spurge=olive
spur=hawk
spur=heeled, etc.
spur=leather
spurling=line
spurnwater (a break-
    water)
spur=pepper
spur=pruning
spur=royal
spur=shell
spur=shore
spurtle=blade

spur=track
spur=tree
spurway
spur=wheel
spurwing (a bird)
spurwort
spyboat
spycraft
spy=glass
spy=hole
spy=money
squab=chick
squab pie
squail=board
squam=duck
squan=fish
square=built, etc.
square=flipper (a seal)
squarehead (a person)
square=leg
square man (who is
    "square")
squareman
squaresail
square=spot, a.
squarespot (a moth)
square=stern (a boat)
square=toes (a person)
squaring=boards
squaring=plow
squaring=shears
squash=beetle
squash=borer†
squash=bug
squash=gourd
squash=melon
squash=vine
squat=snipe
squat=tag
squatting=pill
squaw=berry
squaw=duck
squaw=huckleberry
squawk=duck
squawking=thrush
squaw=man
squaw=mint
squawroot (a plant)
squaw=vine

squawweed
squeezing=box
squid=fork
squid=hound
squid=jig
squid=jigger†
squid=thrower†
squilgee=toggle
squillfish
squint=eyed, etc.
squirrel=bot
squirrel=corn
squirrelcup (a plant)
squirrel=fish
squirrel=grass
squirrel=hake
squirrel=hawk
squirrel=lemur
squirrel=lock
squirrel=monkey
squirrel=mouse
squirrel=petaurist
squirrel=phalanger
squirrel=shrew
squirreltail (a grass)
squirt=gun
stabbing=machine
stabbing=press
stable=boy
stable=call
stable=fly
stableman
stable=room
stable=stand
stack=borer†
stack=funnel
stack=guard
stacking=band
stacking=belt
stacking=derrick
stacking=stage
stack=room
stack=stand
stack=yard
staddle=roof
staddle=stand
staff=angle
staff=bead
staff=captain

staff=commander
staff=degree
staff=duty
staff=herding
staff=hole
staff=man
staff=notation
staff=officer
staff=sergeant
staff=stone
staff=surgeon
staff=tree
staff=vine
stag-beetle
stagbush (a plant)
stag=dance
stage=box
stage=carriage
stage=coach
stage=craft
stage direction
stage door
stage effect
stage=fever
stage=forceps
stage fright
stage=hand
stage=house
stage=manager†
stage=micrometer
stage=plate
stage=play
stage=player†
stage right
stage=setter†
stage=struck
stag=evil
stage=wagon
stage wait
stage whisper
stagewright
staggerbush (a plant)
stagger=grass
staggerwort
stag=headed, etc.
stag=horn
staghound
stag=party
stag's=horn*

stag=tick
stag=worm
stairbeak (a bird)
staircase
staircase=shell
stair=foot
stair=head
stair=rod
stairway
stair=wire
staithwort
stake=boat
stake=driver†
stake=head
stakeholder
stake=hook
stake=iron
stake=net
stake=netter†
stake=pocket
stake=puller†
stake=rest
stalemate
stalk=borer†
stalk=cutter†
stalk=eyed, etc.
stalking=horse
stalk=puller†
stall=board
stall=fed, etc.
stall=feed
stallman
stall=plate
stall=reader†
stamp=affixer†
stamp=album
stamp=battery
stamp=block
stamp=book
stamp=canceller†
stamp=collecting†
stamp=distributer†
stamp=duty
stamp=hammer
stamp=head
stamping=ground
stamping=machine
stamping=mill
stamping=press

stamp-machine
stamp-mill
stamp-moistener†
stamp-note
stamp-office
stanchion-gun
standard-bearer†
standard-bred
standard-grass
standard-knee
standardwing (a bird)
standby
stander-by
stander-grass
standerwort
stand-gall
standing-cypress
standing-ground
standing-press
standing-room
standing-stool
stand-off
stand-offish
stand-pipe
standpoint
stand-rest
standstill, n.
stane-raw
stank-hen
staple-house
staple-punch
staple-right
star-animal
star-anise
star-apple
starbeam
star-bearer
star-blasting
starblind
starboard
star-bright, a.
starbush (a plant)
star-buzzard
star-capsicum
star-catalogue
star-chamber
starch-cellulose
starch-gum
starch-hyacinth

starch-machine
starchroot (a plant)
starch-star
starch-sugar
star-cluster
star-crossed, etc.
star-diamond
star-drift
star-dust
star-facet
starfinch
starfish
starfish-flower (a plant)
starflower (a plant)
star fort
starfruit (a plant)
star-gauge
star-gaze
star-gazer†
star-gooseberry
star-grass
star-head
star-hyacinth
stark naked
starlight
starlike
starlit
star-lizard
star-map
star-moulding
star-netting
starnose (a mole)
star-of-Bethlehem (a
    plant)
star-of-night (a plant)
star-of-the-earth (plant)
star pagoda
star-pepper
star-pile
star-pine
star-proof
star-reed
star-rowel
star-ruby
star-sapphire
star-saxifrage
star-shake
star-shell
starshine

star-shoot
star-shot
star-slough
star-stone
startail (a bird)
star-thistle
starthroat (a bird)
starting-bar
starting-bolt
starting-engine
starting-place
starting-point
starting-post
starting-valve
starting-wheel
star-trap
starve-acre (a plant)
star wheel
star-worm
starwort
statecraft
state-house
state-monger
stateroom
states-general
statesman
statesmanlike
state-socialism
state-socialist
stateswoman
station-bill
station-calendar
station-house
station-indicator
station-master
station-meter
station-pointer
station-pole
station-staff
statuary-brass
statuary-casting†
statue dress
statute-book
statute-fair
statute-roll
stave-bender†
stave-bilging†
stave-chamfering†
stave-crozing†

stave-cutter†
stave-dressing†
stave-howelling†
stave-jointer†
stave-planing†
stave-rime
stave-riving†
staverwort
stave-sawing†
stave-setter†
stave-tankard
stavewood (a tree)
stay-at-home (a person)
stay-bar
stay-bolt
staybusk
stay-chain
staycord
stay-end
stay-foot
stay-gauge
stay-hole
stay-hook
staylace
stay-light
staymaker
stay-pile
stay-plow
stay-rod
staysail
stay-tackle
stay-wedge
steadfast
steady-going, etc.
steady-rest (a back-rest)
steak-crusher†
steak-masher†
stealing-strake
steam-atomizer†
steam-blower†
steamboat
steamboat-bug
steamboat-coal
steamboat-rolls
steamboat-screen
steam-boiler
steam-box
steam-brake
steam-car

steam-carriage
steam-case
steam-chamber
steam-chest
steam-chimney
steam-cock
steam-coil
steam-color
steam-crane
steam-cutter
steam-cylinder
steam-dome
steam-dredger
steam-engine
steamer-cap
steamer-duck
steam-excavator†
steam-fountain
steam-gauge
steam-gas
steam-generator†
steam-governor†
steam-gun
steam-hammer
steam-heat
steam-hoist
steam-house
steam-jacket
steam-jet
steam-joint
steam-kettle
steam-kitchen
steam-launch
steam-motor
steam-navigation
steam-navvy
steam-organ
steam-oven
steam-packet
steam-pan
steam-pipe
steam-plow
steam-port
steam-power
steam-press
steam-printing†
steam-propeller
steam-pump
steam-radiator†

steam-ram
steam-regulator†
steam-room
steamship
steam-space
steam-table
steam-tank
steam-tight
steam-toe
steam-trap
steam-tug
steam-valve
steam-vessel
steam-wagon
steam-wheel
steam-whistle
steam-winch
steam-worm
steam-yacht
stearine-press
steel-blue
steel-bow, a.
steelboy
steel-clad, etc.
steel-engraving†
steel-finch
steelhead (a duck, a
    trout)
steelmaster
steel-mill
steel-ore
steel-press
steel-saw
steelware
steelwork
steel-worker†
steel-works
steelyard
steep-down
steep-grass
steeplebush (a plant)
steeplechase
steeplechaser†
steeple-crowned, etc.
steeple-engine
steeple hat
steeple-hunting
steeple-jack
steepletop (a whale)

steep=to
steep=tub
steep=up
steep=water
steepweed
steepwort
steerageway
steering=apparatus
steering=compass
steering=gear
steering=sail
steering=wheel
steersman
steersmate
stellate=pilose
stem=character
stem=clasping†
stem=climber†
stem=eelworm
stem end
stem=head
stem=knee
stem=leaf
steam=pessary
stem=piece
stem=sickness
stem=stitch
stem=winder†
stench=pipe
stench=trap
stencil=cutter†
stencil=pen
stencil=plate
stent=master
stent=roll
step=back, a.
stepbairn
step=bit
step=box
stepbrother
stepchild
step=country
step=cover
step=cut
step=dame
step=dance
stepdaughter
stepfather
step=fault

step=gauge
step=grate
step=ladder
stepmother
step=parent
stepping=point
stepping=stone
stepsister
stepson
step=stone
step=vein
stereotype=block
stereotype=metal
stereotype plate
stern=board
stern=cap
stern=chase
stern=chaser
stern=fast
stern=frame
stern=gallery
stern=hook
stern=knee
stern=port
stern=post
stern=sheets
sternway
stern=wheeler
sterro=metal
stew=pan
stew=pond
stew=pot
stick=bait
stick=bug
stick=culture
stick=handle
stick=helmet
sticking=place
sticking=plaster
sticking=point
stick=insect
stick=in=the=mud
stick=lac
stickleback (a fish)
stick=play
stickseed (a plant)
sticktail (a duck)
sticktight (a weed)
stiff=borne, etc.

stiffening=machine
stiffening order
stiff neck
stifftail (a duck)
stifle=bone
stifle=joint
stifle=shoe
stigma=disk
still=birth
still=born, etc.
still=burn
still=fish
still=fisher†
still=house
still=hunt
still=hunter†
still=liquor
still=room
still=stand
still=watcher
stilt=bird
stilt=petrel
stilt=plover
stilt=sandpiper
stilt=walker†
sting=and=ling, adv.
sting=bull
stingfish
stinging=bush (a plant)
stinging=cell
sting=moth
sting=ray
stingtail (a sting=ray)
sting=winkle
stink=alive
stink=ball
stink=bird
stink=bug
stinkhorn (a plant)
stinking=weed
stinking=wood (a plant)
stink=rat
stink=shad
stinkstone
stink=trap
stink=turtle
stinkweed
stinkwood (a tree)
stipple=engraving†

stipple=graver†
stippling=machine
stirrup=bar
stirrup=bone
stirrup=cup
stirrup=hose
stirrup=iron
stirrup=lantern
stirrup=leather
stirrup=muscle
stirrup=oil
stirrup=piece
stitch=fallen
stitching=clamp
stitching=horse
stitching=machine
stitch=regulator†
stitch=ripper†
stitch=wheel
stitchwork
stitchwort
stock=account
stock=beer
stock=blind
stock=board
stock=book
stock=bow
stock=breeder†
stock=broker†
stock=brush
stock=buckle
stock=car
stock=dove
stock=duck
stock=eikle
stock exchange
stock=farm
stock=farmer†
stock=father
stock=feeder†
stock=fish
stock=gang
stock=gillyflower
stock=hawk
stockholder†
stock=horse
stock=indicator
stocking=frame
stocking=loom

stocking=machine
stocking=maker†
stocking=yarn
stock=jobber†
stock=jobbery
stock=list
stockman
stock=market
stock=morel
stock=owl ·
stock=pot
stock=printer†
stock=pump
stock=punished
stock=purse
stock=raiser†
stock=ranch
stock=range
stock=rider†
stock=room
stock=saddle
stock=station
stock=still
stock=stone
stock=tackle
stock=taking†
stock=train
stock=whaup
stockwork
stock=yard
stoke=hole
stomach=ache
stomach=brush
stomach=cough
stomach=grief
stomach=piece
stomach=plaster
stomach=pump
stomach=qualmed
stomach=sick
stomach=staggers
stomach=sweetbread
stomach=timber
stomach=tooth
stomach=tube
stomach=worm
stone axe (made of
    stone)
stone=axe (to cut stone)

stone=basil
stone=bass
stone=bird
stone=biter
stone=blind
stone=blue
stone=boat
stone=boilers
stone=boiling
stone=borer†
stone=bow
stone=bramble
stone=brash
stonebreak (a plant)
stone=breaker†
stone=bruise
stonebuck (an antelope)
stone=butter
stone=canal
stone=cast
stonecat (a fish)
stone=centiped
stonechacker (a bird)
stonechat (a bird)
stonechatter (a bird)
stone=climber†
stoneclink (a bird)
stone=clover
stone=coal
stone=cold
stone=color
stone=colored, etc.
stone=coral
stone=crab
stone=crawfish
stone=cray
stone=cricket
stonecrop (a plant)
stone=crush
stone=crusher†
stone=curlew
stone=cutter†
stone=dead
stone=deaf
stone=devil
stone=dresser†
stone=drilling†
stone=dumb
stone=eater†

stone=engraving†
stone=facing†
stone=falcon
stone=fern
stonefish
stone=fly
stone=fruit
stone=gall
stone=gatherer†
stone=gray
stone=grig
stone=grinding†
stone=hammer
stone=hard
stone=harmonicon
stonehatch (a plover)
stone=hawk
stone=head (bed=rock)
stone=leek
stone=lichen
stone=lily
stone=lobster
stone=lugger (a fish)
stoneman
stone=marten
stone=mason
stone=merchant
stone=mill
stone=mint
stone=moulding†
stone=mortar
stone=oak
stone=oil
stone=owl
stone=parsley
stonepecker (a bird)
stone=pine
stone=pit
stone=pitch
stone=planing†
stone=plover
stone=pock
stone=polishing†
stone=quarry
stone=quarrying†
stone=rag
stone=raw
stone=roller (a fish)
stoneroot (a plant)

stone=rue
stone=runner (a bird)
stone=saw
stone=sawing†
stone's cast
stoneseed (a plant)
stone=separator†
stone=shot
stone=shower
stonesmickle (a bird)
stone=snipe
stone=sorting†
stone=sponge
stone=squarer†
stone=still
stone=sturgeon
stone=sucker (a fish)
stone=thrush
stone=toter (a fish)
stone=walling
stoneware
stoneweed
stonework
stone=working†
stone=works
stonewort
stone=yard
stony=hearted, etc.
stool=ball
stool=end
stool=pigeon
stoop=shouldered
stop=cock
stop=collar
stop=cylinder
stop=drill
stop=finger
stop=gap
stop=gate
stop=hound
stop=knob
stop=motion
stop=net
stop=order
stop=over
stopper=bolt
stopper=hole
stopper=knot
stopping=brush

stopping=coat
stopping=knife
stop=plank
stop=plate
stop-ridge
stop=rod
stop=thrust
stop=valve
stop=watch
stopwater
stop=wheel
stop=work
storage=bellows
storax=tree
store=city
store=farm
store=farmer†
storehouse
storekeeper†
storeman
storemaster
storeroom
store=ship
stork=billed, etc.
storksbill
storm=area
storm=beat, etc.
storm=belt
storm=bird
storm=card
storm=centre
storm=circle
storm=cloud
storm=cock
storm=compass
storm=cone
storm=current
storm=door
storm=drum
storm=finch
storm=flag
storm=glass
storm=house
storming party
storm=kite
storm=pane
storm=path
storm=pavement
storm=petrel

storm=proof
storm=sail
storm=signal
storm=stay
storm=stone
storm=track
storm=wind
storm=window
storm=zone
story=book
story=post
story=rod
story=teller†
story=writer†
stout=dart
stouth=and=routh
stout=hearted, etc.
stove=coal
stove=cover
stove=drum
stove=glass
stove=hearth
stove=house
stove=jack
stovepipe
stove=plant
stove=plate
stove=polish
stove=truck
stowaway (a person)
stowdown, n.
stow=wood
strabismus=forceps
strabismus=scissors
straddle=bug
straddle=legged, etc.
straddle=pipe
straddle=plow
straggle=tooth
straightaway, a.
straight=billed, etc.
straight=edge
straightening=block
straightening=machine
straightforward
straighthorn (a cephalopod)
straight=joint, a.
straight=out, a.

straightway, adv.
strainer=vine
straining=beam
straining=fork
straining=leather
straining=piece
straining=reel
straining=sill
strain=normal
strain=sheet
strain=type
strait=hearted, etc.
strait=jacket
strait=waistcoat
strand=bird
stranding=machine
strand=mycele
strand=mycelium
strand=plover
strand=rat
strand=wolf
strangle=tare
strangleweed
strap=bolt
strap=clamp
strap=game
strap=head
strap=hinge
strap=joint
strap=laid
strap=mounts
strap=oil
strap=oyster
strapping=plate
strap=shaped, etc.
strap=skein
strapwork
strapworm
strapwort
straw bed
strawberry
strawberry bass
strawberry=bed
strawberry=blite
strawberry=borer
strawberry=bush
strawberry=clover
strawberry=comb
strawberry=crab

strawberry=finch
strawberry-geranium
strawberry=leaf
strawberry=mark
strawberry=moth
strawberry=pear
strawberry=perch
strawberry=plant
strawberry=roan
strawberry=shrub
strawberry=tomato
strawberry=tree
strawberry=vine
strawberry=worm
straw=board
straw=boiler†
straw=buff
straw=built
straw=carrier†
straw=cat
straw=coat
straw=color
straw=colored, etc.
straw=cotton
straw=cutter†
straw=drain
straw=embroidery
straw=fiddle
straw hat
straw=house
straw=needle
straw=ride
strawsmall (a bird)
strawsmear (a bird)
straw=stem
straw=stone
straw=underwing (a moth)
straw=wine
straw=worm
straw=yard
straw=yellow
stray=line
stream=anchor
stream=cable
stream=clock
stream=current
stream=gold
stream=ice

stream=line
stream=tin
stream=wheel
stream=works
streamwort
street=car
street=door
street=locomotive
street=orderly
street=railroad
street=sprinkler†
street=sweeper†
street=walker†
streetway
stretcher=bond
stretcher=fly
stretcher=mule
stretch=halter
stretching=frame
stretching=iron
stretching=machine
stretching=piece
striate=plicate
striate=punctate
striate=sulcate
stricture=dilator
stridulating=organ
strike=a=light (a flint)
strike=block
strike=fault
strike=or=silent, n.
strike=pan
strike=pay
strike=plate
striker=arm
striker=boat
striker=out
striker=plate
striking=beam
striking=knife
striking=plate
striking=solution
string band
string=bark
string=bean
string=block
string=board
string=course
string=gauge

string=halt
string=minstrel
string orchestra
string=organ
string=pea
string=piece
string=plate
stringwood (a tree)
stringy=bark
strip armor
striped bass
stripetail (a bird)
strip=leaf
strip=lights
stripping=knife
stripping=plate
stroke=gear
stroke=oar
stroke=oarsman
strokesman
strong=back, n.
strongbark (a tree)
stronghold
strong=knit
strongman's=weed*
strong=minded, etc.
strutting=piece
stubble=field
stubble=goose
stubble=land
stubble=plow
stubble=rake
stubble=tunner
stub=book
stubborn=shafted, et
stub=damask
stub=end
stub=feather
stub=iron
stub=mortise
stub=nail
stub pen
stub=short
stub=shot
stub=tenon
stub=twist
stubwort
stucco=work
stuck=up

stuck=bolt
stud=bolt
stud=book
studdingsail
studdingsail=boom
student=parsnip
stud=farm
studfish
studflower (a plant)
stud=groom
stud=horse
stuff=chest
stuff=engine
stuff=gownsman
stuffing=box
stuffing=brush
stuffing=machine
stuffing=wheel
stumbling=block
stumbling=stone
stump=extractor†
stump=joint
stump=puller†
stump=tailed, etc.
stump=tree
style=branch
style=curve
stylewort
styptic=bur
stypticweed
subject=matter
subject=notion
subject=object
subsoil=plow
succirubra=bark
sucker=fish
sucker=foot
sucker=mouthed, etc.
sucker=rod
sucker=tube
suckfish
suck=in, n.
sucking=bottle
sucking=disk
sucking=fish
sucking=pump
sucking=stomach
suckstone (a fish)
suction=anemometer

suction=box
suction=chamber
suction=fan
suction=pipe
suction=plate
suction=primer
suction=pump
suction=valve
sud=oil
sugar=apple
sugar=barrel
sugar=bean
sugar=beat
sugarberry
sugar=bird
sugar=bowl
sugar=bush
sugar=camp
sugar candy
sugar=cane
sugar=clarifier†
sugar=coated, etc.
sugar=cutting†
sugar=drainer†
sugar=evaporator†
sugar=filter
sugar=furnace
sugar=granulator†
sugar=grass
sugar=gum
sugar=house
sugar=huckleberry
sugar=kettle
sugar=loaf
sugarloaf (a hat, a hill)
sugar=louse
sugar=machinery
sugar=making†
sugar=maple
sugar=meat
sugar=mill
sugar=millet
sugar=mite
sugar=mould
sugar=nippers
sugar=orchard
sugar=packer†
sugar=pan
sugar=pea

sugar=pine
sugar=plantation
sugar=planter†
sugar=plum
sugar=press
sugar=refiner†
sugar=refinery
sugar=sifter†
sugar=squirrel
sugar=syrup
sugar=teat
sugar=tongs
sugar=tree
sugar=vinegar
suit=shape
sulky cultivator
sulky harrow
sulky plow
sulky rake
sulky scraper
sullage=piece
sulphur=bottom
sulphur=concrete
sulphur=ore
sulphur=rain
sulphurroot (a plant)
sulphur=salt
sulphur=spring
sulphur=waters
sulphurweed
sulphur=whale
sulphurwort
sulphur=yellow
sultana=bird
sultan=flower (a plant)
sumac=beetle
sumbul=root
sum=calculus
summer day
summer=dried, etc.
summer=fallow
summer=house
summer=like
summer quarters
summer=ripe
summer=shine
summer=stir
summer=stone
summer=time

summer=tree
summer weather
summit=level
sump=fuse
sump=plank
sump=pump
sump=shaft
sump=shot
sumpter=cloth
sumpter=horse
sumpter=mule
sumpter=pony
sun=angel
sun=animalcule
sun=bath
sunbeam
sun=bear
sun=beat
sun=beaten, etc.
sun=beetle
sunbird
sun=bittern
sun=blink
sunbonnet
sunbow
sun=bright
sun=broad
sunburn
sunburned
sun=burner
sunburnt
sunburst
sun=case
sun=crack
sun=cress
sun=dance
sun=dart
sun=dawn
Sunday=school
sunder=tree
sundew
sun=dial
sun=dog
sundown
sundowner
sundra=tree
sundrops (a plant)
sundry=man
sun=fern

sun=fever
sun=figure
sunfish
sunflower (a plant)
sunflower=oil
sunflower=seed
sun=fruit
sun=gem
sun=glass
sun=glimpse
sun=glow
sun=god
sun=gold
sun=grebe
sun=hat
sunlight
sunlike
sun=myth
sunn hemp
sunny=sweet
sunny=warm
sun=opal
sun=perch
sun=picture
sun=plane
sun=plant
sun=proof
sun=ray
sunrise
sunrising
sun=rose
sun=scald
sunset
sunset=shell
sunsetting
sunshade
sunshine
sunshine=recorder†
sun=smitten
sun=snake
sun=southing
sun=spot
sun=spurge
sun=squall
sun=star
sunstead
sunstone
sun=stricken
sunstroke

sunstruck
sun=tree
sun=trout
sun=try
sunup
sun=wake
sun=wheel
sun=worship
sun=worshipper†
sun=year
sun=yellow
supper=board
supper=table
supper=time
supple=jack
supply=roller
supply=train
sur=ancrée
sure=enough, a.
sure=footed, etc.
surface=car
surface=chuck
surface=color
surface=condenser
surface=enamel
surface=fish
surface=gauge
surface=geology
surface=glaze
surface=grub
surface=integral
surface=joint
surfaceman
surface=mining
surface=motion
surface=plane
surface=printing
surface=rib
surface=road
surface=roller
surface=tension
surface=towing
surface=velocity
surface=water
surface=working
surface=worm
surfacing=machine
surfacing=plane
surf=bathing

surf=bird
surf=boat
surf=boatman
surf=clam
surf=duck
surfeit=swelled, etc.
surfeit=water
surf=fish
surfman
surf=scoter
surf=smelt
surf=whiting
surf=worn
surgeon=apothecary
surgeon=aurist
surgeon=dentist
surgeon=fish
surgeon=general
surgeon=generalship
surge=reliever
surge=spring
sur=master
surplice=fee
surprise=cup
sur=royal
surveying=vessel
surveyor=general
suspension bridge
suspension drill
suspension railway
suture=needle
swab=pot
swab=stick
swaddling=band
swaddling=clothes
swaddling=clout
swage=block
swaging=machine
swaging=mallet
swagman
swag=shop
swallow=day
swallow=fish
swallow=flycatcher
swallow=hawk
swallow=hole
swallow=pear
swallow=plover
swallow=roller

swallow=shrike
swallow's=nest*
swallow=stone
swallow=struck
swallowtail (a coat, a
    bird, etc.)
swallow=tailed
swallow=wing
swallowwort
swamp=apple
swamp=ash
swamp=beggarticks
swamp=blackberry
swamp=blackbird
swamp=blueberry
swamp=broom
swamp=cabbage
swamp=cottonwood
swamp=crake
swamp=cypress
swamp=deer
swamp=dock
swamp=dogwood
swamp=elm
swamp=fever
swamp=gum
swamp=hare
swamp=hellebore
swamp=hen
swamp=hickory
swamp=honeysuckle
swamp=land
swamp=laurel
swamp=lily
swamp=locust
swamp=loosestrife
swamp=lover
swamp=magnolia
swamp=mahogany
swamp=maple
swamp=milkweed
swamp=moss
swamp=muck
swamp=oak
swamp=ore
swamp=owl
swamp=partridge
swamp=pine
swamp=pink

swamp=quail
swamp=robin
swamp=rose
swamp=sassafras
swamp=saxifrage
swamp=sparrow
swamp=sumac
swamp=thistle
swamp=warbler
swampweed
swamp=willow
swampwood (a tree)
swan=animalcule
swan=down
swanflower
swan=goose
swanherd
swan=hopping
swan=maiden
swan=mark
swan=marking
swan=mussel
swanneck (end of a
    pipe, a plant)
swan's=down*
swan=shot
swanskin
swan=song
swan=upping
swanwort
swape=well
sward=cutter†
swarf=money
swarm=cell
swarm=spore
swartback (a gull)
swart=rutter
swart=star
swart=visaged, etc.
swash=bank
swash=bucket
swash=buckler
swash=letters
swash=plate
swashway
swash=work
sway=backed, etc.
sway=bar
sway=bracing

swear=word
sweat=band
sweat=box
sweat=canal
sweat=centre
sweat=cloth
sweat=duct
sweat=fibre
sweat=gland
sweat=house
sweating=bath
sweating=cloth
sweating-fever
sweating=house
sweating=iron
sweating=pit
sweating=room
sweating=sickness
sweating=tub
sweat=leather
sweat=lodge
sweat=stock
sweep=bar
sweeping=car
sweeping=day
sweep=net
sweep=piece
sweep=rake
sweep=saw
sweep=seine
sweep=seining
sweepstake
sweepstakes
sweep=washer
sweep=washings
sweet=apple (a tree)
sweet=bay
sweet=box
sweetbread
sweet=breathed, etc.
sweetbrier (a plant)
sweetbrier=sponge
sweet=fern
sweet=flag
sweet=gale
sweet=grass
sweet=gum
sweetheart
sweet=john

sweetleaf (a tree)
sweetlips (a fish, etc.)
sweetmeat
sweet-nancy
sweet-oil
sweet-reed
sweetroot (a plant)
sweet-rush
sweet-sop
sweetsucker (a fish)
sweet-tangle
sweet-water
sweetweed
sweet-william
sweet-willow
sweetwood (a tree)
sweetwort
swell-blind
swell-box
swellfish
swell-keyboard
swell-mob
swell-mobsman
swell-organ
swell-pedal
swell-rule
swell-shark
swell-toad
swift-boat (a certain flat
   boat used in Great
   Britain)
swiftfoot (a bird)
swift-footed, etc.
swift-moth
swill-milk
swim-bladder
swimming-apparatus
swimming-bath
swimming-bell
swimming-belt
swimming-bladder
swimming crab
swimming-fin
swimming-foot
swimming-plate
swimming-pond
swimming-school
swimming spider
swimming-stone

swimming-tub
swinebread (a plant)
swine-cress
swine-feather
swinefish
swine-flesh
swine-grass
swineherd
swine-oat
swine-penny
swine-plague
swine-pox
swine's-bane*
swine's-cress*
swine's-feather*
swine's-grass*
swine's-snout*
swine's-succory*
swinestone
swinesty
swine-thistle
swineward
swing-back
swing-beam
swing-boat
swing-bolster
swing-bridge
swing-churn
swing-devil
swing-buckler
swing-handle
swinging-block
swinging boom
swinging-post
swinging saw
swing-jack
swing-knife
swingle-bar
swingle-staff
swingletail (a shark)
swingletree
swingletree-hook
swingling-knife
swingling-machine
swingling-staff
swingling-tow
swing-motion
swing-pan
swing-plow

swing-press
swing-saw
swing-shelf
swing-stock
swing-swang
swing-table
swing-tool
swingtree
swing-trot
swing-wheel
swipe-beam
swish-broom
swish-swash
switchback, n.
switch-bar
switchboard
switcher-gear
switch-grass
switching-bill
switching-engine
switching-eye
switching-ground
switching-locomotive
switching-neck
switching-plug
switch-lantern
switch-lever
switchman
switch-motion
switch-signal
switch-sorrel
switch-stand
switch-tender†
swivel-bridge
swivel-eye
swivel-eyed, etc.
swivel-gun
swivel-hanger
swivel-hook
swivel-joint
swivel-keeper
swivel-loom
swivel-musket
swivel-plow
swivel-sinker
swizzle-stick
sword-arm
sword-bayonet
sword-bean

sword=bearer†
sword=belt
swordbill (a bird)
sword=blade
sword=breaker†
sword=cane
sword=carriage
swordcraft
sword=cut
sword=cutler
sword=dance
sword=dollar
sword=fight
swordfish
swordfishery
swordfishing
sword=flag
sword=flighted, etc.
sword=gauntlet

sword=grass
sword-guard
sword=hand
sword=hilt
sword=knot
sword=law
sword=lily
swordman
sword=mat
sword=play
sword=player
sword=pommel
sword=proof
sword=rack
sword=sedge
sword=shaped
sword=shrimp
swordsman
sword=stick

swordtail (a bug, etc.)
sword=thrust
S wrench
sycamore=disease
sycamore=fig
sycamore=maple
sycamore=moth
sycee=silver
syllable name
syllable=stumbling
sylph=like
symbol=printing
sypher=joint
syringe=gun
syringe=valve
syrphus=fly
syrup=gauge
system=maker†
system=monger

T

tabby-cat
tabernacle-work
table-anvil
table-bit
table-board
table-book
table-carpet
table-clamp
table-cloth
table-clothing
table-cover
table-cut
table-cutter
table diamond
table-flap
table grinder
table-knife
table-land
table-lathe
table-leaf
table-lifting
table-line
table-linen
table-money
table-moving†
table-music
table-plane
table-rapping†
table-rent
table-saw
table-service
table-shore
table-song
table-spar
tablespoon
table-sport
table-talk
table-talker†
table-tipping†
table-tomb

table-topped, etc.
tabletree
table-turning
tableware
table-work
tac-au-tac
tachina-fly
taching-end
tachylyte-basalt
tack-block
tack-claw
tack-comb
tack-driver†
tack-duty
tack-free
tack-hammer
tack-lashing
tackle-block
tackle-board
tackle-fall
tackle-hook
tackle-post
tack-lifter†
tack-puller†
tack-rivet
tacksman
tack-tackle
tac-locus
tacnode-cusp
tad-broom
tad-pipe
tadpole
tadpole-fish
tadpole-hake
tafferel-rail
tag-alder
tag-belt
tag-boat
tag-end
tag-fastener†

tag-holder†
tag-lock
tag-machine
tag-needle
tag-rag
tag-sore
tagtail (a worm, a
    person)
tag-wool
tail-bay
tail-block
tail-board
tail-bone
tail-coat
tail-corn
tail-coverts
tail-crab
tail-drain
tail-end
tail-feather
tail-fin
tailflower (a plant)
tail-fly
tail-gate
tail-grape
tail-hook
tail-lamp
tail-lobe
tail-muscle
tailor-bird
tailoring-machine
tailor-made
tailor-muscle
tailor-warbler
tail-piece
tail-pin
tail-pipe
tail-race
tail-rope
tails-common

tail-screw
tail-stock
tail-switching
tail-tackle
tail-trimmer
tail-valve
tail-vise
tail-water
tailwort
taint-worm
take-heed, *n.*
take-in
take-off
taker-off
take-up
talc-schist
talebearer†
tale-book
tale-piet
talesman
taleteller†
talipot-palm
talkee-talkee
talking-machine
talking-to
talky-talky
tall-boy
tallicoona-oil
tallowberry
tallow-can
tallow candle
tallow-chandler
tallow-chandlery
tallow-cup
tallow dip
tallow-drop
tallowface (a person)
tallow-faced, etc.
tallow-gourd
tallow-keech
tallownut (a tree)
tallow-nutmeg
tallow-oil
tallow-shrub
tallow-top
tallow-tree
tallowwood (a tree)
tally-ho
tallyman

tallymaster
tally-mark
tally-sheet
tally-shop
tally-stick
tally-trade
tallywoman
talmi-gold
tamarack-pine
tamarind-fish
tamarind-plum
tambor-oil
tambour-cotton
tambour-embroidery
tambour-frame
tambour-lace
tambour-needle
tambour-stitch
tambour-stitcher†
tambour-work
tamburet-stitch
tame-poison
tammy-norie
tam-o'-shanter (a cap)
tamping-bar
tamping-iron
tamping-machine
tamping-plug
tamp-work
tam-tam
tamtam-metal
tan-balls
tan-bark
tan-bath
tan-bay
tan-bed
tan-colored, etc.
tan-extractor
tangleberry
tangle-fish
tanglefoot (liquor)
tangle-picker
tangle-swab
tangle-wrack
tang-whaup
tan-house
tanka-boat
tankard-turnip
tank-car .

tank-engine
tank-furnace
tank-iron
tank-locomotive
tank-pump
tank-vessel
tank-worm
tan-liquor
tan-mill
tanning-apparatus
tanning-cylinder
tanning-materials
tannin-plate
tan-ooze
tan-pickle
tan-pit
tan-press
tan-ride
tan-spud
tan-stove
tan-turf
tan-vat
tan-yard
tao-tai
tapa-cloth
tap-bar
tap-bolt
tap-borer
tap-cinder
tape-carrier
tape-grass
tape line
tape measure
tape-needle
tape primer
taper-candlestick
taper-fuse
taper-pointed, etc.
taper-stand
taper-vise
tapestry-cloth
tapestry-moth
tapestry-painting
tapestry-stitch
tapework
tapeworm
tapeworm-plant
tap-hole
tap-house

tappet-loom
tappet-motion
tappet-ring
tappet-rod
tap-pickle
tapping-apparatus
tapping-bar
tapping-cock
tapping-drill
tapping-gouge
tapping-hole
tapping-machine
tapping-tool
tappit-hen
tap-plate
tap-rivet
tap-room
tap-root
tap-rooted, etc.
tap-screw
tap-shackled
tapsman
tap-wrench
taqua-nut
tarantula-killer†
tar-board
tar-box
tar-brush
tardy-gaited, etc.
targeman
target-card
target-firing
target-lamp
target-practice
tariff-ridden
tar-kiln
tar-lamp
tar-oil
tar-putty
tarry-breeks
tar-vetch
tar-water
tarweed
tar-well
taskmaster
taskmistress
task-work
tasselflower (a plant)
tassel-grass

tassel-hyacinth
tassel-stitch
tassel-tree
tassel-worm
taste-area
taste-bud
taste-bulb
taste-centre
taste-corpuscle
tatterwallop (rags)
tatting-shuttle
tattooing-needle
tau-bone
tau cross
tau crucifix
tau staff
tavern-bush
tavern-haunter†
tavern-keeper†
tavern-token
tax-cart
tax-dodger†
tax-free
tax-gatherer†
taxing-district
taxing-master
taxman
taxpayer†
tax sale
T bandage
T bar
T beard
T-bone
T branch
T bulb
T-cart
T-cloth
teaberry
tea-biscuit
tea-board
tea-bread
tea-bug
tea-caddy
tea-cake
tea-canister
tea-case
tea-chest
teaching-machine
tea-clam

tea-clipper
tea-cloth
teacup
tea-dealer†
tea-drinker†
tea-drunkard
tea-fight
tea-garden
tea-gown
tea-house
teakettle
teak-tree
teak-wood
teal-duck
tea-lead
tea-leaf
team-shovel
team-work
tea-oil
tea-party
tea-plant
teapot
tear-bag
tear-drop
tear-duct
tear-falling
tear-gland
tearing-machine
tea-room
tea-rose
tear-pit
tear-pump
tear-sac
tear-shaped, etc.
tear-thumb
tear-up
tea-scent
tea-scrub
tea-service
tea-set
tea-shrub
teasing-needle
teaspoon
tea-stick
tea-table
tea-taster†
tea-things
teat-like
tea-tray

tea=tree
tea=urn
tea=ware
teaze=hole
teazel=card
teazel=frame
teazelling=machine
teazelwort
teaze=tenon
tec=tec
teel=oil
teel=seed
teeming=hole
teeming=punch
tec=tee
teetertail (a bird)
tee=totum
tee=wheep
teind=master
tein=land
telegraph=board
telegraph=cable
telegraph=carriage
telegraph=clock
telegraph=dial
telegraph=key
telegraph=plant
telegraph=pole
telegraph=post
telegraph=reel
telegraph=register
telegraph=wire
telephone=harp
telescope=bag
telescope=carp
telescope=driver†
telescope=eye
telescope=fish
telescope=fly
telescope=shell
telescope=sight
telescope=table
tell=bill=willy (a bird)
telling=house
telltale (a person)
tellurium=glance
tolpherway
temperature=alarm
temperature=curve

tempering=furnace
tempering=machine
tempering=oven
tempering=wheel
temper=screw
tempest=tossed, etc.
templin=oil
temse=bread
temse=loaf
tenant=farmer†
tenant=right
tenchweed
tender=dying
tender=eyed, etc.
tenderfoot (a person)
tendril=climber
tenebræ=hearse
tenement=house
tenfingers (a starfish)
ten=forties
tennis=arm
tennis=ball
tennis=court
tennis=elbow
tennis=player†
ten=o'=clock (a plant)
tenon=auger
tenoning=chisel
tenoning=machine
tenon=saw
tenon=truing†
tenpence
tenpenny
tenpins
ten=pounder
tension=bar
tension=bridge
tension=fuse
tension=member
tension=rod
tension=roller
tension=spicule
tension=spring
tensor=twist
ten=strike
tentacle=sheath
tent=bed
tent=bedstead
tent=caterpillar

tent=cloth
tenter=bar
tenter=ground
tenter=hook
tentering=machine
tent=fly
tent=guy
tent=maker†
tent=peg
tent=pegging†
tent=pin
tent=pole
tent=rope
tent-stitch
tent=tree
tent=wine
tent=work
tentwort
tenure=horn
tenure=sword
terebinth=tree
term=day
term=fee
term=piece
terne=plate
terra=cotta
terraculture
terrapin=farm
terrapin=paws
terra=plein
terre=tenant
terror=breathing
terror=haunted, etc.
terror=smitten
terror=strike
ter=tenant
teru=tero
terza=rima
tesho=lama
test=box
tester=cloth
test=glass
testing=box
testing=clause
testing=gauge
testing=hole
testing=machine
testing=slab
test=meal

test·meter
test·mixer
test·object
test·paper
test·plate
test·pump
test·ring
test·spoon
test·tube
test·types
tête·à·tête
tête·de·mouton
tête·de·pont
tether·stick
tetrad·deme
tetter·berry
tewing·beetle
text·book
text·hand
text·man
text·pen
textus·case
text·writer†
tcyl·tree
thale·cress
thallium·glass
thane·land
thank·offering
thanksgiver†
thankworthy
thank·you·ma'am (a
    ridge of earth in
    a road)
thatch·grass
thatching·fork
thatching·spade
thatch·palm
thatch·rake
thatch·sparrow
thatch·tree
thatchwood·work
thaw·drop
T·head
theatregoer†
theatre·party
theatre·seat
themselves
thenadays
thenceforth

thenceforward
thencefrom
theodolite·magneto-
    meter
thereabout
thereabouts
thereafter
thereagainst
thereamong
thereanent
thereat
thereaway
therebefore
thereby
therefor
therefore
therefrom
therein
thereinafter
thereinbefore
thereinto
thereof
thereon
thereout
there·right
therethrough
thereto
theretofore
thereunder
thereunto
thereupon
therewith
therewithal
thickback (a fish)
thickbill (a bird)
thick·brained, etc.
thickhead (a person, a
    bird)
thickknee (a bird)
thickleaf (a plant)
thicklips (a person)
thickskin (a person)
thickskull (a person)
thick·stamen (a plant)
thick·wind
thief·catcher†
thief·leader†
thief·stolen
thief·taker†

thief·tube
thigh·bone
thigh·joint
thill·coupling
thill·horse
thill·jack
thill·tug
thimbleberry
thimble·case
thimble coupling
thimble·eye
thimble·eyed, etc.
thimble·joint
thimble·lily
thimbleman
thimble·pie
thimblerig
thimble·skein
thimbleweed
thin·blooded, etc.
T hinge
thingman
thin·gutted, etc.
third·borough
third·class
thirdpenny
third·rate
thirdsman
thirteen·lined, etc.
thirty·second note
thistle·bird
thistle·butterfly
thistle·cock
thistle·cropper
thistle·crown
thistle·digger†
thistle·dollar
thistle·down
thistle·finch
thistle·merk
thistle·plume
thistle·tube
thitherto
thoft·fellow
thole·pin
thorn·apple
thornback (a fish, a
    crab)
thornback·ray

thornbill (a bird)
thorn-bird
thorn-broom
thorn-bush
thorn-devil
thorn-headed, ete.
thorn-hopper
thorn-house
thorn-oyster
thornstone
thorn-swine
thorntail (a bird)
thorough-bass
thorough-bolt
thorough-brace
thorough-braced, etc.
thoroughbred
thoroughfare
thoroughfoot
thoroughgoing
thorough-joint
thorough-pin
thorough-shot
thorough-stem
thoroughwax (a plant)
thoroughwort
thorpsman
thought-executing
thought-reader†
thoughtsick
thought-transfer
thought-transference
thought-transferential
thought-wave
thousandfold
thousand-legs
thread-animalcule
threadbare
thread-carrier†
thread-cell
thread-cutter†
thread-feather
threadfin (a fish)
thread-finisher†
threadfish
threadflower (a plant)
threadfoot (a plant)
thread-frame
thread-gauge

thread-guide
thread-herring
thread-leaved, etc.
thread-mark
thread-moss
thread-needle
thread-oiler
thread-paper
thread-plant
thread-polishing
thread-the-needle (a game)
thread-waxer†
thread-winder†
threadworm
three-aged, etc.
three-birds
three-coat
three-decker
threefold
three-foot
three-light
three-man
three-master
three-out, n.
threepence
threepenny
threepenny piece
three-per-cents
three-ply
three-quarter
three-quarters
threescore
three-square
three-way
thresher-shark
thresher-whale
threshing-floor
threshing-machine
threshing-mill
threshing-place
thrift-box
throat-band
throat-bolt
throat-brail
throat-chain
throat-halyard
throat-jaws
throat-latch

throat-piece
throat-pipe
throatroot (a plant)
throat-seizing
throat-strap
throat-sweetbread
throatwort
throstle-cock
throstle-frame
throttle-damper
throttle-lever
throttle-valve
through-gang
through-going
through-lighted
through-mortise
throughout
through-stone
throwback, n.
throw-bait
throw-crank
throw-crook
throwing-balls
throwing-clay
throwing-engine
throwing-house
throwing-mill
throwing-stick
throwing-table
throwing-wheel
throw-lathe
throw-off
throw-stick
thrum-cap
thrum-eyed
thrumwort
thrush-babbler
thrush-blackbird
thrush-fungus
thrush-lichen
thrush-nightingale
thrush-paste
thrush-tit
thrust-bearing
thrust-box
thrust-hoe
thrusting-screw
thrust-plane
thumb-band

thumb-bird	thunder-storm	tide-rock
thumb-blue	thunderstrike	tide-rode
thumb-cleat	thunderstruck	tide-runner
thumb-cock	thunder-tube	tidesman
thumb-latch	thunder-worm	tide-table
thumb-mark	thwacking-frame	tidewaiter
thumb-nut	thwacking-knife	tide-water
thumb-pad	thwarter-ill	tide-wave
thumb-piece	thwart-hawse	tide-way
thumb-position	thyrseflower (a plant)	tide-wheel
thumb-pot	tib-cat	tiding-well
thumb-ring	tic-bird	tidytips (a plant)
thumb-screw (a screw)	tic-douloureux	tic-bar
thumbscrew (an instru-	tick-bean	tie-beam
ment of torture)	tick-eater	tieboy
thumb-stall '	ticker-in	tic-plate
thumb-tack	ticket-day	tie-rod
thunder-axe	ticket-holder†	tiers-argent
thunder-bird	ticket-night	tier-saw
thunderblast	ticket-porter	tier-shot
thunderbolt	ticket-punch	tie-strap
thunderbolt-beetle	ticket-seller†	tie-tie
thunderburst	ticket-taker†	tie-up
thunder-carriage	ticket-writer†	tie-wig
thunderclap	tick-hole	tiger-beetle
thunder-cloud	ticking-work	tiger-bittern
thunder-crack	tickle-grass	tiger-cat
thunder-darter	tickseed (a plant)	tiger-chop
thunder-dirt	tick-tack	tiger-cowry
thunder-drop	tick-tock	tiger-eye
thunder-fish	tick-trefoil	tigerflower (a plant)
thunder-fit	tickweed	tiger-footed, etc.
thunderflower (a plant)	tide-ball	tiger-frog
thunder-fly	tide-crack	tiger-grass
thunder-gust	tide-current	tiger-lily
thunder-hammer	tide-day	tiger-moth
thunder-head	tide-dial	tiger's-claw*
thunder-headed	tide-gauge	tiger's-eye*
thunder-house	tide-gate	tiger's-foot*
thunder-peal	tide-harbor	tiger-shark
thunder-pick	tide-land	tiger-shell
thunder-plant	tide-lock	tiger's-milk*
thunder-plump	tide-mark	tiger-wolf
thunder-pump	tide-marsh	tiger-wood
thunder-pumper	tide-meter	tightening-pulley
thunder-shower	tide-mill	tig-tag
thundersmith	tide-pool	tile-copper
thunder-snake	tide-predictor†	tile-creasing
thunder-stone	tide-rips	tile-drain

tile=earth
tile=field
tilefish
tile=kiln
tile=laying†
tile=machine
tile=making†
tile=ore
tile=oven
tile=pin
tile=red
tileroot (a plant)
tileseed (a tree)
tilestone
tile=tea
tile=tree
tile=works
tillage=rake
till=alarm
tiller=chain
tiller=head
tiller=rope
tillie=vallie
till=lock
tilly=seed
til=oil
til=seed
tilt=boat
tilt=hammer
tilting=fillet
tilting=gauntlet
tilting=helmet
tilting=lance
tilting=shield
tilting=spear
tilting=target
tilt=mill
til=tree
tilt=up
tilt=yard
tilwood
timber=beetle
timber=brick
timber=cart
timberdoodle (a bird)
timber=frame
timber=grouse
timber=head
timber=hitch

timber=line
timber=lode
timberman
timber=merchant
timber=scribe
timber=tree
timber=wolf
timber=work
timber=worm
timber=yard
time=alarm
time=attack
time=ball
time=bargain
time=beguiling, etc.
time=bill
time=book
time=candle
time=card
time=detector
time=fuse
time=globe
time=gun
timekeeper†
time=lock
timely=parted
timepiece
time=pleaser
time=sense
time=server†
time=sight
time=signal
time=signature
time=table
time=thrust
time value
time=work
timing=apparatus
timothy=grass
tim=whiskey
tin=bath
tin=bound
tinclad (a gunboat)
tincture=press
tinder=box
tinder=like
tinder=ore
tine=grass
tine=stock

tin=floor
tin=foil
tingis=fly
tin=glass
tin=glaze
tin=ground
Tinkar's=root*
tinkershire (a bird)
Tinker's=weed*
tin=liquor
tinman
tin=mordant
tinmouth (a fish)
tinning=metal
tin=penny
tin pint
tin plate (a plate made
    of tin)
tin=plate (tin in plates,
    as a material)
tinplate, v.
tin=pot
tin=pulp
tin=putty
tin=saw
tin=scrap
tinsel=embroidery
tin=shop
tinsman
tinsmith
tinstone
tin=streaming
tin=stuff
tint=block
tint=drawing
tint=tool
tintype
tinware
tin=witts
tin=works
ti=palm
tip=car
tip=cart
tip=cat
tip=cheese
tip=foot
ti=plant
tip=paper
tippet=grebe

tippet=grouse
tipping=wagon
tippling=house
tip=sled
tipstaff
tip=stock
tip=stretcher
tipsy=cake
tipsy=key
tip=tilted
tiptoe
tip=top
tip=up
tip=wagon
tipworm
tire=bender†
tire=bolt
tire=drill
tire=heater†
tireman
tire=measurer†
tire=press
tire=roller†
tire=setter†
tire=shrinker†
tiresmith
tiring=room
tirlie=whirley
tirl=mill
T iron
tissue=paper
tissue=secretion
titanium=green
titan=schorl
tit=babbler
titbit
tithe commissioner
tithe=free
tithe=gatherer†
tithe=owner
tithe=payer†
tithe=pig
tithe=proctor
tithe=stealer†
tithing=man
titlark
title=deed
title=leaf
title=letter

title=page
title=sheet
title=type
titmouse
ti=tree
titter=totter
tittlebat (a fish)
tittle=tattle
tit=warbler
tityre=tu
T joint
toadback (a potato)
toad=back, a.
toad=eater†
toadfish
toad=flax
toadflower (a plant)
toadhead (a plover)
toad=lily
toad=lizard
toad=orchis
toad=pipe
toadrock
toad=rush
toad's=cap*
toadseye
toad's=hat*
toad's=meat*
toad=snatcher
toad=spit
toad=spotted
toadstone
toadstool
toasting=fork
toasting=glass
toasting=iron
toast=master
toast=rack
toast=water
tobacco=beetle
tobacco=box
tobacco=chewer†
tobacco=curing†
tobacco=cutter†
tobacco=dove
tobacco=grater†
tobacco=heart
tobacco=knife
tobacco=man

tobacco=packing†
tobacco=pipe
tobacco=plant
tobacco=pouch
tobacco=press
tobacco=rolling†
tobacco=root
tobacco=stemming†
tobacco=stick
tobacco=stopper
tobacco=stripper†
tobacco=tongs
tobacco=wheel
tobacco=worm
Tobias=fish
toboggan=shoot
toboggan=slide
to=bread
to=come, n.
to=day
toddy=bird
toddy=blossom
toddy=drawer
toddy=ladle
toddyman
toddy=palm
toddy=stick
to=do
tod's=tail*
tod=stove
toe=biter
toe=cap
toe=drop
toe=nail
toe=piece
toe=ring
toe=tights
toe=weight
tofall
toftman
toftstead
toggle=bolt
toggle=harpoon
toggle=hole
toggle=iron
toggle=joint
toggle=lanyard
toggle=press
toilet=cap

toilet=cloth
toilet=cover
toilet=cup
toilet=glass
toilet=quilt
toilet=service
toilet=set
toilet=soap
toilet=sponge
toilet=table
toil=worn
token=sheet
toll=bait
toll=bar
toll=book
tollbooth
toll=bridge
toll=collector†
toll=corn
toll=dish
toll=free
toll=gate
toll=gatherer†
tollhouse
tolling=lever
toll=man
tolosa=wood
tolu=tree
tomato=gall
tomato=plant
tomato=sauce
tomato=sphinx
tomato=worm
tomb=bat
tomb=house
tomboy
tombstone
tom=cat
tomcod
tomfool
tom=hurry
tommy=noddy
tommy=shop
tom=noddy
tom=norry
tom=noup
to=morrow
Tom=piper
Tom=poker

tom=pudding
tomtit
tom=tom
tom=trot
tom=turkey
to=name
tone=color
tone=master
tone=measurer†
tone=painting†
tone=relationship
tone=syllable
tongman
tongsman
tongue=bang
tongue=banger
tongue=battery
tongue=bird
tongue=bit
tongue=bone
tongue=case
tongue=chain
tongue=compressor
tongue=depressor
tongue=doughty
tongue=fence
tonguefish
tongueflower (a plant)
tongue=grafting
tongue=grass
tongue=holder
tongue=hound
tongue=joint
tongue=lashing
tongue=membrane
tongue=shaped, etc.
tongue=shell
tongue=shot
tongue=spatula
tongue=support
tongue=test
tongue=tie
tongue=tooth
tongue=tree
tongue=valiant
tongue=violet
tongue=warrior
tongue=work
tongue=worm

to=night
tonnage=deck
tony=hoop
tool=car
tool=chest
tool=coupling
tool=extractor
tool=gauge
tool=holder†
tool=mark
tool=marking†
tool=post
tool=rest
tool=stack
tool=stay
tool=stock
tool=stone
toothache
toothache=grass
toothache=tree
toothback (a moth)
tooth=backed, etc.
tooth=bearer
toothbill (a pigeon)
tooth=brush
tooth=brush tree
tooth=carpenter
tooth=cress
tooth=drawing†
toothedge
tooth=filling
toothflower (a plant)
toothing=plane
tooth=key
tooth=like
tooth=net
tooth=ornament
tooth=paste
toothpick
toothpicker†
tooth=plugger†
tooth=powder
tooth=pulp
tooth=rash
tooth=ribbon
tooth=sac
tooth=saw
tooth=shell
tooth=violet

tooth=wash
toothwort
tooth=wound
toot=plant
toot=poison
top=armor
topaz=rock
top=beam
top=block
top=boot
top=booted, etc.
top=card
top=chain
top=cloth
top=coat
top=cross
top=drain
top=draining
top=dress
top=dressing
top=flat
top=full
top=fuller
topgallant
topgallant=bulwarks
topgallant=forecastle
topgallantmast
topgallantsail
topgallant=shrouds
top=graining
top=hamper
top=heavy
topknot
top=lantern
top=light
top=lining
toplofty
top=mall
topman
topmast
topmast=head
topmast=shrouds
top=maul
top=minnow
top=minor
top=pendant
topping=lift
top=rail
top=rim

top=rope
topsail
topsail=yard
top=saw
top=sawyer
top=shell
topsman
top=soil
top=soiling
top=stone
topsyturn
topsyturvy
top=tackle
toptail, v.
top=timber
top=tool
torch=bearer†
torch=dance
torch=fishing†
torchlight
torch=lily
torch=race
torch=staff
torch=thistle
torch=wood (wood)
torchwood (a tree)
torchwort
torn=crenate
torn=down
tor=ouzel
torpedo=anchor
torpedo=boat
torpedo=boom
torpedo=catcher†
torpedo=net
torpedo=netting
torpedo=officer
torpedo=school
torpedo=spar
torpedo=tube
torrent=bow
torrent=duck
tortoise=beetle
tortoiseflower (a plant)
tortoise=headed, etc.
tortoise=plant
tortoise=rotifier
tortoise=shell
tortoise=wood

toshnail
tossy=tail
tot=book
tote=load
tote=road
tot=o'er=seas, n.
totter=grass
touch=and=go, a. or n.
touch=body
touch=corpuscle
touch=down
touch=hole
touching=stuff
touch=me=not, n.
touch=needle
touch=pan
touch=paper
touchpiece
touchstone
touchwood
toughbark (a tree)
tough=cake
toughhead (a duck)
tourney=helm
towboat
tow=cock
towel=gourd
towel=horse
towel=rack
towel=roller
tower=clock
tower=cress
tower=mill
tower=mustard
tower=owl
tower=shell
towerwort
towhead (a person)
tow=headed, etc.
tow=hook
towing=bitts
towing=bridle
towing=hook
towing=net
towing=path
towing=post
towing=rope
towing=timber
tow=iron

tow=line	track=clearer†	training=halter
town=adjutant	track=edge	training=level
town=councillor	track=harness	training=pendulum
town=cress	track=hound	training=school
tow=net	track=indicator†	training=ship
townfolk	track=layer†	training=wall
town=husband	trackman	trainman
town land (owned by a	trackmaster	train=mile
town)	track=pot	train=oil
townland (a township)	track=raiser†	train=road
town=major	track=road	train=robber†
town=meeting	track=scale	train=rope
townsfolk	track=scout	train=tackle
townsman	track=walker†	trainway
townspeople	trackway	train=wrecker†
town talk	traction=aneurism	tram=car
town=wall	traction=engine	tram=line
tow=path	traction=gearing	trammel=net
tow=rope	traction=wheel	trammel=wheel
toy=block	trade=hall	tramping=drum
toy=box	trade=mark	tram=plate
to=year	trademaster	trampot
toy man (a toy)	trade=name	tram=pick
toyman (a maker or	tradesfolk	tramroad
seller of toys)	tradesman	tram=staff
toy=mutch	tradespeople	tramway
toy=shop	tradeswoman	tramway=car
toywort	trade=union	tram=wheel
T panel	trade=unionism	transfer=book
T plate	trade=unionist	transfer=day
trace=buckle	trade=wind	transfer=elevator
trace=chain	traffic=manager†	transfer=gilding
trace=fastener†	traffic=return	transfer=ink
trace=hook	T rail	transfer=paper
trace=horse	trail=board	transfer=press
trace=loop	trail=car	transfer=printing
trace=mate	trail=eye	transfer=resistance
trachea=forceps	trail=handspike	transferring=machine
trachyte=tuff	trailing=spring	transfer=work
tracing=cloth	trailing=wheel	transformation=scene
tracing=instrument	trail=net	transfusion=apparatus
tracing=linen	trail=plate	transit=circle
tracing=lines	train=band	transit=compass
tracing=machine	train=bearer†	transit=duty
tracing=paper	train=bolt	transit=instrument
tracing=thread	train=boy	transit=trade
tracing=wheel	train=hand	translating=screw
track=boat	training=bit	transom=knee
track=chart	training=day	transom=window

transport-rider
transport-ship
transport-vessel
transverse-cubital
transverse-medial
transverse-quadrate
trap-ball
trap-bat
trap-bittle
trap-brilliant
trap-cellar
trap-cut
trap-door
trapfall
trap-fisher†
trap-hole
trap-hook
trap-net
trapping-attachment
trap-rock
trap-seine
trap-stair
trap-stick
trap-tree
trap-tuff
trap-valve
trap-weir
trash-house
trash-ice
traveller's-joy*
traveller's-tree
travelling-bag
travelling-cabinet
travelling-cap
travelling-carriage
travelling-chest
travelling-convert
travelling-dress
travel-soiled, etc.
traverse-board
traverse-circle
traverse-drill
traverse-saw
traverse-table
trawl-anchor
trawl-beam
trawl-boat
trawlerman
trawl-fish

trawl-fisherman
trawl-head
trawl-keg
trawl-line
trawl-net
trawl-roller
trawl-warp
tray-cloth
treacle-mustard
treacle-sleep
treacle-wag
treacle-water
treacle-wormseed
tread-behind
tread-board
treadle-machine
treadmill
tread-softly (a plant)
treadwheel
treason-felony
treasure-chest
treasure-city
treasureflower (a plant)
treasure-house
treasure-trove
treble-bar
treble-dated, etc.
trebletree
treck-pot
tree-agate
tree-aloe
tree-asp
tree-azalea
tree-bear
tree-beard
tree-beetle
tree-boa
tree-bug
tree-cabbage
tree-cactus
tree-calf
tree-cat
tree-celandine
tree-climber†
tree-clipper†
tree-clover
tree-coffin
tree-copal
tree-coral

tree-cotton
tree-coupling
tree-crab
tree-creeper†
tree-cricket
tree-crow
tree-cuckoo
tree-digger†
tree-dove
tree-duck
tree-fern
tree-finch
treefish
tree-fly
tree-frog
tree-fuchsia
tree-germander
tree-goldenrod
tree-goose
tree-hair
tree-heath
tree-hoopoe
treehopper
tree-houseleek
tree-iron
tree-jobber
tree-kangaroo
tree-lark
tree-lily
tree-lizard
tree-lobster
tree-lotus
tree-louse
tree-lungwort
tree-lupine
tree-mallow
tree-marbling†
tree-medic
tree-mignonette
tree-milk
tree-moss
tree-mouse
treenail
tree-nettle
tree-nymph
tree-oil
tree-onion
tree-orchis
tree-oyster

tree=partridge
tree=peony
tree=pie
tree=pigeon
tree=pipit
tree=poke
tree=poppy
tree=porcupine
tree-primrose
tree=protector†
tree=pruner†
tree=rat
tree=remover†
tree=scape
tree=scraper†
tree=serpent
tree=shrew
tree=shrike
tree=snake
tree=sorrel
tree=soul
tree=sparrow
tree=squirrel
tree=swallow
tree=swift
tree=tiger
tree=toad
tree=tomato
tree=top
tree=violet
tree=warbler
tree=wax
tree=wool
tree=wormwood
tree=worship
tree=worshipper†
trek=oxen
trek=rope
trek=tow
trelliswork
trembling=jock
trembling=jocky
trench=cart
trench=cavalier
trencher=cap
trencher=coat
trencher=critic
trencher=friend
trencher=knight

trencher-law
trencherman
trencher=mate
trencher=plate
trench=plow
trepanning-elevator
trephine=saw
trespass=offering
trestle=board
trestle bridge
trestletree
trestlework
trewsman
triad=deme
trial=case
trial=day
trial=fire
trial=glasses
trial=ground
trial heat
trial=jar
trial=piece
trial=plate
trial=proof
trial=sight
trial=square
trial trip
tribesman
triblet=tubes
tribute=money
tribute=pitch
tribute=work
trick=dagger
tricker=lock
trick=line
trickmaker†
trick=scene
trick=sword
trick=track
trick=wig
tricot=stitch
trigger=finger
trigger=fish
trigger=guard
trigger=hair
trigger=line
trigger=plant
trip=book
trip=cord

tripe=de=roche
tripeman
tripe=stone
tripe=visaged, etc.
trip=gear
trip=hammer
triple=awned, etc.
triple=grass
tripletail (a fish)
triplet=lily
triplicate=ternate
tripmadam (a plant)
tripod=jack
trippant=counter
tripping=line
tripping=valve
trip=shaft
trip=skin
trip=slip
trithing=reeve
Triton's=horn*
trivet=table
trolley=pole
trollflower
trolling=bait
trolling=hook
trolling=rod
trolling=spoon
troll=plate
troolie=palm
troop=bird
troop=fowl
troop=horse
troop=ship
trophy=cress
trophy=lock
trophy=money
trophywort
tropic=bird
troth=plight
troth=plighted
troth=ring
trot=line
trotter=boiler
trotter=oil
trouble=mirth
trough=battery
trough=fault
trough=gutter

trough=room
trough=shell
trous=de=loup
trout=basket
trout=bird
trout=colored, etc.
trout=farm
trout=hole
trout=hook
trout=line
trout=louse
trout=net
trout=perch
trout=pickerel
trout=rod
trout=shad
trout=spoon
trout=stream
trout=tackle
trowel=bayonet
trowelbeak (a bird)
truce=breaker†
truck=bolster
truck=farm
truck=farmer†
truck=house
trucking=house
truck=jack
truckle=bed
truckle=cheese
truckman
truckmaster
truck=pot
truck=shop .
truck=store
true=blue
true=born, true=de-
    rived, etc.
true=love (one who
    has true love)
truelove (a plant)
truepenny (a person)
true=stitch, *n*.
truffle=worm
truing=tool
trump=card
trumped=up, *a*.
trumpet=animalcule
trumpet=ash

trumpet=banner
trumpet=cail
trumpet=conch
trumpet=creeper
trumpet=fish
trumpetflower (a plant)
trumpet=fly
trumpet=gall
trumpet=gourd
trumpet=honeysuckle
trumpet=jasmine
trumpet=keck
trumpet=lamp
trumpetleaf (a plant)
trumpet=lily
trumpet=major
trumpet=milkweed
trumpet=reed
trumpet=shaped, etc.
trumpet=shell
trumpet=tone
trumpet=tree
trumpet=vine
trumpetweed
trumpetwood (a tree)
trundle=bed
trundle=head
trundle=shot
trundle=tail (a tail)
trundletail (a dog)
trundle=wheel
trunk=alarm
trunkback (a turtle)
trunk=bearer
trunk=brace
trunk=breeches
trunk=cabin
trunk=case
trunk=engine
trunkfish
trunk=hose
trunk=light
trunk line
trunk=maker†
trunk=nail
trunk road
trunk=roller
trunk=sleeve
trunk=stay

trunk=store
trunk=turtle
trunnion=lathe
trunnion=plate
trunnion=ring
trunnion=sight
trunnion=valve
truss=beam
truss=block
truss=bridge
trussing=machine
truss=piece
truss=plank
truss=rod
truss=tackle
trustworthy
truth=lover†
truth=teller†
try=cock
try=house
trying=plane
trying=square
try=pot
trysail
try=square
trysting=day
trysting=place
try=works
tsetse=fly
T square
tubber=man
tubbing=wedge
tube=bearing†
tube=board
tube=breather†
tube=brush
tube=casts
tube=clamp
tube=cleaner†
tube=clip
tube=cock
tube=colors
tube=compass
tube=coral
tube=cutter†
tube=door
tube=drawing†
tube=expander†
tube=fastener†

tube=ferrule
tube=filter
tubeflower (a plant)
tube=flue
tube=foot
tube=form
tube=germination
tube=hearted, etc.
tube=machine
tube=packing
tube=plate
tube=plug
tube=pouch
tube=retort
tuberous=rooted
tube=scaler†
tube=scraper†
tube=shell
tube=spinner†
tube=stopper†
tube=valve
tube=vise
tube=weaver†
tube=well
tube=worm
tube=wrench
tub=fake
tubfish
tub=gig
tub=oar
tub=oarsman
tub=preacher†
tub=race
tub=saw
tub=size
tub=sugar
tub=thumper†
tub=wheel
tuck=creaser†
tucker=in
tuck=folder†
tuck=in
tucking=gauge
tuck=joint
tuck=marker†
tuck=neck
tuck=out
tuck=seine
tuck=shop

Tudor=flower (a plant)
tue=iron
tuff=cone
tuftgill (a fish)
tuft=gilled, etc.
tuft=hunter†
tufting=button
tugboat
tug=carrier†
tug=hook
tug=iron
tugman
tugmutton
tug=slide
tug=spring
tula=work
tule=wren
tulip=ear
tulip=eared, etc.
tulip=poplar
tulip=root
tulip=shell
tulip=tree
tulip=wood
tumblebug
tumble=car
tumble=down, a.
tumbledung (a beetle)
tumble=home   -
tumbler=brush
tumbler=cart
tumbler=dog
tumbler=drum
tumbler=glass
tumbler=holder
tumbler=lock
tumbler=punch
tumbler=stand
tumbler=tank
tumbler=washer†
tumbleweed
tumbling=barrel
tumbling=bay
tumbling=bob
tumbling=box
tumbling=net
tumbling=shaft
tumbling=trough
tumbling=wheel

tumika=oil
tumor=like
tump=line
tum=tum
tun=belly
tung=oil
tung=tree
tunhoof (a plant)
tuning=cone
tuning=crook
tuning=fork
tuning=hammer
tuning=horn
tuning=key
tuning=knife
tuning=lever
tuning=peg
tuning=pin
tuning=slide
tuning=wire
tun=moot
tunnel=borer†
tunnel=disease
tunnel=head
tunnel=hole
tunnel=kiln
tunnel=net
tunnel=pit
tunnel=shaft
tunnel=vault
tunnel=weaver†
tunning=cask
tunning=dish
tun=shell
tup=man
turban=shell
turban stone
turban=top
turbinate=lentiform
turbine=dynamometer
turbine=pump
turf=ant
turf=bound, etc.
turf=charcoal
turf=cutter†
turf=drain
turfing=iron
turfing=spade
turf=knife

turfman
turf-moss
turf-plow
turf-spade
turf-worm
turkeyback (a bird)
turkeybeard (a plant)
turkeyberry
turkeyberry-tree
turkey-bird
turkey-blossom
turkey-buzzard
turkey-call
turkey-cock
turkey-corn
turkey-gnat
turkey-gobbler
turkey-grass
turkey-hen
Turkey hone
turkey-leather
turkey-louse
turkey-pea
turkey-pen
turkey-poult
Turkey slate
Turkey stone
turkey-vulture
Turkman
Turk's-cap*
Turk's-head*
Turk's-turban*
turmeric-oil
turmeric-paper
turmeric-plant
turmeric-root
turmeric-tree
turnabout, n.
turnback, n.
turn-bench
turn-bridge
turnbuckle
turncap
turncoat (a person)
turncock (a person)
turn-down
turned-shells (mol-
    lusks)
turner-harp

turner-hood
turn-file
turning-bridge
turning-carrier
turning-chisel
turning-engine
turning-gauge
turning-gouge
turning-lathe
turning-machine
turning-mill
turning-piece
turning-place
turning-point
turning-rest
turning-saw
turning-steel
turning-tool
turnip-aphid
turnip-cabbage
turnip-cutter†
turnip-flea
turnip-fly
turnip-maggot
turnip-parsnip
turnip-pest
turnip-puller†
turnip-pulper†
turnip-radish
turnip-rooted, etc.
turnip-shell
turnipwood (a tree, its
    wood)
turnkey
turnout, n.
turnover, n.
turnpike
turnpike-man
turnpike-stair
turn-pin
turnplate
turn-poke
turn-row
turn-screw
turnsick
turnside
turnsole-blue
turnspit
turnstile

turnstile-register
turnstone
turntable
turn-under, a. or n.
turn-up, a. or n.
turn-wrest
turpentine-back
turpentine-moth
turpentine-oil
turpentine-still
turpentine-tree
turpeth-mineral
turquoise-green
turret-gun
turret-head
turret-lathe
turret ship
turtleback (something
    like a turtle's
    back)
turtle-cowry
turtle-crawl
turtle-deck
turtle-dove
turtle-egging
turtle-footed, etc.
turtle-grass
turtle-head
turtle-peg
turtle-run
turtle-shell
turtle soup
turtle-stone
tusk-shell
tusk-tenon
tusk-vase
tussah-silk
tusser-silk
tusser-worm
tussock-caterpillar
tussock-grass
tussock-moth
tussock-sedge
tut-nose
tutty-more
tut-work
tut-worker
tut-workman
tu-whit

tu-whoo
twain-cloud
twa-lofted
twayblade
'tween-brain
'tween-deck
'tween-decks
tweezer-case
Twelfth-cake
Twelfth-day
Twelfth-night
Twelfth-tide
twelvemonth
twelvepence
twelvepenny
twelve-score
twenty-fold
twentyfourmo
twenty-second
twice-stabbed, etc.
twick-bine
twiddling-line
twig-blight
twig-borer†
twig-bug
twig-girdler†
twig-insect
twig-pruner†
twig-rush
twin-born
twin-cylinder
twine-cutter†
twine-holder†
twine-machine
twine-reeler†
twinflower (a plant)
· twinleaf (a plant)
twinning-axis
twinning-machine

twinning-plane
twinning-saw
twin pair
twin-shell
twin-spot
twin-stock
twisted-flower (a plant)
twisted-horn (a plant)
twisted-stalk (a plant)
twisted-stick (a plant)
twisting-crook
twisting-forceps
twisting-machine
twisting-mill
twist-joint
twist-machine
twist-stitch
twist tobacco
twist-velocity
twitch-grass
twite-finch
twit-lark
twitter-bit
twitter-bone
twitter-boned
twit-twat
'twixt-brain
two-cleft, two-edged,
    etc.
two-decker
two-eyes (a plant)
twofold
two-hand, a.
two-line, a.
twopence
twopenny
two-ply, a.
two-speed, a.
two-throw, a.

two-tooth, a.
two-valve, a.
two-way, a.
tye-block
tyleberry
tymp-plate
tymp-stone
type-bar
type-block
type-case
type-casting†
type-chart
type-cutter†
type-cylinder
type-dressing†
type-founder†
type-foundry
type-gauge
type-high
type-holder†
type-matrix
type-measure
type-measurer†
type-metal
type-mould
type-punch
type-scale
typesetter†
type-wheel
typewrite
typewriter†
typh-fever
typh-poison
typo-etching
tyrant-bird
tyrant-chat
tyrant-flycatcher
tyrant-shrike
tyrant-wren

U

U bolt	under=clay	undergo
udalman	under=clerkship	undergore
udder=cloud	under=cliff	undergown
uggur=oil	underclothed	under=grade, *a.*
uji=fly	underclothes	undergraduate
ule=tree	underclothing	underground
umber=bird	under=coat	undergrove
umbra=tree	under=color	undergrow
umbrella=ant	under=colored	undergrowl
umbrella=bird	under=crest	undergrown
umbrella=fir	undercroft	undergrowth
umbrella=grass	undercurrent	underhand
umbrellaleaf (a plant)	undercurved	underhanded
umbrella=man	undercut	underhang
umbrella=palm	undercutter	underhew
umbrella=pine	under=dealing	underhole
umbrella=shell	underditch	underhung
umbrella=stand	underdo	under=kind, *n.*
umbrella=tree	underdoer	under=king
umbrellawort	underdone	under=kingdom
underact	underdose	underlay
underaction	underdrain	underleaf
underagent	underdraw	underlease
underaid	under=dressed	underlet
under=back	under=driven	underlie
underbearer	underestimate	under=life
underbid	underestimation	underline
underbill	under=exposed	underlock
underbind	underfeed	underlooker
underbitten	underfilling	underlying
underbrace	under=fired	underman, *v.*
underbred	underfloor	undermasted
underbrush	underflow	undermentioned
underburn	underfoot, *a., adv., v.*	undermine
underbush '	underfurnish	underministry
under=butter	underfurrow	undernamed
under=buy	undergarment	undernote
undercast	undergear	undernoted
undercharge	undergird	underpart
under=chord	underglaze	underpay

underpeopled
underpin
underpinning
underplay
underplot
underpraise
underprize
underproduction
underproof
underprop
underproportioned
underquote
underrake
underrate
underreckon
underripe
under=roof
underrun
underscore
under=scribe
under=searching
under=secretary
undersell
undersense
under=servant
underset
undershapen
under=sheriff
undershirt
undershoot
undershot
undershrub
undersign
undersized
underskirt
under=sky
undersleep
undersleeve
undersoil
undersong
undersparred
undersphere
underspread
understand
understate
understatement
understock
understrapper
understratum

understroke
understudy
undersuit
undersward
undertake
undertaker
under=tenancy
under=tenant
undertimed
undertint
undertone
undertow
undertreated
undertrump
undervaluation
undervalue
undervest
underviewer
underwater, n.
underwear
underwent
underwing (a moth)
underwinged
underwitted
underwood
underwork
underworker
under=workman
underworld
underwrite
ungulite=grit
unhairing=beam
unhairing=knife
unhairing=machine
unicorn=beetle
unicorn=bird
unicorn=fish
unicorn=moth
unicorn=plant
unicorn=root
unicorn=shell
unicorn's=horn*
unicorn=whale
union=bow
union=cord
union=grass
union=joint
union=pump
union=room

unloading=block
unloading=machine
up=and=down, a.
upas=tree
upbear
upbind
upblaze
upbraid
upbreak
upbringing
upbuild
upburst
upby
upcast
upclimb
upcoil
upcoming
up=country, a. and adv
upcurl
upcurved
updive
updraw
upend
upfill
upfling
upflow
upfolded
upgather
upgaze
upgirt
upgoing
upgrow
upgrowth
upgush
uphand
uphang
uphasp
upheap
upheave
upheld
uphoard
uphold
upholsterer=bee
uphurl
upland
uplay
uplead
uplean
upleap

uplift
uplook
uplooking
uplying
upmaking
up=peak
uppergrowth
upper=leather
upper=machine
uppertendom
up=pile
up=plight
up=plow
up=pluck
up=pricked
up=prop
up=putting
upraise
uprear
upridge
upright
uprise
uproar
uproll
uproot
uprouse

uprun
uprush
upseek
upsend
upset
upshoot
upshot
upside
upsnatch
upsoar
upspring
up=stairs
upstare
upstart
upstay
upstream, *v.*
up=stream, *a.* and *adv.*
up=street
upsway
up=sweep, *n.*
upswell
uptake
uptear
upthrow
upthrust
upthunder

uptilt
uptoss
up=town
uptrace
uptrill
upturn
upwafted
upwall
upwell
upwhirl
upwind, *v.*
up=wind, *adv.*
upwreathe
uran=glimmer
uran=mica
uran=ochre
urchin=fish
urchin=form
uredo=fruit
uredo=gonidium
ure=ox
urnflower (a plant)
urn=shaped
utility=man
U tube
uva=ursi

V

vaccination-scar
vaccine-farm
vaccine-point
vacuum-brake
vacuum-filter
vacuum-gauge
vacuum-pan
vacuum-pump
vacuum-tube
vacuum-valve
vade-mecum
vainglorious
vainglory
valise-saddle
valley-board
valley-piece
valley-rafter
valonia-oak
valve-bucket
valve-chamber
valve-cock
valve-coupling
valve-file
valve-gear
valve-motion
valve-pallet
valve-seat
valve-stem
valve-tailed
valve-view
vamper-up
vampire-bat
van-courier
van-foss
vanga-shrike
vanguard
vanilla-bean
vanilla-grass
vanilla-plant
vanner-hawk

vanning-machine
vantage-ground
vantage-loaf
vantage-point
vantage-post
van-winged
vapor-bath
vapor-burner†
vapor-douche
vapor-engine
vaporer-moth
vapor-inhaler†
vaporizing-stove
vapor-lamp
vapor-pan
vapor-plane
vaporspout
vapor-tension
vare-headed
vare-widgeon
variety-planer
variety show
variety theatre
varnishing-day
varnish-polish
varnish-tree
varnish-wattle
vase-clock
vase-painting
vat-blue
vat-net
vault-cover
vaulting-capital
vaulting-horse
vaulting-pillar
vaulting-shaft
vaulting-tile
vault-light
vault-shell
vault-work

vaza-parrot
V bob
V croze
veal-skin
vein-like
veinstone
vein-stuff
velvetbreast (a duck)
velvet-bur
velvet-cloth
velvet-ear (a mollusk)
velvetflower (a plant)
velvet-grass
velvetleaf (a plant)
velvet-loom
velvet-moss
velvet-painting†
velvet-paper
velvet-pile
velvet-satin
velvetseed (a tree)
velvet-work
veneer-cutter†
veneering-hammer
veneer-mill
veneer-moth
veneer-planing†
veneer-press
veneer-saw
veneer-scraper
veneer-straightening†
venire-man
venom-albumin
venom-duct
venom-fang
venom-gland
venom-globulin
venom-mouthed, etc.
venom-peptone
venom-sac

vent=bit	vesper=mouse	vicugna=cloth
vent=bushing	vesper=sparrow	vida=finch
vent=cock	vestry board	vide=poche
vent=cover	vestry clerk	view=halloo
vent=faucet	vestryman	viewpoint
vent=feather	vestry=room	view=telescope
vent=field	Vesuvius=salt	vignetting=glass
vent=gauge	V gauge	vignetting=mask
vent=gimlet	V gear	vignetting=paper
vent=hole	V hook	village=moot
ventilating=brick	vice=admiral	vine=black
ventilating heater	vice=admiralty	vine=borer†
ventilating millstone	vice=agent	vine=bower (a plant)
ventilating saw	vice=bitten	vine=clad
ventilator=deflector	vice=chairman	vine=culture
ventilator=hood	vice=chairmanship	vine=curculio
vent=peg	vice=chamberlain	vine=disease
vent=piece	vice=chancellor	vine=dresser†
vent=pin	vice=chancellorship	vine=feeder†
vent=pipe	vice=constable	vine=forester
vent=plug	vice=consul	vine=fretter†
vent=punch	vice=consulship	vine=gall
vent=searcher	vice=dean	vinegar=cruet
vent=stopper	vicegerent	vinegar=eel
vent=tube	vice=governor	vinegar=fly
vent=wire	vice=king	vinegar=maker†
Venus's=comb*	vice=legate	vinegar=plant
Venus's=navelwort*	vice=presidency	vinegar=tree
Venus's=pride*	vice=president	vinegar=yard
Venus's=shoe*	vice=presidentship	vine=grub
Venus's=slipper*	vice=principal	vine=hopper
verbena=oil	vice=queen	vine=land
verd=antique	vice=rector	vine=leek
verdigris=green	viceregal	vine=louse
verge=board	vice=regent	vine=maple
verge=escapement	. viceroy	vine=mildew
verge=file	viceroyal	vine=pest
verse=anthem	viceroyalty	vine=plumb
verse=colored, etc.	viceroyship	vine=puller†
verse=maker†	vice=sheriff	vine=rake
verseman	vice=treasurer	vine=slug
verse=monger	vice=treasurership	vine=tie
verse=mongering	vice=warden	vine=weevil
verse=service	victualling=bill	vinewort
verse tale	victualling=house	vineyard
verticillate=pilose	victualling=note	vingt=et=un
vervain=mallow	victualling=office	viol=block
vesper=bell	victualling=ship	violet=blindness
vesper=bird	victualling=yard	violet=blue

violet≠cress
violet≠ear (a bird)
violet≠ears (a bird)
violet≠shell
violet≠snail
violet≠tip
violet≠wood
violin≠bow
violin≠piano
violin≠player†
viper≠fish
viper≠gourd
viper's≠bugloss*
viper's≠grass*
viper's≠wine*
virgin≠born
virgin≠knot
virgin's≠bower*
Virgin≠worship
virola≠tallow
vis≠à≠vis

vise≠bench
vise≠cap
vise≠clamp
viseman
vise≠press
visit≠day
visiting≠ant
visiting≠book
visiting≠card
visiting≠day
vision≠weasel
vlack≠vark
V≠moth
voice≠part
voice≠thrill
volant≠piece
vol≠au≠vent
volley≠gun
volt≠ammeter
volt≠ampere
volt≠coulomb

volt≠meter
volute≠compass
volute≠spring
volute≠wheel
vomic≠nut
vomit≠nut
vooga≠hole
vortex≠filament
vortex≠motion
vortex≠tube
vortex≠wheel
vote≠recorder†
voting≠paper
vow≠breach
vow≠break
vow≠breaker†
vow≠fellow
V≠point
V tool
vulture≠raven
V vat

W

wabble=saw
wabronleaf (a plantain)
wad=cutter†
wadding=sizer
wad=hook
wad=punch
wadset
wafer=ash
wafer=bread
wafer=cake
wafer=iron
wafer=tongs
waffle=iron
wage=earner†
wage=fund
wagen=boom
wager=cup
wages=fund
wages=man
wage=work
wage=worker†
waging=board
wagon=bed
wagon=boiler
wagon=bow
wagon=box
wagon=brake
wagon=breast
wagon=ceiling
wagon=coupling
wagon=drag
wagon=hammer
wagon=headed, etc.
wagon=hoist
wagon=jack
wagon=load
wagon=lock
wagon=master
wagon=roof
wagon=tongue

wagon=top
wagon=train
wagon=tree
wagon=vault
wagonway
wagonwright
wagtail (a bird)
wagwant
wag=wanton
wag=wit
waif=pole
wain=house
wain=load
wain=rope
wainscot=chair
wainscot=clock
wainscot=oak
wainscot=panel
wain=shilling
wainwright
waist=anchor
waistband
waist=belt
waist=boat
waist=boater
waist=cloth
waistcoat
waist=deep
waist=high
waist=panel
waist=piece
waist=rail
waist=torque
waist=tree
wait=fee
waiting=maid
waiting=room
waiting=woman
wait=service
wait=treble

wake=robin
wake=time
wakon=bird
waldflute
waldgrave
waldhorn
wale=piece
walk=around
walking=beam
walking=cane
walking=dress
walking=fan
walking=fern
walking=fish
walking=foot
walking=leaf (a plant,
    an insect)
walking=papers
walking=staff
walking=stick
walking=straw
walking=sword
walking=ticket
walking=twig (insect)
walking=tyrant (a bird)
walking=wheel
walkover
wallaby=bush
wallaby=grass
wall=arcade
wall=barley
wall=bearing
wall=bird
wall=box
wall=clamp
wall=clock
wall=crane
wall=creeper
wall=cress
wall=desk

wall-drill
wall-engine
wall-eye
wall-eyed, etc.
wall-fern
wallflower (a plant, a
   person)
wall-fruit
wall-gecko
wall-germander
wall-gillyflower
wall-grenade
wall-hawkweed
wallhick
wall-ink
wall-knot
wall-lettuce
wall-light
wall-lizard
wall-louse
wall-moss
wall-net
wall-newt
wall-painting
wall-paper
wall-pellitory
wall-pennywort
wall-pepper
wall-pie
wall-piece
wall-plat
wall-plate
wall-pocket
wall-rib
wall-rock
wall-rocket
wall-rue
wall-saltpetre
wall-scraper†
wall-space
wall-spleenwort
wall-spring
wall-tent
wall-tooth
wall-tower
wall-tree
wall-vase
wall-washer†
wall-wasp

wallwort
walnut-moth
walnut-oil
walnut-scale
walnut-sphinx
walnut-tree
walrus-bird
wamble-cropped
wampum-snake
wandering-sailor (a
   plant)
wane-cloud
want-hill
want-thriven
wapper-jaw
war-axe
warble-fly
war-cart
warcraft
war-cry
war-dance
ward-holding
warding-file
ward-mote
ward-penny
wardrobe
wardroom
wardsman
wardwit
warega-fly
ware-goose
warehouse
warehouseman
wareroom
war-fain
warfare
war-flail
war-flame
war-fork
war-hammer
war-horse
warkloom
war-knife
warlike
war-man
warm-blooded, etc.
warning-pan
warning-stone
warning-piece

warning-wheel
war-office
war-paint
war-path
warp-beam
warp-dresser†
warp-dyeing†
warp-frame
warping-bank
warping-block
warping-chock
warping-hook
warping-jack
warping-machine
warping-mill
warping-penny
warp-lace
warp-land
war-plume
warp-machine
warp-roller
war-proof
warp-stitch
warp-thread
warrant-officer
warrior-ant
warri-warri
war-saddle
war-scythe
war-ship
war-song
war tax
wart-cress
wart-grass
wart-herb
wart-hog
war-thought
wart-pock
wart-shaped
wart-snake
wart-spurge
wartweed
wartwort
warty-faced
war-wasted, etc.
war-whip
war-whoop
warwolf
wash-back

wash-ball
wash-basin
wash-basket
wash-bear
wash-beetle
wash-board
wash-boiler
wash-bottle
wash-bowl
wash-brew
wash-cloth
wash-day
wash-dirt
washdish
wash-drawing
washer-cutter†
washer-gauge
washer-hoop
washerman
washerwoman
wash-gilding
wash-gravel
wash-house
washing-bear
washing-crystals
washing-drum
washing-engine
washing-gourd
washing-house
washing-machine
washing-powder
washing-rollers
washing-shield
washing-table
washing-trommel
washing-vessel
wash-leather
washman
wash-off
washout
wash-pot
wash-rag
wash-stand
wash-stuff
washtail (a bird)
wash-tub
wasp-bee
wasp-beetle
wasp-fly

wasp-grub
wasp-kite
wasp-waisted
wassail-bout
wassail-bowl
wassail-bread
wassail-candle
wassail-cup
wassail-horn
waste-basket
waste-board
waste-book
waste-card
waste-duster†
waste-gate
waste-pallet
waste-picker†
waste-pipe
waste-preventer†
waste-trap
wasteway
waste-weir
waste-well
watch-bill
watch-box
watch-candle
watch-case
watch-case cutter
watch-chain
watch-clock
watch-dog
watch-fire
watch-glass
watch-guard
watch-gun
watch-header
watch-house
watching-candle
watch-jewel
watch-key
watch-light
watchmaker†
watch-mark
watch-meeting
watch-night
watch-officer
watch-oil
watch-paper
watch-peel

watch-pocket
watch-pole
watch-rate
watch-spring
watch-stand
watch-tackle
watch-telescope
watch-tower
watchword
watchwork
water-adder
water-agrimony
water-aloe
water-analysis
water-anchor
water-antelope
water-apple
water-arum
water-ash
water-avens
water-back
water-bag
water-bailiff
water-balance
water-bar
water-barometer
water-barrel
water-barrow
water-basil
water-bath
water-battery
water-bean
water-bear
water-bearer†
water-bed
water-beech
water-beetle
water-bellows
water-bells
water-betony
water-bird
water-biscuit
water-blackbird
water-blast
water-blebs
water-blink
water-blinks
water-blob
water-blue

water-board
water-boat
water-boatman
water-borne
water-bottle
water-bouget
water-hound
water-box
water-brain
water-brash
water-braxy
water-break
water-breather†
water-bridge
water-brose
water-buck
water-buckler
water-budget
water-buffalo
water-bug
water-butt
water-cabbage
water-calamint
water-caltrop
water-can
water-cancer
water-canker
water-cap
water-carpet
water-carriage
water-carrier†
water-cart
water-cask
water-cat
water-cavy
water-celery
water-cell
water-centiped
water-charger
water-chat
water-check
water-chestnut
water-chevrotain
water-chicken
water-chickweed
water-chinkapin
water-cicada
water-cistern
water-clam

water-clock
water-closet
water-cock
water-colly
water-color
water-colored, etc.
water-coloring
water-colorist
water-comparator
water-cooler
water-core
watercourse
water-cow
water-cracker
water-craft
water-crake
water-crane
watercress
water-crow
water-crowfoot
watercup (a plant)
water-cure
water-deck
water-deer
water-deerlet
water-devil
water-dock
water-doctor
water-dog
water-dragon
water-drain
water-drainage
water-dressing
water-drinker†
water-drip
water-drop
water-dropper
water-dropwort
water-dust
water-eagle
water-elder
water-elephant
water-elevator
water-elm
water-engine
water-eringo
water-ermine
water-extractor
waterfall

water-farming
water-feather
water-featherfoil
water-fennel
water-fern
water-fight
water-figwort
water-filter
water-finder†
water-fire
water-flag
water-flannel
water-flaxseed
water-flea
water-float
water-flood
water-flounder
waterflow
water-flowing
water-fly
water-foot
water-fowl
water-frame
water-fright
water-fringe
water-furrow
water-gauge
water-gall
water-gap
water-gas
water-gate
water-gavel
water-germander
water-gilder†
water-gillyflower
water-gladiole
water-glass
water-god
water-grampus
water-grass
water-gruel
water-guard
water-gull
water-gum
water-gut
water-hairgrass
water-hammer
water-hare
water-haze

water-heater†
water-hemlock
water-hemp
water-hen
water-hickory
water-hoarhound
water-hog
water-hole, *n.*
waterhole, *v.*
water-horse
water-horsetail
water-hyssop
water-ice
water-inch
water-indicator
watering-bridle
watering-bucket
watering-call
watering-can
watering-cart
watering-house
watering-place
watering-pot
watering-trough
water-injector
water-jacket
water-joint
water-junket
water-kelpie
water-lade
water-laid
water-language
water-laverock
waterleaf (a plant, paper)
water-leg
water-lemon
water-lens
water-lentil
water-lettuce
water-level
water-lily
water-lime
water-line
water-liverwort
water-lizard
water-lobelia
water-lock
water-locust

water-lot
water-lotus
water-lung
water-lute
water-main
water-maize
waterman
water-mantle
water-maple
water-marigold
water-mark, *n.*
watermark, *v.*
water-meadow
water-measurer†
watermelon
water-meter
water-milfoil
water-mill
water-mint
water-mite
water-moccasin
water-mole
water-monitor
water-monkey
water-moss
water-moth
water-motor
water-mouse
water-murrain
water-net
water-newt
water-nixy
water-nut
water-nymph
water-oak
water-oats
water-opossum
water-ordeal
water-organ
water-ouzel
water-oven
water-ox
water-padda
water-pang
water-parsley
water-parsnip
water-parting
water-partridge
water-passage

water-pennywort
water-pepper
water-persicaria
water-pewit
water-pheasant
water-piet
water-pig
water-pillar
water-pimpernel
water-pine
water-pipe
water-pipit
water-pitcher
water-plane
water-plant
water-plantain
water-plate
water-platter
water-plow
water-poise
water-pore
water-post
water-pot
water-power
water-pox
water-press
water-prism
water-privilege
water-proof, *a.*
waterproof, *n.*
water-propeller
water-pump
water-puppy
water-purple
water-purslane
water-qualm
water-quintain
water-rabbit
water-radish
water-rail
water-ram
water-ranny
water-rat
water-rate
water-rattler
water-reed
water-rent
water-reservoir
water-ret

water-retting
water-rice
water-robin
water-rocket
water-room
water-rose
water-rot
water-route
water-sail
water-salamander
water-sallow
water-sapphire
waterscape
water-scorpion
water-screw
water-seal
water-sengreen
water-serpent
watershed
water-shell
water-shield
water-shoot
water-shrew
waterside
water-silvering
water-sink
water-skin
water-skipper
water-sky
water-slater
water-smartweed
water-smoke
water-snail
water-snake
water-soak
water-socks
water-sodden
water-soldier
water-sorrel
water-souchy
water-space
water-spaniel
water-sparrow
water-speedwell
water-spider
water-spike
water-spinner
waterspout
water-sprite

water-stairs
water-standing
water-star
water-stargrass
water-starwort
water-stream
water-strider
water-supply
water-system
water-tabby
water-table
water-tank
water-tap
water-target
water-tath
water-telescope
water-thermometer
water-thief
water-thistle
water-thrush
water-thyme
water-tick
water-tiger
water-tight
water-tower
water-treader†
water-tree
water-trefoil
water-trunk
water-tube
water-tupelo
water-turkey
water-twist
water-twyer
water-vacuole
water-varnish
water-vascular
water-vine
water-violet
water-viper
water-vole
water-wagtail
waterway
water-weed (any weed
    in water)
waterweed (a particu-
    lar weed)
water-weevil
water-wheel

water-white
water-whorlgrass
water-willow
water-wing
waterwitch
water-withe
water-wood
water-work
water-worker†
water-works
water-worm
water-worn
waterwort
water-wraith
water-yam
water-yarrow
wattle-bark
wattle-bird
wattle-crow
wattle-gum
wattle-jaws
wattle-tree
wattle-turkey
wattlework
wattmeter
wave-action
wave-breast
wave-front
wave-goose
wave-length
wave-line
wave-loaf
wave-moulding
wave-motion
wave-offering
wave-path
waver-dragon
waver-roller
wave-shell
wave-surface
wave-trap
wave-worn
waving-frame
wavy-barred
waw-waw
waxberry
waxbill (a bird)
wax-bush
wax-chandler

wax=cloth
wax=cluster
wax=dolls (a plant)
wax=end
waxflower (a plant)
wax=gourd
wax=insect
wax=light
wax=modelling
wax moth
wax=myrtle
wax=painting†
wax=palm
wax=paper
wax=pine
wax=pink
wax=plant
wax=pocket
wax=polish
wax=red
wax=scale
wax=tree
waxweed
waxwing (a bird)
waxwork
waxworker
wax=worm
way baggage
way=barley
way=beaten
way=bill
way=bit
wayboard
waybread (a plantain)
waybung (a bird)
wayfare
wayfarer†
wayfaring=tree
way=gate
waygoing
waygoose
way=grass
waylay
way=maker†
way=mark
way passenger
way=post
way=shaft
wayside

way=sliding
way station
way=thistle
way=thorn
way train
way=warden
way=wise
wayworn
waywort
weak=built, weak=
     handed, etc.
weakfish
weal=balanced
weapon=smith
wearing=apparel
wear=plate
wease=allan
weasel=cat
weasel=coot
weasel=duck
weasel=faced, etc.
weasel=fish
weasel=lemur
weasel=snout
weasel=spider
weather=beaten, etc.
weather=bitt
weather=board
weather=boarding
weather=box
weather=breeder†
weather=cast
weather=caster
weather=cloth
weather=cock, n.
weathercock, v.
weather=contact
weather=cross
weather=dog
weather=eye
weather=fend
weather=fish
weather=gauge
weather=gall
weather=glass
weather=gleam
weather=head
weather=house
weather=map

weather=moulding
weather=notation
weather=plant
weather=proof
weather=prophet
weather=report
weather=roll
weather=service
weather=shore
weather=sign
weather=spy
weather=stain
weather=station
weather=strip
weather=symbol
weather=tile
weather=vane
weather=waft
weather=wind
weather=wise
weather=work
weather=wreck
weave=house
weaver=bird
weaver=finch
weaver=shell
weaver's=shuttle*
weber=meter
web=eye
web=eyed, etc.
web=foot
web machine
web press
web=saw
web=wheel
web=worm
wedding=bed
wedding=cake
wedding=cards
wedding=chest
wedding=clothes
wedding=day
wedding=dower
wedding=dress
wedding=favor
wedding=feast
wedding=flower
wedding=garment
wedding=knife

wedding-ring
wedding-song
wed-fee
wedgebill (a bird)
wedge-bone
wedge-cutter†
wedge-micrometer
wedge-photometer
wedge-press
wedge-shaped, etc.
wedge-shell
wedge-valve
wedge-wise
wedging-crib
wedlock
weeder-clips
weed-grown
weed-hook
weeding-chisel
weeding-forceps
weeding-fork
weeding-hoe
weeding-hook
weeding-iron
weeding-pincers
weeding-rim
weeding-shears
weeding-tongs
weeding-tool
week-day
week-work
weenong-tree
weeping-cross
weeping spring
weeping-widow (plant)
weese-allen
weet-bird
weever-fish
wee-wow
weft-fork
weft-hook
weigh-bank
weigh-beam
weigh-board
weigh-bridge
weigh-can
weigh-house
weighing-cage
weighing-house

weighing-machine
weighing-scoop
weigh-lock
weighman
weigh-shaft
weight-nail
weight-rest
weir-fishing
weir-table
weld-bore
welding-heat
welding-machine
welding-powder
welding-swage
weld-iron
weld-steel
well-acquainted (with
   noun following),
   etc.
welladay
wellaway, *interj.*
well-being
well-boat
well-borer†
well-bucket
well-chain
well-curb
well-deck
well-decker
well-doer†
well-drain
well-dressing†
well-drill
well-flowering
well-found
well-grass
well-head
well-hole
well-house
well-meaner†
well-nigh
well-packing
well-room
well-set
well-sinker†
well-smack
well-spherometer
well-spring
well-staircase

well-sweep
well-to-do (always)
well-tome
well-trap
well-tube
well-water
well-wisher†
Welshman
welt-cutter†
welter-race
welter-stakes
welter-weight
welt-guide
welt-leather
welt-machine
welt-shoulders
welt-trimmer†
wentletrap
were-angel
West-Virginian
wet-bird
wet-broke
wet-cup, *v.*
wet-cupping
wether-hog
wet-nurse
wet-pack, *v.*
wet-press, *v.*
wet-shod
wetter-off
wetting-machine
whaleback (part of
   a ship's deck)
whale-barnacle
whale-bird
whale-boat
whalebone
whalebone-whale
whale-brit
whale-built, etc.
whale-calf
whale-fin
whale-fisher†
whale-fishery
whale-flea
whale-food
whale-head
whale-hunter†
whale-lance

whale=line
whale=louse
whaleman
whale=oil
whale=rind
whale's=foot*
whale=shark
whale=ship
whale=shot
whale's=tongue*
whaling=gang
whaling=gun
whalingman
whaling=master
whaling=port
whaling=rocket
whaling=station
whang=leather
wharf=boat
wharfman
wharfmaster
wharf=rat
wharrow=spindle
whatabouts
whatever
what=like
what=not
what=reck
whatsoever
whay=worm
wheal=worm
wheat=bird
wheat=brush
wheat=bug
wheat=caterpillar
wheat=chafer
wheat=cracker
wheat=drill
wheat=duck
wheat=ear (ear of
    wheat)
wheatear (a bird)
wheat=eel
wheat=field
wheat=fly
wheat=grader†
wheat=grass
wheat=land
wheat=maggot

wheat=midge
wheat=mildew
wheat=mite
wheat=moth
wheat=pest
wheat=riddle
wheat=rust
wheat=scourer†
wheatsel=bird
wheat=separator†
wheat=thief
wheat=thrips
wheat=weevil
wheat=worm
wheel=animal
wheel=animalcule
wheel=band
wheel=barometer
wheelbarrow
wheel=base
wheel=bearer†
wheel=bird
wheel=boat
wheel=box
wheel=bug
wheel=carriage
wheel=case
wheel=chain
wheel=chair
wheel=colter
wheel=cross
wheel=cultivator
wheel=cut
wheel=cutting†
wheel=draft
wheel=engraving†
wheel=fire
wheel=fixing
wheel=guard
wheel=head
wheel=hoe
wheel=horse
wheel=house
wheel=jack
wheel=jointer†
wheel=lathe
wheel=lock
wheelman
wheel=ore

wheel=organ
wheel=pit
wheel=plate
wheel=plow
wheel=race
wheel=rib
wheel=rope
wheel=seat
wheelseed (a plant)
wheel=shaped
wheelsman
wheel=spicule
wheel=stitch
wheelstone
wheel=swarf
wheel=tire
wheel=tooth
wheel=tree
wheel=urchin
wheelway
wheel window
wheelwork
wheel=worm
wheelwright
wheen=cat
whelk=tingle
whence=ever
whencesoever
whenever
whensoever
whereabout
whereabouts
whereagainst
whereas
whereat
whereby
wherefore
wherefrom
whereinsoever
whereinto
whereof
whereon
whereout
whereover
whereso
wheresoever
wherethrough
whereto
whereunder

whereupon
wherever
wherewith
wherryman
whet=slate
whetstone
whetstone=slate
whew=duck
whey=beard
whey=face
whey=faced
whey=wig
whey=worn
whichever
whichsoever
whickflaw
whidah=bird
whidah=finch
whiffing=tackle
whiffletree
whilly=wha
whilly=whaw
whim=gin
whimsey=shaft
whim=shaft
whimwham
whin=axe
whinberry
whin=bruiser†
whin=bushchat
whinchacker (a bird)
whinchat (a bird)
whincow (a bush)
whin=gray
whin=linnet
whin=lintie
whin=rock
whin=sill
whinstone
whip=and=derry
whipcat (a person)
whip=cord
whip=cordy
whip=crane
whip=crop
whipfish
whip=gin
whip=graft
whip=grass

whip=hand
whip=handle
whip=hanger
whip=hem
whipjack (a person)
whip=lash
whip=maker†
whip=net
whipper=in
whipper=snapper
whipping=boy
whipping=hoist
whipping=post
whipping=snapping
whipping=top
whippletree
whippoorwill
whip=ray
whip=rod
whip=roll
whip=row
whip=saw, n.
whipsaw, v.
whipsawing
whip=scorpion
whipsey=derry
whip=shaped, etc.
whipsnake
whip=socket
whip=staff
whip=stalk
whip=stick
whip=stitch, n.
whipstitch, v.
whipstitching
whip=stock
whip=tail
whip=tom=kelly (a bird)
whip=top
whipworm
whirl=about
whirlbat
whirlblast
whirlbone
whirling=table
whirling=machine
whirl=pillar
whirlpool
whirlwind

whirl=worm
whiskey=frisky
whiskey=jack
whiskey=john
whiskey=liver
whispering=gallery
whistle=belly
whistle=cup
whistle=drunk
whistle=duck
whistle-fish
whistlewing (a duck)
whistlewood (a tree)
whistling arrow
whistling buoy
whistling=shop
whist=play
whist=player†
whit=bee
white alloy
white=armed, etc.
whiteback (a duck, a tree)
whitebait (a fish)
white=baker (a bird)
white bass
whitebeam (a tree)
whitebeam=tree
whitebeard (a man)
whitebelly (a bird)
whitebill (a bird)
white=bird
whiteblow (a plant)
whitebonnet (a person)
whitebottle (a plant)
whiteboy (a person)
white brass
whitecap (a bird, a person, etc.)
whitecoat (a seal)
white=ear (a mollusk)
white=eye (a bird)
whitefish
white=flesher (a grouse)
white=grass
white=grub (a beetle)
white=gum (a disease)
white=hass
whitehause (a fish)

whitehead (a bird, etc.)
white-horse (a shrub, etc.)
white-hot
white-leg (a disease)
white-line, a.
whitening-slicker
whitening-stone
white-pot (a food)
white pudding
white-rock
whiterump (a bird)
whitescop (a bird)
whiteside (a duck)
whitesmith
whitespot (a moth)
whitespur (a person)
whitestone
whitetail (a bird, a deer)
whitethroat (a bird)
whitetip (a bird)
whitetop (a grass)
white-tree
whitewall
whitewash
white-water (a disease of sheep)
white-wave (a moth)
whiteweed
whitewing (a bird)
whitewood (a tree)
whiteworm
whitewort
whithersoever
whiting-pollack
whiting-pout
whitleather
whitlow-grass
whitlowwort
Whit-Monday
Whitsun
Withsun-ale
Whitsunday
Whitsun-farthings
Whitsun-lady
Whitsun-lord
Whitsuntide
Whitsun-week

whit-tawer
whittie-whattie
whittle-shawl
whity-brown
whizzing-stick
whoever
whole-colored, etc.
whole note
wholesale
whole-snipe (a snipe)
whole stitch
whomsoever
whoop-hymn
whooping-cough
whooping-crane
whooping-swan
whoop-la
whortleberry
whosesoever
whosoever
whunstane
wickerwork
wicket door
wicket gate
wicket-keeper†
wicket-work ·
wick-trimmer†
wide-awake
wide-chapped, etc.
widegab (a frog)
wide-spread
wide-work
widgeon-coot
widgeon-grass
widow-bench
widow-bird
widow-burning
widow-duck
widow-finch
widow-hunter†
widow-maker†
widow's-cross*
widow-wail
wife-bound
wife-carl
wifelike
wife-ridden
wig-block
wiggen-tree

wiggletail (a person)
wig-maker†
wigtail (a bird)
wig-tree
wigwag
wig-weaver†
wildbrain (a person)
wildcat, n. and a.
wild-fire
wild-flying
wild fowl
wild-williams (a plant)
wild-wood
willie-fisher
willie-hawkie
willie-man-beard (a fish)
willing-hearted
will-in-the-wisp
will-o'-the-wisp
willow-beauty
willow-bee
willow-beetle
willow-cactus
willow-caterpillar
willow-cimbex
willow-curtain
willow-dolerus
willow-fly
willow-gall
willow-garden
willow-ground
willow-grouse
willow-herb
willowing-machine
willow-lark
willow-leaf
willow-machine
willow-moth
willow-myrtle
willow-oak
willow-peeler†
willow-ptarmigan
willow-sawfly
willow-slug
willow-sparrow
willow-thorn
willow-warbler
willowweed

willowwort
willow=wren
will=willet
will=with=a=wisp
will=worship
will=worshipper†
willying=machine
willy=mufty
willy=nilly
willy=wagtail
wimming=dust
wim=sheet
winberry
win=bread
wince=pit
wince=pot
wincing=machine
windbag (a person)
windball
wind=band
wind=beam
windberry
wind=bill
wind=bore
wind=bound, etc.
wind=brace
windbreak
wind=changing
wind=chart
wind=chest
wind=colic
wind=contusion
wind=cutter†
wind=dial
wind=dog
wind=dropsy
wind=egg
windfall
windfallen
windfanner (a hawk)
wind=fertilized
windfish
windflower (a plant)
wind=furnace
wind=gauge
wind=gall
wind=gap
wind=gun
wind=hatch

windhawk
wind=herb
wind=house
windhover a (hawk)
winding=engine
winding=pendant
winding=rope
winding=sheet
winding=stairs (a gas-
　　tropod)
winding=sticks
winding=tackle
winding up
wind=instrument
windlestraw (a bird,
　　etc.)
wind=marker†
windmill
windmill=cap
windmill=grass
windmill=plant
window=bar
window=blind
window=bole
window=curtain
window=frame
window=gardening†
window=gazer
window=glass
window=jack
window=latch
window=lead
window=lift
window=martin
window=mirror
window=opener†
window=oyster
window=pane
window=sash
window=screen
window=seat
window=sector
window=shade
window=shell
window=shutter
window=sill
window=stile
window=stool
windpipe

wind=plant
wind=pole
wind=pox
wind=pressure
wind=pump
wind=record
wind=rode
wind=root
wind=rose
wind=sail
wind=scale
windseed (a plant)
wind=shaft
wind=shake
wind=shaken
wind=shock
wind side
wind=spout
wind=storm
windstroke
windsucker (bird, etc.)
wind=sucking
wind=swift
windthrush
wind=tight
wind=trunk
wind=up
windway
wind=wheel
windy=footed
wine=bag
wineberry
wine=bibber†
wine=bibbery
wine=biscuit
wine=blue
wine=bottle
wine=bowl
wine=bush
wine=carriage
wine=cask
wine=cellar
wine=colored, etc.
wine=conner
wine=cooler†
wine=fat
winefly
wine=fountain
wine=glass

wineglassful
wine=grower†
wine=marc
wine=measure
wine=merchant
wine=oil
wine=palm
wine=party
wine=piercer
wine=press
wine=room
wine=sap
wine=skin
wine=sour
wine=stone
wine=taster†
wine=vault
wine=vinegar
wine=warrant
wing=band
wing=bar
wing=bay
wing=beat
wing=bow
wing=case
wing=cell
wing=compass
wing=conch
wing=cover
wing=covert
wing=feather
wing=fish
wing=footed, etc.
wing=gudgeon
wing=membrane
wing=nervure
wing=net
wing=pad
wing=passage
wing=pen
wing=post
wing=quill
wing=rail
wing=scale
wingseed
wing=sheath
wing=shell
wing=shooting†
wing=shot

wing=snail
wing=spread
wing=stopper
wing=stroke
wing=swift
wing=tip
wing=tract
wing=transom
wing=wale
wing=wall
wink=a=peep
winker=leather
winker=muscle
winker=plate
winker=strap
winking=muscle
winking owl
winkle=hawk
winning=headway
winning=post
winnowing=basket
winnowing=fan
winnowing=machine
winnow=sheet
winter=beaten, etc.
winterberry
winter=bloom
winter=bonnet (a gull)
winter=bound
winter=cherry
winter=clad
winter=clover
winter=crack
winter=cress
winter=flower (a plant)
wintergreen
wintergreen=oil
winter=ground
winter=kill
winter=lodge (a bud or
    bulb of a plant)
winter quarters
winter=rig, v.
winter=settle
winter sports
winter=tide
winterweed
wire=bent, wire=
    edged, etc.

wire=bird
wire=cutter†
wire=dancer†
wiredraw
wire=edge
wire=finder†
wire=gauge
wire=grass
wiregrub (a worm)
wire=heel
wireman
wire=micrometer
wire=pan
wire=pegger†
wire=puller†
wire=road
wire=silver
wiresmith
wire=straightener†
wire=stretcher†
wire=tramway
wire=twist
wireway
wireweed
wirework
wireworker†
wire=works
wireworm
wiring=machine
wiring=press
wisdom=tooth
wiseacre (a person)
wise=hearted, etc.
wise=like
wish=bone
wishing=bone
wishing=cap
wishing=rod
wish=wash
wishy=washy
witch=alder
witch=ball
witch=bells
witch=chick
witchcraft
witch=doctor
witch=elm
witches'=bells*
witches'=besom*

witches'-broom*
witches'-butter*
witches'-thimble*
witch-grass
witch-hag
witch-hazel
witch-knot
witch-meal
witch-ridden
witch-seeker†
witch-stitch
witch-wife
witchwood (a tree)
withdrawing-room
wither-band
withering-floor
withe-rod
wither-wrung
within
withinside
without
without-door
withstand
withwind
witloof
witmonger
witness-box
witness-chair
witness-stand
wit-starved
wit-tooth
wizen-faced
woad-mill
woadwaxen
woebegone
woe-wearied, etc.
wolfberry
wolf-dog
wolf-eel
wolf-fish
wolf-moth
wolf-net
wolf-note
wolf robe
wolf's-bane*
wolf-scalp
wolf's-claws*
wolf's-fist*
wolf's-foot*

wolf's-head*
wolfskin
wolf's-milk*
wolf-spider
wolf-tooth
wolf-trap
woman-body
woman-born, etc.
woman-guard
woman-hater†
womankind
womanlike
woman-queller†
woman-suffrage
woman-suffragist
womb-grain
womb-passage
womb-stone
women's-tree*
wonderland
wonder-net
wonder-stone
wonder-stricken
wonder-work
wonder-worker†
wonder-wounded
wonga-wonga
wood-acid
wood-agate
wood-alcohol
wood-almond
wood-anemone
wood-ant
wood-apple
wood-ashes
wood-awl
wood-baboon
wood-barley
wood-beetle
wood-betony
wood-bill
woodbine
woodbind
wood-bird
wood-block
wood-boiler
wood-borer†
wood-born
wood-bound

wood-brick
wood-broney (a tree)
wood-broom
wood-bug
wood-calamint
wood carpet (carpet
   made of wood)
wood-carpet (a moth)
wood-carver†
wood-cell
wood-charcoal
woodchat
woodchat-shrike
wood-chopper†
woodchuck (an animal)
wood-chuck (a chuck
   in a lathe)
wood-coal
woodcock (a bird)
woodcock-eye
woodcock-fish
woodcock-owl
woodcock-pilot
woodcock-shell
woodcock-snipe
wood-copper
wood-corn
woodcracker (a bird)
woodcraft
wood-crash
wood-cricket
wood-culver
woodcut
wood-cutter†
wood-dove
wood-drink
wood-duck
wood-eater†
wood-embossing†
wood-end
wood-engraver†
woodenhead (a person)
wooden-headed, etc.
woodenware
wood-evil
wood-fern
wood-fibre
wood-flour
wood-francolin

wood=fretter†
wood=frog
wood=gas
wood=germander
wood=gnat
wood=god
wood=grass
wood=grinder†
wood=grouse
woodhack (a bird)
wood=hagger
wood=hawk
wood=hen
wood=hewer†
wood=hole
wood=honey
wood=hoopoe
wood=horse
wood=ibis
wood=inlay
woodjobber (a bird)
wood=kingfisher
woodknacker (a bird)
woodland
wood=layer
wood=leopard
wood=lily
wood=liverwort
wood=lock
wood=louse
wood=louse milleped
woodman
wood=march
wood=measurer†
wood=meeting
wood=mill
wood=mite
wood=mouse
wood=naphtha
wood=nightshade
wood=note
wood=nut
wood=nymph
wood=oil
wood=opal
wood=owl
wood=paper
wood=parenchyma
wood=partridge

wood =avement
wood=pea
wood=peat
woodpecker (a bird)
wood=pewee
wood=pie
wood=pigeon
wood=pile
wood=pimpernel
wood=pulp
wood=quail
wood=quest
wood=rabbit
wood=rat
wood=reed
woodreeve
wood=robin
wood=rock
wood=rush
wood=sage
wood=sandpiper
wood=sanicle
wood=saw
wood=sawyer
wood=screw
wood=shed
woodshock
wood=shrike
wood=shrimp
wood=skin
wood=slave
woodsman
wood=snail
wood=snake
wood=snipe
wood=soot
wood=sorrel
wood=sour
wood=spack
wood=spirit
wood=spite
wood=spurge
wood=stamp
wood=star
wood=still
wood=stone
wood=stork
wood=stove
wood=strawberry

woodsucker (a bird)
wood=swallow
wood=swift
woodtapper (a bird)
wood=tar
wood=thrush
wood=tick
wood=tin
woodtopper (a bird)
wood=tortoise
wood=vetch
wood=vine
wood=vinegar
wood=violet
wood=wagtail
wood=walker
wood=warbler
wood=wasp
woodwax
woodwaxen
wood=widgeon
wood=wool
woodwork
wood=worker†
wood=worm
wood=wren
wood=wroth
wool=ball
wool=bearing†
wool=burler†
wool=carder†
wool=cleaner†
wool=comber†
wool=driver†
wool=duster†
wool=dyed, etc.
wool=extract
wool=fat
woolfell
wool=gathering†
wool=grass
wool=grower†
wool=hall
woolhead (a duck)
woollen=cord
woollen=draper
woollen=matelassé
woollen=printer†
woollen=scribbler†

woolly=but
woolly=haired, etc.
woolly=head (a person)
wool=mill
woolmonger
wool=moter
wool=needle
wool=oil
wool=oiler†
woolpack
wool=packer†
wool=picker†
wool=powder
woolsack
wool=sale
wool=scribbler†
wool=shears
wool=sorter†
wool=sower†
wool=sponge
wool=staple
wool=stapler†
woolstock
wool=winder†
woolwork
word=blind
word=book
word=bound, etc.
word=building
word=catcher†
word=deafness
word=form
word=formation
word=making
word=memory
word=painter†
word=picture
word=square
word=strife
workaday
work=bag
work=basket
work=box
work=day
worker ant
worker bee
worker=bobbin
worker=cell
workfellow

work=folk
work=folks
work=girl
work=holder
workhouse
workhouse=sheeting
working=beam
working class
working=day
working drawing
working=face
working=house
working man
working party
working plan
working=point
working=rod
work=lead
workman
workmanlike
workmaster
workmistress
work=people
work=roller
workroom
workshop
work=stone
work=table
workwoman
world=hardened, etc.
world=language
worldly=minded, etc.
worldly=wise
world=old
world=wide
worm=bark
worm=burrow
worm=cast
worm=cod
worm=colic
worm=dye
worm=eat
worm=eaten
worm=eatenness
worm=eater†
worm fence
worm fever
worm=fisher†
worm=gear

worm=grass
worm=gut
worm=hole
worm=holed, etc.
worming=pot
worm=larva
worm=like
worm=oil
worm=pipe
worm=powder
worm=punch
worm=rack
worm=safe
wormseed
wormseed=mustard
wormseed=oil
worm=shaft
worm=shell
worms' meat
worm=snake
worm=tea
worm=track
worm=wheel
wormwood
worn=out
worsted=work
wort=condenser
wort=cooler
wort=filter
wort=refrigerator
would=be
wound=fever
wound=gall
woundwort
wourali=plant
wow=wow
wrack=grass
wrain=staff
wrapping=paper
wrapping=silk
wrap=rascal
wrasse=fish
wreath=animalcule
wreath=shell
wreck=chart
wreckfish
wreck=free
wrecking=car
wrecking=pump

wreck=master
wreck=wood
wren=babbler
wrench=hammer
wrench=handle
wrenning=day
wren=tit
wrest=block
wrest=plank
wringing=machine
wring=staff
wrinkle=beaked
wrinkling=machine
wristband
wrist=bone
wrist=clonus
wrist=drop
wristfall

wrist=guide
wrist=joint
wrist=link
wrist=pin
wrist=plate
write=of=hand
writing=book
writing=box
writing=cabinet
writing=case
writing=chambers
writing=desk
writing=folio
writing=frame
writing=ink
writing=machine
writing=master
writing=paper

writing=reed
writing=school
writing=set
writing=table
writing=telegraph
wrong=doer†
wrong=head
wrong=headed, etc.
wrought iron
wrought=iron, a.
wrybill (a plover)
wry=billed, etc.
wrymouth (a fish)
wryneck (a disease, a
  bird)
wych=elm
wych=hazel
wylie=coat

Y

yacca-tree
yacca-wood
yacht-built
yacht-club
yachtsman
yam-bean
yang-kin
Yankee gang
yard-arm
yard-grass
yardkeep
yard-land
yard-limit
yardman
yardmaster
yard measure
yard-rope
yard-slings
yardsman
yardstick
yard-tackle
yard-wand
yarn-beam
yarn-clearer†
yarn-dresser†
yarn-meter
yarn-printer†
yarn-reel
yarn-roll
yarn-scale
yarn-spooler†
yarn-tester†
yarn-winder†
yate-stoop
yate-tree
yawweed
Y branch
Y cartilage
Y cross

yea-forsooth
year-bird
year-book
year-long
yeast-beer
yeast-bitten
yeast-cell
yeast-fungus
yeast-plant
yeast-powder
yell-house
yellow-backed, etc.
yellow-beak
yellowbelly (a fish)
yellowbill (a duck)
yellowbird
yellowcrown (a bird)
yellow-duckwing, a.
yellowfin (a fish)
yellowfish
yellow-golds (a plant)
yellow-gum (a disease)
yellowham (a bird)
yellowhammer (a bird)
yellow-jack
yellow-jacket (a wasp)
yellowleg (a bird)
yellowlegs (a bird)
yellow-legger
yellow-line, a.
yellowpoll (a widgeon)
yellow-rocket (a plant)
yellowroot (a plant)
yellowrump (a bird)
yellow sally
yellowseed (a plant)
yellowshank (a bird)
yellowshanks (a bird)
yellowshell (a moth)

yellowshins (a bird)
yellowtail (a fish)
yellowthroat (a bird
yellowtop (a turnip)
yellowweed
yellowwood (a tree)
yellowwort
yellow-wrack
yerba-mate
yercum-fibre
yester-year
yew-pine
yew-tree
ylang-ylang
Y-level
Y-moth
yoke-arbor
yoke-bone
yoke-devil
yoke-elm
yokefellow
yoke-line
yokemate
yoke-rope
yoke-toed
yolk-bag
yolk-cleavage
yolk-duct
yolk-gland
yolk-sac
yolk-segmentation
yolk-skin
young-eyed, etc.
youthlike
Y track
yttrium-garnet
yucca-borer
yucca-fertilizer
Yule-tide

Z

zaffer blue
zand=mole
Zante=wood
Z crank
zebra=caterpillar
zebra=opossum
zebra=parrakeet
zebra=plant
zebra=poison
zebra=shark
zebra=spider
zebra=swallowtail
zebra=wolf

zebra=wood
zebra=woodpecker
zebu=cattle
zenith=collimator
zenith=distance
zenith=sector
zenith=telescope
ziment=water
zinc=amyl
zinc=blende
zinc=bloom
zinc=colic
zinc=ethyl

zinc=methyl
zinc=plating
zinc=salt
zinc=spinel
zinc=vitriol
zircon=syenite
Z iron
zoëa form
zoëa stage
zone=axis
zoöphyte=trough
Zouave=jacket
Zulu=kafir